'This remarkable book occupies a unique position in its capacity to show the *how* of learning what might be best called a psychoanalytic attitude. This particular orientation towards a patient and towards mental suffering has a very wide reference, as this book amply demonstrates. Foundational to this, is that such an attitude cannot be learnt as if it were a technique to be applied, but instead requires an engagement with an evolving process, a process that any trainee necessarily goes though, and something that continues throughout one's professional life. It shows how the trainee learns from experience, makes mistakes but then finds that understanding the mistake, really thinking it through rather than dismissing it, provides a new insight into the nature of the work and of one's own relation to it. This dialectical way of thinking, where a "mistake" is not just something to be avoided or corrected but becomes the basis for an evolution of thought, has been part of psychoanalysis since Freud's very early papers where what seemed at first like mistakes, became the source of a new orientation to the work.

Having established this central theme of the work, the book goes on to show its very wide reference. We are given a kind of window on the development of the trainees as psychanalytic psychotherapists and this encompasses some very varied themes and situations including those that affect the setting such as the therapist's pregnancy, issues of cultural and sexual diversity, etc. The whole book is held together by the editors' overarching vision in the provision of an introduction to each section. In this way they give us not only a model way of presenting this work but one gets a profound sense of their extraordinary skill and commitment in leading this world renowned training which has been the absolute core of adult psychoanalysis at the Tavistock.

It is a unique book—an overused word I know but there really is nothing to compare to it in terms of proving a model for training in psychoanalytic thinking. As such it will occupy a very important position in the psychoanalytic literature of considerable relevance not only to psychoanalytic psychotherapy and to psychoanalysis but broadly but to all those varied settings in which psychoanalyse can make a contribution. Any mental health practitioner will also find a great deal to stimulate thought about their work.'

David Bell

'This important book describing the training of psychoanalytic psychotherapists will interest all those involved in education or indeed anyone wishing to foster curiosity and learning. It gives priority to learning from experience rather than from books and teachers and specifically focuses on what has become known as the psychoanalytic attitude. The central aim in training is to understand the patient and the interaction with the therapist, setting to one side the question of how to help the patient directly. The authors show that for many trainees this means the unlearning of the more usual approach of directly trying to offer relief and reassurance. This commonly means that pain and sorrow have to be endured at least until they are better understood.

The authors admirably illustrate the personal struggle that must be worked through in chapters provided by both trainees and trainers. It is a fascinating account that is all the more remarkable from an NHS service that continues to be underfunded and undervalued.'

John Steiner

'This is a brave and uncompromising book. Learning how to become a psychoanalytic psychotherapist is its main theme. This book should be an inspiration to those who value in-depth approaches to mental health and well-being.'

Michael Rustin

LEARNING AND UNLEARNING THROUGH THE CLINICAL ENCOUNTER

This book examines the learning process involved in becoming a psychoanalytic practitioner and presents training experiences at the Tavistock and Portman NHS Foundation Trust through the lens of both teachers and trainees.

The book describes the relevant history at the Tavistock and how psychoanalytic knowledge is acquired through a process of *learning from experience* and the fostering of a *culture of enquiry*. The contributors also present their interpretations of what is meant by *analytic learning* and how this is acquired for a psychoanalytic attitude to become possible. The book includes a mix of chapters by more experienced clinicians setting out what can be useful in training, balanced by other chapters from more recent trainees who reflect on their development and experience of that training. Other important sections focus on the experience and importance of supervision and on how to respond to clinical challenges in training and practice, specifically public-sector-based trainings.

With rich clinical vignettes and personal reflections on training experiences, this book is key reading for all psychoanalysts and psychotherapists involved or interested in training.

Francesca Hume worked for over 25 years at the Tavistock, where, for 14 years, she ran the Adult Psychoanalytic Psychotherapy Training (M1). She first trained as a clinical psychologist and is now a Training Analyst of the British Psychoanalytical Society. She supervises and teaches in the United Kingdom and abroad.

Helen Barker is a psychoanalyst, now in full time private practice, with a background in psychiatry. She worked in the Adult Department of the Tavistock Clinic as a clinician and supervisor for 18 years.

Tavistock Clinic Series
Founding Editor: Margot Waddell,
Series Editors: Jocelyn Catty & Kate Stratton

Titles in the Tavistock Clinic Series include:

A for Adoption: An Exploration of the Adoption Experience for Families and Professionals, *by Alison Roy*
Assessment in Child Psychotherapy, *edited by Margaret Rustin & Emanuela Quagliata*
Childhood Depression: A Place for Psychotherapy, *edited by Judith Trowell, with Gillian Miles*
Child Psychoanalytic Psychotherapy in Primary Schools: Tavistock Approaches, *edited by Katie Argent*
Complex Trauma: The Tavistock Model, *edited by Joanne Stubley & Linda Young*
Conjunctions: Social Work, Psychoanalysis, and Society, *by Andrew Cooper*
Couple Dynamics: Psychoanalytic Perspectives in Work with the Individual, the Couple, and the Group, *edited by Aleksandra Novakovic*
Doing Things Differently: The Influence of Donald Meltzer on Psychoanalytic Theory and Practice, *edited by Margaret Cohen & Alberto Hahn*
Exploring Psychoanalytic Concepts through Culture, the Arts, and Contemporary Life: Learning from Observation and Experience, *edited by Margaret Lush and Kate Robertson*
Group Relations and Other Meditations: Psychoanalytic Explorations on the Uncertainties of Experiential Learning, *by Carlos Sapochnik*
Inside Lives: Psychoanalysis and the Growth of the Personality, *by Margot Waddell*
Internal Landscapes and Foreign Bodies: Eating Disorders and Other Pathologies, *by Gianna Williams*
Melanie Klein Revisited: Pioneer and Revolutionary in the Psychoanalysis of Young Children, *by Susan Sherwin-White*
Mourning and Metabolization: Close Readings in the Psychoanalytic Literature of Loss, *by Rael Meyerowitz*
New Discoveries in Child Psychotherapy: Findings from Qualitative Research, *edited by Margaret Rustin & Michael Rustin*
On Adolescence: Inside Stories, *by Margot Waddell*
Organization in the Mind: Psychoanalysis, Group Relations, and Organizational Consultancy, *by David Armstrong, edited by Robert French*
Perspectives from a Psych-Oncology Team Working with Teenagers and Young Adults with Cancer: Thrown Off Course, *edited by Jane Elfer*
Psychoanalysis and Culture: A Kleinian Perspective, *edited by David Bell*
Researching the Unconscious: Principles of Psychoanalytic Method, *by Michael Rustin*
Sexuality and Gender Now: Moving Beyond Heteronormativity, *edited by Leezah Hertzmann & Juliet Newbigin*
Surviving Space: Papers on Infant Observation, *edited by Andrew Briggs*
Sustaining Depth and Meaning in School Leadership: Keeping Your Head, *edited by Emil Jackson & Andrea Berkeley*
The Anorexic Mind, *by Marilyn Lawrence*
The Learning Relationship: Psychoanalytic Thinking in Education, *edited by Biddy Youell*
Therapeutic Care for Refugees: No Place Like Home, *edited by Renos Papadopoulos*
Therapeutic Interventions with Babies and Young Children in Care: Observation and Attention, *by Jenifer Wakelyn*
Thinking Space: Promoting Thinking about Race, Culture, and Diversity in Psychotherapy and Beyond, *edited by Frank Lowe*
Turning the Tide: A Psychoanalytic Approach to Mental Illness. The Work of the Fitzjohn's Unit, *edited by Rael Meyerowitz & David Bell*
Understanding Trauma: A Psychoanalytic Approach, *edited by Caroline Garland*
Waiting to Be Found: Papers on Children in Care, *edited by Andrew Briggs*

LEARNING AND UNLEARNING THROUGH THE CLINICAL ENCOUNTER

On Becoming a Psychoanalytic Psychotherapist

Edited by
Francesca Hume & Helen Barker

Foreword by
Jane Milton

Taylor & Francis Group
LONDON AND NEW YORK

Designed cover image: © "Chaos" by David Hume

First published 2025
by Routledge
4 Park Square, Milton Park, Abingdon, Oxon OX14 4RN

and by Routledge
605 Third Avenue, New York, NY 10158

Routledge is an imprint of the Taylor & Francis Group, an informa business

© 2025 selection and editorial matter, Francesca Hume & Helen Barker; individual chapters, the contributors

The right of Francesca Hume & Helen Barker to be identified as the authors of the editorial material, and of the authors for their individual chapters, has been asserted in accordance with sections 77 and 78 of the Copyright, Designs and Patents Act 1988.

All rights reserved. No part of this book may be reprinted or reproduced or utilised in any form or by any electronic, mechanical, or other means, now known or hereafter invented, including photocopying and recording, or in any information storage or retrieval system, without permission in writing from the publishers.

Trademark notice: Product or corporate names may be trademarks or registered trademarks, and are used only for identification and explanation without intent to infringe.

ISBN: 9781032909066 (hbk)
ISBN: 9781032901916 (pbk)
ISBN: 9781003560432 (ebk)

DOI: 10.4324/9781003560432

Typeset in Palatino
by Apex CoVantage, LLC

We dedicate the book to our trainees, past and present from whom we continue to learn.

CONTENTS

SERIES EDITORS' PREFACE	xiii
ACKNOWLEDGEMENTS	xvi
ABOUT THE EDITORS AND CONTRIBUTORS	xviii
PREFACE	xxii
Francesca Hume	
FOREWORD	xxv
Jane Milton	

Introduction   1
  Francesca Hume

PART I: Teaching and learning   5
  Francesca Hume

1   Education at the Tavistock and the development of an adult psychoanalytic psychotherapy training   7
  Francesca Hume

| 2 | On the acquisition of psychoanalytic knowledge and attitude: fostering development and learning from experience
Francesca Hume | 14 |

PART II: Learning and unlearning — **23**
Francesca Hume

3	Trainee selection and the challenge of experiential learning *Francesca Hume*	27
4	On not knowing *Era Trieman*	32
5	Up or down; life or death *Anne McKay*	44
6	The elephant tied up with string *Simon Shaw*	55
7	There are two in the room *Malika Verma*	67
8	One groove's difference: on unlearning psychiatry *Alan Baban*	75
9	Becoming a psychoanalytic psychotherapist: learning and unlearning, identity and citizenship *Rachel Hodgins*	82
10	Learning through supervision *Francesca Hume*	88

PART III: Learning about the transference and countertransference — **103**
Francesca Hume

| 11 | Transference and countertransference
Francesca Hume | 105 |

12	Not just any old bowl *Michelle Washington*	113
13	Should I stay or should I go? *Thomas Hillen*	125
14	The shape of things to come *Viv Walkerdine*	135
15	From incorporation to introjection and mourning: parallel processes in both patient and trainee *Diane Turner*	146
16	On being guided by the countertransference *Carolyn Walker*	157

PART IV: Learning through clinical challenges — **167**
Helen Barker

17	A death during the pandemic *Louise Barnard*	171
18	When the worst thing happened *Susan Baldock*	179
19	The impact of the therapist's pregnancy in a training case *Avgoustina Almyroudi*	189
20	"I would prefer not to": a man in terror of his own mind *Devayani Shevade*	198
21	The Ghost Ship: a reflection on working in the Tavistock during the Covid-19 pandemic *Alan Baban*	209
22	Lost in the dark: my first training patient and working on the telephone *Denise Hurst Hastings*	219

PART V: Diversity 227
Francesca Hume

23 Insiders and outsiders: some thoughts on diversity and psychoanalysis 229
Poul Rohleder

24 Thinking about sexual diversity in psychoanalytic training 232
Poul Rohleder

25 Hiding in plain sight: a personal experience of being black on the M1 course 244
Diane Turner

26 On my diversity and the M1 training 252
Reziya Harrison

PART VI: Some final reflections 259

27 A changing NHS and threats to the integrity of the M1 training: can we keep a culture of enquiry? 261
Francesca Hume

28 Final reflections 269
Francesca Hume

REFERENCES 275
INDEX 287

SERIES EDITORS' PREFACE

Since it was founded in 1920, the Tavistock Clinic—now the Tavistock and Portman NHS Foundation Trust—has developed a wide range of developmental approaches to mental health, which have been strongly influenced by the ideas of psychoanalysis. It has also adopted systemic family therapy as a theoretical model and a clinical approach to family problems. The Tavistock is now one of the largest mental health training institutions in Britain. It teaches up to 600 students a year on postgraduate, doctoral, and qualifying courses in social work, systemic psychotherapy, psychology, psychiatry, nursing, and child, adolescent, and adult psychotherapy, along with 2,000 multidisciplinary clinicians, social workers, and teachers attending Continuing Professional Development courses and conferences on psychoanalytic observation, psychoanalytic thinking, and management and leadership in a range of clinical and community settings.

The Tavistock's philosophy aims at promoting therapeutic methods in mental health. Its work is based on the clinical expertise that is also the basis of its consultancy and research activities. The aim of this Series is to make available to the reading public the clinical, theoretical, and research work that is most influential at the Tavistock. The Series sets out new approaches in the understanding and treatment of psychological disturbance in children, adolescents, and adults, both as individuals and in families.

Learning and Unlearning through the Clinical Encounter: On Becoming a Psychoanalytic Psychotherapist, edited by Francesca Hume and Helen Barker, focuses on how to enable psychoanalytic learning and how to impart a psychoanalytic attitude—or a mode of thinking and receptivity—through the experience of the clinical encounter. Like another recent book in our Series, *Exploring Psychoanalytic Concepts through Culture, the Arts, and Contemporary Life: Learning from Observation and Experience*, edited by Margaret Lush and Kate Robertson,[1] the present volume uses insights derived from a highly regarded Tavistock programme—the Adult Psychotherapy Training—to illuminate the rewards but also the difficulties of learning from experience. Here the central focus is on the intellectually and emotionally destabilizing aspects of clinical psychotherapy, and we go with them as the authors, drawing on their training experiences at the Tavistock, enter clinical situations filled with problems for patients and therapists alike and wrestle with the complex mix of transference and countertransference that informs the clinical process.

Learning and Unlearning through the Clinical Encounter thus complements a number of key publications in the Series that have been developed from teaching and training conducted at the Tavistock, including [*New Discoveries in Child Psychotherapy: Findings from Qualitative Research*, edited by Margaret Rustin and Michael Rustin,[2] and Jenifer Wakelyn's *Therapeutic Observation with Babies and Young Children in Care: Observation and Attention*,[3] work that has now given rise to the internationally employed intervention Watch Me Play! (https://watchmeplay.info). Other recent volumes have described the ways in which training at the Tavistock has inspired pioneering work in other areas of the National Health Service (NHS),[4] or the use of the Tavistock model in the primary school sector.[5] But by bringing the focus back to psychoanalytic training itself, Hume and Barker foreground "what is meant by *analytic learning* and how this may be acquired", and what it is to gain such learning in the context of a public health service, here the NHS, which provides the trainee with "immersion in a rich breadth of clinical work, ... diverse clinical populations ... [and] many areas of applied psychoanalytic work from which to learn".

As Jane Milton comments in her Foreword, the contributors are brave in their inclusion of accounts of work where clinicians lost patients to illness or suicide. The book also challengingly, and often movingly, includes chapters that raise important questions about aspects of diversity in the clinical and training encounter. While Frank Lowe's edited collection, *Thinking Space: Promoting Thinking about Race, Culture, and Diversity in Psychotherapy and Beyond*,[6] has been seminal in promoting thinking about diversity in psychoanalytic clinical practice, the complexity of such issues is increasingly being highlighted in Series titles, not just in the award-winning *Sexuality and Gender Now: Moving Beyond Heteronormativity*, edited by Leezah Hertzmann and Juliet Newbigin,[7] but also here.

The rootedness of psychoanalytic training in a public health service setting is essential to this book. Inevitably, then, and helpfully, the editors reflect on some of the vicissitudes of delivering both a training and clinical work itself, in the setting of an NHS wracked by the twin evils of a global pandemic and, in the United Kingdom, "austerity" and relentless real-terms funding cuts. While they leave us in no doubt about the very real nature of these threats, they also convey a feeling of challenge and hope in the rigour and precision of the approach the Adult Psychotherapy Training embodies, in the breadth and depth of the Tavistock training method, and in the invaluable contribution that psychoanalytic psychotherapy can make to public mental health.

We are delighted to welcome *Learning and Unlearning through the Clinical Encounter* to our Series.

Notes

1. Margaret Lush & Kate Robertson (Eds.), *Exploring Psychoanalytic Concepts through Culture, the Arts and Contemporary Life: Learning from Observation and Experience* (London: Routledge, 2025).
2. Margaret Rustin & Michael Rustin (Eds.), *New Discoveries in Child Psychotherapy: Findings from Qualitative Research* (London: Routledge, 2019).
3. Jenifer Wakelyn, *Therapeutic Observation with Babies and Young Children in Care: Observation and Attention* (London: Routledge, 2020).
4. Alison Roy, *A for Adoption: An Exploration of the Adoption Experience for Families and Professionals* (London: Routledge, 2020). Jane Elfer (Ed.), *Perspectives from a Psych-Oncology Team Working with Teenagers and Young Adults with Cancer: Thrown Off Course* (London: Routledge, 2023).
5. Katie Argent, *Child Psychoanalytic Psychotherapy in Primary Schools: Tavistock Approaches* (London: Routledge, 2022).
6. Frank Lowe (Ed.), *Thinking Space: Promoting Thinking about Race, Culture, and Diversity in Psychotherapy and Beyond* (London: Karnac, 2014).
7. Leezah Hertzmann & Juliet Newbigin (Eds.), *Sexuality and Gender Now: Moving Beyond Heteronormativity* (London: Routledge, 2020).

ACKNOWLEDGEMENTS

The M1 training upon which this book is based has involved the collaboration of numerous people over its history and still today. This book reflects the input and efforts of all those people. Some are directly reflected in these pages, but there are many others whose support over the years has been vital to our work in running the M1 training and maintaining its quality as a place to acquire an analytic education. They are too many to name but include all those working in the Adult Department clinical service and in the Department of Education and Training. We want to highlight those with whom we worked most closely and productively over many years on our small M1 team: at different points they were Rael Meyerowitz, Shirley Borghetti-Hiscock, Elisa Reyes-Simpson, Michael Mercer, Hiroshi Amino, Marcus Evans, and Peter Hobson. Then there are those who over the years have been vital in supporting both the training and the clinical service: David Taylor, Julian Lousada, Caroline Garland, Phil Stokoe, Dave Bell, and John Steiner. Finally, our most important analytic teachers and mentors both at the Tavistock and at the Institute of Psychoanalysis: Irma Brenman Pick, Edna O'Shaughnessy, Michael Feldman, Betty Joseph, and Priscilla Roth.

With regards to the book itself, very many thanks go to our friend and colleague Jane Milton, who read and commented upon the entire manuscript in draft form and was a huge encouragement to us; also, to Derek Summerfield, Andreas Banki, Caroline Garland, and Michael Rustin, who read early drafts and offered valuable ideas; and to those who provided information in relation to the history of the M1 training at the Tavistock: Vic Sedlak, David Millar, and Marcus Evans.

Most important of all, we want to thank our main contributors, without whom this book would not exist: the current and past trainees, along with their patients, upon whom their chapters are based. The clinical encounters described are at the heart of the book and illustrate how and where the learning took place. We are deeply indebted to them for their honesty and openness in sharing their experiences and also to their patients who made this possible. In addition, we thank Louise Wardle and Holly Hassell, who have assisted us by providing valuable material that was included in some of the editors' chapters.

Finally, we thank the sterling work of our Series Editors, Jocelyn Catty and Kate Stratton, who have read and re-read our book in draft form, offering steady encouragement and clarity.

ABOUT THE EDITORS AND CONTRIBUTORS

Avgoustina Almyroudi is a psychoanalytic psychotherapist and psychiatrist. Since completing her training at the Tavistock, she has been working as a consultant psychiatrist in psychotherapy in the West London NHS Trust.

Alan Baban is a consultant psychiatrist in medical psychotherapy and general adult psychiatry. He is a psychoanalytic psychotherapist, having completed the M1 course at the Tavistock clinic. In 2023 he was the Chief Investigator of Research within Health Education England (HEE) that studied the impact of Covid-19 on trainee psychiatrists' ability to learn psychotherapy competencies and their experience of learning psychotherapies in general. He chairs the Arts and Psychiatry Special Interest Group within the Royal College of Psychiatrists.

Susan Baldock is a psychoanalytic psychotherapist working in a number of settings: as a group and individual therapist for the mental health charity CPU London, in a variety of teaching roles, and as a founding partner of a family law mediation service, the Mediation Space LLP.

Helen Barker trained in medicine and psychiatry in Manchester, where she worked as a consultant psychiatrist in psychotherapy. She then trained as a psychoanalytic psychotherapist at the Tavistock, working in the Fitzjohn's Unit for 15 years. She trained at the Institute of Psychoanalysis and is currently a psychoanalyst in full-time private practice.

Louise Barnard trained as a psychoanalytic psychotherapist on the M1 training programme. She has worked for many years in the adult and trauma units at the Tavistock as well as for CPU, the British Red Cross, Scotscare, and also in private practice.

Reziya Harrison was a Chancery barrister before qualifying as a psychoanalytic psychotherapist. She has a private psychotherapy practice in central London.

Thomas Hillen is a consultant medical psychotherapist based at the Camden and Islington NHS Foundation Trust. Since qualifying as a psychoanalytic psychotherapist, he has been providing consultations and therapy to numerous NHS and private patients. In his role as psychotherapy tutor, he helps psychiatric trainees develop their listening, reflective, and therapeutic skills.

Rachel Hodgins is a psychologist and psychotherapist working in the NHS with individuals, families, and groups, and with training, experiential, and reflective practice groups for staff. She is the book reviews editor for the journal *Psychoanalytic Psychotherapy* and an Honorary Teaching Fellow at UCL.

Francesca Hume is a training analyst of the British Psychoanalytic Society. She studied psychology at UCL in the 1980s and then trained as a clinical psychologist. She went on to specialize as a forensic clinical psychologist before training at the Tavistock as a psychoanalytic psychotherapist and at the Institute of Psychoanalysis as an analyst. She worked for 26 years in the Tavistock's Adult Department, where one of her main roles was to run the M1 training in psychoanalytic psychotherapy for 14 years, until she left in 2021. She now works in private practice and teaches and supervises extensively in the United Kingdom and abroad. She has lectured and published on various psychoanalytic topics and has a particular interest in Kleinian theory.

Denise Hurst Hastings is a psychoanalytic psychotherapist who qualified from the M1 training in July 2024. She worked for 16 years as an honorary psychotherapist in the NHS, at The Gordon Hospital and at the Tavistock Clinic, and now works in private practice. She works with adults in individual intensive psychotherapy and also co-facilitates a private psychotherapy group.

Anne McKay is Principal Psychodynamic Psychotherapist in the Southwark Psychology and Psychotherapy team at the Maudsley Hospital, in South London. Since qualifying as a psychoanalytic psychotherapist, she has been working with perinatal and community mental health teams and has developed a special interest in treating patients with complex trauma and personality disorder.

Jane Milton, who has a background in NHS psychiatry, is a retired Fellow and training analyst of the British Psychoanalytical Society. Among other analytic publications her writings include, jointly with Julia Fabricius and Caroline Polmear, *A Short Introduction to Psychoanalysis*. She is part of a team who have for many years been helping with the development of psychoanalysis in Ukraine.

Poul Rohleder is a clinical psychologist and psychoanalytic psychotherapist. He has taught on various clinical trainings and is currently an honorary senior lecturer at the Department of Psychosocial and Psychoanalytic Studies, University of Essex.

Simon Shaw is Principal Psychotherapist and service Lead for SLAM's Croydon Personality Disorder Service at The Touchstone Centre, and Psychological and Operational Lead for the Personality Disorder Pathway in Croydon. He has worked for many years with adults with personality disorder and is an MBT therapist and MBT supervisor, accredited with the Anna Freud Centre.

Devayani Shevade is a clinical psychologist and psychoanalytic psychotherapist working in a secondary care psychotherapy service in the NHS. Since qualifying as a psychoanalytic psychotherapist, she has been working primarily with patients with a diagnosis of personality disorder and has developed a special interest in primitive states of mind and the use of countertransference to understand these states.

Era Trieman trained at the Tavistock. He is now a candidate at the Institute of Psychoanalysis and works in full-time private practice.

Diane Turner is a consultant psychoanalytic psychotherapist and psychoanalyst. She originally trained as a general and psychiatric nurse. She works in the T1DE Team (Type 1 diabetes and disordered eating) at Kings College University Hospital Foundation Trust, and in private practice at the South London Centre for Psychotherapy and Psychoanalysis. She has a special interest in psychosomatic disorders.

Malika Verma is a clinical psychologist based in Melbourne. Since qualifying as a psychoanalytic psychotherapist, she has worked in India and established the Tara Institute. She is now doing the psychoanalytic training with the Melbourne branch of the Australian Psychoanalytic Society.

Carolyn Walker is a psychoanalytic psychotherapist, clinical supervisor and group relations consultant. She teaches on the M1 and other training programmes at the Tavistock and Portman NHS Trust, where she was previously consultant adult psychotherapist and social worker.

Viv Walkerdine is a psychoanalytic psychotherapist, currently working in private practice in the North West of England. She previously worked for the NHS within Child and Adolescent Mental Health Services. Since qualifying, she has also worked as a clinical supervisor and tutor for the Tavistock psychotherapy training course based in Leeds.

Michelle Washington is a mental health nurse based within the Lewisham Integrated Therapies Team (South West London and Maudsley NHS Trust). Since qualifying, she has become the Psychodynamic Psychotherapy Lead in her service. She provides psychoanalytic psychotherapy to patients who present with severe and enduring complex emotional and mental health needs, which span the diagnostic spectrum.

PREFACE
Francesca Hume

This book is about the learning and training involved in becoming a psychoanalytic practitioner. The main contributors are the trainees themselves, who reflect upon their training experiences. Some are still training, while others are now qualified. In all cases, their accounts of how they came to acquire psychoanalytic knowledge and skills sit at the heart of the book. The book describes a particular public sector setting: the UK's National Health Service (the NHS). But what we discuss is of relevance and importance to anyone interested in, or currently undertaking, a psychoanalytic training, as well as those involved in delivering a training to others, whatever setting or country they are in.

Our primary focus has been to convey the trainees' experiences of their own development. Their 20 chapters are organized around various themes, together with introductory and concluding chapters in which we explore and develop the themes that have emerged and reflect, at times, on what we have learnt ourselves as their teachers. The introductory chapters give a broader and more theoretical focus: we discuss what is meant by *analytic learning* and how this may be acquired so that a psychoanalytic attitude becomes possible. We point to how the trainees' accounts of their clinical encounters illustrate this. Putting this book together has made us examine closely the process of *learning from experience*. We examine the trainees' accounts and try to understand and formulate them in clinical and theoretical terms.

The training we base our experience upon is the *Four Year Advanced Adult Training in Psychoanalytic Psychotherapy*, based at the Tavistock and Portman NHS Foundation Trust in London. We have gathered and examined the experiences and accounts of the trainees, to help us understand more about the processes of learning involved in any analytic training. The training was one of the first trainings at the Tavistock and, for this reason, became widely known as the *M1 Training*. We use this shorthand throughout.

A secondary focus of the book is concerned with the context surrounding this particular training. We describe the relevant history at the Tavistock and in the NHS that enabled the M1 training to evolve and the rather unique qualities that emerged from this. In the Introduction we give an account of some of the rewards and benefits that arise from a public sector-based training like this one: the quality of immersion in a rich breadth of clinical work, the diverse clinical populations encountered, and the many areas of applied psychoanalytic work from which to learn. But, later in the book, we also reflect upon the more recent history and the significant threats now faced by public sector trainings like this one. The penultimate chapter, "Threats to the Integrity of the M1 Training: Can We Keep a Culture of Enquiry?", describes some specific challenges inherent in undertaking a training in Britain's currently resource-poor and beleaguered NHS. While it is likely that there are similar challenges for psychoanalytic trainings outside Britain, we highlight the fraught situation that exists for this particular training and the implications for the trainees undertaking it.

Both editors are psychoanalysts. We began our training with M1 and then went on to train at the Institute of Psychoanalysis in London. We come to this book from the position of having worked as senior staff consultants. I was the M1 Course Lead for 14 years, until 2020, and Helen Barker was, for many years, a senior member of the M1 team around me. Along with others, we were involved in the strategic planning and implementation of the training, and also the teaching, supervision, and decision making around the trainees' progression and qualification.

Although I wrote most of the introductory and linking chapters, Helen Barker has been responsible for the lion's share of the editorial work. We have worked closely together holding the whole of the book in mind in a way that has been essential to an integrated approach to our thinking about the different parts.

The book contains many clinical accounts describing confidential analytic treatments. Much attention has been given to the anonymization of the clinical material. Although in some cases the authors also chose to seek permission from their patients, these cases, too, have been anonymized.

In some cases, where trainees struggles are particularly sensitive, we have chosen to describe the difficulties encountered using composite cases.

Finally, the cover painting is by the artist David Hume (Francesca Hume's late father). It's title, "Chaos", reflects one of the main themes of the book—Bion's notion that creative learning evolves out of catastrophic change. New thoughts are potentially disruptive and shattering, but out of this chaotic state may come the opportunity for new learning.

FOREWORD
Jane Milton

I am delighted to be writing this foreword to what is an important and unique book, describing the work of a National Health Service centre of excellence in London. Most psychoanalytic psychotherapy trainings and treatment of patients take place in the private sector, with access limited to those who can afford it. As this book so vividly shows, this particular training in psychoanalytic psychotherapy is inextricably linked to the free clinical service provided to adult patients referred to the Tavistock Centre on London. The treatment offered here gives people who are often suffering terribly an all-too-rare opportunity to make fundamental changes to their lives and relationships. For trainees, an NHS service offers a breadth of experience in both direct clinical and applied psychoanalytic work.

Francesca Hume and Helen Barker, the senior clinicians who brought this book together, asked their current and recently qualified trainees to focus their chapters on the experiential learning process with their training cases. They were interested in ascertaining: how had they acquired their psychoanalytic skills, and what difficulties were encountered along the way. Although the context of these questions was a London-based NHS service, the book is highly relevant for all teachers and students of psychoanalysis and psychoanalytic psychotherapy, in the United Kingdom and beyond.

What has been so vital about this service and training is something Francesca, referencing the work of Tom Main, returns to repeatedly: a "culture of enquiry" where trainees can learn and develop through clinical encounters with patients. The culture of enquiry needs to exist at all levels, from the individual clinician to the whole institution, and this requires us to remain on the alert for degradation into what Main describes as ritualized and stale "knowledge" of how things are or should be done.

Clinical work is supported by skilled analytic supervision, which is, in turn, supported by a creative and thoughtful group of senior clinicians who think more broadly about the patients, the trainees, the service itself, and their part in it. This needs to exist within a management structure that can trust and protect the whole enterprise.

The psychoanalytic stance, a socially unfamiliar one, is a most difficult one to learn, and the challenges are illustrated in this book beautifully and in a myriad ways. You are not supposed to be a teacher, a trainer, a friend, or a "better parent" to your patient, though under pressure you may long to be, even feel you should be. As many of the clinical authors here show strikingly, you may have to "unlearn" a more familiar and comfortable position you adopted previously—for example, as a doctor, a psychologist, nurse, or social worker. Maintaining a stance of sympathetic neutrality and observation attracts intense transferences that may puzzle, confuse, even frighten the new trainee, who may feel helpless or silly or even worried that they are behaving absurdly. Without skilled supervision to achieve some sense of conviction about your work, it is easy to collapse from being someone potentially new and transformative for the patient into someone more socially ordinary, responding "normally" to the patient with reassurance, explanation, exhortation, and so on. At this point, alas, you become exactly like the people already around the patient, unwittingly acting out the roles assigned to you from the patient's troubled inner world in a way that simply repeats their lifelong experiences.

I particularly like the way that the chapters by Francesca Hume, explaining concepts and the principles of learning, are then so vividly complemented and exemplified by the trainees. I am impressed by how carefully the authors show, from the point of view of the teacher and the student, that the psychoanalytic stance is painstakingly learnt anew by each apprentice clinician, struggling as they are in the sea of seen and unseen transferences, often with pain and struggle and against their own resistance. There is a freshness, honesty, and humility that shines through the clinical chapters. Patients and their struggles are described with respect and empathy. In these pages there is a real sense of learning together with the patient, and often a sense of impressive change and development taking place in both.

I found Part IV, about learning through clinical challenges, particularly moving: I admire the honest and articulate way that the authors describe how they struggled through and negotiated some of the most difficult clinical situations that any of us can face, particularly the death of a patient through illness or suicide. I am pleased that there are two chapters here on the sudden disorientating switch to online work necessitated by the pandemic, and what this meant for the work.

Psychoanalytic learning, as we see, takes place not just by listening to lectures or reading books, but by becoming a participant-observer in the clinical process. It is often when we are most at a loss, most confused and doubtful, that change can take place—something that I have always personally found a refreshing surprise and that makes this work so rewarding, but difficult.

I have worked in the NHS since 1975, and although I have seen many negative changes, I have seen a huge positive shift in perspective about respect and inclusion for disadvantaged groups and minorities. This book is exemplary for the way it devotes a part to diversity and psychoanalysis, inviting some colleagues from minority groups to be straightforward and honest about their experiences of training. Indeed, they were honest, and the rather sobering accounts of the experiences of clinicians from various sorts of minority groups show us that there is no place in our discipline for complacency.

Following five years as a senior member of staff at the Tavistock, my later ten-year-long role as external examiner for M1 training meant that I attended meetings of the whole staff group several times a year, giving my observations, feedback, or advice. I was impressed at first hand by the quality of thinking in these meetings, where the trainees and their work with patients were thought about in such depth by a group of dedicated senior colleagues. They worked hard, thinking about how to support junior colleagues in their next steps of learning, all the while keeping the welfare of the patients as the fundamental goal. I also, for a long time, read and commented on the trainee qualifying papers, something I found very rewarding. I have been delighted to see how some of the excellent papers I read then have been developed into book chapters here.

I did come to find disquieting over those ten years how the diameter of the circle of colleagues in these meetings diminished, slowly but inexorably. First there was no longer a need to search for extra chairs. Then, progressively, so few chairs were needed that we found ourselves allocated to ever smaller rooms. Senior staff were retiring in the normal course of events, but, perturbingly, they were often not replaced. And where they were, less experienced clinicians were often taken on at lower salary points. The Tavistock, like so many trusts, was under huge pressure to cut costs. In a way, how could the organization resist using such opportunities; but, then again, how could this not lead to a vicious circle of loss of morale, loss of expertise, in a much-prized training?

In her chapter on the changing NHS, Francesca outlines the series of seismic changes to the service during the gradual but determined imposition upon what was essentially a community of clinicians of a quasi "market" or "business" model and, together with this, piecemeal privatization. Internal fragmentation has led to situations where, following an unthought-out change of management structure, an artificial and disastrous division has been made between what are in fact indivisible parts of M1, threatening the core of the training and risking setting different groups of good, well-meaning people against each other.

Some of my own NHS training took place at a centre of excellence similar in some ways to the Tavistock. The Maudsley Psychotherapy Unit, where I was fortunate enough to learn on the job from excellent senior colleagues in the 1980s, was later disbanded as a department, its senior staff divided and sent out "to the community". In practice, this often means being taken *away from* a vibrant community of colleagues, who learn together, do excellent work with patients, and enrich each other's work, while training the next generation, to struggling in a small team, isolated and stretched to breaking point. The same would, strikingly, not be tolerated in physical medicine. World-class heart units are not habitually fragmented and allocated in bits to "the community". It is an interesting thought experiment to compare the steady improvements in treatment for those with physically "broken hearts" alongside the piecemeal and deteriorating provision for those whom we see as suffering from hearts that are broken, perhaps through childhood neglect and abuse, leaving the sufferer chronically depressed and anxious, maybe trapped in a miserable relationship, struggling to parent their own children.

Whatever our current troubles in the UK health service, the wisdom and thinking distilled in this book will be long-lasting, applying, as it does, not just to one service at one time. What we hear about in this book is how we learn and teach the craft of psychoanalytic psychotherapy. With each new therapist and patient, with each new supervisor, we see how it must be discovered and learnt anew. Each training organization has to go on learning too, keeping a "culture of enquiry" alive.

Introduction

Francesca Hume

In this book we illustrate the experiential learning involved in undertaking an adult psychoanalytic psychotherapy training. Much of what we describe is true of any psychoanalytic training, even if aspects of the context may be different. We hope, therefore, that the book will be of interest to anyone concerned with analytic learning and training. The setting we use to develop our ideas is a London-based public-sector training, in the UK's National Health Service (the NHS). This training is unique in the United Kingdom, as it embraces the whole breadth of psychoanalytic applications relevant to working across the public sector but does this alongside training its students to work intensively (three times per week) with long-term cases. This second aspect has been richly fed by the Tavistock's historical closeness with the Institute of Psychoanalysis, which has meant that Institute-trained psychoanalysts have always held prominent consultant-level positions at the Tavistock and have been involved in all aspects of the training.

Through a series of chapters written by the psychoanalytic psychotherapists who trained with us, we seek to illustrate their learning. We refer to them as "trainees", because the work they describe took place during their training, but most of the chapters were written towards the end of their training. We offer our thoughts about what was important in how they acquired their psychoanalytic knowledge and the type of experiential learning involved. As editors, we have not seen it as our role to explain to our trainees how they should learn or do learn, but, instead, we asked them to think about this for themselves and describe it to us through their chapters. Of course, we have had many discussions with them along the way and have invited them to talk to each other too. But these conversations have always started with what they have brought to us. A few seemed clear from the outset about what they wanted to say. Many started off wanting to write about a piece of work they felt particularly proud of. But, in general, and with encouragement, they have all been able to think about where the real learning took place for them, and, very often, they realized that this was where they had encountered some difficulty or other that needed to be understood. What we got back from them impressed us with its honesty and openness, many describing in very personal terms what they felt in themselves had hindered them and the impact this had had. Some allude to aspects of their own make-up, which, they felt, had interfered with being able to use their supervision or make better contact with their patients. Several felt they had had to "unlearn" old ways of thinking before they could engage in this new approach. For some, giving up the status and knowledge they already possessed, for the uncertain gains of a new approach, felt unwelcome. This was particularly true for those coming from other mental health disciplines, especially psychology and psychiatry. But mostly, when such struggles could be engaged with, there was a feeling of hard-won success. It will be obvious, too, that this sort of process mirrors in some way the experience that they were each involved in through the personal development taking place in their individual analyses. For all, their contribution was something that evolved as they got going with the thinking and writing.

And for us, the editors, there has been a similar evolution in our thinking. At the outset, we also started off with the rather simple idea that we would like to showcase the learning that was possible through the M1 training, at a time when one of us (FH) was stepping down from the leadership of the training, by publishing a book that included some of the best qualification papers written by our trainees. But we moved away from this notion, feeling that, while a series of clinical studies might be compelling, it would be far less informative than an account in which the student's own learning and development through their clinical encounters was at the heart.

This got us interested in thinking more deeply about the learning involved in becoming a psychoanalytic practitioner. My own development through this work was to examine, for the first time properly, what the process of *learning from experience* involves when applied to psychoanalytic training, to try to understand some of the anxieties that I was observing in the trainees, as well as a phenomenon that seemed so important: their exposure to a state of not knowing what was going on, and the capacity to tolerate this, rather than clinging to old knowledge and old ways of managing. This seemed to involve what I have referred to in the book as the *unlearning* of previously held knowledge—knowledge and experience that might continue to have a value in different contexts but was being used defensively now. I have offered my own thoughts about this in some of my chapters, referencing established theoretical works that have been helpful to me.

Book contents

The book is divided into six main parts.

Part I outlines the history of the M1 training and then presents the main theme of the book: how we come to acquire psychoanalytic knowledge in the process of psychoanalytic training. I discuss the complexity that exists for the trainee in being open intellectually and emotionally to new ideas and experiences, and some of the reasons why this can fail. I draw upon Bion's notion of learning from experience and suggest that didactic learning has little place in a psychoanalytic training. The question I address is the role of the trainer in encouraging learning and individual creativity. Permitting a trainee to take his or her own initiative requires us at times to think more deeply about what we are doing and can be felt to compete with the need to maintain a consistent approach to psychoanalytic teaching and practice and to keeping the needs of the patient at the centre of our minds.

Part II develops the theme of how we acquire analytic knowledge and looks more closely at what we mean by learning from experience. I start by addressing the selection of trainees: how we might think about their suitability and readiness to train, and some of the personal and intellectual qualities we look for. I then describe my understanding of the process of learning that is involved, and why we have chosen to use the term *unlearning* in the title of this part.

This is followed by six chapters by trainees describing their experience of training. Several focus on the challenges of giving up previous ways of engaging with psychological distress and disorder to be open to a new (psychoanalytic) approach. The central task of understanding the importance of unconscious processes and phantasy and recognizing enactments as they emerge in the analytic encounter are exemplified in many of these chapters. Some authors describe the difficult work involved in becoming competent in the application of this learning and what they came to feel had impeded them from doing so.

At the end of Part II, I describe the role of the clinical supervisor in assessing progress and fostering the trainee's development and some of the obstacles encountered by the supervisor. I give three vignettes from my experience as a supervisor.

Part III concerns the central topic of learning to understand and use the transference and the countertransference. I introduce the part with a brief historical look at the evolution of these concepts and how many analysts think about them today. The chapters that then follow convey how uncomfortable it is for trainees to have to bear the experience of not understanding their patients, or not understanding them well enough, often for a long time. Registering and tolerating this deeper experience is what we ask of our trainees if they are to develop analytically and work effectively with the transference and countertransference.

Part IV, introduced by Helen Barker, addresses the topic of "learning through clinical challenges". The challenges described include breakdowns and interruptions in treatment, the deaths of patients (from illness or suicide), and the ordinary but difficult experience when the therapist becomes pregnant during the course of a treatment. As Helen Barker puts it, "It is part of our everyday work to face difficulties. Sometimes these can be worked through and result in a sense of achievement and progress. At other times, there is an impasse or breakdown." The part concludes with two chapters that describe the impact of the Covid-19 pandemic and lockdown on trainees' experience of training.

In Part V we turn our attention to the important topic of diversity: sexuality, race, and ageing. We invited our contributors to tell us about any aspects of the training that made their experience more difficult than it needed to be, due to our own failings. We were particularly interested to hear from trainees who might feel marginalized or discriminated against due to some aspect of their identities. This part is introduced by Poul Rohleder, who also contributes a chapter on sexual diversity.

Finally, Part VI addresses some of the pressures and storms that the M1 training has had to withstand in recent years, and the concern these pose for the future of the M1 training and of the place of psychoanalysis in the public sector. I consider the ways in which a culture of enquiry (as described by Tom Main), so essential to psychoanalytic learning at the individual level, is also essential at the level of the whole institution and can become degraded or lost.

The book closes with some final reflections, pulling together the themes that have emerged.

PART I

TEACHING AND LEARNING

Francesca Hume

Chapter 1 describes the Tavistock's inception and then gives an account of how adult psychoanalytic psychotherapy training developed there, culminating in the establishment of the M1 training in the 1970s. We give a sense of the prevailing cultural and political ethos at its start and how a training evolved to educate clinicians whose careers involved the implementation of psychoanalytic treatments in the public sector, across a broad spectrum of clinical situations. Chapter 2 moves away from the specific training at the Tavistock and addresses the topic of analytic learning more broadly. It describes how a capacity to learn experientially lies at the heart of all analytic training. It requires a particular immersion in all the areas—one that exposes the trainee to both emotional and intellectual challenges.

CHAPTER ONE

Education at the Tavistock and the development of an adult psychoanalytic psychotherapy training

Francesca Hume

A brief history of education at the Tavistock

The Tavistock Clinic was established in 1920 by Hugh Crichton-Miller, following his experience of working with shell-shocked soldiers in the First World War. At the start its doctrine was to "have no doctrine", instead emphasizing flexibility of approach. The clinic provided free outpatient treatment for adults and children suffering from neuroses. From 1920 it was based in a small building in Tavistock Square, Bloomsbury, but, swamped by the immense demands for clinical services and training, it moved to larger premises in 1932 and, again, in 1945. The Tavistock Clinic joined the new National Health Service at its inception in 1948. The move to its current building in Belsize Lane came in 1967.

In his book *Fifty Years of the Tavistock Clinic* (1970), Dicks describes the approach to educational activities at the Tavistock. Until the start of the war, under the auspices of J. R. Rees, the Tavistock was still distanced from psychoanalysis but, in 1947, Jock Sutherland took over as director, remaining in post until 1968. It was under his leadership that the Tavistock became more firmly psychoanalytic in its approach. While in post, Sutherland instituted a model of on-the-job training which included weekly case conferences plus theoretical seminars.

Battles over money were present from the start of the NHS, absorbing the time and energy of the clinic leadership. But the fact that these analytically trained officers were the ones involved in those struggles protected the analytic culture at the Tavistock, allowing for its development in a way that is much harder today, when many managers are no longer mental health practitioners.

In 1948, John Bowlby and Esther Bick developed a Child Psychotherapy training which included the first infant observation programme and was accessible to health professionals from diverse backgrounds. In the Adult Department progress was slower, with training restricted to the psychiatrists employed by the clinic who were concurrently training at the Institute of Psychoanalysis. Over time, and in response to the expressed demand from psychiatric trainees, a programme was developed in the Adult Department which consisted of a personal analysis for the trainee, together with supervised intensive individual and group experience, supplemented by seminars and attendance at staff meetings. This programme aimed to provide an understanding of the basic psychodynamic doctor/patient relationship. The course extended over two years, was very popular and always over-subscribed.

In the 1950s there was on-going discussion about the dependence of Adult Department trainees upon the training given at the Institute of Psychoanalysis for the acquisition of analytic skills. Sutherland took the view that, if psychoanalytic expertise were necessary in the NHS, then the NHS itself should provide it. In the end it was agreed that "the real task of the Tavistock was to provide training which was different from, but complementary to, the training given by the Institute of Psychoanalysis" (Dicks, 1970, p. 255). So, the decision was made to complement the analytic training with experience and teaching in brief psychotherapy, work with groups, families and marriages, all to be delivered by exponents of psychoanalysis.

In 1957 the Tavistock Institute of Human Relations launched the first group relations experiments, in partnership with Leicester University. The Leicester Conferences signalled the start of another area of training at the Tavistock which, along with infant observation, established a unique approach based on Bion's theory of learning from experience. Both these developments, over ensuing years, have richly influenced the adult training programmes too.

By the 1960s the adult training programme was extended, so that, as well as doctors, psychologists and social workers could train too. Moreover, trainees were now required to take on patients for intensive (three-times-weekly) training. This four-year training was starting to resemble today's M1 training.

Increasingly, those undertaking the Tavistock training programmes were expressing the need for some kind of formal accreditation and paper qualification. Links started to be made with the relevant professional organizations, including the ACP (Association of Child Psychotherapy), BCP (now the BPC or British Psychoanalytic Council) and BPS (British Psychological Society).

The M1 training: a broad education to prepare for a career in the public sector

The M1 Tavistock qualification in adult psychotherapy (TQAP) was, from its informal beginnings in the 1950s and 1960s, an apprenticeship training, which was completely embedded in the adult department's clinical service. The clinical service was home to the patients who passed through its doors and to the students who were there to learn their trade from a large group of senior staff delivering teaching and supervision. The training sat at the very centre of this public sector clinical service, and the trainees who belonged there enjoyed a symbiotic relationship in which they were looked after, supervised, and taught by a clinical service who benefitted from a workforce of intelligent and committed trainees. The senior staff comprised medical doctors, clinical psychologists, and social workers. All were qualified psychoanalysts from the Institute of Psychoanalysis. The Adult Department evolved with three clinical units, each comprising staff from all the mental health disciplines and led by one of the senior staff. As well as offering the rare provision in the NHS of long-term, individual, intensive, three-times-weekly psychoanalytic therapy, patients were also seen for once-weekly therapy for shorter periods of time. There was also the tradition of analytic group psychotherapy (a legacy of Wilfred Bion's from his time at the Tavistock Clinic); trainees ran their own psychotherapy groups for three years and were also encouraged to apply group analytic principles to working with organizations and institutions. In addition, trainees were required to undertake a large number of closely supervised clinical consultations, to learn the complex skills involved in psychoanalytic assessment.

Well into the second decade of the twenty-first century, all trainees undertaking the M1 training were able to benefit from this full apprenticeship in the application of psychoanalysis to working in the NHS: the model of learning spelled out above, in which knowledge was derived through the lived experience of working on a clinical unit, seeing diverse types of patient under supervision, all alongside more formal channels of academic teaching and supervision.

Trainees would attend all the regular meetings in which complex clinical problems were discussed, always with an analytic understanding at the centre but at which relevant psychiatric aspects and any risk management issues would also be considered. In this way, trainees would witness the struggles involved in reaching clinical formulations, making difficult clinical decisions, and agreeing appropriate treatment requirements. The seniors were there not just to showcase their greater knowledge and experience, but as colleagues engaged and struggling with their day-to-day clinical work.

Over the decades, many specialist units were developed and led by senior practitioners: a Trauma Unit (started by Caroline Garland and later developed by Jo Stubley), a Couples' Therapy Unit (Joanna Rosenthal and others), a Brief Psychotherapy Unit (Peter Hobson), the Fitzjohn's Unit (for more severely ill psychotic and personality disordered patients started by David Taylor and led for many years by David Bell), units for patients suffering with eating disorders (Marilyn Lawrence), researching and treating severe refractory depressive illness (David Taylor), and more. There were workshops established that combined clinical presentation with academic teaching on Assessments (John Steiner), an internationally famous Borderline Workshop (John Steiner), a Groups Workshop (led at different times by Caroline Garland, Francesca Hume, and Liz Gibb), a Transference Workshop (led by Francesca Hume and Peter Hobson), and a "Thinking Space" Workshop addressing diversity (Frank Lowe and Maxine Dennis). Many of these units have resulted in publications in the Tavistock Series (Garland, 2002, 2010; Lawrence, 2008; Lowe, 2013; Meyerowitz & Bell, 2018; Stubley & Young, 2021; Taylor, 2017).

Competition for salaried trainee posts was fierce, and trainees were assessed on both their commitment to psychoanalysis as well as a future career in the NHS. By the late 1980s, salaried apprenticeship posts were available across all four professions (medicine, psychology, social work, and nursing), and post-holders were encouraged to maintain links with their core professional disciplines, in the hope of disseminating analytic ideas and applications further afield.

As post-holders were undertaking a training in delivering three-times-weekly psychoanalytic psychotherapy, it was an expectation that they would themselves receive psychoanalysis or psychoanalytic psychotherapy at a minimum frequency of three times a week (though mostly five times weekly).

By the time the British Confederation of Psychotherapists (the forerunner of the British Psychoanalytic Council) was set up in 1992, the training was well placed to become an important member and has been so since then.

Ties with the Institute of Psychoanalysis remained informal but strong, and, because the M1 training was unique in equipping its trainees with a public-sector-based education, people often chose to train both at the Institute (with its focus on depth through five-times-weekly analytic treatment) as well as benefiting from the clinical breadth and application provided by the M1 training.

So, the M1 training evolved to be a precious and rare NHS provision. It equipped those who undertook it to work at a consultant level in the NHS and, in turn, provided the NHS with a highly experienced workforce conversant with the application of psychoanalytic ideas to everyday clinical problems. There are many threats to the continuing existence and quality of the M1 training, and some of these are described here. We hope that the rich personal accounts that follow will make a cogent case for the protection of this kind of 360-degree apprenticeship-style education.

The M1 training and the current context of psychoanalytic training in the NHS

Sadly, the environment for the analytic apprentice has become increasingly challenging. Today, some of the clinical activities and applications have been lost, and others are available only to those entering the training as junior psychiatrists.

For this reason, a concern for us, as editors, was whether this book would stand as a positive account of an exceptional training that *still is*—something that continues to feel vital and solid—or whether we were writing about something that *once was*. Were we describing a training that continues to have a credible place in today's beleaguered public sector, or would this come to feel like an obituary to a golden era of yesterday? Our hope is to inspire future generations of trainees when they read the many vivid clinical accounts given in this book. But we have had to reflect also on the current state of affairs, the wider context of an under-resourced NHS, and the place of psychoanalysis within that, as well as the currently politically troubled condition at the Tavistock Centre, and the difficulties that that poses for the M1 training based there. While it is beyond the scope of this book to describe all the current struggles—financial, cultural, and political—some of the chapters allude to these. In the penultimate chapter (chapter 26), I address the serious impact of recent changes upon the viability of the training and upon the culture in which trainees now have to operate. I suggest that there is a very real risk of losing a thoughtful culture of enquiry, and of this being replaced by a culture of action and doing, as staff seek to manage the anxiety that arises from institutional pressures: fears about financial and resource realities and ever-increasing demands. A culture of enquiry needs to exist at every level, from the trainee learning his trade, to the trainers and to the whole institution. This requires us to remain vigilant to the possibility of degradation into what Tom Main describes as ritualized and stale "knowledge" of how things are or should be done.

In chapter 9, a trainee, Rachel Hodgins, touches upon the impact of recent changes on her training: "At the time of writing there are changes happening at every level, from the staff and structure of the course itself, to the organization of clinical services in the Trust where we're based, to national and international changes to public health provision [such as the Health and Care Bill 2021] and the aftermath of Covid-19 on NHS staff and services."

The population of patients has also become more complex as the survival of the service has depended upon a shift from being a generic adult service to a "complex-needs" service managing more troubled patients, often in shorter treatments. Such patients do not make straightforward training cases, and, not infrequently, trainees have had to manage anxiety about a patient's risk from self-harm, psychiatric breakdown, and suicide while trying to maintain an analytic frame. There are examples of such cases in the chapters that follow.

More recently, there has been the Covid-19 pandemic to contend with, and many trainees have been obliged to take on training cases remotely using the internet or the telephone. Several chapters allude to this challenge and to the eerie experience of returning to an empty Tavistock "Ghost Ship"—the Institution that had once been a vibrant, containing "Brick Mother" (Rey, 1994, quoted by Alan Baban in chapter 8).

But, in the end, we wanted to convey our feeling that, while the future of analytic training within the NHS is uncertain, there is much that is worth fighting for, and there remains an identifiable place for analytic approaches and training in the public sector. No one closely observing the impact of analytic treatments on our patients can seriously doubt the value of such work, and many of the contributions in this book are a testimony to that. Some chapters refer to this aspect directly. For example, in chapter 6 Simon Shaw draws upon the contrast that can be made with the grandiose claims of proponents of other treatment modalities. He reviews some of the research evidence that suggests that long-term psychoanalytic psychotherapy might be particularly justified as a treatment of choice for more complex mental disorders and may be cost-effective when other factors, such as decreased presentations and costs to other parts of the NHS, such as to GPs and A&E departments, are considered.

And, for now, The M1 training still exists, and new generations of trainees remain as passionate, talented, and committed as they ever were, even if they find themselves frequently embroiled in trying to defend aspects of the training that they hold dear and rightly fear they could lose. We (the editors) completed the training ourselves many years ago and at a time when we were able to benefit from the full richness it then provided. Along with the sorrow and anger of seeing the current threats and difficulties the training faces is the guilt that comes from witnessing so many gifted trainees having to struggle to acquire what we benefitted from with less difficulty.

Perhaps we can draw some comfort from a piece written in 1969 by J.D. Sutherland (officer in charge at the Tavistock Clinic between 1947 and 1968). Then, as now, he described the forces working against the establishment of a psychoanalytic centre, forces that pointed to a need to remain creative to ensure their relevance and survival:

> I have tried to show in these "working notes" what I perceive to be the forces coming into more prominence in our society, and which are impinging upon us with increasing urgency. Far from being on the "way out", psychoanalytic knowledge could, and should, be more than ever on the "way in". It is incumbent upon psychoanalysts, especially those in specialist centres, as many of us now are, to study the current scene as carefully as we can and to act constructively to the best of our ability. I believe that, if we do not innovate in regard to our own roles, our mental health centres will shrivel and hence the welfare and development movements will be impoverished. [Sutherland, 1969, p. 682.]

Whatever the future of the M1 training, it has also given us the opportunity to examine this question of how we acquire analytic knowledge and expertise. The fact that there have been many new challenges to face has also given us and the trainees some striking situations to think about and learn from.

CHAPTER TWO

On the acquisition of psychoanalytic knowledge and attitude: fostering development and learning from experience

Francesca Hume

The question of how much psychoanalysis can be taught has occupied many authors, with several (e.g., Ekstein, 1969) preferring the notion of a psychoanalytic *education* rather than a *training*. But the notion of an education *per se* doesn't capture the particular nature of the learning involved in psychoanalysis, or the complex interplay between emotional and intellectual aspects, personal qualities, and psychological readiness in developing a psychoanalytic attitude. There is also little consensus as to the relative emphasis that should be given to the acquisition of theoretical facts versus clinical understanding. Different views are expressed across the continents, as well as differences about how best to teach either.

Freud goes to the heart of the problem in a letter to Fritz Wittels, where he writes, "I cannot make any use of ideas that are suggested to me when I am not ready for them" (in E. L. Freud, 1960, p. 346). This might strike a note of caution in the over-zealous teacher hoping to circumvent the issue of the trainees' state: their readiness, maturity, and the particular meaning and impact that psychoanalytic ideas will have upon them.

This more theoretical chapter examines the question of how analytic learning is acquired and evolves. But I want to start with three quotes from the chapters that follow that convey vividly something of the trainees' inchoate and confused state of mind when they first begin with a patient:

In chapter 5, Anne McKay writes: "I felt I was losing my way. I also felt that I was being boring and cruel. For months I was stuck, unable to find a way to talk to her. I think I did not take seriously enough her experience that feeling so dependent upon the therapy was humiliating. My supervisor observed that she was experiencing my attempts to help as a weapon that I was using to bring her down, to prove *my* superiority. This very wise advice did not sink in until much later. I felt stupid, and I felt shame, and I did not see that my patient did too."

In similar vein, Michelle Washington writes, in chapter 12: "The disruptive nature of her projections, and the force and accuracy with which they were delivered, made it easy to lose sight of their communicative function. At such times my interpretations felt like amalgamations of words, inauthentic and devoid of substance. I recall how often my supervisor needed to point out my tendency to take Ms L and her narrative at 'face value', thereby only reaching the more adult part of my patient's personality. Thus, when we were operating within this environment and Ms L would tell me that I had 'nearly but not quite understood', she was absolutely correct!"

And, finally, in chapter 6, Simon Shaw: "I was right at the start of learning a new way of listening and responding: one that involved trying to think about the patient's associations, while not getting too caught up in the content of what I was being told. I was also becoming aware of the changing mood in the room and the connections (and disconnections) between this and what was being said. This free-floating attention was hard to maintain when I felt so lost in these early sessions. My anxiety caused me to speak prematurely at the start of the session or to grasp for some concrete point of understanding. I recall my supervisor suggesting that, if I didn't understand what was going on in a session, I should wait before speaking. I remember thinking that, if I did that, I'd never say anything at all!"

As well as feeling inept and unskilled, these trainees convey how, at this early stage, it was difficult to take in the advice they were being given, advice that later could feel helpful.

Freud himself recognized that psychoanalysis could only be taught when it came at the right time and was met in the trainee by a need to satisfy his own curiosity (Freud, 1913c). He seemed to favour an approach that trainees should not be taught in a technically prescriptive fashion, but be permitted to take the initiative, to be actively engaged with the work, and face the difficulties as they emerge: "The candidate who understands the case will know what to do since that *'ergibt sich von selbst'* [follows by itself]" (Ekstein, 1969, p. 316).

So, for Freud and his immediate followers, supervision was an informal affair, and, while stressing the place of intellectual understanding, he seems to have relied upon the educative power of the personal analysis in reaching an emotional and intuitive understanding, paying less attention to pedagogy. Even in relation to personal analysis, however, he appears to have had a fairly laissez faire attitude. Ekstein (1969) describes how Freud's student, Siegfried Bernfeld suggested to Freud that he might have some analytic treatment as preparation before embarking on seeing a patient. Freud's answer: "Nonsense. Go right ahead. You certainly will have difficulties. When you get into trouble, we will see what we can do about it" (in Ekstein, 1969, p. 314).

In fact, in relation to didactic learning, Freud wrote:

> Anyone who hopes to learn the noble game of chess from books will soon discover that only the openings and end-games admit of an exhaustive systematic presentation and that the infinite variety of moves which develop after the opening defy any such description. This gap in instruction can only be filled by a diligent study of games fought out by masters. [Freud, 1913c, p. 123]

Bernfeld (1952) suggests, however, that Freud had discovered the futility of passing on information didactically, as the very nature of the analytic process taught him that learning implies change, and that change is resisted, only coming about experientially by working through, not by hearing bits of information, no matter how correct.

The central point has to do with this capacity to learn *experientially*. The three trainees quoted above illustrate that it is not enough for us to simply impart knowledge: the trainee must engage with it himself, tussle with it, and cathect it. And while this begins with a personal analysis and the insight that comes from that, it extends far beyond it. It requires a particular kind of immersion throughout a training that exposes the trainee to emotional and intellectual challenges that come from the clinical and theoretical components of the training. These challenges must then be met by certain essential personal qualities: patience and a capacity to bear frustration and anxiety, as well as curiosity, intuition, and empathy, to mention some of the important ones.

Tom Main (1967) who has written about experiential learning describes the importance of the learner's state of mind, He reminds us that the fate of knowledge when it reaches the other is not at all ensured by its truthfulness or its usefulness in reality, and:

> An assiduous teaching of theories and facts, an honest sharing of discoveries and a liberal training in skills give no guarantee that any will be learned and used appropriately. Even when they are well learned, there can be no certainty that the student will understand them in the manner intended by the trainer, still less that he will use them in

the service of further thought. We can never be sure whether knowledge will form the basis of later initiative in thinking, learning and the growth of techniques, or whether thorough training, far from equipping the individual for independent work, will only increase his dependence on the trainer and his appetite for further passive experience, and thus inhibit his own thinking. [Main, 1967, p. 64]

He vividly describes the possible sequelae of a more prescriptive form of didactic teaching, using digestive metaphors:

If the object is forcibly fed into the mind, it may be internalised in a particular oral way, mentally swallowed whole, thereafter, to lie as an unassimilated foreign body, disturbing and preoccupying the mind, later perhaps to be mentally vomited, evacuated or digested with more or less pain. The starved learner in particular may swallow an idea with eager undiscriminating delight, and thereafter be preoccupied with it, in windy indigestion to the exclusion of all other interests. Mental food may be used to create idle mental fat, or great energy and activity, or to whet the appetite for more. [p. 66]

We can see in these passages that, while Main does not state it explicitly, he is addressing the relationship that exists between the trainer and trainee. And in this book, which is about analytic learning, we also address this relationship at various points. What is our role as teachers in helping to determine a favourable outcome? Even if we understand the dangers of a didactic approach, do we consider how we facilitate the trainee's learning and the importance of not interfering with their own efforts to learn? When is criticism constructive, and when does it lead to the trainee feeling discouraged? Are we facilitating a creative space to learn from experience, to develop a psychoanalytic identity that feels authentic? In general, I would say we are often guilty of a certain laziness, passively following the ways of our own teachers. We may also be guilty of enjoying rather than questioning the general tendency among trainees to idealize us, rather than seeing it as evidence of a passivity that is inimical to creative learning. Main wrote that "enthusiasm or popularity in a trainer is . . . no criterion of excellence. The popular trainer may be one who simply creates dependency" (Main, 1967, p. 67). He suggests that forceful, sure teaching by an authority seems to hasten the process whereby an idea degenerates into a belief by hierarchical promotion, and that the clear expositor who knows best is most likely to produce this result.

Encouraging individual creativity and permitting the trainee to take their own initiative requires us to think more deeply about what we are doing and can be felt to compete with the need to maintain a consistent approach to teaching psychoanalytic practice. Moreover, we are always mindful of the patients and their need for a competent professional clinician.

The epistemophilic instinct and the trainee's capacity for creativity and learning

Any analytic discussion of the trainee's capacity to learn might usefully include some reference to what psychoanalysts have had to say about the "epistemophilic instinct" (variously described as the "desire for truth", the "drive for knowledge" or the "instinct of curiosity"). While not actually an instinct in the narrow sense of the word, Freud saw the epistemophilic instinct as related to the sexual instinct: "We have learnt from psycho-analysis that the instinct for knowledge in children is attracted unexpectedly early and intensively to sexual problems and is in fact possibly first aroused by them" (Freud, 1905d, p. 194). In his view, a thirst for knowledge was inseparable from sexual curiosity (Freud, 1909b).

Later, in 1925, writing about the response to novelty, Freud describes this as ranging "from fear through curiosity and exploration [and] is shown to be very much present in the psychoanalytic situation" (1925f, p. 213). He tells us that the "source of this unpleasure is the demand made upon the mind of anything that is new, the psychical expenditure that it requires, the uncertainty, mounting up to anxious expectancy, which it brings along with it" (p. 213). Freud discusses novelty with reference to the timing and phrasing of interpretation. Novelty, then, signals danger, and defences are aroused against it, which can interfere with the desire and acquisition of new learning.

While Freud focused on the links between infantile sexuality (libido) and curiosity, Klein was concerned with the way in which the child's very earliest anxieties both interfere with and promote intellectual development (Klein, 1921, 1928). She was struck by the violence of the infant's phantasized attacks on the mother's body, the anxiety this gave rise to, and the relationship between these two things and the child's capacity to feel curious. It was her observations of young children that led to her conclusion that their central anxiety was associated with their phantasies about exploring the inside of the mother's body and destroying its contents. She observed that the ensuing anxiety provided a huge impetus to the development of interests and sublimations, acting as a continuous incentive to observe and learn about the external world, as a way of understanding the internal world better. But if anxiety was too overwhelming, this could interfere with the child's intellectual curiosity and development. Severe difficulties arose when the internal world so dominated the child that anxieties could not be disproved.

Unconscious drives, then—libidinal and aggressive—lie behind curiosity. This, and the need to negotiate developmental conflicts, is the motivating force in acquiring knowledge for both Freud and Klein. Despite their different explanations, both maintain that an interest in the environment is imposed on infants: they are obliged to negotiate powerful anxieties if they are to deal with a reality that frightens or frustrates them and is felt to conflict with the drive to satisfy their own needs. In the course of normal development, curiosity loses its sexual component and helps in mastering the external world: the real world in which the infant lives. All of this involves active engagement, and it will be obvious that a good-enough resolution of these early struggles is what is needed to remain curious and to learn.

In his own discussion of curiosity, Bion (1959) suggests that Freud's analogy of an archaeological investigation with a psychoanalysis is helpful 'if it were considered that we were exposing evidence not so much of a primitive civilization as of a primitive disaster'. He attributes a lack of progress in analysis to the destruction of a capacity for curiosity and the consequent inability to learn. He reminds us that early curiosity develops in the paranoid-schizoid phase in which both the self and the other are experienced in part-object ways and not as whole objects. The preoccupation at this stage is with function rather than structure ('feeding' rather than 'breast') which is why there is the impression of a dynamic disaster rather than a static situation. He suggests that problems and understanding that depend upon an awareness of causality, 'cannot be stated, let alone solved'. This is because the question 'why is something?' has been split off through guilt (guilt being an affect that can only be managed later in the depressive position). Returning to the trainee, I suggest that under the pressure of managing primitive anxieties in themselves and in their patients they may be exposed to earlier struggles associated with an inhibition in thinking and curiosity and a concreteness of thought. I think this is particularly true when the anxieties in question are associated with guilt and frustrated reparative urges in the face of clinical dilemmas that are felt to be too big and their own sense of mastery of them, too small.

Bion hugely enriched our psychoanalytic understanding of the instinct to know and its relationship with the development of the capacity to think. For him, the experience of 'knowing' is rooted in an object-relationship— that of being known by another person. The fascinating implication is that emotional knowledge precedes cognitive understanding and underpins all knowledge that follows. He takes us back to the very start of life and the emotional experience of striving to know. It is this striving that he felt underpinned cognitive development. His theory of thinking is based upon his view that "pure thoughts" (or "preconceptions") exist in us before there is a mind to think them. This is what he means when he tells us that thoughts precede being able to think (Bion, 1962b, p. 306). It is the infant's contact with the external world (through the sense organ of consciousness) that stimulates development. He must create a thinking apparatus to deal with the pressure of primitive thoughts. In other words, he develops a mind that can become a container to think the thoughts it contains.

Bion describes this as the outcome of emotional events between mother and infant (in the early feeding situation). It begins when the infant projects his uncontainable fear, discomfort, and anxiety into the mother. At first, it is she who must act as a container for her child's experience. She receives these projections, and, at an unconscious level, she modifies them so that the infant can re-introject their experience in a manageable form (a form that could be felt and thought about by her). Her "reverie" is her ability to modify her child's tensions and anxieties in this way. The mother and the child form a "thinking couple", which is the prototype of the thinking process that continues developing throughout life.

Bion's concern therefore was with *thinking* as a human link and the emotional experience of trying to know oneself or someone else, to comprehend the reality of both. He distinguished the process of coming to know oneself through such experience (the *getting to know*) from the more static position of being *in possession of* knowledge. The extent to which this succeeds or fails depends upon both constitutional aspects in the infant—the capacity to manage frustration or not—and the pivotal role of the mother's capacity to facilitate this through her capacity for reverie. Being unable to bear frustration has major consequences for the infant's cognitive development and subsequent emotional adjustment. One very important implication of Bion's theory is that knowledge of the psychological precedes knowledge of the physical.

Returning to the psychoanalytic trainee, it will be clear that the capacity to *know*, or, rather, to *get to know*, in the sense of *learning from experience*, will depend upon the success or otherwise with which these early experiences have been negotiated, and whether any difficulties have been amenable to subsequent psychoanalytic treatment. Development through analysis is uneven and never complete, and we should expect that trainees will have areas of vulnerability and may lack awareness of many of their own unconscious responses.

Moreover, although all learning interacts with a trainee's unconscious struggles and resistance, it has been suggested (Keiser, 1969) that the acquisition of psychoanalytic knowledge holds a unique position in this regard. The emotional and personal significance of what the trainee has to learn has been specifically repressed (or otherwise defended against) and is likely once to have been a prime source of anxiety. Arguably, the trainee for whom this has no affective significance may be too insensitive to be suited to the profession. In ordinary teaching, there is little concern given to the emotional impact of the theoretical content. This is left to the trainee's personal analysis. But the latter may also coincide with the subject matter, increasing the anxiety and leading either to a difficulty in tolerating knowing or what Steinberg (1993) has described as a *hyper-cathexis of the drive to know*: a psychological inability to tolerate not knowing.

One trainee I supervised, expressed the problem thus: "I spent the first six months with my patient trying to avoid knowing what I was feeling—that I was more similar to him [the patient] than I cared to believe. But once that penny had dropped, I felt I saw evidence of my own psychopathology in everything the patient said and everything I read. No amount of reading and researching was enough to relieve me of the anxiety that I was as troubled and disturbed as him."

Perhaps the best we can do as teachers and supervisors is to emphasize the mutative emotional experiences involved in training over the acquisition of facts, and to keep in mind the uncertain journey taken by analytic knowledge as it passes from teacher to trainee and its fate within the trainee once it arrives there. But what we are most concerned to see is that a trainee is able to move away from a position of simply possessing factual knowledge and to engage with the struggles and frustrations involved in coming to know.

Another aspect to consider is that whatever the talents of the trainee, psychoanalytic training must also have ways of teaching through which trainees can grow beyond their training. Only then can they contribute to the development of the profession rather than just becoming technically competent and useful to their patients.

With regards to nurturing talent and creativity in our profession Keiser (1969) suggested that

> the history of the "genius" usually reveals that the conventional rules for education and/or training simply do not apply. Out of a synthesis of knowledge of the past such unique individuals create something new. Then "ordinary" mortals must be trained to develop and apply the new knowledge. Others with a quantum of giftedness (only by comparison) will be educated to expand, enrich, clarify, and fulfil the intellectual potential of the gift offered to the world by the genius. That is the most an educational institute can do. It cannot "produce" a genius. At best, it can give him or her a home." [Kreisler, 1969, p. 240]

Freud, as a teacher, gave us not only many new thoughts, but also a *way of thinking about these thoughts,* to keep them alive and able to evolve. Ekstein suggests that Freud gives us a way to look at analytic facts, citing what he has to say about analogies: they are useful "but we have constantly to keep changing these analogies for none of them lasts us long enough" (Freud, 1926e, p. 195). He suggests that this "spirit of enquiry" in relation to scientific conceptualization

> make(s) it possible for Freud not to get caught in a closed system, but constantly to change it, and to build into psychoanalytic science that open-mindedness, that possibility for creative advance, which is necessary if one wants to follow his spirit, and not merely accept analogies as a static, final body of knowledge, but to teach them in such a way that the total field can develop and expand. [Ekstein, 1969, p. 319]

He says that we should try to be alert to this if we are to avoid "falling into the trap of the kind of training orientation which maintains the Institution, the profession, but closes the inherent possibility of change."

Later, I return to this theme of how important it is to keep the training institution alive and creative in its thinking, and I also comment on some of the serious problems facing our institutions and the damaging impact they are having. I refer to Main's "culture of enquiry" so that ideas that start out as thought-provoking don't become degraded into meaningless rituals or even dogmas to be worshipped. Organizations are particularly vulnerable to this at times when there is anxiety and uncertainty about the future. A thoughtful, enquiring culture becomes replaced by ritualized practices as a defence against the primitive dread of "not-knowing".

To conclude

I have been discussing the complexity that exists for the trainee in being open intellectually and emotionally to new ideas and experiences, and some of the reasons why this can fail. I have particularly emphasized Bion's notion of learning from experience, one that many have found important and have developed. Even for Bion, however, this idea was derivative. It comes from Freud, who was himself much inspired by another, Goethe, and quoted these famous lines several times in his works: "*Was du ererbt von deinen Vätern hast/Erwirb es, um es zu besitzen*" ["What thou hast inherited from thy fathers, make not only thine but thee"] (Goethe, 1808).

While Freud was mostly discussing the passing down of different aspects of the psychological disposition (the working through, for example, of a sense of inherited unconscious guilt) it is true also of the inheritance of knowledge: it is not enough to passively receive information that is given to you: received knowledge needs to be reasserted and engaged with, and only then does it properly become yours. This is the process of internalization, integration, and consolidation that is of such interest to us in this book.

The chapters that follow capture the experience of some of our trainees and the struggles and challenges they faced in acquiring new psychoanalytic knowledge through experience.

PART II

LEARNING AND UNLEARNING

Francesca Hume

On learning and unlearning, knowing and not knowing

Part II is based on trainees' accounts of their experiences of training and, specifically, the learning and unlearning involved.

In Chapter 3, I set the scene with some general remarks about the selection of trainees and my analytic understanding of the nature of the process of learning that is involved, and why it is that we use the term *unlearning* in the title here.

To exemplify the kind of learning encountered at the start of the course, we asked six trainees to write about their experiences. In different ways, they describe grappling with feelings of inadequacy and feeling professionally at loss, as well as the strategies they used to protect themselves against these feelings. But they all go on to demonstrate the learning that can occur if these difficult states can be tolerated and understood. Several also allude to the role their supervisor played in their development.

Era Trieman (chapter 4) reflects upon his experience with his first training case, when he was new to the training and in the throes of his own analysis. Patient and student feel lost and persecuted and find themselves retreating into an idealized relationship with one other in which supervisor and analyst are felt to be interfering and undermining.

Anne McKay (chapter 5) describes what happens when patient and therapist are caught in a struggle to give up that which is familiar to them:

the security and status felt to lie in what is already known and the pleasure of feeling in a "one-up" position in relation to another. She examines her feelings of vulnerability in the face of a training that challenges her prior knowledge, and how this makes her unable to be properly receptive to her patient. She must recognize and metabolize this experience before she can help her patient. In the end, patient and therapist start to embrace the unknown and hold out for the uncertain gains that might come from learning something new.

Simon Shaw (chapter 6) describes a very troubled man who engaged in risky and aggressive sado-masochistic sex with men he found on the internet. The chapter describes his own development from his nursing identity to a psychoanalytic one. In addition, he makes a compelling case for the importance of being able to offer long-term NHS analytic treatment for such patients.

Malika Verma (chapter 7) focuses on the difficulty for a new therapist and a new patient to share space. Both feel vulnerable and exposed. She reflects upon the way her own defensive armour shields her from feelings of inadequacy but makes it difficult for her to recognize her patient's predicament and the need to hold on to her narcissistic and omnipotent defences. In her moving chapter she describes the journey of the patient and therapist couple in reaching the person behind the defences and the role of the supervisor who holds compassion and sanity on behalf of the warring couple.

Alan Baban and Rachel Hodgins, in their chapters, approach the topic of learning and unlearning from a different perspective, that of joining the Tavistock as staff members from previous careers in psychiatry and psychology, respectively.

Alan Baban (chapter 8) describes his discomfort as he rotates to the Tavistock from an all-action psychiatric service in which there is a premium on moving quickly and solving clinical crises by doing "something", without really understanding the nature of the patient's predicament. Alan's initial confusion on arrival at the Tavistock ultimately gives way to his realizing that a manic approach to understanding patients runs the risk of dangerous enactments. Psychotic processes that may originate in the patient come to pervade the functioning of those trying to help them. This insight helps him move towards a different kind of understanding, but only when he can bear the feeling that he must slow down and wait for meaning to emerge through deeper understanding. His experience reminded me of the words of the White Rabbit in Alice in Wonderland, who shouts, "Don't just do something, stand there!"

Rachel Hodgins (chapter 9) also describes the relief she came to feel when she started to have an analytic framework for thinking about powerful pressures and dynamics in an inpatient unit. Her interest in analytic ideas seems to have begun early in her career as a clinical psychologist, and she describes the tension involved in holding on to two very different frameworks: an analytic one and mainstream clinical psychology. She explores how, in her words, she has to "re-think authority, power, and expertise in the therapy room".

At the end of this part, in chapter 10, I examine the role of the supervisor in helping the students in their learning, giving several examples from my own experience as a supervisor.

CHAPTER THREE

Trainee selection and the challenge of experiential learning

Francesca Hume

Albert Einstein (1931) wrote that "Information is not knowledge. The only source of knowledge is experience. You need experience to gain wisdom."

Trainee selection

I suspect that we are not particularly good at selecting analytic trainees, as, in my experience, we are often surprised by how an individual develops. Unpromising trainees sometimes blossom and others struggle more than anticipated. Despite this, trainees pursuing the M1 training have all been through a rigorous selection process, and, to some extent, this ensures that those who are either entirely unsuitable or unready do not begin. Temperamentally, we are interested in whether a trainee appears to have a passion for the subject. This is very important, given the emotional and intellectual demands of the training. Having a certain kind of intellect is important too: a preparedness to take time to understand, an interest in the attention to detail and a dislike of glib or hasty conclusions. Emotional depth and breadth, and a wish to explore emotional states in others is essential. But, most of all, we are looking for a certain mental attitude: one in which there is a willingness to step into the unknown, to recognize that one feels relatively unskilled, to be thoughtful about what emerges, and its impact upon oneself. We are interested in an openness to new learning, alongside a willingness to "unlearn" what is already known, if it prevents new learning from taking place. We try to gauge this by inviting the applicant to present some recent clinical work and then follow this up with some discussion. Are they interested in new ideas, especially those that challenge their existing views? Do they relish the opportunity to discuss and take on a different perspective? Can they bear to feel that someone might know more than they, without becoming deflated? In my experience, if these qualities are largely present, many of the problems associated with different personalities, and even certain psychopathologies, can be managed, enabling the trainee to develop.

Being open to learning may, however, be difficult for the trainee who is narcissistic, envious, or rivalrous. An overly critical superego is a problem, too, because feeling persecuted and criticized can lead to a defensive closing down. Occasionally, during the course of the training, a trainee may become emotionally troubled, or their external circumstances might interfere in some significant way. Problems may be picked up by the tutor or, more commonly, by the clinical supervisor.

While trainees struggle in many different ways, I would draw attention to two rather common difficulties we encounter:

1. Those who are prone to becoming overwhelmed by a patient's state, sometimes to the extent that they feel taken over, their own minds failing them: these trainees let their patients down, because they feel confused, fragmented, and unable to contain the patient's projections. They can be perplexing, too, for the supervisor. I describe such a situation Chapter 10, where I discuss the role of the supervisor.
2. Those who fail to make contact with a patient, remaining emotionally unresponsive or impervious: these trainees may have a well-developed or even precocious intellectual understanding, but they struggle to be in touch with the patient's psychic reality, remaining emotionally cut off and unavailable. Later, I describe a case where we came to feel, in the end, that the trainee was unable to learn and develop, and his training was discontinued.

I also describe a more ordinary experience in which students have to struggle for a while in supervision but can eventually make use of it, with good results.

An analytic perspective on the challenge of learning

> The psychoanalyst should aim at achieving a state of mind so that at every session he feels he has not seen the patient before. If he feels he has, he is treating the wrong patient. [Bion, 1967, p. 138]

This powerful and provocative quote, suggesting an impossibly ambitious state of mind, might have been intended to jolt the reader out of a feeling of complacency. Certainly, the idea was greeted with scepticism, and even anger, at the time Bion published his paper "Notes on Memory and Desire" (1967). But the important point that he was trying to convey was that we will never experience the same situation more than once. Nothing remains static in the clinical encounter, and, even if a moment has certain similarities with a previous one, every moment is unique and needs to be thought about afresh.

The contention that creativity involves being able to dismantle previous views and theories, so that new ideas might form, is an important one in analytic theory. Bion was making use of Klein's concepts of the paranoid-schizoid and depressive positions to illustrate the on-going relationship between processes of fragmentation and re-integration, which he regarded as being essential to all creative learning. He described fragmentation (or "dissolution") as having the quality of a small "psychic catastrophe"—an experience akin to falling apart. In this respect, it is a movement into the paranoid-schizoid position. The re-forming of a new set of views and theories is a synthesizing move, like that of the depressive position. Creative effort can, therefore, be viewed as an on-going process of movements to and fro between these two positions. Bion thought that the mathematician Henri Poincaré was describing something similar in his account of the creative process involved in arriving at a mathematical formula.

Poincaré (1914) writes:

> If a new result is to have any value, it must unite elements long since known, but till then scattered and seemingly foreign to each other, and suddenly introduce order where the appearance of disorder reigned. Then it enables us to see at a glance each of these elements in the place it occupies in the whole. Not only is the new fact valuable on its own account, but it alone gives a value to the old facts it unites. Our mind is as frail as our senses are; it would lose itself in the complexity of the world if that complexity were not harmonious; like the short-sighted, it would see only the details and would be obliged to forget each of these details before examining the next, because it would be incapable of taking in the whole. The only facts worthy of our attention are those which introduce order into this complexity and so make it accessible to us. [p. 30]

Bion's notion, then, is that creativity and learning involve "catastrophic change". New thoughts, by their nature, are potentially disruptive and shattering and lead to the experience of anxiety, doubt, and even fragmentation. But this state contains an opportunity too: seemingly disparate, chaotic elements can accumulate around a "selected fact", and this process gives new meaning to both the chaotic elements and the fact selected. For Bion, this "selected fact" is the name of an *emotional* experience. If it can be tolerated, there is the possibility of creative development. Bion compares the state needed to achieve this as being akin to Keats's notion of "negative capability", which I allude to in chapter 10, on supervision.

All the same, the wish to have arrived at a hard-earned position of having requisite knowledge is an understandable one in the trainee, and, indeed, in all of us. Not to have any background feeling of conviction would make it impossible to work. However, too heavy a reliance on having "arrived" at an understanding is antithetical to the kind of flexible position one needs to strive for in an analytic training. There, understanding and meaning need to be kept in a state of provisionality. The reason for this relates to the kind of attitude one needs to cultivate in the psychoanalytic encounter with a patient.

Michael Feldman (2009) describes this complex attitude thus:

> What I will argue is that if analysts believe they have arrived at a particular place, reflected for example in the notion of having hold of a 'selected fact' this can itself become an overvalued idea, rather than a useful way of organizing and integrating their observations and experiences for the time being. Conversely, while it may be useful to recognize a state of doubt, if the formulation that arises out of this recognition is itself seized upon and treated as a fact, a defined and hence static mental state, analysts' flexibility and openness are restricted. [p. 233]

And:

> ... the pressure the analyst is under may induce him to reach for a structured formulation about the situation that offers relief. Indeed the very recognition of a state of doubt itself may become rigidified into an "overvalued idea." This reaching for such a structured formulation may be a necessary, perhaps inevitable part of the analytic process and represents one of the ways in which the analyst strives to organize his observations and experience, thereby preserving his analytic functions: but his real analytical functioning depends on his also constantly striving to maintain, or recover an openness and the capacity for flexibility and movement. [p. 231]

Feldman is describing the pressure on the analyst that will apply throughout his analytic career. For the trainee, it may seem impossibly challenging. Trainees are likely to feel overwhelmed by how much there is to learn, the myriad stimuli (intellectual and emotional) that need to be made sense of, and the juxtaposition of developing analytic understanding of themselves and of the patient. In fact, it is an almost universal experience for trainees to feel deskilled and at a loss at times. Some, as we will see, experience this very acutely, even feeling as if their minds are falling apart. For others, it is more manageable. In some cases, there may not be such a conscious experience of dissolution, but this is what is being defended against. In these cases, the student may feel persecuted, their supervisor experienced as unhelpful or judgemental. (Era Trieman describes this rather vividly in chapter 4.) More worrying is when there is a complete denial of the difficulty and where a quest for truth is replaced by false knowledge. Again, I give a brief example in chapter 10, on supervision.

CHAPTER FOUR

On not knowing

Era Trieman

The initial encounter

The initial encounter with a therapist is a strange and bewildering experience, involving a gamut of unconscious communication that cannot yet be known. Wilfred Bion writes, "When two personalities meet, an emotional storm is created" (1979, p. 321). The patient enters into the preliminary meeting with a multitude of fears, anxieties, and wishes. They will already have a transference towards the therapist (the one they expect to find in phantasy), as well as preconceived notions about the therapeutic process. From the assessor's notes and formulation, the trainee will have their own countertransference before they meet the patient. Priscilla Roth, quoting David Foster Wallace, illustrates the dynamics of the transference and countertransference with an evocative metaphor: "Deeply unconscious phantasies are, like the water [that] fishes swim in, invisible and un-apprehendable, at least for a long time" (Roth, 2009, p. 13).

Clinical example: Ms O

When I met Ms O for a preliminary meeting, everything appeared to flow without friction. We seemed to evade any notion of a beginning to avoid confronting the inherent unknown-ness of the situation. Though I could not have known it at that time, we were already swimming in a total situation (Joseph, 1985).

Ms O, a woman in her late twenties, came into treatment following the catastrophic loss of her partner, Y. She introduced herself amiably, with a cogent narrative of recent events and an expressive description of her family and upbringing. Ms O felt she needed to be "the good child", precocious, helpful, and well-behaved. She described her beleaguered mother, who suffered a depressive breakdown when Ms O was a child, and who she has "always worried about. . . ." Her father was said to be "stoic", and that he responded to their subsequent divorce by adopting an attitude that "in life we are all ultimately on our own. . . ."

I was struck that Ms O could not rely on her objects for fear of causing damage, sensing that they would not be robust enough to withstand her attacks or demands. She worried that fragile objects and precarious relationships could collapse. Her modus operandi was to manage on her own. When she *did* try to depend on others, she felt that they were unable to mitigate her anxiety; instead, they became stricken by anxiety themselves. And yet, I had the feeling that I was being situated in contrast to these brittle and undependable objects.

It is said that the kernel of the patient's difficulties emerges during the initial meeting in an inchoate form, so that we are only able to comprehend these central anxieties in retrospect. Elizabeth Spillius (2007) suggests that a patient will turn to "the repetition of infantile defences" in an "attempt to draw the analyst into behaviour that will evade painful emotional experiences" (p. 55). With hindsight, I understood what an important communication was being made by Ms O during our preliminary meeting. From the outset, she manoeuvred to make things coherent and familiar between us. With evident enthusiasm, she exclaimed, "It's just a couch! I've been through worse!" Once again, she became a precocious and uncomplicated child, inviting me into a harmonious union, to prevent any "fuss" that could destabilize her psychic equilibrium. The worries and the unpredictability were split off into other figures, while I became the "good therapist", both of us wishing that I could somehow be different from her precarious internal objects. Unconsciously, I was only too willing to take on the role of an object who understands and knows what to do. The repetition of this infantile defence was intended to turn me into an ideal object, reliable and understanding, to evade a painful emotional experience of being with an unavailable object, who does not contain hostile, vulnerable, and undesirable feelings.

Getting drawn into manifest content

The following session Ms O greeted me in a cheerful way, with an expectant pause that I did not respond to. Eventually she said, "I'm feeling a bit nervous. . . . I don't know why. . . . This is the worst part . . . not knowing where to start. . . ." Responding to her subtle nudge, I felt prompted to speak: "It's an invitation for me to say something to make this more comfortable. . . ." Ms O laughed, any potential discomfort now vanished. With hindsight, we effectively colluded in our avoidance of awkwardness. Rather than struggling with the acute anxiety of not knowing what to say or where to start, I responded to Ms O in a convivial way that lowers the tension. Neither of us can bear the "worst part", and so, instead, by putting things into words, we shift towards a "comfortable" dialogue.

Within minutes, Ms O was talking emotively: "after Y died, I read lots of books on grief. . . . I didn't have anyone to talk to about what had happened. . . ." Ms O managed to alleviate any tension in the present by deftly moving to the past. Instead of "not knowing where to start", she could pivot to the "books on grief". She was now on the familiar ground of bereavement, talking about the loss of Y. At the time, I felt swayed by the apparent emotionality of her words, which I considered to be a poignant communication. Perhaps I had wanted to take Ms O's tears at face value? By nudging me subtly towards the manifest content, we had lost track of the affect in the room. Moreover, I was lulled into a narrative: that the only reason Ms O came to therapy was because of the tragic loss that had befallen her.

Although only our second meeting, I was feeling validated as a psychotherapist. We had apparently established a therapeutic alliance, in which a distraught Ms O was telling me about her sense of loss. I was aware of the somewhat rehearsed quality of Ms O's account, that she *already* knew all about what was wrong and needed to reiterate for my sake. Nonetheless, glad that we had alighted on something, and equally eager to dispel anxieties about not knowing where to start, I responded to Ms O in a way that avoided the immediacy of being together in this unfamiliar situation. Each of us had dived straight in, with a premature sort of pseudo-understanding. We now had some palatable manifest content to discuss, rather than needing to get in touch with more primitive anxieties around contact and closeness. By getting drawn into the past, we did not need to expose the fears, ambivalence, or indeed excitement that each of us felt upon embarking on this new therapeutic relationship.

Listening to the affect

Twelve months into therapy, Ms O started the session casually telling me about a scary dream. She went on to enumerate several other things, before neatly concluding, "so that's four things to talk about. . . ." I was struck by the breadth of what Ms O had started with, and remarked that, "it does not seem clear what feels most relevant". There seemed to be some incongruity between the apparently disturbing dream and Ms O's nonchalant mood. She decided to go elsewhere, neglecting the dream content, which seemed to have been left behind like a sacrificial offering. Curious about the overlooked dream, eventually I asked: "What do you make of the dream?" She responded with apparent surprise, before considering the dream from various angles. I felt swayed by Ms O's apparent insight and impressive thoughtfulness. However, on writing up my notes afterwards, I had an inkling of searching for clues in a detective story. With content to nibble on, I was left trying to make it all tangible, trying to understand meaning, essentially playing an analytic game. Meanwhile the affect was gone.

Each week my supervisor would question what was *actually* going on in the transference/countertransference relationship. Had this become "a soporific sort of contact, disarming and comfortable, drifting into the realm of ideas", thus preventing anything fresh or disturbing from emerging? When my supervisor asked me, "what did you *feel*? . . . " I felt thrown by this deceptively simple question. I started to notice some contradictory responses within myself. The sessions with Ms O could appear lively and engaging, and yet in supervision I often found myself doubting my own impressions. Initially I thought that I'd been offered an engrossing dream, whereas my supervisor would suggest that I was being "drawn in by the compelling material", while "much more immediate was the incongruity. . . ." The dream was not so detailed, neither was it so disturbing. There *was* a discrepancy between the content and affect, so that the dream somehow didn't come to life.

Most troubling of all, my supervisor would call into question which of Ms O's communications felt genuine. The problem was that I no longer knew. I *had* felt engaged and curious. The patient *had* seemed emotive and present. So why did I feel so shaken by my supervisor's probing question? I found it disturbing not knowing whether to trust my own intuition. I began to listen to Ms O with scepticism, alert to any slight change in her tone. When she spoke, I would ask myself whether it felt emotionally resonant, or intellectual and hollow, or performative and melodramatic. I became exceedingly preoccupied with questions around authenticity. Often my supervisor would seem unconvinced by apparently emotive material. I would ask myself whether something might be getting lost in translation. These doubts did not feel helpful; instead, I was left feeling despondent.

Why could I not perceive the emotional texture within our sessions? I had always assumed that I was a person who *knew* what he felt, who was emotionally attuned; now I was not so sure. It was disheartening. Had I kept myself at the safe distance of intellectual detachment? I was confronted with the challenging, somewhat unsettling experience of questioning what I thought I knew about psychoanalytic technique. Suddenly the academic background, the armour of acquired theoretical knowledge, seemed more hindrance than help. What was going on?

Doubt and confusion

To examine our personal experience, to distinguish what could be relevant as a countertransference communication is an integral and ongoing task in the analytic process. For the trainee, it can be an especially challenging thing to work out. Irma Brenman Pick has suggested that one's capacity to understand is diminished whenever the patient corresponds too closely to some aspect of the analyst: "We see clearly here how difficult it is to differentiate in such a situation what part of the transference/countertransference problem is coming from the patient and what from the analyst; the one elides into the other" (2012, p. 56).

Was I struggling to perceive the affect owing to my own confusion *or* as a response to Ms O's sense of being at a loss? In retrospect, it is possible to see that it was both. On one level, my inexperience would certainly have contributed to the shock that I felt at the uncomfortable dismantling of my intellectual defences. At the same time, my response did reflect something important about Ms O: we were talking *about* feelings and yet it was unclear what the *actual* feeling was in the room.

Gradually, I came to recognize the interplay of several factors between Ms O and myself. Each of us was trying to keep our own anxieties at bay, cautiously hiding behind words, flaunting our insights, keeping the disturbance of emotional contact *out there*. I started to perceive a well-established mechanism in Ms O, whereby she could use emotionally articulate language to show understanding of others, enabling her to take refuge from knowing about her own emotional vulnerability.

Only much later could I perceive that my own countertransference *did* convey something significant about Ms O's internal world: a profoundly lost state of not knowing. In the midst of the emotional storm, I could not comprehend the forces of projective identification at play in our fishbowl. By projecting the doubt and confusion elsewhere, Ms O could maintain an apparently casual air. Meanwhile, in this intense turmoil of self-doubt, I had become identified with that part of my patient who does not know what she feels.

Idealization

Until now, the work with Ms O had felt relatively comfortable, whereas any sense of uncertainty or frustration seemed instead to emerge in the context of supervision. I had felt disconcerted by my supervisor's suggestion that some form of seduction was going on, reluctant to contemplate the alleged "romance", which I quickly dismissed, for fear of being deemed unprofessional or lacking in self-awareness. Now the exceedingly positive transference was gradually starting to be called into question.

Slowly I became more aware of the displacement of affect and the projection of confusion. I also became more curious about what needed to be kept *out*. For Ms O it was a way to stave off the negative affect, to not disrupt the idealization: bad objects were located *out there*, not in the room. Perhaps a different kind of affect needed to be kept out, one of a more sexual nature, which could equally be experienced as something dangerous to be avoided. Without being conscious of doing so, I too must have been committed to keeping the badness and the potential of an erotic transference firmly outside. By not allowing space for intense affect to emerge, it had to continually be split off or suppressed. Our hesitance, or unwillingness to go there, could then become a self-perpetuating cycle, each of us feeling too timid to really deepen the analytic relationship.

Function of the third

Initially I felt reluctant to disrupt the idealized rapport, protective of our bond, and suspicious of an interfering supervisor. "Try not to have ideas about Ms O", my supervisor would suggest, "You need to stop talking . . . to allow the disturbance and anxiety in. . . ." It was difficult not to hear this as an injunction, from an excluded supervisor (third) who was determined to spoil the positive transference, who was being jealous, begrudging, cruel. Nevertheless, I was determined to be a good supervisee (counterpart to Ms O, determined to be a good patient) and so I approached the following session rigidly, reluctant to say anything that was not absolutely essential.

> When I did not respond to the usual cues, Ms O proceeded cautiously, like an animal that suspects a trap. She talked about some argument with her partner: "So he has been a bit short with me . . . because of something that has nothing to do with me! . . ." Perhaps, she seemed to ponder, something foreign had got into me too? In a way, that is a correct assumption: my superego *had* been injected with the figure of a strict supervisor. In her attempt to preserve me as a good object, Ms O attributed the change to something foreign, some bad object

from outside. Simultaneously I was left feeling guilty, as though I had become withholding and severe, reneging on our earlier pact.

What was actually going on when I did not respond as usual? Ms O did, indeed, become more anxious, and the disturbance undoubtedly came into the room. When I stopped talking, she could not discern what I was thinking. Struggling to locate her object, Ms O was put in touch with that awful state of being lost. Within the transference a significant shift was starting to take place. Before it was as though (in phantasy) we were of one mind. Now we had become two separate minds, confronted with the difficulty of getting to know one another. Ms O evidently found it unbearable. To be left in an unknown situation evoked immense anxiety: "It's like being in a dark room with a blindfold . . . just swinging a sword around . . . it's like stabbing in the dark!"

When my supervisor cast doubt on the mutually supportive dynamic, it had the effect of disrupting the idealized dyad. Instead, a triangular situation was formed. Initially my supervisor had been experienced as the mean-spirited, bad object who evokes suspicion, who is accused of jealousy, and elicited a protective impulse in me to defend against the intrusion. With a growing awareness of my countertransference, the wary and somewhat paranoid distrust of an intruding supervisor (third) and the wish to guard against this disruption, I was one step closer to recognizing the anxiety Ms O experienced when she did not know what I was thinking.

In tandem with this shift in the transference, there was a parallel process going on between myself and my supervisor. Whereas initially I had regarded my supervisor with awe and admiration, these feelings now became suffused with frustration. The desire to impress gave way to a sense of disappointment, as I struggled beneath the weight of my own expectations, feeling unable to get it right. These exacting standards were then projected onto my supervisor, who became the strict superego figure who was impossible to satisfy.

With hindsight, I came to appreciate that my supervisor was encouraging me to slow down, to make more space, to allow something to emerge beyond the apparently coherent dialogue. Otherwise, we were at risk of going through the motions, a pseudo-engagement, dancing around rather than getting into contact with the unconscious communication.

I had embarked on a first training case with high hopes, and now I had to accept the loss of what I initially thought was attainable. I had to reckon with my own idealization and subsequent disillusionment *before* I was able to comprehend or address the transference situation between

ON NOT KNOWING

myself and Ms O. When my own idealization had been punctured, some frustration had been worked through, and more realistic expectations had set in, it was only then that I was ready to accompany Ms O through an equivalent process of mourning, towards the depressive position.

Clinical vignettes

Gradually I became aware of Ms O's acute anxieties around trust and dependency. What now became much more apparent was Ms O's ambivalence about letting anyone get too close. This shift in the transference is shown in two brief vignettes, six months apart, in the therapy.

First vignette

> After the winter break, a midweek session at a later hour than usual, Ms O began: "It's odd coming here at this time. The waiting room is empty . . .", followed by a long pause. "Picking up where we left off on Monday . . ." she continued seamlessly, "I was quite angry at mum as a teenager, because she had a boyfriend who I hated!" Evading the "odd" feeling at the start, Ms O diverted us back to "Monday", while the hatred could be split off into the distant "boyfriend". Instead of following Ms O into the past, on this occasion I tried to stay with her ambivalence in the here-and-now: "I think it feels weird being here with me, especially today, at a later time, so you need to find something to diffuse the uncomfortable feeling . . . "
>
> P: "It *does* feel weird . . . maybe it will always feel that way? Lying down, when I can't see you . . . needing to do most of the talking . . . I do try to find something to run with . . . I can't stand it, not knowing what to say . . . sometimes afterwards I think to myself, 'Do I really feel that way?' . . ."

Outwardly Ms O's response appeared genuine, so that I felt we had made emotional contact. Only later, with the help of supervision, did another perspective arise. I came to see that despite her pervasive feelings of anxiety, Ms O had nonetheless managed to find a way to remain comfortable with me: *by going along with my suggestion*. Initially she could acknowledge that "It *does* feel weird". This was followed by what had felt to be a genuine communication: "Maybe it will always feel that way?" Yet before long, Ms O crescendos with dramatic intensity: "I can't stand it." Not able to "see" me or to know what was in my mind left her feeling uncomfortable, and so she needed to find something for us "to run with". Conjuring something for me to engage with, she could now control what I was thinking. I could be pulled into an apparent closeness, while the intense, uncomfortable feelings were kept elsewhere. In this way, we were left with a pretence of intimacy, while actually a distance had been maintained.

Second vignette

> Six months later, Ms O arrived, with some disquiet. "Today I'm feeling stressed and irritable. . . . Yesterday [my partner] lost his job. The thing to do is stay calm. . . . There is no point getting into a panic. . . ." Listening to Ms O, I felt aware that she snuffs out any anxiety, reassuring herself with a reasonable and pragmatic attitude. I initially tried to take up the defence: "Feeling stressed and irritable, you fear that you might get into a panic—it feels safer to keep all those feelings at bay." As in the previous example, Ms O responded by following my cue, adding intensity and getting increasingly worked up about zero-hour contracts, the housing crisis, and her fears about the relationship with her partner. In a trembling voice, she spoke about feeling unable to allow the anger out: "I'm scared that I'm going to screw this up!" With exasperation she exclaimed, "I don't want to lose *another* person because there is something wrong with me!"

On this occasion, I felt more able to gauge the different strands of Ms O's communication. Rather than getting drawn in by the content or apparent intensity of Ms O's words, I remained attentive from a third position. While Ms O grappled with my invitation to bring her angry and irritable feelings, the affect was left out of the room, leaving her unable to allow a more real contact to emerge. I felt that the central anxiety for Ms O was that she would make herself hateful and unloveable if I were to witness her rage. Staying with the affect in the room, I said, "You fear that I would not stand your aggression and that I would leave you. . . ." What followed was a tense pause.

> P: " . . . Era . . . would you hold on a moment? . . . I have to go pee. . . ."
> [*returning quickly*] "Why do I still feel so angry after eighteen months of therapy?! . . .
> I don't know how to be open with my emotions . . . I want to trust you, but I can't do it! . . .
> It's like all this bitterness inside of me. . . ."
> T: "As you felt this intensity inside, you had to go to the bathroom . . . It needed to be released elsewhere. . . ."

P: "[*genuine*] I did actually think that if this conversation goes on I would actually piss myself . . . [*laughs*] I had all sorts of mad thoughts! . . . It would have gotten messy. . . ."
T: "You feel nervous that things cannot be kept in . . . it might get too messy in here. . . ."
P: "Maybe that's the point of therapy . . . to allow those emotions out. . . ."

In this vignette, I could clearly see that Ms O struggled to bring her intense feelings into our relationship. I felt that she was afraid of losing her object because "there [was] something wrong" with her. Her hidden bitterness and mad thoughts felt too dangerous to be known. I was helped in supervision to think about the urethral attacks that had to be averted and my need to keep it that way to remain the "good object". Interrupting at the point of utmost anxiety, Ms O had to prevent the urine (or an intangible sense of badness) from spilling into the session, unsure whether I could be a container who could tolerate her "messy" feelings,

Through the transference/countertransference relationship, Ms O's primitive object relations became clearer. In her internal world, she felt stuck with an object who could not take her in fully. She did not know how to enliven her objects, feeling that she needed to keep her real self at bay. This, in turn, confirmed that her objects were frail and unreliable. With my own difficulties in acknowledging the negative transference, I was indeed acting as a frail and unreliable object who could not bear the messy feelings in the room. Once I was able to recognize this, Ms O could start to wonder about the real point of therapy.

Learning from experience

This case study aims to illustrate a journey that every analytic couple experiences: the establishing of an analytic position from which things can start to be known. In developing an analytic attitude, one must be open to not knowing. I would suggest that learning how to take up a third position is especially demanding for a trainee who does not yet know their own analytic mind.

Early in my training, I would often find myself drifting towards a cognitive and intellectual sort of understanding, rather than waiting to see what emerges. Similarly, Ms O could be described as a patient who desperately wanted knowledge, although she found intolerable the process of getting to know. The central anxiety around "not knowing" could initially be disguised by premature knowledge, as if she and I *knew* what was going on. I assumed the role of an ideal object who "understands".

The function of role-responsiveness (Sandler, 1976) was especially effective in this transference scenario, because it had a certain resonance for me too: as a trainee and a beginner who desperately wanted to know about his patient and to feel that he *did* know what he was doing.

Reflecting in supervision on the struggles in my clinical work provided a timely dose of humility and doubt and shook something up in my own analysis. I felt like a child needing to re-learn everything, to start again with a foreign language. Thomas Ogden advises that "If the analyst allows himself perpetually to be the beginner that he is, it is sometimes possible to learn about that which he thought he already knew" (1992, p. 225). When I could get in touch with my own internal sense of being a beginner, when I could start to recognize my own defences against not knowing, such as a propensity to intellectualize to avoid emotional contact, only then was I able to learn something of Ms O and the dynamic between us.

Ms O's predicament was that she could not allow us to find out where she was. While internally she may have been feeling lost, she was struggling to bring that part of herself into the room. By attempting to stay coherent and make sense of things, for fear of getting lost in the confusion, neither she nor I envisaged that we would somehow muddle through it together. It was difficult for Ms O to trust me to help find her.

It is, however, only through the *lived experience* in the analytic process that learning can take place.

Only when I could allow *myself* to feel lost could I start to countenance the primitive anxiety that both Ms O and I had been warding off. Only now were we getting to a place where things could start to be known about. We were moving from a state of paranoid-schizoid certainty towards an awareness of depressive pain and ambivalence. To do so, I had to learn to slow down. I also had to learn to tolerate confusion and helplessness, to make room for the unknown. Over time I would discover that one of the most difficult things for an analyst to do is to keep things simple. When a trainee talks a lot, usually this does not come from a place of knowing or understanding; more likely, it is an expression of their anxiety about not knowing.

Eventually, and with some difficulty, we could allow something more real to emerge. One cannot engage with the unconscious from a safe distance. For Ms O it could feel almost unbearable, like being "stabbed in the dark". Once things began to unravel, flooded by anxieties, feeling lost at sea, I, too, felt the turmoil and despair of uncertainty. Yet it is only by negotiating that journey that we can (eventually) emerge from it. In our analytic process, there is only mutative value in things that are affectively present, not in absentia.

The trainee is plunged into an emotional storm. They will depend on their supervisor to find a third position, while their clinical identity is still in the making. Our patients enable us to go through a journey with them: that is how we learn to know our own analytic mind. Each of us must face the difficulty of not knowing before we are able to learn from experience.

CHAPTER FIVE

Up or down; life or death

Anne McKay

Betty Joseph captures beautifully the dilemma for my training patient:

> I get the impression from the difficulty these patients experience in waiting and being aware of gaps and aware of even the simplest type of guilt that such potentially depressive experiences have been felt by them in infancy, as terrible pain that goes over into torment, and that they have tried to obviate this by taking over the torment, the inflicting of mental pain on to themselves and building it into a world of perverse excitement, and this necessarily militates against any real progress towards the depressive position. It is very hard for our patients to find it possible to abandon such terrible delights for the *uncertain pleasures of real relationships*. [Joseph, 1982, p. 455, italics added]

In this chapter, I also address the other side. Alongside the patient's task of abandoning "terrible delights for the uncertain pleasures of real relationships", the trainee therapist also struggles to abandon that which is familiar to her: her existing experience and skills, her sense of who she is and how she operates, for the uncertain pleasures and rewards of a daunting psychoanalytic training and a fresh knowledge that comes from a new and real experience. In this therapy, both patient and therapist were struggling, both preoccupied with being either in the "one-up" or "one-down" position. This reality had to become known and metabolized by both sides for the work to succeed.

The aqueduct

There was a painting, by the artist Jeff Makin, at the end of the north corridor on the fourth floor of the Tavistock centre, of an aqueduct linking two hills, which I really liked. Warm brown stone links two warm green hills. There is sunlight and growth, and the idea of water flowing from one community to another. Taken further, there is a social organization that built this link between two places where resources are shared in an organized way. My patients and I saw this undramatic but lovely painting every time we walked towards the consulting room.

A common theme with many patients is how "linking" (the bridge in the painting) can be experienced as psychically dangerous: a giving up of a spurious place of safety in superiority for the "uncertain pleasures" of ordinary relationships. One patient dreamed of flying up high above ancient bridges. One person talked of being high above the city, with street door locked; another of being high on a stage looking down on (and spurning with her jewelled heel) the ordinary people; another of floating high above the world in space. I came to understand that, for those who felt the world of other people was to be avoided, the idea of a bridge, a link, was replaced by a sort of psychic see-saw, where one was either up or down. Fear of the catastrophic consequences of connection with the other was replaced by something tentative, a fragile balance, which could be withdrawn at any moment, by a jumping up to a superior state of mind (and also being vulnerable to being brought low by any authentic encounter).

Bridging internal and external worlds

When I first came to the Tavistock looking for a training, it was a confusing experience, I think, on both sides. I came looking for help in thinking about the work I was doing with young people affected by political violence in South African townships. I had come to rely more and more on a psychoanalytic way of thinking. I was lucky to have a supervisor who recommended Anton Obholzer's 1994 book on unconscious stress in organizations, which really helped. But the book that stayed in my mind was a random find in a second-hand bookshop in Johannesburg: *Loss of the Good Authority: The Cause of Delinquency*, co-written by Tom Pitt-Aikens, a psychoanalyst who had worked at the Tavistock and the Cassel (Pitt-Aikens & Ellis, 1989). It is difficult to convey the impact of this text in the early 1990s, when the ANC was negotiating with the "no-good-authority" apartheid government, in which murderers were still in power, and the country had entered the process of the Truth Commission, where the horror of state-sanctioned violence was laid bare. I really needed this book. I really needed this way of thinking, to keep my head above water. I started to think seriously about leaving home to train at the Tavistock.

It was not easy to find a common language. Visiting psychoanalysts came to Johannesburg to lecture; they spoke of patients with violent thoughts and feelings. In the clinics where we worked as interns, our patients had experienced all kinds of state, social, and interpersonal violence: weapons were all around; poverty was racially entrenched; state actors were violently persecutory. The whole setting was unsafe; the external was always dramatically and traumatically present. A lucky introduction to a psychoanalyst working at the Portman clinic helped me to connect the world I came from and the United Kingdom. It seemed also to be a place of understanding of the connection between the internal and the external.

In late 2021 I attended an online conference, where an eminent analyst reported on a treatment of an adolescent presenting with psychosis. She introduced the work without a biography or family history. In the question time, someone asked about the parents, and she replied, without pause, that she had not met them and did not know—or, by implication, *need* to know—anything about what had happened "outside"; what was happening between patient and analyst "inside" the consulting room was sufficient for understanding and treatment. I was struck, deeply. I had always started my thinking about patients from the outside inwards: family and social history, attachment disruption, intergenerational transmission of trauma, class, racism and sexism, sexuality and gender, the impact of the social, including how I might be experienced by a patient. I had never even wanted to let go of these anchors in working with patients. But what the M1 offered was a training in understanding, much more deeply, the internal worlds of our patients and ourselves.

The Tavistock seemed to me to be a bridge, with one foot in the NHS and, by extension, the social world, and the other in what I thought of as "pure" psychoanalysis. I circled around the idea of training as a psychotherapist, doing short courses here and there, working in the NHS, hesitating to take the plunge. When I finally did apply to the M1, my interviewer asked why I did not go straight to the Institute of Psychoanalysis, as I already had NHS experience, so didn't need another NHS-based training? I think I needed the NHS, the rootedness in a world I had already come to understand, the connection to society, the link to a universal service. It was impossible for me to imagine private practice: my fantasy was that *I* would be unhoused.

Up or down—superior/inferior

I had come to learn. What I found difficult, though, was having to unlearn or put aside what I had already learned elsewhere. It was also hard because I had to retain my capacity to do adapted psychodynamic work for the rest of my working week. I had to learn to let some things go to be receptive enough for psychoanalytic psychotherapy. I thought this would be easy, but it was really difficult, partly because I had to let go of what I felt good at, something creative and useful, to take up the role of a new learner (again, and again). It was uncomfortable and difficult.

I felt (not always consciously) cross that I was giving up everything, and the staff were not that interested in understanding where I was coming from (they seemed strangely unfascinated by my thoughts). I was trying, on my own, to make a meaningful bridge between my applied work and the training, perhaps to bolster my lack of confidence, and as if no one had made these links before. I did persist for a while but had to learn to drop it. "It alienates you when you keep talking about the work you did in South Africa", a senior trainee said to me kindly. "If you talk about MBT, your supervisor will think you are psychotic", said another. "Is DIT even psychoanalytic?" a supervisor asked me with curiosity, and kindness. Struggling with irritated humiliation in analysis, I was bemoaning not being understood by "the English" when my analyst remarked, to my amusement, "But, how many people actually *are* English at the Tavistock at the moment?" Everyone, even "the English", will have had this experience, of leaving something behind, to learn something new.

Thinking about it now, though, this may contribute to the inferior/superior status anxiety, which does seem to be everywhere in the psychotherapy community. There is a hierarchy. Training as a psychoanalytic psychotherapist is a huge undertaking, yet never really good enough: that good-enoughness is only to be found in training for five-times-weekly psychoanalysis, and so on, illustrating Kernberg's point that the only good-enough training is the one you are not doing at the present time.

> It may be very helpful to point out that psychoanalysis is understood and carried out properly only in places far away from your own institution, and preferably in a language not known by many of your students. If the demands of the training are such that the students would not be able to spend an extended part of the time in that distant ideal land, they may become convinced that it is useless to attempt to develop psychoanalytic science in a place so far from where the true and only theory and technique are taught. And that conviction will last. [Kernberg, 1996, p. 1034]

Yet the M1 was good enough to be a seduction to also start feeling superior in my turn, towards others.

Nevertheless, I was a long way away from having access to feelings of superiority. I just had to give in, give up holding onto what I was already good at, give up hoping someone would be interested in what had learned elsewhere, to find that something deeper. Returning to my work with my patients, there were echoes of this struggle with ordinary (inferior)/special (superior), a real struggle to find the special in the ordinary, to find love and affection, rather than admiration, and we struggled on together through most of the two years.

Clinical example: Ms Z

Flying above the crowd

Ms Z (all identifying details disguised) was a talented businesswoman who had succeeded against many odds. Her parents, survivors of colonial wars, had learned to survive by putting up a good front, their glamorous and expensive lifestyle masking financial and emotional vulnerability. Ms Z had been successful, before ill-health and the breakdown of her marriage precipitated a financial collapse, and a long, painful withdrawal from work and creativity. The sudden death of a close friend, lost to an illness she had ignored for years, shocked her out of her numbness. She was determined to regain the lucrative career she had set aside, and, at the start of therapy, she was engaged in a new business venture that put her house, her savings and her health at risk.

From the beginning, I felt we, patient and therapist, moved in and out of being able to be in touch with how scared and out of control she felt, and how scared and incompetent I felt as a trainee. In sessions she liked to tell me of the excitement of her encounters with wealthy people, and the enticing possibilities that were opening up for her. The only relationships she invested in were those where there was a joint admiration, where she could feel in control of how people viewed her. Her brand depended on being in connection with the elite in her homeland and Europe. This was held onto fiercely; awareness of her immense vulnerability was disavowed (Steiner, 1993). I kept talking as if to a patient who wanted to know about how to manage anxiety, failing to realize that I was the one who was meant to feel, and did feel, the anxiety and loneliness, the fumbling attempts to keep my balance, while her conversation floated above my concern.

The stress was located in me, and she chided me for "making her take care of my anxiety". She said, with kind insistence, that she had no time for this inadequate, good-enough, ordinary life with ordinary relationships, which she thought was my goal for the therapy. I often felt irrelevant. She came late to sessions, having had meetings with people who "cancelled everything" for her. When I said that she might be contrasting this to my miserly sticking to the 50 minutes, she gently said that I was missing the point. She described elite parties, in tall glass buildings in the City. I felt that the Tavistock and I were small and drab in comparison. She also poignantly told me of hurting her feet walking miles to the underground in high heels because that month she could not afford a taxi.

It was often hard to keep going. In supervision I had to face what felt like my incompetence every week and, in sessions, I was with a patient who appeared to feel that I was interrupting more interesting thoughts with my banal observations. It was very different from the rather comforting "working on this together" of brief psychological therapies in the NHS, which, for the most part, elicit and work with a positive transference (see chapter 9, by Rachel Hodgins).

Her psychotherapy revolved around a central issue: whether the wish for superiority, with which she managed her loneliness and anxiety, could be given up in favour of experiencing "the uncertain pleasures of real relationships" (Joseph, 1982, p. 456). I tried to think with her about her rejection of ordinary concerns, her wish to be superior to others, to me, to everyone. She responded with anger, sometimes contempt, for my limited vision.

I felt I was losing my way. I also felt that I was being boring and cruel. For months I was stuck, unable to find a way to talk to her. I think I did not take seriously enough her experience that feeling so dependent upon the therapy was humiliating. My supervisor observed that she was experiencing my attempts to help as a weapon that I was using to bring her down, to prove *my* superiority. This very wise advice did not sink in until much later. I felt stupid, and I felt shame, and I did not see that my patient did too.

A turning point

One cold winter morning, she told me that she had thought about me a little during the Christmas break. She talked about a book she had read about attracting "the best" into your life for real success, and that if you thought about failure, you were attracting it. I took up her binary structure, that you were either success or failure, best or worst. She said, kindly, that that *is how people think.* She said that, on the way to the clinic, she had passed a homeless woman on the street who was selling plastic items: she didn't want to buy anything, but she bought her a sandwich from a nearby kiosk, saying it had felt good to be able to help her out in a practical way.

I said I thought that her cold and loneliness and feeling of not being useful were projected into the woman sitting on the street/her therapist, that she felt in a better place than that, able be generous. She said something surprising: that she *had* felt the cold that morning: "I could have just gone back to bed. But I came. Look, I know what you are saying; we were talking about this before the break. I am protecting myself. I feel like I'm high up, looking out everyone else."

I felt that this was a retreat to an old position of unassailable superiority, where I and the homeless woman on the street were in need of her somewhat impersonal kindness, while our paltry goods were not worth much. I said something about this, and she said, with absolute seriousness, that next winter she would have no therapy to come back to. She said that therapy was like blood pressure pills, all she had to do was take them every day, and she would be stable. Again, I interpreted this as a pushing away: "I think you would like me to be like that, to keep you stable, high above, not let disturbance or pain in." She protested hotly that she didn't like psychic pain. I pushed on, saying that when she was in touch with her pain and her loneliness, that was when she was, in a way, most sane. She quietly shut down the thread, saying that I was giving her a lot of metaphors. I felt I had lost her then.

I think in my misery of not being good enough, my plastic goods not worth buying, I really did miss that point. To this patient, I was the warm smug elite in the high building of the Tavistock, offering food that she could not afford. In my trainee "one-down" position I was out of touch with actually how much I was being supported and held by the clinic, while the patient had little enough other than her imagination to feed her. Her relentlessly optimistic defence masked such a vulnerability and loneliness, a despair that she would never be able to find the "more-than-ordinary" life she wanted, and that if she did not have it she would, in her eyes, have failed completely. I continued to interpret her holding onto superiority, missing what Steiner calls "the embarrassment of tenderness" (2011a, p. 61). She had told me that she had remembered what we had talked about before the break, that she could have stayed in bed but came out in the chill, that she recognized the cold and hunger of another. Her flat note that I had given her "a lot of metaphors" was right: there was no taking up of her shyly offered moments of connection.

This was a turning point in the therapy, although I did not find it or understand it until it had been repeated in different ways. In the interim, we returned to the stalemate. At times she said my help was useful, at other times she felt humiliated, accused me of laughing at her. She was exhausted, I felt stale. She came late, rejected my observations, even missed sessions for the first time. I kept trying not to but often fell into a knee-jerk "telling her off". I felt lost, filled with something horrible, perhaps akin to the "terrible masochism" described by Joseph (1982). I became full of concern for what might happen when the therapy finished, afraid that, if she experienced any external blows, she might let herself fall to bits, and that it would be my fault. However, the pressure of the ending did, I think, help us break this impasse.

The turning point: start with the "hello", not "goodbye"

> For some patients, their courage to risk love, and to value understanding, takes precedence over their wish not to know. In other cases, the admiration and social rewards for their way of being are considerable, the fear of a deeper commitment in an intimate relationship threatens to be quite overwhelming. They do not risk experiencing failure, never face this very uncertainty; they are impelled, instead, to always be on the run, to preserve this defensive structure, the very opposite of commitment and working through. [Brenman Pick, 2012/2018, p. 190]

The breakthrough came at a time when the media was full of the debates around Brexit, and she was hotly angry that the United Kingdom had decided to "go it alone", and how it would affect her new venture. We were able to link that with her own fear of relying on other people. I started to think about this in relation to her frequent coming late and her throwing away some of the therapy that remained, as, for her, to value it would indicate that she needed something outside herself. One day, when she had arrived 40 minutes late, I again took this up. She said wearily that I was wasting our time banging on about it: after all, she had got here, hadn't she? Even if it was only to say, "hello and goodbye".

My supervisor suggested what, for me, was the turning point of the work, and of my training: that I should start to focus on the "hello" rather than the "goodbye". This felt invigorating.

The following session she was again late and apologized with the air of someone who was going to be told off. I, instead, said that perhaps it would be useful to think about how she made the effort to be there, but that coming late kept the session half alive, protecting her from something she feared would hurt her. She was interested. I said that I thought she had "an immense capacity for warmth and loving", but that letting people see that felt dangerous, that perhaps she would prefer to be the one seeing the loneliness of another and, bringing her own coffee, that this felt safer than knowing she needed something from me. She was quite taken aback, then asked if I thought this therapy relationship "was personal". What did this mean if it was ending? (A question many NHS patients ask of their psychotherapists: "Am I just a job to you?")

I thought that this was the beginning of a capacity to let me know that she took in something, that the "personal relationship" of therapy could be a reliable connection. By my noticing the connection *she had created*, just by her turning up, we could both think about the dangerous idea that this was a meaningful relationship. The encounter with connectedness involves a simultaneous encounter with the pain of separateness. And, in an NHS therapy, neither party is in control of the ending. While this can make space for real mourning of loss (Steiner, 2011c, p. 149), it is a lot for a patient to have to bear, and it explained some of the resistance.

This led to a conversation about bridges. This idea emerged in a session where she had spoken with ill-concealed triumph about the demise of a longstanding business that she hoped to replace. I said that it seemed that, in her mind, there was room for only one person to be "up". She asked whether what I said was an observation or a criticism: "because I'm still not satisfied with ordinary 'good-enough'." I said I thought she was often in a state of mind where either she or the other is superior or inferior. I used the image of a seesaw that can only go up and down—not a bridge that can connect two people. She argued with me, saying she had to keep a superior image, it was what her business depended on.

A bridge between us would bring the potential for her to feel real vulnerability. It was a recognition that she could not control the end point of the therapy, that she could not control my thoughts about her or what I saw, and that I might really hurt her with my gaze (she used the image of me pouring acid on her wounds with her eyes). It was another perspective on her need to deny and undo a link between us. I thought about Britton's observation that for many patients, thoughts are kept apart, not only or even by envy, but by fear that bringing them together would result in "explosion and disintegration" (1989).

Later in the week she talked about her longing to be free from the drudgery and stress of daily life. She used grand metaphors, but this time I did not remark on that, saying, rather more simply than everyone, me included, must work with the mess of the world as it is. She accused me of patronizing her, then became interested: "Does everyone, really?" She allowed herself to be surprised, perhaps because I was including myself. She asked, so very quietly, why I thought she might have ended up so afraid of connection. Some weeks later she said that she had been performing all her life and was "tired, tired, tired". From then on, to the end a few months later, I felt I had patient who wanted to be in contact with my mind. Once she saw that a connection was between two ordinary people, not an oscillating relationship of beggar–queen, we were able to do some work around allowing others to know her, to be supportive, and to give her connection rather than admiration.

The aqueduct and the Brick Mother

Going back to the aqueduct painting, I started to wonder how the patients made sense of it, whether they noticed it? I was thinking about how several patients had used images of high buildings or high places, towering over others, imagery that was the antithesis of the warm brown and green curves of the painting of a low and useful bridge bringing water from one breast-like hill to another. Perhaps the valleys connected by the aqueduct were the therapist and the clinic, two parts of something connecting and enabling more life, a container much bigger than myself (Henry Rey's "Brick Mother": Steiner, 2012).

One potential difficulty with the aqueduct image is that the flow of water *is* only one way, from high to low, but perhaps one might think of an aqueduct also as a bridge built from both sides of the flow, a social contract, a co-operative two-way flow of conversation, thought and gratitude between patient and therapist, student and institution. Symbolically, this painting was placed between the consulting room and the room where the Unit meetings were held. My Brick Mother, the Tavistock, the team of the M1, the other students, the Unit meetings, the department of staff, had held me together through all those years. Or perhaps we held each other in different ways.

Like this patient, I needed some respite from anxiety about being inferior (or wishing to be superior), to see that the Tavistock centre was not the glazed, unperceiving glass tower of her/my dread, where she or I were up or down. The Adult Department was not in the business of delivering me to a superior place. It was a thoughtful, steady, bread-and-butter NHS clinic where patients were taken very seriously. My work as a trainee was to learn, and to work, while still having much left to learn. To be steady, plodding, good enough, turning up, as Winnicott (1969) observes, alive and undestroyed and not retaliating, holding the loving as well as the destructive aspects of both me and my patients in mind. Connecting psychoanalysis and the NHS, this Brick Mother also made it possible for me to find a way through my training. I had to hold, but not hold onto, what I already knew. To sit with not knowing, and not understanding, and letting that work become the bridge and perhaps even, on good days, an aqueduct between myself and the patient—and to allow the teaching and supervision at the clinic be the aqueduct for me too.

In the end, "We all hope our patients will finish with us and forget us, and that they will find living itself to be the therapy that makes sense" (Winnicott, 1969, p. 712).

CHAPTER SIX

The elephant tied up with string

Simon Shaw

The title of this chapter refers to an association made by my training patient, Mr E, early in his therapy, when talking about his long-standing fear of rejection due to his sexual orientation. He likened himself to the captive elephants in a TV documentary, who were attached to a tree by a chain. As they grew older and became accustomed to the restriction on their movement, their keepers replaced the chain with a thin piece of rope or string. The elephants could, of course, have easily broken free, had it occurred to them to try.

This poignant metaphor seemed to contain multiple meanings: the chain/string represented Mr E's unthinking attachment to a repetitive, schematized personal history (he was an elephant with an unhelpfully rigid memory), but I discovered, soon enough, through the transference, that it also stood for the nature of his relationships, which limited his contact with me and others by tying us to a particular way of relating. The string might also represent an umbilical cord, albeit a fragile one, and a wish for a healthier attachment to a parental figure who might restrain him, as well as care for him.

Working out what kind of "string" or "connection" was dominating our contact at any given time was a challenge for the trainee psychotherapist I was then. At times, when I hoped to find a patient who was concerned about himself, I would be surprised by the emergence of someone contemptuous and undermining, apparently excited by the way he could triumph and reject my efforts to help him. I remembered reading Rosenfeld who described how it is essential in narcissistic states to find the sane part of the self that recognizes the need for a dependent relationship and to help that part to see how he is turning to destructive omnipotent solutions as a source of strength and superiority (Rosenfeld, 1971a).

Working with Mr E taught me just how difficult this was.

Clinical example: Mr E

Mr E was a 40-year-old man who had had a lot of previous help. He had seen private therapists and NHS counsellors and had tried antidepressants, CBT and once-weekly psychotherapy. But, as he put it, "No cure has lasted."

He had worked in marketing, but was, at the time of assessment, unemployed. He felt hopeless and aware that he lacked meaningful, intimate relationships. He also described transient psychotic symptoms and, at times, felt that his mind was fragmented. Much of his time was spent making contact with men online, arranging to meet them for violent sado-masochistic sex.

At the consultation with a senior colleague, Mr E said that his difficulties were related "not to what has happened but to my essential core identity"—not to any trauma, but to something that felt intrinsic in him, which, he felt, led to him feeling and getting rejected. The assessor noted that Mr E's relentless "entertaining" conversation served to control the consultation. However, he was also able to talk about feelings of loneliness, desperation, and emptiness. It was hoped that an intensive treatment might "hold" him, allowing him to open himself to his psychic reality.

So, Mr E was offered a three-times-weekly individual psychotherapy with me, for two years.

History

Mr E was his mother's favourite. He said at the start that she was loving and "perfect", though he came to feel she was subtly demanding in relation to his behaviour and achievements. He described his father as aggressive, rejecting of him and his sexuality and preferring his two conventionally masculine older brothers. Mr E had, in turn, rejected his father from early on, even saying he "had no father".

He was bright and was sent to a public boarding school he hated, where he was bullied by staff and pupils alike. Suffering from asthma, he was taken to the school sick bay, where he overheard a nurse saying that the children there "just wanted a day off school". He recalled, with pleasure, how he had wheezed audibly, causing the staff to freeze in panic then jump to care for him. I thought this was an early example of his triumphing over his object, creating both alarm and obfuscation so that knowledge of his dependence and vulnerability were lost to all. In fact, I was often similarly faced with his confused and confusing communications, and I had to tolerate very disturbing feelings that were generated in me, often without understanding them for long periods. On top of this was the frequent anxiety I had to carry about his potential for harming himself through his actions.

Although the achievements that can be made in two years of intensive psychotherapy are likely to be modest, I hope to demonstrate, through my work with Mr E, the value of this kind of work in the public sector—and I will say more about this at the end.

Early phase of treatment

The first six months of treatment felt like a search for the part of Mr E that might genuinely be in touch with his difficulties and his need for help. But what dominated was something in him that seemed to want to destroy the contact between us.

Although he presented as outwardly cooperative, he used various means to make himself unknowable to me. He was extremely talkative, filling the sessions with a stream of stories and vignettes, often lurid, dramatic, or gossipy in tone. When I spoke to Mr E about this, he would talk about his "jigsaw puzzle mind" as something special, unique, and fascinating to others.

In response to this I often felt lost, and, as a trainee, this left me anxious. I was being presented with a vast amount of material and somehow felt that I should know how to respond to it. In retrospect, I had an idealized sense of what was expected: that I might register and understand my countertransference quickly and then speak to this with authority and composure. This made tolerating feeling lost and confused all the harder. I was right at the start of learning a new way of listening and responding: one that involved trying to think about the patient's associations, while not getting too caught up in the content of what I was being told. I was also becoming aware of the changing mood in the room and the connections (and disconnections) between this and what was being said. This free-floating attention was hard to maintain when I felt so lost in these early sessions. My anxiety caused me to speak prematurely at the start of the session or to grasp for some concrete point of understanding. I recall my supervisor suggesting that, if I didn't understand what was going on in a session, I should wait before speaking. I remember thinking that, if I did that, I'd never say anything at all!

It took some time for me to realize that I was not simply lost, struggling to find my way through the patient's confusing mind, but that this was also an important part of the patient's communication: his experience projected. As well as feeling something of his lost state, I came to understand that generating this feeling in me was his unconscious way of keeping us both confused and lost, thus reproducing the sense of a merged closeness he described with his mother. It was almost impossible to free up a part of my mind that could observe Mr E and think about what was going on.

Acting out in the early phase

Mr E seemed both anxious and excited about an intimacy he anticipated from our contact. This would lead to various kinds of acting out in the early phase, including arriving at sessions drunk or having cut himself, cancelling sessions, or insisting on bringing a friend into a session with him.

One Friday afternoon, Mr E arrived in a very agitated state, ostensibly in a crisis. He aggressively demanded that I admit him to a psychiatric ward, telling me that he could not go on and was not safe to be on the street. He implied, in a vague but intense way, that some harm would come to him or someone else.

He went on to describe the beeping noises of other people's personal stereos on the bus driving him mad. He shouted and slammed his hand and forearm hard against the wall next to the couch, making a loud "thwack". I felt bullied by this intense pressure and uncertain whether I was with a patient at breaking point or with a histrionic patient. I conducted the session as best I could, trying to work with him to understand what was happening and struggling at the end to help him to leave.

The weekend was a long one for a trainee psychotherapist! I felt under terrific pressure to keep him in mind, worrying about the level of risk he posed to himself. My mind became home to various anxious fantasies about what disaster might have befallen him and the consequences for me too.

On the Monday morning, I checked Mr E's electronic patient records. There had been no presentation over the weekend. In the next session he appeared calm and told me in a casual tone that following the session, he had thought to himself, "Should I go to A&E, or just get that taxi home?" A taxi had driven past, and, on a whim, he had hailed it and gone home, where he had got drunk. The weekend had been uneventful. I had mixed feelings in response to this: on the one hand, relieved that there had been no catastrophe but, at the same time, angry at the apparent abuse of my concern for him. I was reminded of how he had elicited panic in his school nurse by his apparent wheezing attack, and I felt foolish. Helped by supervision, I came to see that when Mr E was faced with our separation (the weekend break), he felt lost and deprived of the merged state described earlier. I think he was compelled to project his anxiety and fear into me as we each went our separate ways. I became identified with his vulnerable self and the feelings associated with this: feeling small, inadequate, and confused. In fact, there were many such occasions, and it was striking that Mr E appeared to enjoy what he accurately sensed he had elicited in me. At such times, I felt cruelly controlled by my patient, who seemed now to be dominated by a quite destructive part of himself, one that attacked his perception of his need as well as the connection between us and our work. It was as if Mr E had thrown the pieces of the jigsaw puzzle down and triumphantly watched me struggling in vain to put them together. In this way, in the early part of the treatment, Mr E's vulnerability was hijacked, controlled, and triumphed over as, indeed, were my attempts to help him.

While there was an internal invitation to dismiss him as a "histrionic" patient with little the matter with him, I realized that he posed a real dilemma: would I admit him to the mental hospital in my mind, where his problems would be taken seriously, even when he could not do so himself?

Mr E's introduction of sexually explicit material

During another Friday session, Mr E began by saying, in a thoughtful tone, that he had been thinking about our previous session, recognizing that he looked at problems in other people rather than in himself. He then began moving quickly from subject to subject leaving me unclear how they were connected.

He announced that he had left the previous session feeling thoughtful but had then arranged to go and have sex with a stranger in the town where he had spent the first eight years of his life. The trip had brought back various memories. After a brief silence, he said sadly, "What a journey—growing up in that place but then returning there for sex—when I woke up the next morning, I felt really depressed." He seemed again, for the briefest of moments, to be struggling with sadness and regret. But, continuing in a more excited tone, he started describing the encounter: there was an electrician working in the house who would have "seen them at it with their sex toys". His sexual partner was disabled and disfigured, his face and body covered in a terrible skin condition. They had had violent sex, which had involved penetrating each other with large objects. He had been very excited and still was, as he described it.

It was hard to keep thinking. I felt oddly guilty: pulled into a voyeuristic encounter, like the electrician who was trying to go about his work. I felt disoriented by the description of these sado-masochistic acts involving the body that was lying there in front of me on the couch. It was hard to know what to believe and what, or how, to think. When I tried to take up how he seemed engaged in damaging himself, he replied triumphantly, "You have a Daily Mail mindset", telling me that I was being prejudiced and narrow minded. But, in the end, I managed to take up the way in which I was made to witness an exciting sex scene like the electrician, and how this was stopping me from getting on with my (repair) work. To my relief, he became quieter again and, in a sadder voice, said he wondered whether he would ever have a fulfilling relationship. I said I thought he felt sad now about our relationship, realizing how difficult it was to feel that my understanding and concern could interest him more than the excitement. He remained silent until the end of the session and left looking crestfallen.

Middle phase of treatment

In the second year, something started to shift. There were moments when he seemed anxious about how he was using me and genuinely worried about himself, acknowledging his confusion, loneliness, and anger. While such moments were generally short-lived, he would return to these feelings more readily. The acting out greatly reduced, and the introduction of sexually explicit material in the sessions largely stopped.

Supported by supervision, I tried to focus less on the content of Mr E's communications and more on the here-and-now of the transference, helping him to see what he did to the contact between us. I realized that this was the only thing I felt I could address with any degree of conviction or authenticity. Both he and I seemed to recognize that we needed something to tether us together, the contact made through elucidation of the transference: the elephant and the string.

End phase

It seemed to me that the ending of Mr E's therapy was the battlefield on which the fate of the treatment would ultimately be decided. He was torn by the pull of his destructive self, which sought a masochistic solution: twisting the ending to mean that he was the victim of a rejecting, dismissive therapist, rather than holding onto his knowledge of me as concerned and decent. But as the therapy neared the end, something more thoughtful seemed to take hold. He found himself wondering whether I could tolerate him when he had been so difficult. He mentioned a character in the TV programme "Casualty". He said: "There was a nurse who used to be really strict with everyone, not nice at all. She didn't try to make herself popular, but when one of the other nurses got cancer, it was this nurse who really stood by her." I reminded him that he had often described his psychological problems as a kind of cancer, and I suggested that he might feel that I had stuck by him through some difficult times. He said "Yes, I do think you've stood by me, I have felt supported coming to these sessions." The "cancer", of course, was his cruelty—something he knew I had had to bear.

But the reality that we had to end was still enormously difficult for Mr E and a source of anger and distress. In a Friday session he began by telling me, in a light tone, that he was cancelling all his sessions the following week to attend a yoga course. I took up how unbearable it felt to be left by me, and how rejecting he became. He then told me that he had recently attended a marketing conference: "It was all slick and professional, but when I went round the back to talk to someone, I found myself in this really ugly backstage area. It was all concrete pipes and things, not like the beautiful front-stage area at all. It was really shocking." I said I thought he had a lot of "backstage" feelings about the ending: angry, hurt, and disappointed feelings, which felt awkward and ugly to him and which had to be hidden away behind an acceptable front. He agreed and associated it to someone being sacked. I said, "A part of you feels I've sacked you unfairly. By going away next week, I think you're getting back at me by sacking me and the therapy." He then told me how lonely he had felt one evening earlier in the week, having just got back from visiting his parents. He had desperately wanted a drink but had abstained. He said, "The sobriety made me feel the loneliness even more intensely. My mother told me that my father was really upset about me leaving last weekend, which is weird, as he didn't say that to me."

This felt poignant, with a shift from angry, disappointed feelings having to be hidden away completely to the possibility of sad feelings being acknowledged between Mr E and the father he had "sacked" from a very young age.

He went on, "My father is never properly in the present. He only talks about things that happened years ago. He is this broken man, drinking too much. I noticed it particularly when he told me about a friend of his, who was very ill in hospital. Despite being so close to death, his friend was able to talk about politics and remain interested in what was going on in the world. I'm just like my father; I'm always thinking about my future, but I'm not very good at just being in the present."

This was a real moment of insight into his own stuck way of seeing himself and his relationships.

Later, I found myself wondering whether the shocking and ugly backstage he referred to was a reference to the sexual behaviours he had enjoyed describing to me to earlier in the therapy. While it is probable that he continued to indulge in these activities, and certainly to fantazise about them, what had changed was that he appeared more worried now by the gratification he derived from it all and how he had exposed me to this. Becoming aware of this now put him in touch with feelings of regret and an anxiety that he had driven me away.

As the end of the treatment approached, I was struck by these significant developments but wondered whether he would be able to maintain them when I was gone. In the final session he was sad but grateful to me for having persevered with him.

Final reflections

I met Mr E for a follow-up review six months after the treatment ended. His mood was positive: he had not become depressed again, and he felt more connected to other people. He had remained in work too.

Just over two years later, Mr E wrote to me, saying that he felt "much more solid" in himself. He felt his reactions to others were "less extreme" and more manageable. He had continued working and was in a new relationship.

Reflecting on my experience as a trainee, I am struck now how vividly I remember the sessions that made up Mr E's treatment: what was said and how I felt, even now, several years later. The feelings evoked in me were intense, difficult, and, at times, overwhelming, but they widened the palette of emotional experiences that I could allow myself to have and share (and learn that I could survive) with the patient. I was helped to develop as a psychotherapist, as much by this as by the analytic theory and knowledge I acquired. I think the integration of the two came later and in an on-going way.

I think it will be evident that some modest but real achievements were made in Mr E's two years of intensive psychotherapy.

Postscript

Finally, I would like to share some of my thoughts about the value of this kind of work in the public sector.

The influence of Professor Richard Layard's Depression Report (Centre for Economic Performance's Mental Health Policy Group, 2006), arguing for greater provision of psychological therapy for people suffering with depression and anxiety, using "evidence-based interventions", largely Cognitive Behavioural Therapy (CBT), is well known. Equally well known is the economic aspect of his rationale, with increased provision of treatment to be funded out of reduced incapacity benefit payments, and increased income tax revenues as people return to work (Layard, Clark, Knapp, & Mayraz, 2007).

There are certain aspects of Layard's thinking that most psychotherapists, psychoanalytic or otherwise, would agree with: the need for wider provision and greater funding for psychological therapies; the importance of talking therapies rather than the reliance on medication alone; and the idea that many people on incapacity benefits have psychological problems needing help, rather than being simply either physically ill or work-shy (Marzillier & Hall, 2009). More problematic, however, are some of the conceptual foundations of Layard's thinking and conclusions, such as the over-simplistic "medical model" reduction of complicated psychological, social, and economic circumstances to a single symptom, such as depression, and the belief that, once this symptom is treated, a person will then be able to return to work (Marzillier & Hall, 2009).

Equally problematic was Layard's emphasis on CBT as the evidence-based "therapy of choice", based on then-current National Institute for Health and Clinical Excellence (NICE) guidelines (NICE, 2004) for the treatment of depression, which considered only randomized control trials (RCTs) as acceptable evidence, and the way in which this has been taken up by politicians and has become the basis of the IAPT programme, which continues to dominate planning decisions to this day.

The revised 2009 NICE guidelines included a welcome widening of the range of short-term treatments recommended. There is also, however, a need for NHS provision of intensive (three-times-weekly) but *time-limited* (in this case, two years) individual psychoanalytic psychotherapeutic treatment, something now only rarely available to NHS patients, and, even if it is available, almost always with a psychotherapy trainee. I would argue the case for such treatments, as opposed to shorter-term treatments such as CBT, or once-weekly psychodynamic treatments, for two reasons. First, because there is a group of patients who require this particular treatment to make a real difference to their difficulties, due to the complex personality pathology that is the foundation of their problems, and that make them highly unlikely to be helped by other forms of treatment. Second, that because shifts can be made in such patients' psychopathology, even within a time-limited treatment such as this, a strong economic argument of the type made by Layard can be made to justify the provision of such treatments. Such patients are expensive in terms of unemployment and incapacity benefits, but also in terms of multiple psychological treatments, which rarely have a lasting effect.

As Bell (2010) states, the psychoanalytic perspective does not think about a patient having many illnesses, but as having "only one illness which expresses itself in different ways, and which is inseparable from his character" (p. 191). As described, my patient, Mr E, had a highly disordered personality structure, which led to multiple difficulties, including depression, suicidality, and deliberate self-harm, anxiety, hallucinations, and the potential for psychotic breakdown, alcohol abuse, problems with interpersonal relationships, and poor day-to-day functioning. This underlying personality pathology makes it ineffective to try to treat one of the presenting symptoms, such as depression, in the focused way that Layard suggests doing with short-term treatments.

The other aspect of Mr E's difficulties that psychoanalytic treatment aimed to address, which others do not, was his perversity. Bell makes clear how important it is to differentiate between patients with significant levels of perversity, and those without. This is a crucial element to engage with, as every clinician working with patients knows, and yet, as Bell says, it is "more or less independent of psychiatric diagnosis", and so remains relatively independent of treatments focused on traditional diagnostic categories.

Research findings suggest the effectiveness of longer-term psychodynamic psychotherapy (LTPP) compared to shorter treatments. Fonagy (2010) cites two systematic reviews to this end. The first, De Maat, de Jonghe, Schoevers, and Dekker (2009), studied a large number of patients treated with LTPP and found good effect sizes, which increased at follow-up. The second study cited was the well-known but methodologically controversial meta-analysis of 23 studies of LTPP (individual psychodynamic psychotherapy of at least one year) conducted by Leichsenring and Rabung (2008). Their follow-up (Leichsenring & Rabung, 2011) included fewer studies, but with stricter control conditions, and found pre–post effect sizes consistently high, compared with those for short-term therapy. Fonagy (2010) describes these findings as "of enormous importance [being] the first set of strong signals that suggest that LTPP is superior to less intensive treatments when directed towards complex mental disorders" (p. 27). More recently, the Tavistock Adult Depression Study (TADs) (Fonagy et al., 2015) compared once-weekly psychoanalytic psychotherapy over 18 months with a control group receiving the treatments currently approved by the NICE depression guidance. The results provided compelling evidence for the effectiveness of psychoanalytic therapy. After two years of follow-up, depressive symptoms had remitted in 30% of those receiving the psychoanalytic therapy, whereas in the control group this figure was only 4%. Additionally, those receiving the psychoanalytic psychotherapy saw significantly more benefits to their quality of life, general wellbeing, and social and personal functioning.

While it seemed clear that Mr E benefitted from his therapy at the time, one can never be certain what a patient will do internally with any treatment once it is finished. This is true of any treatment modality. There is, however, evidence of a "sleeper effect" in psychoanalytic therapy in which the patient continues to make use of the treatment and to make progress after the treatment has ended (de Maat et al., 2009; Fonagy et al., 2015). Turning once more to Mr E, I think that he was ultimately able to take in the treatment, and that the follow-up information suggested he was able to hold onto and build on the progress he made, in terms of his own psychic functioning, his interpersonal relationships and work. It is hard to think what other treatment modality could have achieved this, with a patient with Mr E's level, and complexity of difficulties.

Clearly, psychoanalytic treatment costs more than shorter-term, less intensive treatments, but, in being effective with this group of patients with complex mental disorders, can be justified compared to multiple cheaper but ineffective treatments. In fact, Leichsenring and Rabung (2008) conclude that LTPP may be a cost-effective treatment for complex disorders, due to its greater effectiveness, than short-term treatments. In addition, the resulting decreased presentations and costs to other parts of the NHS, such as to GPs and A&E departments, must be considered, along with the economic benefits of treated patients being able to work. In terms of NHS resource provision, this type of treatment might be thought of as being positioned between the short-term treatments recommended by NICE for depression and the structured psychological treatment programmes recommended by NICE for treatment of borderline personality disorder, provided by specialist teams, regularly offering programmes of between three and five days a week for up to two years.

The psychoanalytic psychotherapy perspective recognizes the limitation of viewing "getting patients back to work" as a concrete goal in itself and understands that, unless the underlying problems which made work unbearable are addressed, any return to work is likely to be temporary at best.

Mr E had taken significant time off work due to depression, anxiety, exhaustion, and thoughts of suicide and self-harm in the year prior to beginning his treatment with me. As we began, he was only working occasionally, in a very limited way. During his treatment, Mr E made progress on several aspects of his difficulties, which made work more bearable and satisfying. He was able to be less preoccupied with others' views of him at work and so felt less pressure to "make others like him" by working obsessively, which had left him exhausted. Many of his work relationships had a sexualized flavour, which undermined his authority, and he became more able to maintain clearer boundaries at work, to hold a more authoritative position. He was also able to develop less conflictual relationships with bosses and authority figures, mirroring the growing sense of his ability to work in our sessions, to be productive and creative.

Mr E returned to work partially during this treatment with me. At the six-month review, he was continuing to work, and was developing a business idea with collaborators that he had had during the treatment. Two years after the treatment ended, he described now being financially independent of outside support. He also talked about making future career plans, to develop something more manageable and more stable.

I was pleased to have worked with Mr E, despite being aware that longer term therapy might have been needed for his progress to continue. But I was also aware that, in the current NHS financial climate, this would be unrealistic and inequitable. In the event, two years of intensive treatment did enable us to work together meaningfully, with some real therapeutic gains, for a patient who had previously found making real gains very difficult.

Note

An earlier version of this chapter was published as S. Shaw (2014), "The elephant tied up with string: A clinical case study showing the importance of NHS provision of intensive, time-limited psychoanalytic psychotherapy treatments." *Psychoanalytic Psychotherapy, 28*: 379–396.

CHAPTER SEVEN

There are two in the room

Malika Verma

My work with Ms D helped me to learn about sharing space with my patient: the room itself, our thoughts and experiences, and the space in which to develop something new.

Clinical example: Ms D

Ms D was a 22-year-old white woman, attractive, charming, and likeable. She came from a well-to-do, successful family. She had recently finished her postgraduate studies and had been offered a sought-after internship at a prestigious company. She came to therapy because she was experiencing difficulties at work, feeling that her supervisors and superiors were bullying her. After some negotiation, she had been given an ultimatum: if her work did not improve, she would have to leave the internship.

Both her parents were well-known figures in their field. Within the family, there was a sense that father always came first, and the children were expected to fall in line and accommodate him. Ms D believed that she was mother's favourite, and that mother would have liked to give her more time, had she not been overwhelmed by father's demands.

The first nine months

The preliminary meeting went smoothly. Ms D was pleasant and well-mannered. She spoke intelligently and articulately. We had both thought we were ready for this. Two years together gave us enough time to rethink initial impressions.

The sessions became very intense very quickly, which took me by surprise. Ms D was very dramatic, her speech full of exaggerations. At times, her words sounded nonsensical, and I struggled to understand her. In one session, she described how enlivened she felt after a short nap, just before coming to the session. I commented that this had made her late. She became furious, saying that she was probably falling in love with me but that I was cold and stone-hearted. I found it very difficult to make sense of what was happening.

She would start the session with something prepared: either an experience, or her own analysis of this experience, or a dream. Her script would include what I was allowed to say. The moment she would start speaking, I would become tense. Every word felt like an attack on my capacity to think, understand, and interpret. Eventually, I would collect myself and manage to say a few words. Those few words, however, were always the worst, the most misplaced, the most destructive words imaginable: I had ruined everything, I had stolen her thoughts and made them my own, I was pushing my thoughts into her, I didn't understand her.

Bion explains that, if the patient's projections are unbearable, the therapist may eject them out quickly in the form of unprocessed interpretations (Bion, 1959). I began to wonder if this accounted for my patient's accusations. Was this my inability to contain my patient's distress? At times, I would feel both accused and guilty, and we would get into a tussle about who was trying to get rid of what. With other patients, difficult moments would come and go, but with Ms D there was just no easing up. Her intense and agitated reaction would confuse me, make me tense and rigid. I would be scared to open my mouth, and also my mind, both because of how she would turn on me but also because I was afraid that I was causing her distress. It took many months to begin to understand what was being communicated during these moments.

At work she submitted an unsatisfactory piece of work and was asked to leave. I felt that her bosses had tried their best to help but that her stubbornness had defeated their efforts. It was only later that I noticed that my sympathies were always with her adversaries, never with her. At the time, I tried to be conscientious and dutiful, but I wasn't truly available, perhaps very much like her mother. My supervisor had to work very hard to help me see how painful this experience might be for her, how humiliating. It would often not make sense to me. This was an indication of how disconnected I was from her experience.

At this early stage of my training, I had thought that patients were supposed to talk about their life and that I was supposed to bring in the transference. She, however, could only ever talk about me, and I would find myself paralysed by her. It took time for me to understand that this *was* the transference, being lived out between us rather than talked about.

The next nine months

> In a Monday session Ms D began with a dream that she had had the afternoon before. The setting of the dream was her room, which she described in detail, in the way that a stage is described in the script of a play. Her sister was in the dream, and there was some friction between them, but soon they were laughing, and the tension was eased. I said that there was tension between us after I announced the break the previous week, but today it was gone. She was suddenly furious with me. She said that she had held on to the memory of how we had smiled at each other when she entered the room today, but that now I had robbed her of that by mentioning the break again.

This was a typical exchange at this point in the treatment. She came hoping for a dreamy cosiness but then found me coarse and harsh. When I made an interpretation, she would say that I had stolen her thoughts, fractured and shattered her mind. Interestingly, this was also my experience with her. Bion writes that, irrespective of its destructive effect, projective identification is always a communication—*provided* that the object/therapist is ready to receive, hold, contain, and process this (Bion, 1959). As a beginner therapist, my response found more sympathy in Paula Heimann's observations that, when at the receiving end of such powerful projections, the intuitive response is to push back, rather than hold and contain (Heimann, 1950).

Often in the sessions I would feel that it was a conversation between two people in different rooms. It seemed there was no link between what we were saying to each other. How frustrating it must have been for her. She experienced me as a mad brick wall. In her frustration she would hurl insult after insult at me and storm out of the room. The next session she would come back, frightened and pleading: I was the only one who could understand her, and she hoped I would not throw her out. It was very difficult to speak to a patient who attacked my mind so aggressively, but also very difficult to work with a therapist whose mind collapsed so easily.

She would comment on what I was wearing, how I looked or spoke, which would disturb me, perhaps a lot more than I understood. I would try to hide myself from her by never smiling, being cautious about what I wore, entering the building and completely ignoring her as she stood by the reception. At the time, this was the only recourse available to me.

I felt so intruded upon that I had to take physical precautions against her. I was, of course, doing the same with my mind, but that was more difficult to see.

One day I laughed in the session. She had said something funny. It was an uninhibited, spontaneous moment, perhaps the first of this kind. She talked about it for many days—first sexualizing it: "your laughter was so warm, so beautiful", and eventually acknowledging how disturbing the experience was for her. In her mind, if I could become uninhibited, that made me very dangerous.

My supervisor helped me to see that my patient was very attached to me, that she really needed me. I wasn't convinced, but I would hold on to my supervisor's words and sit with them in front of me like a shield. At times, we were two very frightened people in a room. The fact that she desperately needed access to me made me more uptight and defended. She would say that I was like her mother, in her head all the time but so distant and unavailable.

I spoke to her about how enraged she felt if I did not follow the script that she had prepared for me. As punishment, she would try to push me out and exclude me. She agreed, but, as she continued to talk, she was rather shocked to see that there were feelings of disdain and scorn for me, hidden behind all the apparent praise and idealization.

As we got to know each other better, I began to understand more about the unbearable anxiety that Ms D carried inside her. In addition to her innate disposition, I wondered about her early experiences of containment. Winnicott describes how *disillusionment* (or Klein's depressive position), which lies at the foundation of our relationship with reality, cannot be achieved unless the child has had a full and satisfactory *Illusion* of omnipotence and unchallenged narcissism (Winnicott, 1953).

The violence with which Ms D would attempt to take possession of my mind made me wonder whether one had ever been available to her. Had she wrestled similarly with her mother and felt constantly pushed out, defeated? Did her mother, very much like me, feel overwhelmed and under-resourced?

In my supervisor I had a partner with experience, patience, and skill, who, every week, put my mind together and helped me to see that my ordinariness was nothing to be ashamed of. Her mother, perhaps, had had no such support.

It took me a while to appreciate how humiliated and disturbed Ms D felt by my presence. I had been preoccupied by my own disturbances and humiliations. Steiner writes that we underplay the impact of shame on our capacity to be seen (Steiner, 2011c). The stripping of defences, both hers and mine, left us shying away from each other. I also became painfully aware of the fact that we are just human: that sexual thoughts and aggression belonged to me also and that I had often used my position as the professional in the room to protect myself from ordinary experiences.

My patient and I struggled with our respective sense of shame. There was such a wish to be seen and understood, and yet we both felt that it was the other who made things complicated, who refused to understand. When I began to understand this better, I was able to see, and to help her see, that something particular happened when she tried to communicate with me. If she felt distressed, she could not tell me about this in a straightforward way; instead, she would start *acting* distressed, for my benefit. She would then become completely involved with this acting, leaving the distressed person, and me, far away. She could see this, and, briefly, we were together in our struggle. These moments continued to be rare, but their memory, the impression they made, helped to develop some trust between us.

Ms D found a new job—another internship—which meant that we had to negotiate new session times. Her sessions were moved from mid-morning to 6 pm in the evening. My own family life meant that leaving work at 7 pm to reach home by 8 pm was very difficult for me. I think the strain this caused in me made it difficult to fully appreciate the effort my patient was making. The truth was that both of us could be tired and resentful by 6 pm, both feeling they were doing the other a big favour, and the stage would be set for us to snap at each other. My own guilt regarding my neglected roles as mother and homemaker could make me want to shove gratefulness and awareness into her prematurely. It took some time for me to work this through before I could regain my analytic equilibrium.

Ms D's job was to provide administrative help to people for whom English was not their first language, often refugees with very traumatic backgrounds. Their lives in this new country were also often difficult. Many of them lacked experience of someone really taking an interest in them. She started telling me about her work, and I recognized my patient in every story: a person who was troubled, feeling exposed, needing care and protection but unable to trust anyone. Ms D said that the people she worked with wanted to trust her, but that something within them caused them to act with suspicion and hatred. This description brought to mind Rosenfeld's description of "the gang" (Rosenfeld, 1971a): a part which is clingy and attached but controlled by another part, which is hostile and bullying. She used the sessions as a refuge from the real world, where she was expected to be an adult, but in the sessions the feelings of need and vulnerability were unbearable. She would then become a bully to herself and to me.

She was having a hard time at work. She was evidently more privileged than those she was meant to help, and she assumed that she would be treated like a saviour. She was taken aback by the rage, suffering, and shame she encountered. They were aggressive. They insulted her. They ridiculed her. She wanted to help them, but they would not let her. They evoked hatred in her. But, over time, she began to understand the parallels with her own situation, and she began to feel protective of them. She began to laugh when they made fun of her. She could see how they all needed her to be genuine. It was unbearable for them to be vulnerable with someone who was so guarded.

This experience began to allow her to take in my interpretations about how she treated me. The refugees became the connection that we had been struggling to make. We both became more aware of how we struggled in the other's presence. I started trusting myself more with her, to be less guarded. Something between us had eased.

She carried on with the internship for a year and then resigned because the organization had made unrealistic promises, which they were in no position to fulfil. This led her to face her own difficulties in accepting external reality, when she preferred a manic optimism. She struggled with the acceptance that reality kept her rooted to the ground, rather than floating grandiosely, like an overblown balloon. Then, when reality hit, there was a crash. It was more manageable for her to respond to disappointment with denigration, than with an acknowledgement of her disappointment and pain. And for once it was possible to address this.

The last nine months

A month before the ending, it was Ms D's birthday. She told me how she had gone out for a birthday meal with her friends. One friend took over: he was boasting and showing off and left without paying his share. I said that she saw a glimpse of herself in this friend and that this had disturbed her. She became livid: I had nothing good to say about her, ever. She said that she knew I was mocking her, complaining about her, because the two years of therapy had been a waste of time.

It was very painful to hear her say this, and it made me sit back and think. I said that it was very painful and humiliating that I ask her to look at herself, even today, when she had hoped that I would remember that she is the special birthday girl. Instead, I treated her like an ordinary patient and expected her to get on with the work.

She responded—first angrily, but then with more regret. She spoke about how the evening had not gone as planned, and that she did not, could not, thank her friends.

Slowly, the sessions began to focus on the relationship with her sister, the envy and rivalry between them, the tendency to blame the other. She had moved in with her sister, and every day there was a story about how terrible she was: a bully, aggressive, hostile. How difficult it was to be in the same room with her. These outbursts gave me the courage to talk about my experience of her, that she also tended to be aggressive and hostile. She was stunned: her entire life had been built upon differentiating herself from her sister. It was frightening for her to recognize that some of the ills she saw in others were, in fact, projections of her own feelings. However, it was also an achievement that she was able to recognize this.

Ms D described numerous fights between the sisters about who ate what and what belonged to whom. It seemed impossible to share and coexist. Now, looking back, I remember how I had felt at the start of the therapy, when she hung her coat on top of mine. I had felt violated. I wanted her out of *my* room. It had been difficult to allow ourselves a shared space. This recurrent sense of feeling overwhelmed, intruded upon, started to take on a new meaning.

Sometimes I felt that she was the older sister, that she ate up all I gave greedily and then accused me of stealing her ideas to cook the interpretation that fed her. Klein says that sometimes we may get caught up with the patient's hatred and destruction, at the cost of acknowledging the patient's love (Klein, 1957). We fail to see how hard the patient is trying to accomplish what in fact is very hard for them. The patient can use the therapist in the only way she knows how, and, in the using, the patient reveals herself and makes herself available for being understood.

At first, I had found it very hard to share the room with her, sometimes becoming very possessive of it, but mostly forgetting that I was also present in the same room, part of the dynamic, and contributing to it. Paula Heimann (1950) observes that *psychotherapy is, first of all, a relationship between two people,* but sometimes this went missing. I largely spoke to her about how *she* experienced me, and I think she found this very accusatory. As my capacity to work with my countertransference developed, this changed how I was able to understand her and to talk to her. We would, increasingly, find a few moments when we could cook and eat the food together.

From the very beginning of our last year together, Ms D was preoccupied with the ending. She was in a panic and trying to find a substitute for her therapy and for me. She was also looking for a career. She managed to get herself an interview with a senior executive in a respected organization. Once again, there was a risk of this being hijacked by a manic excitement. She got the job, and was given her first assignment, at which point things became much more difficult. The boss was demanding and did not mince her words in telling her that she was a disappointment. Her work was shoddy and incomplete.

The therapy was coming to an end, and she felt shoddy and incomplete. She felt that I was leaving her, and she tried hard to find an immediate replacement. Initially, she tried to manage the ending in the only way she knew how, by controlling and attacking, and idealizing me in turns:

"You have not helped me."

"You are the only one who understands."

"Why are you leaving me? Why can't I continue as your private patient?"

Silences became even more unbearable for her: I was not talking to her, not telling her anything, I was not helping her.

There was truth in all the feelings she expressed, yet she still tended to dramatize them, still unsure whether she was talking to a figure who could hear and understand her. I said that it was sad and painful for her that, after the end of her therapy, I would not be there to enjoy her successes. This seemed to calm her, and she could acknowledge the loss of something of value.

I was getting better at judging the temperature of her outbursts and learning how to respond without retaliating in kind.

Although she was taken aback by the dressing-down the boss had given her, Ms D also responded differently. She did not become overwhelmed but talked about having bitten off more than she could chew. This experience helped her to decide that she needed to undertake some more training, and with that in mind, she applied for a course. She explained to me what the course entailed, what it required, and what it would lead to. It all sounded very down-to-earth and ordinary. She seemed to be comfortable with it.

She began talking about how much the therapy had helped. We discussed her continuing it, either in a low-fee clinic or privately. In the last session she left me speechless. She cried soundlessly for the entire 50 minutes. Anything I could have said felt meaningless, and so I sat with her for our last 50 minutes, eventually able to share the room quietly, together in our sadness and loss.

She was seen for a review by my supervisor six months after the end of the therapy. Ms D said that she was doing well and, although she knew that more work was needed, for now she would like to digest the two years she had had with me.

CHAPTER EIGHT

One groove's difference: on unlearning psychiatry

Alan Baban

I have often wondered what a medical training might sound like if it were a piece of music. Over a bed of cellos slowly bleeding into feedback, there is a repeated phrase trying to achieve blast-off. The music seems to surge forwards then resolve, like an Escher painting: we are moving, but we are also back where we started. Progress is slow, if it (arguably) ever happens, but the process is meant to be fun, like avant-garde disco is meant to be fun. There are canned horns.

I remember, on becoming a doctor, that I felt in my own way that some sort of "blast-off" was imminent—that after six years of nuzzling anatomy textbooks and nurturing a sense of personal and professional disarray, the "rocket" would cohere, and we would finally be going somewhere. In fact, there was only more chaos. Despite the on-going pressure to do more, see more, get that experience, go to that course, I did not feel that "every step [was] moving me up". It felt more like every step was moving me sideways, at a slant, and on some sort of vague, shifting incline. It's probably clear that in those days I did not really know where I was going: of course, I ended up in psychiatry.

These days, when you are a junior psychiatrist, you spend a lot of time around people, but you also spend a lot of time in front of a computer: typing discharge summaries, organizing TTAs, sifting through pages and pages of pdfs that detail, in shorthand, someone's "history." ICD terms like W61.61XD become depressingly familiar. It was a great relief, then, to find a vibrant psychotherapy community in my local hospital: the idea that you could sit with a patient, week after week, for an hour, and be expected simply to understand—not medicate, or try to describe, but understand—was mind-blowing: if not a "blast-off", then a slip into a new dimension, like pushing on a false wall that gives way to reveal an entirely new room. But none of that really prepared me for starting work at the Tavistock.

Usually, when one starts a medical job, there are things to do. You move from ward to ward, carrying around a "jobs list", like a newspaper baton. Bleeps go off. You turn a corner and run into someone who gives you more work. Lunch becomes the meagre findings of what is in the "reduced" aisle of Sainsbury's. Every now and then a well-heeled drugs rep arrives like a Roman god and treats the entire team to a bulk order of Domino's pizza. And, in the background, always, one is faintly aware of the system buzzing away: peristaltically pushing the patients through. In short, you start a job, and things are already happening.

It was a great shock, then, to start work at the Tavistock, and find that nothing was happening. No one was there; it was the August analytic break. For the first time in my career, I had a great swathe of space in front of me that I, at once, set about trying to anxiously fill up. I wandered the corridors looking for things to do, because I was so used to "doing things." It did not occur to me that work here might be about something other than "doing." Still, I tried. In the sweltering summer heat, I un-boxed and put together two desk fans for Adult Complex Needs. They did not work. I tried to fix them, but my concerned line manager intervened and let me know that I was not approved yet to use the departmental screwdriver. The professionals were brought in. At this point I really was at a loss. Eventually I gave up and started reading Freud.

Now I can look back and realize there was something so apposite about that time of "doing nothing" and the struggle against "doing nothing" that, in its own way, this conflict taught me a lot about the quality of a psychoanalytic encounter where we might have to negotiate between many different demands, where it wasn't so much about the "doing" but about being and understanding. But, at that point, all this was protean. The desk fans whirred. When people returned to work after the break, the unit meetings started, and the true weight of my ignorance hit me. I did not understand what anyone was saying. I had used the term "projective identification" in my interview, but now I realized I did not understand what it meant, let alone "introjective identification" or "container-contained."

Occasionally I felt like piping up with something psychiatric, but then I remembered the words of warning from the previous trainee: "Never", they said, "*never* speak of a psychiatric diagnosis. They will swat you over the head for it." Of course, in those days, the diagnoses were like pink elephants in my mind; I could not stop seeing or thinking about them, they were so embedded in my mind as ways of structuring things.

This, then, is the central challenge of coming to a psychotherapy training from psychiatry: slowly coming to an understanding of how much one does not know, and then being OK with that. Rather than jumping to diagnostic labels, sitting and waiting for meaning to emerge: a process that is difficult to explain in words and, which, I think, one simply needs to submit to—with curiosity, of course. As one scatter-brained character says to another in Thomas Pynchon's *Inherent Vice* (2009):

> What goes around may come around, but it never ends up exactly the same place, you ever notice? Like a record on a turntable, all it takes is one groove's difference and the universe can be on into a whole "'nother song". [p. 334].

When I returned, having spent some years in the M1 training, to doing psychiatric on-calls, it did feel, disturbingly, as if I was knowing places (situations, people, things) for the first time that I had *thought* I'd known before. I felt sensitized to what was going on, but in a painful way that made me miss and yearn for the states of dissociation that had previously allowed me to function in these environments: churning out the discharge summaries, writing the drug charts, e-mailing pharmacy. To bear thinking about psychotic processes, between patients and staff, between the staff themselves, processes rebounding within the Institution at large, was and is a constant challenge. I found myself saying less in assessments, listening more, sometimes to the chagrin of other clinicians who thought me absent-minded. But it is a purposeful absent-mindedness that I believe has allowed me to approach things in the acute setting in a new way.

Clinical example 1

A 51-year-old man was undergoing a Mental Health Act Assessment. He had been brought in by police, having been found wandering in his nightgown in a dishevelled state, muttering something about aliens. Medical investigations had ruled out any organic cause for his presentation. There was no previous contact with psychiatric services. During the assessment, the man spoke rapidly, moving from topic to topic in a stream. He stalked the assessment room, occasionally doing karate kicks, in a way that obviously made me, the other doctor, and the social worker assessing him, anxious. There was the disquieting sense that asking him specific questions, or prodding too much around the wheres and whys of what brought him in, might end in violence. The man himself said he just needed to go home. To my surprise, we were about to let him. In our discussion outside the assessment room, the other doctor acknowledged that, yes, this patient was very unwell, but that there was no acute risk or risk history, which meant (in his mind) that there were no grounds to bring this man into hospital against his will. It felt, though, to me, that we were in danger of colluding with powerful psychotic projections from the patient and in the realm of denial and rationalizations. I found myself speaking about this sensitively, not wanting to anger the other doctor, who I felt was identifying with something from the patient. After thinking through and exploring these processes with the team, this man, who was in an acute psychotic crisis, was ultimately detained and admitted to a psychiatric hospital.

The title of this piece is a little gauche. Is it really "unlearning psychiatry"? What is being learned or unlearned here? I would contend that something must be given up in this work and this way of doing things, and that is the omnipotent belief that one already knows. Because, regardless of the amount of emergency assessments, section papers, drug charts, and early-hours conversations with beleaguered colleagues one has done, one still doesn't really know. It is terrifying sometimes to return to psychiatry and feel those pressures between "knowing" and "not knowing".

At a certain point in my career I was on the rota to do a night shift that split me between five different hospitals at the same time—that is, during the 12-hour shift I would be the person you called from any of those hospitals if someone was very sick in A&E, or if someone was brought in against their will and needed an emergency assessment. Very often I would get calls from junior psychiatrists about drug management and other calls from medical and surgical doctors about rapid tranquilization, sedation, and the small numbers on ECGs that say something about the heart, and which go up and down depending on what drugs someone is taking. This was work, and at 4 am, work definitely feels like work. But my point is that this work—which, as you recall, is very often centred on the containment of *psychotic states*—was itself beset by a sort of fragmenting, psychotic process. I was split between five different sites, zipping around London in a sort of manic patient-assessing free-flow.

No sooner had I arrived at one site than I got a call to go to another. In the middle of seeing one patient, I would be pulled aside and told about three more. Referrals abounded. Often the patients were described by staff in highly memorable "bite-sized" ways that emphasized only their demographics and their perceived dangerousness, in an effort that, I believe, was on some level designed to get me to see them first. Would I see the man who had been running with a hammer, swinging at people in central London? Or was it the young woman recovering in A&E from a Paracetamol overdose, whom I had to prioritize? There were also the so-called "frequent attenders", who had come to various EDs so many times and with such force that the system tended to treat them and their appeals for help with the organizational equivalent of a shoulder-shrug. "We know them, they'll be OK." "Just let them sleep." I could go on.

The effect of all this external pressure could be a frittering of the perceiving mind: patients bleed into each other, people are described as if they were things (composites of risk histories, scans, and blood tests), and bad decisions are made. The work itself becomes impossible, because there can be no work in that state, where work is just a constant piecing together of where one has to be, when, and for what. The who is under threat of disappearing.

There is a lot I have learned from my M1 training, but if there is one thing I had to pick out that has been important for me, it is the essential value of that "who". That, to do this sort of work—whether it is in the therapy room, or out of the room in the heart of the psychiatric on-call—one should have, more or less, a robust internal frame. Or, in other words, one hopefully is rooted in a secure sense of "who" one is, while at the same time being comfortable with the fact that there are limits, there is room for growth, new discoveries, and new losses. In essence: an ongoing and dynamic process.

Clinical example 2

A 45-year-old woman had been detained under Section 136 by the police and then conveyed to the Emergency Department for a psychiatric assessment. She had contacted emergency services while inebriated, saying she was going to slash her neck. While under medical investigation in A&E, she had taken her hospital dressing gown and made it into a ligature, which she tied around her neck. By the time I arrived as the duty psychiatrist on-call, she had been moved to a side room, where she sat cross-legged and hidden behind a mattress that she had turned on its side, shielding her from view. A camera in the room meant that she was constantly observed by the staff in A&E. They let me know that the patient would occasionally throw two fingers up at them through the screen. During the few hours which it took for me to arrive, she had reportedly settled and said she wanted to go home. There was some pressure on me to go along with this, that this obviously difficult-to-manage patient needed to be discharged quickly from the department. There was, however, a complex history of several previous suicide attempts, dating back to the tragic death of her new-born son 15 years prior, and the subsequent loss of her long-term relationship with her ex-partner. The patient had previously worked in a well-paid and regarded job, but since these devastating losses she had been in a financial, reputational, and relational tailspin, with several admissions to in-patient units, some abandoned attempts at psychotherapy treatments, and a fluctuating dependence on alcohol and drugs, all detailed in her notes—making for depressing heart-sink reading before I had even gone to speak with her. In short, I felt she was going to put me in a difficult position.

> After I entered the room and introduced myself, there was a pause, and she said she couldn't hear me. I was too far up. How on earth could I expect her to engage in this so-called "psychiatric assessment" when I was the one standing up—standing above her—and she was the one sitting down on the floor. No, she told me quite emphatically, if I wanted to take this any further, then I would have to be the one sitting down with her on the ground, like a normal person, and then maybe we could talk. And no, she looked at me and smiled coyly, pre-empting what I was about to ask her—she *definitely* wasn't going to be the one who stands up. And so I knelt down to listen to her.
>
> Immediately the patient seemed quite surprised by my actions, and I could feel the atmosphere in the room softening. The respite was brief, though, and when the patient started speaking, it was with a very blaming tone. She spoke to me about all the ways she had been let down and abandoned over the last 15 years, with the implication that I was going to be yet another incompetent person in a long line of incompetent people who had not managed to help her. It was difficult material for me to listen to. The fact that I was crouching on my knees made it physically taxing. There were quite a few moments I wanted to stand up and leave, wondering why I was listening to this woman, who, in her manner and bearing, seemed to do-down and complain about everything and everyone, almost inviting me to leave. Is it too much for you? she would say. Yes, I almost said. It is.

I remember feeling guilty that I was even entertaining these thoughts and that, as a clinician, I wanted to move away from my patient, that she was, indeed, too much, and that I did have to be the one standing, giving my knees a rest. I gradually began to understand these as important communications from the patient—that in fact there was something she desperately wanted to move away from and stand above, as it were, leaving her in a state both of terror and of unresolved guilt. Just as I felt myself being killed off in our interactions, I became aware of the poignant absence in her material of her dead son. I remember feeling very sad and in touch with her suffering, in a way that made me want to stay and help her.

When I pointed out to her that we had gone half an hour and she had not mentioned the most devastating losses that had happened in her life, and that perhaps it was too painful for us to think about, she looked at me with genuine surprise and feeling.

My comment to her was, I believe, a psychoanalytic interpretation that was able to help the patient understand something about herself and her suffering in that moment. There were still difficulties—how could there not be difficulties?—but the assessment began to move slowly in a new direction. The outcome was that she later engaged with Alcohol Services in a bid to stop her damaging pattern of dependent drinking.

I bring this as an example of something I don't think I would have said at the start of my psychiatric training. At the very least, it wouldn't have come spontaneously to my mind, and, given the bureaucracy-on-wheels aspect of some medical trainings, where there is always something "to do", even if it did come to my mind, I might not have had the space inside to pay it any attention. I might have stood in front of this patient and felt so overwhelmed by her powerful projections that I would have had to leave, not really understanding what had just happened and probably blaming it all on the patient. Another depressing night shift. But luckily, that wasn't the case, and I have my training to thank for it.

The more experience I have, the more convinced I am that this sort of psychoanalytic understanding, when deployed at the right times, can be of genuine help to the patients we see. It might just be one groove's difference, but it is a groove that takes us into a whole other song.

CHAPTER NINE

Becoming a psychoanalytic psychotherapist: learning and unlearning, identity and citizenship

Rachel Hodgins

It feels particularly difficult to write this chapter at the moment. Even a snapshot of the institutional and political context of the M1 training would be blurred. At the time of writing, there are changes happening at every level, from the staff and structure of the course itself, to the organization of clinical services in the Trust where we're based, to national and international changes to public health provision and the aftermath of Covid-19 on NHS staff and services.

These circumstances, in combination with the profound work that M1 asks of trainees, both in the academic and clinical components of the training and in their analyses, can feel bewildering. However, it is also not unusual to hear trainees and graduates talk about the ways that the training has changed their lives, their careers, their relationships, and their minds, deepening their engagement with their patients, grounding their clinical judgement in theory and in the experience of long-term close supervision, and introducing them to friends and colleagues whom they may know for the rest of their lives.

In this chapter I outline my own experience of coming to the M1 training from a background in clinical psychology. I also say something about the experience of being a trainee (again), the challenges inherent in that position, and the importance of peer support and solidarity.

Just be careful how you phrase it: psychoanalytic clinical psychology

In my first job after qualifying as a clinical psychologist, the lead Consultant Clinical Psychologist in the service heard that I wanted to specialize in psychoanalytic therapy, and shook her head, saying "No, no: that's a cul-de-sac." I had already been advised to be cautious about requesting a psychoanalytic placement, which would be at the top of my CV when applying for clinical psychology jobs: "Just be careful how you phrase it. Some employers will like it . . . but some will really not like it." When we interview trainee clinical psychologists who are applying for a specialist placement in this service, we often ask them, "What draws you to psychoanalytic ways of working, at a time when shorter, more symptom-focused treatment is more prevalent?" By the time we start M1, we will have had to find some sort of answer to this question for ourselves, but that does not mean that our identity as clinicians, in relation to the NHS, our core training, or the psychoanalytic community, feels comfortable or fixed. I certainly had concerns about specializing in psychoanalytic therapy while also hoping to work in the NHS, but by that point it was too late: I was already finding both psychoanalytic thinking and my own therapy to be too helpful to turn away from.

My first contact with psychoanalytic thinking came before my clinical psychology training, when a local psychiatric nurse started to run reflective groups at the hostel for homeless women where I was a keyworker. Although I was certainly feeling the effects of powerful pressures, tensions, and displaced feelings among residents and staff, these were not talked about in supervision or handover meetings. We would find ourselves full of anxiety or irritation, mismanaging routine tasks, and often in conflict with one another over concern for, or suspicion of, "difficult" residents. I'm not sure we ever used words like projection or splitting in those reflective groups, but I remember how enlivening it was, and what a relief to begin to have a framework for thinking about what was happening.

Psychoanalytic ideas can feel both immediate and quite intuitive, and also very complicated. Some years later, after finishing the DClinPsy, I started the D59 Psychodynamic Psychotherapy training at the Tavistock and was very conscious of how much I didn't know. I still felt like this when I started M1, but at that point I was also beginning to see that there was a lot that I hadn't even known that I didn't know. It is not entirely easy to sign up to this sort of uncertainty at a point when you had hoped to feel "qualified".

Clinical psychology is a broad discipline: you could invest your professional energies in assessing brain injuries, campaigning to replace diagnoses with formulations, or working to promote treatment adherence in physical medicine services, among many, many other things. For this reason, it is hard to summarize one overarching clinical psychology stance, and I can only talk from my own experience as a trainee and clinician, as a supervisor of clinical psychology trainees, and as a staff member on Tavistock trainings for psychologists. From that perspective, it seems to me that some of the immediate challenges of starting to work in an analytic way are to do with recognizing and letting go of assumptions about your stance and your identity and having to re-think authority, power, and expertise in the therapy room. This is a big ask: having a familiar-feeling stance or role in the therapy room can be one of the ways we gird ourselves for this difficult work at the "emotional coalface" (Obholzer, 2021).

In her chapter on psychoanalysis and cognitive behavioural therapy (which was the dominant modality during my psychology training), Jane Milton suggests that:

> The stance of the therapist in CBT is a socially acceptable one, which makes immediate intuitive sense. The psychoanalytic stance is much harder to swallow, and is maintained against the resistance of both the analyst and the patient. . . . The analyst is pushed constantly from without and within either into being more "cognitive" or into a simpler counselling stance—in such ways the analytic stance is frequently in danger of being lost and having to be refound. [Milton, 2001, p. 432]

I had a sense that, as psychology trainees, we were aiming to become a sort of competent, efficient, friendly, and engaging jack-of-all-trades (and emerging master of any of the ones we were using in our current placements). It seemed advisable to encourage a good collaborative engagement with patients by relating to them in a way that would reassure them that I was a competent, trustworthy, and attentive helper. My psychology placement at the Tavistock was the first time that I was (strongly) encouraged to examine what I was setting up here: to consider that if you are broadcasting so many reassuring messages about what sort of figure you are, you are not receiving much information at all about the internal objects or relational dynamics that your patient has brought with them. Two of the papers that helped me to think about this, and that I now recommend to clinical psychology trainees, are those by Jane Milton (1997) and Jane Temperley (1984). Temperley describes the "internal setting" required for psychoanalytic work, giving an example of resisting a patient's pressure to be a motherly and consoling figure and, instead, letting something more complicated and difficult emerge in the consulting room in the form of an identification with cold and indifferent objects: "This was not the sort of insight he could get from barmaids." Milton's 1997 paper on psychoanalytic assessment in the NHS caricatures two assessment styles, Dr A and Dr B, and considers the implications of adopting Dr A's more analytic stance:

> ... my personal view is that I do [patients] a better service by not responding to their social cues, and thereby engaging more directly with their disturbance. After all, by maintaining neutrality and working in the transference, we have the opportunity often of becoming quite a fresh and unexpected figure in the patient's life. [Milton, 1997, p. 49]

During my clinical psychology training we were encouraged to see our clients as the experts and to take a "one-down position" of curiosity, and psychology trainees on placement with us are often very good at asking skilful questions. They are far more hesitant to offer an interpretation: a claim to having, at the very least, a hypothesis about something less conscious, something that the patient may not be able to recall, or guess, in answer to a question. One of my peers on my psychology training once joked that if a psychoanalytic patient agrees with an analyst's interpretation, it is right; if they disagree, it is right, but the patient is in denial. To interpret patients' material, then, feels like quite an assertion of something—Expertise? Authority? My own experience has been that there is something important about owning your expertise and authority, and letting the patient own theirs and challenge yours, which is harder if you're being so nice all the time. My feeling was that the reality of authority in the therapy room could sometimes be obscured, but not escaped, in more overtly collaborative models. During my psychology training I attended an externally organized CBT "bootcamp" in which the speaker focused at some length on techniques for the important task of keeping clients on-topic, sticking to the agreed agenda for the session. In contrast, in an analytic therapy session, an unexpected diversion might be welcomed as an illuminating association. Even if you suspect the patient is dodging something, this is still helpful information to be curious about, rather than a cue to steer them politely back to whatever it is that *you* thought you should be talking about. Like Socrates, we can sound like we're asking questions, when, in fact, we know which answers we're steering towards.

Being a trainee, being a citizen

The Tavistock and Portman clinics have an early history of democratic decision making, with staff as engaged citizens of the organization (see Armstrong & Rustin, 2020). There is also a longstanding connection between this service and the Tavistock Group Relations Conferences, with many staff involved in the conferences and writing and thinking about how we function in groups and how groups relate to one another (Stokoe, 2010). These traditions provide some basis for thinking and talking to each other about how we are functioning in relation to the task of offering a public sector psychoanalytic psychotherapy service. Weighing in on the other side, however, are all the external and internal pressures and forces that make it difficult to think together, or to find one's voice to talk about what it is like to be here, doing this work.

Clinicians in any NHS service have to find a way to work under pressure. The financial pressures and survival anxieties are apparent, however much service managers may wish to protect trainees from them. Institutions can deal with these pressures in all sorts of defensive ways: Rizq (2014) suggests that "mental health services that are subject to neo-liberal regulatory and performance management systems offer a perverse organizational solution to the anxieties and difficulties of dealing with psychologically distressed patients" (p. 249).

Trainees are also subject to all of the additional pressures of learning and being assessed, of being open to not knowing, and being helped, at the same time as taking up your authority in the role of psychoanalytic psychotherapist and at times advocating for yourself, your peers, or your patients within the service. As a trainee in a department with many established and senior staff members who are also involved in assessing you and making important decisions about your progression through the training, it can be hard to feel free to speak candidly in team discussions or feedback about the training. Writing about psychotherapy trainees' experiences of supervision, Penelope Crick describes "the student's adolescent position in relation to the training, the pains of learning, and the discomforts of being assessed" (Crick, 1991, p. 9). Perhaps a degree of formality and hierarchy in psychoanalytic traditions contributes to this: Kernberg (1996) has written a tongue-in-cheek (or head-in-hands?) paper about the institutional and cultural processes that can inhibit the creativity and confidence of psychoanalytic trainees, including some of the ways that supervisors and trainers can defend themselves against the considerable challenges and anxieties of their own roles.

Hitherto, the M1 curriculum involved at least one term of study groups during the four years of teaching. These were experiential groups led by a consultant external to the department (someone not involved with assessing or managing the trainees), with the task of looking at the experience of being a trainee on the M1 course and understanding dynamics within the study group. A recurring theme in the group I was in seemed to be the immense difficulty of speaking up with the authority of our position in the service, however junior that position might be, and not only about things that might constitute complaints, but about appreciation, concern, or investment in the future of the service. Around this time I also heard the saying, "he who lives in the attic knows where the roof leaks": trainees have a unique vantage point on the training and the clinical service and, as Stokoe describes, "encounters between people that preserve communication ... must be positively valued and embraced by the organization and rigorously protected, because they will be the first things to go under stress" (Stokoe, 2019, p. 9). The Psychotherapy Trainee Group (PTG) is one of the ways that these sorts of encounters can be promoted, not only among us but between us and the two different structures that govern our role as trainees: the clinical service and the department of education and training. There are, of course, differences and rivalries within the trainee cohort, but if these can be talked about, they can be fertile ground for acknowledging our own positions, and perhaps challenging the assumptions that they foster.

The trainee group is an invaluable source of support during a demanding and lengthy training, and solidarity from my M1 colleagues and friends has been essential for me. One of the lessons of remote working during the pandemic was the cumulative importance of even the most momentary greetings and exchanges in the corridor or the kitchen: brief breaks from the emotional coalface. In recent times it hasn't always been easy to keep in touch with one another, and both the formal and informal "encounters ... that preserve communication" continue to be under pressure from all sides (the trainees are busy and tired, the service and the training timetables are very full. . . .). However, in holding on to our own capacity to take an interest in each other, to stay in contact and keep thinking and talking, we are also preserving something valuable for the organization, and for our patients. I hope that we will continue to find and to nurture these opportunities to be good colleagues and good friends to one another.

CHAPTER TEN

Learning through supervision

Francesca Hume

The clinical encounter and clinical supervision

In chapter 2 I described the importance of fostering an analytic attitude and the capacity to learn experientially. The chapters by trainees in this section focussed on the key area where this applies: the trainee's encounter with the patient. Now I look at the interplay between this and the role of the clinical supervisor.

The role of the analytic supervisor is a complex one. We have two subjects—trainee and patient—and we try to reach an adequate understanding of them both and of what is going on between them. We work with the trainee towards a clinical understanding of the patient based on what is known about the patient and what we see going on in the transference, subjecting this to our theoretical understanding of clinical phenomena. All the while, we try to remain attuned to our own affective responses—to the trainee and to the material we are hearing. We try to indicate how we have reached our understanding, with the intention that trainees will learn to become more receptive to the emotional communications coming their way and subjecting these to intellectual scrutiny too. Through this process, trainees learn to use their minds and bodies to register and respond to the patient's projections. In practice, it is an education in becoming clinically sensitive, of becoming aware of impressions that were previously unobserved.

The gulf in understanding between a supervisor and trainee generally feels wide at first, and while it can be inspiring for the trainee to witness the supervisor's deep and confident understanding of unconscious processes, this may feel impossible to emulate. With regard to the relationship between supervisor and trainee, it helps to remember that we are a transference object for them, and their experience of us will be coloured by important relationships they have known. Otto Kernberg (2010) notes that some degree of idealization of the supervisor is probably unavoidable under conditions of a good supervisory experience, particularly if the supervisee is simultaneously experiencing regressive reactions in their own analysis. But, he suggests, it may be helpful for the supervisor to keep in mind that, in all interpersonal situations in which there is a role distribution between one who "knows" and one who "needs to know", an implicit de-skilling of the latter may occur, with the consequent attribution of all knowledge and skills to the supervisor and a self-devaluation of the supervisee. This is important to bear in mind in relation to the question of how best we foster an active stance in the trainee, enabling them to engage with examining their own thoughts, feelings, and countertransferences. Group supervision and clinical seminars can be helpful in this regard, as there is an opportunity to examine the clinical aspects of a case from many different perspectives, including those of other trainees.

The trainee–supervisor couple come to some understanding of the patient, so that clinical interventions and interpretations might suggest themselves, and the task of thinking more broadly about technique may follow. How we do this should depend, to some extent, upon the trainee's progress and their personality. Development is often quite uneven, with intellectual understanding outstripping emotional capacity. When this is true, it may be better not to turn to the theory too quickly. In contrast, a trainee who is easily overwhelmed by the patient's emotions may feel anchored by theoretical ideas. Whether we succeed or fail in helping trainees to develop will largely depend upon their pre-existing capacities: a willingness and suitability for analytic work and a readiness for this. As supervisors, our role is in fostering this. Here, it is worth being aware of our own capacity for doubt and anxiety, especially anxiety born of a superego demand to get things right. We also misunderstand patients and trainees, and often this is in the context of an enactment. It helps to remember the value of enactments and to see them as opportunities for new learning, rather than simply as mistakes.

The fact that the supervisor is involved in evaluating and reporting on the trainee's performance serves to complicate things. Fostering development on the one hand and judging progress on the other make uncomfortable bedfellows. We must consider how best to impart knowledge while maintaining a facilitating atmosphere conducive to learning. In my experience, being open with trainees in reporting on their progress is essential: sharing concerns about difficulties as they arise and being transparent about what is written in the report to assessment boards.

Theoretical teaching: the application of analytic theory and technique

There are some analysts who demonstrate an impressive capacity to engage with a broad range of theoretical ideas and schools of thought and to impart this knowledge and approach in supervision. For most supervisors, analytic understanding and knowledge will come broadly from one of the analytic traditions (Kleinian, Contemporary Freudian, Independent), and, while ideally we should try to be receptive to other traditions, the feeling of having a solid analytic identity based in one place is not a bad thing: it is containing for us and reassuring for the trainee. This is provided it doesn't interfere with the individual's freedom to decide in their own time which theories most inspire them and help them with their work. This is particularly important if the trainee's own analyst is from a different group from that of the supervisor.

While supervisors differ in the extent to which they allude to analytic theory directly, it is important that they are thoroughly conversant with the body of psychoanalytic theory and its application to clinical work. In my experience, the kind of knowledge needed is not generally well embedded in the analyst by the end of their own training but takes some years to consolidate. It relies upon our ongoing learning through reading and teaching, alongside keeping up a clinical practice. I have no doubt that my own competence as a clinical supervisor has been assisted by the many years that I have been teaching analytic theory in weekly seminars. The reason a thorough training in theory is needed is because you want to largely forget about it while you are actually working and supervising. Only then does the theory enter your mind spontaneously, as an association to what you are hearing from the trainee, rather than because you are attempting to "match" what you are hearing to something that may be a theoretical "fit". The more deeply the theory is embedded in the supervisor's background knowledge, the more possible it is to respond intuitively and imaginatively to the clinical material, associating to it freely. We listen to the trainee and to what they have to say about the patient in as fresh a way as we can, hoping each time to discover not a known situation but a new one. In this way, we are like the trainee: relying not on being in possession of theoretical "facts" but "learning from experience."

With regard to teaching analytic technique, supervisors differ in how much they address this directly. It is beyond the scope of this chapter to describe the various aspects of analytic technique that might get discussed during supervision. It is also potentially misleading to suggest that a technique is what a trainee is engaged in acquiring. It is precisely the absence of prescriptive measures that make an analytic apprenticeship most challenging. However, this does not mean that we leave the trainee without any clinical anchors. There are many basic principles that are crucial in fostering the right kind of environment for the trainee to become competent. These start with the fundamental principles around the setting and boundaries. Then there are all the other issues where an understanding of the rationale for a particular stance can assist the trainee in getting started. For example, understanding the reasons why we don't rush to reassure a patient can help a trainee to bear their own anxiety and recognize that they are often reassuring themselves rather than the patient, avoiding the experience of being experienced as a bad or depriving object. Understanding the importance of allowing a patient's anxiety to become manifest so we might examine its nature is also helpful. I feel that theoretical input in relation to technique is very important, but this should not come at the start of a training.

Styles of supervision: the good supervisor

Our supervisory style is likely to start off as an amalgam, based on our identification with our own supervisors and analyst. In the end, it will also be determined by our own personality, talents, and clinical experiences. There have been many excellent analytic teachers, all with quite unique styles of their own.

Hanna Segal, for example, was very spontaneous in her style. One would witness her rich imagination at work, her intuitive understanding of unconscious phantasy emerging in response to a presentation. This could be extremely inspiring by helping you to know your patient better, but it was also very hard to emulate.

By contrast, Betty Joseph's style seemed to promise a kind of apprenticeship experience. You felt that to follow her method closely might help you to become a better analyst yourself. This didn't require you to be exceptionally clever, but it did require you to be scrupulously honest with yourself. A personal example was her response to my telling her that I didn't know which of two interpretations to make to my patient. She replied "the correct interpretation is the one that you don't want to give. It reflects less well upon you." Her approach to supervision came from the technique she had developed from her own analytic practice, one that required great discipline in attending to the immediate emotional contact with the patient and an understanding of enactment by patient and analyst. This involved a scrutiny of the analyst's evolving countertransference and changed throughout a session in building up a picture of the ever-evolving transference. This is difficult to achieve, but aspects of her approach could, to a certain extent, be learnt from her example.

Trainees also pick up our general stance towards patients. A good supervisor will evince a compassionate but unsentimental understanding that recognizes the patient's predicament with feeling. Sometimes this will involve recognizing the frequently encountered internal struggle between aggression and hatred of dependence, on the one hand, and their longing for a good emotional connection on the other. Irma Brenman Pick (2018) would refer to this as "interpreting with two hands" (p. xi).

Finally, a supervisor's capacity to express complex analytic ideas and formulations using ordinary language, free from jargon, is also very important. It encourages trainees to speak in a more ordinary way to their patients and avoids the emotional distance that can be created by using language that is hard to understand.

Three vignettes

What follows are three vignettes. Two of them are from my own experience as supervisor. In the first case (Ms A), I describe a challenging situation for the supervisor, where it was difficult to know what was going on in either the trainee or the patient. After a significant struggle, some limited progress was possible. The second, (Mr B), was much more straightforward and demonstrates the kind of learning that is possible when things are going well-enough. I have also included a brief account of a trainee (Mr C), where things could not be resolved, and his training ultimately was brought to an end.

Ms A

Often as supervisors we struggle to know what is going on, and where, or in whom, a difficulty lies. With this trainee, various options seemed to present themselves, and the situation felt confusing for a long time. Both trainee and supervisor had to tolerate a baffling state of not understanding before some progress became possible.

Ms A was a beginner: conscientious but anxious. Despite this, she and the patient appeared to make a reasonable-enough start. The patient was a troubled young woman with a poor relationship with a cut-off, disturbed-sounding mother. There were some borderline features, and she experienced panic attacks and psychosomatic problems, especially eczema, about which she felt very self-conscious. At a deeper level, the eczema reflected a fear that she was falling apart, unable to hold her body and its insides together. Shortly after the therapy started, near the start of the pandemic, the trainee (Ms A) developed Covid, requiring hospitalization. This was followed by "long Covid" (at that time poorly understood). The severity of her memory impairment, migraines, and attention deficit took some time to become clear. It was also unclear whether the symptoms were entirely Covid-related or were linked to her anxiety starting with her patient. Thus, the work with the patient resumed rather sooner than it might have done (after a couple of months), with lots of absenteeism from the patient, as well as some further disruption caused by the trainee's ongoing poor health. For a while the sessions as well as our supervisions were also conducted by phone.

I felt concerned for both patient and trainee and was worried whether Ms A should be back at work. I was also worried about my own difficulty making sense of what was going on, and where the problem was located. My usual capacity to feel the interaction between trainee and patient was missing, and many things didn't add up. For example, Ms A complained of remembering nothing, and yet her session notes were long and detailed. Her report of her own affect was often at odds with what was suggested from her process notes. The patient spoke of feeling desperate for help, but, despite her best efforts, Ms A felt guiltily unmoved, of no use to the patient, and plagued by self-doubt. This quality of desperation seemed much like the one the patient spoke about, and yet I felt oddly disconnected too. My supervisory comments sounded correct, yet hollow, leaving me feeling I hadn't been of much help. I encouraged Ms A to take up with the patient her experience of an unreliable and damaged therapist, and her fear that she had caused the damage. All of this was powerfully suggested by the patient's material. Yet, when she followed this sort of approach, there was little to suggest this was helpful, and the trainee herself remained anxious and out of her depth.

All the while, I struggled to know where the primary problem lay: was it in the trainee or in the patient, or in some failure in my own understanding? The disturbed and cut-off mother appeared everywhere. Ms A, for her part, seemed to want to attribute it to her own failings: the problem, she felt, lay either with the Covid or with some pre-existing psychopathology of her own.

She told me later: "I feared that my life-long tendency to use my mind in an intellectual way might have been a way of compensating for some major emotional deficit now being exposed by an intellect dimmed by the infamous Covid 'brain-fog'."

I tried my best to explore in greater detail what Ms A was feeling in the sessions: "Nothing", she would say, "I just drew a blank . . . wiped out". But it was unclear what this "nothing" was. We wondered whether the patient was "wiping her out" with projections she couldn't make sense of, or whether it was she, Ms A, wiping out the patient whom she could not allow in, sensing it would be too much for her. As Ms A spoke of her symptoms, I invited her to tell me more about them. Here, she was more forthcoming: "The neurologist's tests scored my 'immediate attention' in the lowest tenth percentile", she said, and "My skin hurts all the time . . . I've been told my face is 'stone-like' because I can't sense my expressions."

This perplexing and difficult situation remained unchanged for some months. All the while, I struggled with my own feeling of being overwhelmed by Ms A's predicament, my duty of care to both her and the patient, and my enduring struggle to make any coherent sense of what was going on. How much was the disembodied experience of phone sessions and supervisions responsible for our struggle? At this point, I think Ms A's sense of having lost her mind was so profound that she didn't know, in an ordinary way, how lost she was feeling: hence the need to project this and have me experience it. Assisted by Ms A's honesty that she was failing her patient, I was able to discuss my dilemma with her: that my plausible-sounding ideas felt to me lacking in conviction and didn't appear to be helping her. The fact that we could share this dilemma seemed important in what followed.

Ms A reported a spontaneous moment of better understanding, which took place during a telephone session: "Taking the call just gave the impression that there was someone there at the other end of the phone, but I doubted how much of a mind I had to hold the mind of my patient." Here, she seemed less taken up with her physical state and could recognize something of her own mental predicament, registering her own failure as an emotional container for the patient. The experience of being the detached cut-off mother had shifted from being an intellectual idea to an experience that could be emotionally registered. We now had a mental representation that indicated some proper insight.

Shortly after, she reported having the distressing thought: "I have lost myself: I will no longer be able to be a psychoanalytic psychotherapist." But this was followed by the recognition that "There was a me who could know and feel myself to be lost." This was important: it was the insight that was lacking earlier. She seemed to have recovered, to some extent, an ego that could observe itself in this terrible state. Gradually, she seemed less overwhelmed by anxiety about her own function and could allow herself the freedom to let her imagination wander. Once, with the patient, she found herself spontaneously remembering a painting by Titian, "The flaying of Marsyas". In the painting, an unfortunate faun is held upside down while his skin is sliced open and peeled off in strips. She recalled the gory account in Ovid's *Metamorphoses* (Book 6, lines 382–400: Tarrant, 2004) where he cries out, "Why do you tear me from myself?" The faun dies (Ovid's description is blood-curdling), but not before he acquires insight. The imaginative association that she brought to supervision, "This training is skinning me alive", struck me as full of emotional connection, aliveness, and even a bit of humour. There was now a better symbolic basis upon which to explore her own state in relation to her patient's.

We thought about the disturbing nature of her patient's experience: the eczema that left her feeling so exposed. The feeling of being "torn from herself", we realized, was also the patient's predicament, past and present. In fact, it was something the patient frequently suggested, when she said, "I don't know who I am"—words that had seemed, until then, to belong only to the trainee. We now were able to think together about the patient's need to have her therapist understand the primitive experience of being lost, and how this had been powerfully projected into Ms A. The fact that Ms A so willingly identified with this projection was because it so closely mirrored her own post-Covid state. Unable to know this at the time, it became a feeling that Ms A was forced to project into me, so that the experience of feeling lost was everywhere.

We wondered also whether the situation had been exacerbated by the patient's awareness of a non-receptive mother–therapist who, for her own reasons, couldn't properly register her patient–infant's projections in a mind that was, for reasons different from her mother's, also broken. As the patient sensed this failure in her therapist, her projections became increasingly violent and broken. These fragmented parts of the patient's personality were even more difficult to apprehend by a trainee therapist who had lost what capacity she had to do so. The fact that, for a while, the sessions had to be conducted by phone only made matters more difficult.

In contrast to the patient's fragmentation, there was a coherence taking shape in our understanding. We started to notice how the patient's eczema flair-ups almost always occurred when she felt in a panic, and that this often coincided with times when Ms A's state was compromised. It was striking, too, that Ms A herself had been experiencing severe skin pain earlier in the therapy, and we now wondered whether this reflected Ms A's struggle to contain an unbearable experience.

This was an extreme situation, owing to the trainee's state: her traumatic and perplexing illness and her pre-existing anxiety. The severity of her patient's difficulties also served to complicate things. Brenman Pick describes how unmanageable feelings may be projected into the trainee and, if not managed, may then be projected into the supervisor. In other words, trainees can also communicate through unconscious actions and not just through words. Another observation of Brenman Pick's is that the trainee's capacity to understand their patient is always diminished when the patient corresponds too closely to some aspect of the therapist. She writes, "How difficult it is to differentiate in such a situation what part of the transference/countertransference problem is coming from the patient and what from the analyst: the one elides into the other" (2012, p. 56).

It is also not uncommon for anxious trainees to become detached from the affective reality of the transference and from their patient's predicament. They then can lose their symbolic understanding of what is going on. Certainly, serious life events of the sort this trainee experienced can cause a regression in emotional functioning, precipitating more concrete thinking and temporary states of persecution or even fragmentation inimical to analytic work. Then we have a problem, and, as supervisors, we need to be thoughtful about how best to intervene.

It was crucial for this trainee to acknowledge how disturbed and incapacitated she had become and to discuss this candidly in supervision. It was also crucial that the supervisor could be in touch with feeling lost, and inadequate and to remain in a state of anxious not-knowing, rather than settling for plausible-sounding explanations. Development was also facilitated by allowing the trainee's apparently irrelevant and anxious associations to come in. Allowing her imagination to wander freely meant that we could eventually start thinking about her patient in a more meaningful way. Describing her experience to me later, she said, "I might have more usefully noticed the fear that my mind was not going to survive this and taken that seriously."

In the end, this trainee was able to gain quite a lot from this experience, and the patient, too, showed some progress.

Mr B

I will now describe a more straightforward experience of supervision in which a competent trainee was able to learn from supervision and use it in his work. At times, though, Mr B could be sensitive to my comments, experiencing them critically. Moreover, the patient's and the trainee's superegos seemed to function in ways that left both feeling easily criticized and undermined.

The therapy with a 35-year-old male patient had been going on for two and a half years and was due to end in six months' time. The transference had, until recently, been dominated by the patient's rivalry and hostility and by doubts about his therapist's capacity to be either a benign paternal figure or a robust-enough maternal one. Lately, however, there had been some development, the patient appearing much more attached to his therapist and making better use of him. There was a history of rivalrous relationships with male friends.

Mr B came to supervision feeling unhappy and worried about a Monday session. The patient told him about meeting a friend. It was the first time the friends had met since they'd quarrelled, and many sessions had been taken up with how much the patient wished to repair things between them. They had arranged to meet near a prestigious institution where the patient was soon to be interviewed for a job. He hadn't told the friend about the interview, ostensibly because he didn't want rivalry to re-enter their friendship. Their reunion had gone well, but he had found himself letting the friend know that he was acquainted with the department and those who worked there.

Mr B reported saying to the patient, "It was hard for you to resist dropping a hint." The patient, in response, had become upset saying, "I feel you are telling me I got it all wrong."

Mr B suggested that he experienced him as cruel in that moment. He commented on how hard it was to escape this dynamic and look at what had happened. The mood had remained tense and unhappy.

In supervision, we discussed how easily the fragile sense of a better contact could get obliterated, after the weekend. I felt touched by the patient's sensitivity and impressed by his more direct way of sharing how he felt with his therapist. I suggested that Mr B felt anxious for the patient, who would be ending his therapy soon and who does, indeed, continue to "get it wrong" with his friends. Mr B agreed but now seemed a bit deflated, feeling that he had also "got it wrong" by failing to acknowledge the patient's difficulty with the weekend and the more touching aspect of the contact between them.

In the next session, the patient was a bit late and, when he arrived, spoke of feeling that the session wouldn't help him. He had his job interview the next day, and, if he were successful, it would mean that coming for his sessions would be more difficult.

Mr B took up how much pressure his patient was under to feel better before the therapy ended. The patient then spoke about a female friend who was already married and had a child. This friend was practicing what she called "attachment-based" parenting with her first child, allowing the baby to breastfeed as long as he liked and to share the parental bed. The patient had been impressed and touched by her capacity to tolerate her son's infantile needs. However, he noticed that when the second child was born, the mother seemed brisker and more irritable with her first child.

The patient then reported a dream:

He was back in his parent's house, talking with his father. He found himself being childish and annoying, at which point his father said, "Isn't it time you grew up, got a decent job, and moved out?"

Mr B invited the patient to bring his associations. The patient remained silent but then, in a distressed way, blurted out:

"I don't feel you are helping me. I felt you undermined my confidence when you said on Monday that I was dropping hints with my friend."

Mr B replied,

"You felt I was saying, 'You are getting caught up in childish games when you should be getting ready to move on from therapy.' And in the dream you goad your father to become cruel to you 'til he tells you to hurry up and leave home."

Here, I thought the trainee was probably correct in his formulation and, certainly, was describing a familiar, cruel-feeling quality present in the patient's material. However, he wasn't responding to what was emotionally most important: the hurt patient, who was with him right now and who had had the courage to talk about the demands of "attachment-based parenting" and say directly, "I don't feel you are helping me." Mr B did notice, however, that he wasn't very happy with the session, and he brought this feeling to his supervision the following week.

Once again, I felt touched by the couple's struggle and by the patient who seemed so much more attached to his therapist than before. I drew attention to the patient's courage in being able to tell his therapist that he felt hurt and in bringing a helpful dream.

Mr B again felt he had been insensitive towards his patient and looked despondent. He realized that he had also forgotten to refer in the session to a half-term break he was taking the following week. But he was able to say all this to his supervisor, perhaps in the same way as the patient was able to talk to his therapist. The trainee then spoke about his anxiety that the patient would not be ready to leave by the summer.

When we thought about the patient's dream, it struck us as connected to the material about the friend who practiced "attachment-based mothering" but then felt irritated with this child when the next child came along. We wondered whether the patient felt he had a therapist–mother who had encouraged him to become "attached" but who now wanted to go on and have other patients. Was there a therapist who wanted him to move out of his consulting room (over half-term) and make his own home in a relationship that might be a cruel one? Mr B felt moved as we discussed this and was then able to tell me that he felt he, too, might still need supervision after he qualified but was worried that his supervisor also wanted him to move on, so she could offer her time to another trainee.

In the following session, speaking from a position of real empathy, he could say to the patient that his comment had hurt the patient who was working so hard to be ready to leave. They could then think together about how the forthcoming break might be affecting him.

Mr B suggested that the patient might feel that he (the therapist) was over-invested in the patient "getting it right", and that that had interfered with his understanding just how anxious the patient was about "leaving home" for somewhere less safe, cruel even.

The patient seemed thoughtful and then reminded his therapist that he had his driving test that day. He had felt torn: should he get up very early and have his session, or get some rest? In the end, he'd come, because he felt it was more important to feel that he had his therapist properly by his side. He had also noticed that his therapist's car in the Tavistock car park had an L-plate on it. He'd assumed previously that someone else in the therapist's family must be learning to drive, but yesterday he'd suddenly wondered whether the therapist himself was the learner-driver and needed to be accompanied to work.

Now, the trainee was able to say that perhaps the patient felt sometimes that his therapist still had things to learn about being a therapist. He added that the patient had found a way of saying these important things to him, rather than repeating his experience with his parents, who, he felt, were too fragile to talk to.

I think we can see here that, when the patient finally felt more convinced that he was with a therapist who could tolerate his own feeling of "getting it wrong", he was able to talk with greater courage about his need for his therapist, and his doubts that his therapist could bear this and not wish to move on to new experiences of his own.

Mr C

Just occasionally, there are profound difficulties. A more deep-seated psychopathology emerges that wasn't spotted earlier, and we realize that the trainee is never likely to develop unless substantial shifts occur in their analysis. One painful example was of a male trainee whose entire analytic persona was based on a simulacrum of an analytic identity and understanding—one in which he copied his supervisors, while mostly remaining out of touch with the patient's predicament. He seemed largely unaware of this and impervious to feedback. This was not the sort of temporary problem that disappears as the trainee's analytic identity develops, and his difficulties didn't alter with time. In sessions with his patients, he adopted a kindly but lofty superiority, oblivious of the patient's distress at the emotional distance he unconsciously conveyed they must keep. Instead, he would intervene with interpretations that seemed to have been assembled from seminars or books and that appealed to him intellectually by giving him a spurious sense of mastery. He brought disturbing-sounding encounters to the supervision, leaving his supervisors feeling frustrated and worried, sometimes even wanting to retaliate in a punishing way. The tenacity with which he resisted help occasionally led to supervisors becoming exasperated, reprimanding him instead of being able to think with him; repeating an experience of "not taking the patient in" but now with the trainee in this position.

We work very hard as supervisors to help trainees with these sorts of deep-seated difficulties. But there has to be honesty and willingness on both sides, and, on this occasion, it was very hard to find. It was eventually decided that Mr C could not be allowed to continue with the training. He was encouraged to think about an alternative career path that might make better use of his considerable intellectual abilities. He has since made a successful career for himself as an academic scientist.

Final comments

In chapter 2, on *The Acquisition of Psychoanalytic Knowledge*, I discussed some of the challenges facing the trainee in psychoanalytic psychotherapy. I suggested that, just as coming to know oneself in analysis depends upon a capacity to "learn from experience", so too, the acquisition of psychoanalytic knowledge during training depends upon a willingness to be open to an evolving experience, rather than the more static position of being in possession of factual knowledge. Whether this is possible will depend upon how the trainee was able to negotiate their infantile experiences, whether the environment around them was broadly supportive, as well as their constitutional capacity to tolerate frustration. Thereafter, it also depends upon whether any difficulties have been helped by their experience of personal analysis. Development through psychoanalysis is uneven and never complete, and we should expect that the trainee will have areas of vulnerability of which they may yet only be partially aware. Although all learning interacts with trainees' unconscious struggles and resistance, psychoanalytic knowledge holds a unique position in this regard. In normal circumstances, the emotional and personal significance of what trainees now have to learn is likely to have been repressed or otherwise defended against.

In the introduction to this part I described Bion's notion that creativity and learning involve "catastrophic change". New thoughts are, by their nature, potentially disruptive and shattering, leading to the experience of anxiety, doubt, and even fragmentation. Bion explains that it is precisely this disruption that contains the opportunity for creative development, if this situation can be tolerated. Seemingly disparate chaotic elements can accumulate around a "selected fact", and this process gives new meaning to both the chaotic elements and to the fact selected. Bion compares the state needed to achieve this as being akin to Keats's notion of "negative capability".

The vignettes from three supervisory experiences, above, have been selected for how they exemplify different aspects of these struggles. Ms A vividly captures the experience of feeling that her mind was fragmented by an experience of "catastrophic" learning. In her case, this was felt quite concretely, as if her brain had been damaged. In this state, it was impossible for her to embrace her patient's disordered mind or, indeed, the thoughts and reflections of her supervisor. While it remained unclear how much the situation was exacerbated by her illness, it was obvious that the anxieties she was contending with felt shattering to her and were, at least in part, a function of the anxiety generated by this new situation. The supervisor also had to be receptive to Ms A's projection of feeling at a loss and stuck, and this had to be endured by both of us for a long time. Eventually, assisted by her willingness to be helped, an emotional interest in the truth, and an honest appreciation of her limitations, Ms A was able to recover her functioning enough to feel that she could learn from this experience and also help her patient to some extent.

By contrast, Mr B, a more advanced trainee, could mostly tolerate the discomfort and frustration in getting things wrong without evading it. He came to recognize a tendency in himself to grasp prematurely at convincing explanations that missed the emotional heat of the session. We came to see that by holding on to ideas too tightly his capacity to listen was compromised in a way that created an enactment in which he was experienced by the patient not as knowledgeable, but as too definite. For the patient this was associated with his clever but imperious father—a father with a rather settled view of his son's inadequacies. I suspect too that the patient projected this object relationship in a way that subtly prompted Mr B to respond as he did so that there was a marriage this and the patient's need to recreate his father. But over time, Mr B was able to wait with his insecurity and doubt until his next supervision, and then had to tolerate his dependence on his supervisor, who could understand more than he did and could help him. Ultimately, his capacity to resist a static understanding of his patient enabled him to embrace new ideas and to develop. He could also be helped to face the impact upon his patient when he didn't quite get things right. Moreover, when the patient intuitively registered Mr B's availability and honesty, he, too, was able to use his mind flexibly to respond and develop.

Later, the patient's experience of a more uncertain 'learner' therapist and the fact that this could be faced by both parties, gave the patient a new experience of being taken in by an object who was able to entertain doubts and anxieties without either collapsing or becoming too rigid. Paradoxically and less obviously, Mr B's acknowledgement at the end when he spoke of the patient experiencing him also as a 'learner' movingly conveyed not just that the patient registered that he still had things to learn but the patient's unconscious knowledge that his therapist was engaged in a positive and active state of learning—evolving in his knowledge of himself and his patient.

The vignette involving Mr C is much more condensed, but I include it because it demonstrates a more serious problem. In his case, there appeared to be a characterological unwillingness or inability to tolerate a state of not-knowing and, instead, a misuse of his supervisors whose ideas he mimicked and copied. This problem is generally temporary and disappears as the student's own analytic identity develops. But Mr C appeared not to be able to move on from this position, even when it became clear that his training was in jeopardy. "Possession of knowledge", truthful or otherwise, was, for Mr C, more appealing than "coming to know", with all the attendant struggles this might have been felt to include.

In Part III we look in more depth at one very central area of the learning: the transference and countertransference.

PART III

LEARNING ABOUT THE TRANSFERENCE AND COUNTERTRANSFERENCE

Francesca Hume

While all the chapters in the book touch in different ways upon the use of the transference and countertransference, the chapters selected for this part give a rather clearer description of the trainees' experience of becoming analytically competent in the use of these key concepts in their clinical work.

In chapter 11 I outline the historical development of the concepts of transference and countertransference.

Michelle Washington's chapter 12 gives a lively account of her struggle in tolerating provocation from a contemptuous and superior patient. She had to survive the experience of being repeatedly devalued and to understand what this signified for the patient. This was difficult for her as a beginner, struggling with her own doubts about her work. Ultimately her efforts were rewarded, and the patient was able to get in touch with her hatred of dependency and need and, ultimately, her appreciation of her therapist.

Thomas Hillen (chapter 13) gives an eloquent account of his experience of working with a man who is unable to tolerate psychic pain. There is constant pressure to provide an analysis that is pain-free, and yet the analyst has to bear a great deal. It becomes clear to him that pain is not kept out of the analytic treatment, but is managed by projecting it into the trainee. Eventually the patient drops out of treatment, and the author describes what this premature ending evokes in him.

Viv Walkerdine (chapter 14) focuses on the treatment of a young woman with an eating disorder. She works sensitively and patiently, experimenting with different ways of interpreting to try to make contact with her patient. Developments in the therapist's mind and her growing confidence as a clinician seem to be mirrored by a growing capacity for symbolization in the patient.

Diane Turner (chapter 15) describes a patient with psychosomatic symptoms who had been unable to mourn the loss of her mother. The chapter describes the way in which the patient's failure to adequately introject her object as an infant contributed to the object becoming incorporated at the point of her mother's death in a magical, omnipotent way. This led to the patient feeling taken over by a toxic internal corpse, which rotted within her, causing the somatic pain. The author discusses her own developing understanding and recognition of this complex and serious psychopathology.

Carolyn Walker's chapter 16 focuses on the developments in patient and therapist that take place as her understanding of her countertransference deepens. She has to manage feelings of being useless, suspicious, and helpless, with a tricky, controlling patient. Again, good progress is made in both the patient and student.

These chapters richly illustrate a point made by Money-Kyrle in his important 1956 paper on countertransference. He suggests that "understanding fails whenever the patient corresponds too closely with some aspect of himself [the analyst] which he has not yet learnt to understand" Money-Kyrle, 1956, p. 36). For example, if the patient needs to project feeling incompetent, this may become mixed up with the analyst's own feeling of being professionally incompetent. In response to a patient's projections, several of the trainees struggle with feeling useless and helpless, or with pained and anxious feelings that belong both to them and to their patients. Money-Kyrle suggests that the degree to which the analyst is emotionally disturbed by periods of non-understanding may also depend upon the severity of their own superego. If the superego is predominantly friendly, limitations can be better tolerated. But the sense of failure may be overwhelming when this is more severe. Brenman Pick says, "The patient's projective identifications are actions in part intended to produce reactions" and "The analyst may deal with this so quickly as not to become aware of it: yet it is a crucial factor . . . if it is being dealt with that quickly, we may have to ask whether the deeper experience is in fact being avoided" (1985, p. 157). These chapters convey how uncomfortable it is for trainees to have to bear the experience of not understanding their patients, or not understanding them well enough, often for a long time. Registering and bearing this deeper experience is what we ask of our trainees if they are to work with the transference and countertransference to help their patients. As Strachey reminds us, the full transference experience is overwhelming to the analyst too, who would like to avoid it.

CHAPTER ELEVEN

Transference and countertransference

Francesca Hume

Transference

Wilfred Bion writes that "When two characters or personalities meet, an emotional storm is created" (Bion, 1979, p. 321). Meeting the "emotional storm" of the transference is, for all of us, the most demanding aspect of our work. For the beginner, it is the hardest part in becoming psychoanalytically competent. It sits at the centre of the training and involves all the learning in relation to the associated phenomena of the countertransference, unconscious phantasy, enactment, projection, introjection, and projective identification.

It is emotionally demanding for the trainee to direct themselves to the point of maximum urgency or difficulty in an analytic session. I gave an example in an earlier chapter of my own experience of supervision with Betty Joseph, who pointed out that when I had two possible "interpretations" I felt I could give to the patient, I found myself giving the more palatable of the two. The "correct" interpretation, she explained, is very often the one that is more difficult for us to give: it may feel more embarrassing, or intimate, or make us anxious about what it will provoke in the patient. Or it may simply reflect less well upon us or cast us in a less flattering light. The challenge is to resist distancing ourselves from the patient in time and space, and to get into the *emotional storm* of the transference, with its immediate and specific importance.

Trainees can become very persecuted or dispirited by how difficult it can be to take up and work in the transference, sometimes taking the demand to attempt transference interpretations too literally, as an injunction to do so at all times and at any cost. This is even when all will have had experience from their own analyses of being spoken to in other, more ordinary ways too. At these times, I have sometimes found it helpful to remind them of how Strachey himself concluded his paper on the mutative interpretation with the statement "a cake cannot be made of currants alone"!

To give an idea of the challenge for the trainee in engaging with the transference in ways that we regard as analytically significant, I now say something about the concept, and how it has evolved.

Freud's discovery of the transference and the evolution of his thinking about it will be familiar to most trainees when they start. They will know that first he thought of it as an "untoward event" (1914d, p. 12), the patient's way of resisting help, and how he came to recognize it as the main means of understanding and intervening. I remember my feeling of awe, as a new trainee, when I learnt how Freud had been able to be so flexible to change his mind and revise his theory in light of what he was observing; abandoning his previous ideas to accommodate his new insight.

In Freud's original model, the focus was on historical reconstruction, and the transference was understood by him as the route by which we gain access to repressed memories in the patient's past. This, Freud contended, could unlock the associated affect, which was what he thought carried the potential for analytic change (1914d, p.10). The interactions between patient and analyst were central in elucidating the transference but were not regarded as important in themselves in leading to change.

In 1934, Strachey was to address this issue. He coined the notion of a "mutative interpretation": an interpretation that, itself, leads to psychic change. His important point was that an interpretation succeeds in this when what it addresses is something of immediate and specific emotional importance *in the transference*. The patient's impulses and feelings must be currently alive and directed towards the figure of the analyst and experienced "as something actual". By contrast, extra-transference interpretations (ones not pertaining to the transference) are not directed to the analyst and are therefore not given at the point of urgency. They will always be distant in time and space.

Klein was very taken with Strachey's focus. In her own seminal paper, "The Origins of Transference" (1952a), she draws upon her theories of infant emotional development. She highlights the nature of the infant's experience of his primary object. The young infant experiences the mother, not as one object, but as many objects, which are constantly shifting. This helps us to understand the patient's view of the analyst. She says we need to take account of the way in which the infant experiences the object in multiple ways if we are to understand the nature of the splits and fragments that emerge in the transference. This is also true of the adult patient in analysis, in their unconscious mind. Klein alludes to the way in which bits of the object can find themselves elsewhere and the analyst's function in gathering all of this up. She draws attention to the need to recognize who or what we represent to the patient moment by moment and to link this to the patient's phantasies about the situation he finds himself in with the analyst. This is the *total situation* of the transference. Klein points out that, as the transference is there from the start of an analytic treatment, transference interpretations should also begin at the start of an analysis. We represent *specific figures in specific situations* and must understand what we represent unconsciously *at any given moment*. This is an extremely demanding task—especially for a beginner.

In her 1985 paper, "Transference: The Total Situation", Betty Joseph develops Klein's notion of this concept, emphasizing all the ways in which the patient's internal situation is expressed. She notes the patient's tendency to try to maintain their emotional equilibrium, despite a conscious desire for change. She is perhaps most associated with the concept of acting out in the transference and also demonstrates that patients use the transference not just for gaining satisfaction of their impulses, but also to support their defensive positions, drawing us into these positions in extremely subtle ways. She uses Klein's term "the total situation" to characterize the way patients express their conscious and unconscious thoughts and experiences in the transference relationship.

Use of the patient's history

A limited understanding of the transference often goes along with a limited way of thinking about the patient's history. For example, it is not uncommon for trainees to focus almost exclusively on what they know of the patient's *actual* history and to search for it in the transference relationship. This, of course, is a departure from Freud's classical approach, with his focus on maintaining an evenly suspended attention and not privileging any particular area of the patient's communication. I am not suggesting at all that the patient's actual history isn't important. It is. However, I want to emphasize this aspect, which trainees don't always understand when they start: that it is the patient's psychic history that primarily concerns the psychoanalyst, and we arrive at it through an understanding of the transference and countertransference, and not the other way round.

Michael Feldman, in his 2007 paper, "The Illumination of History", gives an excellent account of the ways in which our use of the patient's history and of the transference have evolved since Freud first's model, and some of the confusion that has arisen at times. He explores the role that elucidating history has in promoting psychic change, and the more nuanced approach we take to this today. Feldman describes how we have come to see that the patient's history, their *psychic* history, is embodied in their internal object relationships. If the patient's view of reality is not too distorted, we might also be looking at their actual history, but our focus is on this internal version of reality. Exploring the transference and how the internal object relationships are played out often gives rise to a different historical perspective, or even several perspectives that evolve as treatment goes on. The point is that the history, the psychic history, reconstructs itself through the transference. Psychic change, Feldman argues, is promoted when patients are freed up to feel connected with their psychic history and to tolerate the meaning of what emerges, illuminating the past in the present. This, of course, involves making links between the transference and past experiences and phantasies, and change is possible when interpretation of the transference leads to the patient's ego becoming strengthened and more integrated. This implies that the patient is less driven to split off and project these unwanted aspects and to own what belongs to them.

Of course, there is always a balance to be struck between recognizing the importance of the patient's actual history and the patient's psychic history. Moreover, as Feldman and others have pointed out, it is enriching for both analyst and patient to form links with the past, and it gives the patient a greater sense of integration and meaningful continuity. But the point I want to make is that the trainee is generally very familiar with the easier-to-grasp conventional approach to the history and struggles with this more slippery version, which can change from session to session, or even moment to moment, according to the patient's state and whom, or what part of whom, the analyst may represent for them at any particular time.

For trainees to gain an understanding of the transference, they also need to get to grips with some other related concepts. It is to these that I now turn.

Countertransference

As with the concept of the transference and its relationship with history, the perception and use of the countertransference has evolved significantly. It, too, was originally regarded as an obstacle to understanding the patient, and this point of view lasted much longer. Both Freud and

Klein used the term *countertransference* to describe the misperception of the patient caused by some problem or psychopathology of the analyst's and did not recognize that feelings evoked in the analyst could be of clinical value. It was not until the 1950s that the term "countertransference" was re-defined to include all the analyst's perceptions, accurate as well as distorted. An early pioneer in this area was Paula Heimann (1950), who, in her seminal paper "On Countertransference", defined countertransference as "an instrument of research into the patient's unconscious" and "not only part and parcel of the analytic relationship, but it is the patient's creation, it is part of the patient's personality" (pp. 81 & 83).

She, along with Heinrich Racker (1953), drew attention to the aspect of the countertransference that is a specific response to the patient, as opposed to the intrusion of the analyst's own neurosis into the analytic work.

Racker, in his important "Psycho-Analytic Technique", described it thus:

> . . . a technical instrument of great importance, since it is, in great part, an emotional response to the transference, and as such can indicate to the analyst what occurs in the patient in his relation to the analyst. [1968, p. 18]

And:

> . . . just as the transference, according to Freud, is the field in which the principal battles are fought in order to conquer the resistances, so the counter-transference is the other half of this field, and on it the principal battles are fought to conquer the analyst's resistances, that is, the counterresistances. [p. 19]

The struggle for the trainee in getting to grips with the countertransference mirrors, in some ways, the evolution of the concept itself. It is difficult for the new trainee to differentiate between responses to the patient that come from the patient's projections (and which might legitimately be put to the service of understanding them) and emotional responses to the patient that result from some problem or difficulty in themselves.

Along with the problem of being able to differentiate what belongs to whom, there is the emotional challenge in coping with strong experiences when we might wish to dispassionately avoid them. Brenman Pick discusses this in her paper "Working Through in the Countertransference" (1985), where she suggests that the analyst, like the patient, has a primitive part of himself that wishes not to know, not to think, that wants to get rid of the new thing, the noxious element that the patient has introduced into his mind. She maintains that this primitive part is in identification with the primitive parts of the patient or the patient's internal objects and is in conflict with the more mature part of the analyst that wants to understand. She uses the notion of "working through" in the analyst to describe the process the analyst needs to go through to achieve containment of the patient's projections, which, she assumes, are continuously going on.

She concludes with a very important idea and one that is linked to the capacity to learn from experience that I have been highlighting: she suggests that, unless this internal conflict in the analyst is addressed, he will not be able to mobilize his own capacity to accept psychic truth (the unwanted idea) and therefore to help the patient accept his own truth: unwanted ideas. It seems to me that this once again refers to the particular acquisition of psychoanalytic knowledge that needs to develop during training: one that depends upon a willingness to be open to an evolving experience, rather than the more static position of being *in possession* of factual knowledge (truthful or not).

At the Tavistock, there has been considerable focus on learning to undertake psychoanalytic consultations. The reason for this is that we rely on our junior staff (the trainees) to do much of the assessment work, and they need to be able to do it well. Their supervised assessments will determine whether or not a patient is taken into treatment, and, if they are, whether this will be in a group, or in individual (non-intensive) or intensive psychoanalytic psychotherapy. The whole area of the analytic consultation is too broad to be included here, but I refer to it because for the trainee a key area of learning has to do with gauging the patient's difficulties and psychopathology through a growing knowledge and use of the transference and countertransference. And, of course, it is this understanding that will then be carried into the rest of the analytic work.

A number of analysts have been very interested in how we might understand the patient by assessing their level of functioning, and using this awareness to determine how we listen to their communications, respond to them, and measure change. Joseph, in particular, noted that if patients are primarily functioning in a more primitive way (at a paranoid-schizoid level) they will be using splitting and projection more, and we can mostly pick this up by the impact it has upon us in our countertransference responses. If, on the other hand, the patient has reached a position of relative developmental maturity (the depressive position), they will be able to relate to us as a whole object. We may feel "seen" by the patient in a more realistic and complex way, as a sum of many parts, good and bad, and the patient will be using more ordinary neurotic defences (like repression) more. They will be able to introject more freely and won't be communicating primarily in a non-verbal manner.

For a capacity to gauge the level of functioning to develop in the trainee, they will need some understanding of human emotional development and will be greatly assisted by some knowledge of projective identification. This concept has hugely enriched our understanding of the unconscious communication, *beyond words*, even if words remain the primary vehicle by which affects are communicated. To quote Edna O'Shaughnessy, from her 1983 paper "Words and Working Through", the patient's "psychic predicament unfolds in a dual way, divided between words and communications beyond words" (p. 282). She describes how, by using diverse modes of communication, verbal and more primitive, a patient can bring "his unevenly developed personality into analysis". He can use words not as words to express meaning, but, along with other non-verbal aspects, "to engender projections into the analyst".

Without this understanding, Joseph suggests that there is a danger that we take the patient's words too literally on those occasions when the patient is not able to use them in a symbolic way, and it is then that we are in danger of "understanding the material but not the patient".

A trainee who has arrived at a sophisticated understanding of psychoanalysis will recognize that the content of the patient's conscious verbal utterances may be significantly at odds with communications that emanate from elsewhere in the patient. The task is to become more clinically sensitive to the impact on one's own mind and body of these communications and to learn to scrutinize them in as undefended a way as possible.

The trainee comes to learn about the transference in three ways: through their personal psychoanalytic treatment, from clinical supervision, and from the academic teaching. The personal analysis puts the trainee in contact with their primitive self, with all its attendant needs and demands, and allows for some recognition of the defensive strategies used to manage difficult or disturbing feelings. Over time, they will recognize how their analyst is used as a vehicle for understanding themselves, the important figures (whole and part-object) that the analyst comes to represent, and the many ways in which parts of the self that need to be understood or expelled get projected into the analyst. All of this takes place at an emotional rather than at an intellectual level, some of it consciously recognized, and other aspects not so. A deep appreciation of the analyst's capacity to metabolize the more difficult aspects of their character and still remain involved is also important if the trainee is to enter into their own clinical work with the respect and humility this requires. This is the trainee's own lived experience of being at the receiving end of the analyst's reverie.

The role of the clinical supervisor in fostering the application of learning about the transference has been touched upon in Part II. We help the trainee to become receptive to the myriad communications—verbal and non-verbal, conscious and unconscious—that come from the patient and to use these, along with a growing awareness of countertransference responses, to develop a picture of what is going on between them. Through supervision, the trainee becomes more aware of the constantly evolving nature of the transference: how it is not a static thing with static connections to the patient's past, but one that changes moment by moment. The process of exploring the trainee's countertransference in supervision needs to be undertaken with care and respect.

The academic teaching gives the historical context to the understanding of the transference and the evolving ways in which it has been thought about and used, culminating in the modern focus on the transference as described above. The theoretical understanding of human emotional (psychic) development helps the trainee to appreciate the importance of unconscious phantasy and early object relationships and the way these are enacted during an analytic treatment.

If all goes well, the trainee is enabled through these different means to become more emotionally discerning about the affective stimuli being received: ones that may not have previously been registered at all, or that might only have been at the edge of awareness before now. The trainee starts to differentiate what might be coming from the patient and what comes from him or herself; to register and balance affects that might be quite troubling and that have the potential to disturb analytic functioning and stance. The task that follows is to find a way of responding to the patient in a way that conveys an understanding of this complexity and that facilitates the patient's own understanding too.

CHAPTER TWELVE

Not just any old bowl

Michelle Washington

Ms L, a 54-year-old white woman from a middle-class background, requested psychotherapy to address a severe depression, her tendency towards extreme hoarding, and because, despite being a very artistic and creative person, she had found herself unable to create anything for several years.

Clinical example: Ms L

Ms L had been adopted in early infancy and had only unsubstantiated ideas about the circumstances surrounding her adoption. Her adoptive father had died some years previously; her mother was still alive and living in a nursing home. Ms L had a younger brother (B), also adopted in infancy from the same biological parents. Ms L was in a long-term relationship with G) and had two grown-up children from a previous marriage. She didn't work and had previously supported herself on the proceeds of trust funds and inheritances, but, having exhausted these, she was being supported by her brother.

Ms L was my first intensive patient, and we met three times weekly for three years.

First phase

During the first phase of the work, Ms L began to emerge as the type of patient who was difficult to reach. She had been described by her assessor as having "good ego strength, a considerable capacity for depressive functioning", and one who would be an "excellent training patient". Instead, I found myself with a patient who was firmly embedded in the paranoid-schizoid position, and primitive modes of functioning were powerfully operative. Her approach to her therapy was cavalier, while her attitude towards me was characteristically condescending, even rude. My task, to understand this and how it was linked to her presenting problems, was hindered by her repertoire of manic defences which attempted to avoid potential anxiety and psychic destabilization. Therefore, the kind of investigation and understanding in the service of facilitating psychic development was extremely difficult to achieve.

Ms L's very first session enabled immediate insight into her anxieties, phantasy life and a sense of the objects/object relationships in her internal world. She worried that I might be offended by her "smelly feet" and that I would be looking at her stomach, which, she felt, was fat and which continuously rumbled loudly. Each time this happened, she would press down on her stomach, repeating that she was hungry. I suspect that she was conveying her phantasy of herself as someone whose abnormal greed/need overwhelmed and damaged her objects and whose repulsive, smelly, unpleasant impulses ultimately led to a painful rejection. The vulnerable part of her who arrives at the session in a starving hungry state is crushed psychically and concretely with the pressing of her stomach. I thought that this represented her deep unconscious terror that I might be repulsed by her vulnerability and need.

Poor punctuality, poor attendance, and the abrupt, premature ending of sessions led to an atmosphere of unpredictability and unreliability, which left me feeling furious and frustratingly impotent. My attempts to investigate this generated powerful persecutory guilt or were met with mindless oblivion. Yet this unconscious communication seemed connected to a psychic injury caused by an abrupt and painful severance of the link between herself and her first object (her biological mother), an object with whom she was strongly identified at the same time. I wondered whether the mindless oblivion that I sensed was in fact another identification with this mother. She held an unfounded belief that her birth mother was a "crack whore" and imagined her to have a drug-addled mind, unconcerned about the vulnerable baby she had irresponsibly bought into the world. The strength of this identification meant that that it was a long time before we were able to attend to the task of understanding the vulnerable baby-part of her in a serious-minded way.

Typically, she filled the sessions with details about her external life. I found myself frantically trying to discern who was who, what was what, and when was that? This was accompanied by an overwhelming feeling that, if I could just make sense of it all, then I might begin to understand her. Primitive idealization and pathological splitting meant that she was consistently placed in the position of the entirely benign person who was mercilessly bullied and exploited for her internal and external resources. Similarly, her childhood/early life was depicted as materially privileged, idyllic, and characterized by perfect family relationships. All her disturbance and unwanted impulses were powerfully projected outwards and lodged into the external world.

Ms L talked grandiosely about her large house, her considerable wealth, her expensive antiques, culture, famous artists and esteemed psychoanalysts who were "close/dear" friends, and such. She would sympathize with my position of "having to work", insinuate that I wasn't especially bright and exploit any opportunity to denigrate people from other cultures. This was in stark contrast to the broken-down, dishevelled patient in the room, who often couldn't pay bills or afford a basic standard of living. Her partner appeared frequently in her narrative as someone who "understood her perfectly without even words". My offerings, on the other hand, were always "nearly but not quite right, dear". At such times, I imagined her sitting on a perch, delivering these soliloquies down to me from a height. She habitually referred me to as "dear", which I thought was, among other things, a manic attempt at denial of need, value, and a defensive condescension.

The disruptive nature of her projections, and the force and accuracy with which they were delivered, made it easy to lose sight of their communicative function. At such times my interpretations felt like amalgamations of words, inauthentic and devoid of substance. I recall how often my supervisor needed to point out my tendency to take Ms L and her narrative at "face value", thereby only reaching the more adult part of my patient's personality. Thus, when we were operating within this environment and Ms L would tell me that I had "nearly but not quite understood", she was absolutely correct!

The following material, I think, powerfully illustrates our struggle:

P: "... While walking the dog, we started chatting with another couple, who also had a dog. The dogs seemed to be playing together and communing nicely. Then, suddenly, that dog just attacked my dog and ripped a chunk from its throat. The lady asked if there was anything she could do to help but she was completely useless. The second thing is that I have decided to end my treatment. It's not really working. . . ."

T: "I think we may need. . . ."

P: "I am so scared that my dog won't survive, he's very old and has a heart condition."
T: "There is something that we are not able to. . . ."
P: "I am so angry that the lady hasn't even offered a contribution to my vet bills. She has called four times, but I have refused to speak to her. I am that upset."
T: "By not accepting her calls, you have cut off the possibility that she can be helpful. Here you also cut me off, and so I cannot be helpful. Then you tell me that you want to cut off my help permanently, but the possibility to think. . . ."
P: "I called to check on my dog before I came in, he's comfortable."
T: "Like the lady, you need me to work very hard to make contact with you. Perhaps this is the only way you feel you can remain comfortable and survive this therapy."
P: "You know full well that I don't understand when you talk to me like that. It's not personal, but I think you have a problem making yourself clear, dear."

Her communication suggested that the therapy, which, she had imagined, would be a walk in the park, a nice communing between us, had turned into a scene where we are at each other's throats to the point where survival is questionable. This material helped me to see how desperately she needed me and my help, but also her difficulty in accepting the help that I was offering. I began to realize that Ms L was in a very desperate state indeed.

The fact that her formidable defensive systems were ultimately connected with ideas of her psychic survival was often obscured by the sense that they were tricky and duplicitous. Therefore, it was so very difficult to discern what was happening from moment to moment.

This material from is from the third session after our second break and illustrates this:

P: ". . . I came across an article my dad had written when he was a journalist for a newspaper. You are familiar with *The Times*, aren't you, dear? He also translated the works of Walt Whitman for academics. I don't suppose you know his works. He also helped to adapt the cartoon character Charlie Brown, but specifically for the newspapers. I expect you'll know Charlie Brown. On Easter Sunday B (brother) and K (sister-in-law) came for dinner. I really struggle with K. She's a nasty, selfish woman, and I don't know what B sees in her. They always bring a hamper from Fortnum and Mason, and I really look forward to it, because I could never afford to shop there. Anyway, this year she forgot the hamper. I think she did it on purpose. I think she just wanted to punish me for that argument we had. But that was because she had left all the hard work to me. She's just lazy and just lives off of B's money. Silly cow. . . ."

The first part of her narrative felt entirely inauthentic and seemed to be delivered from her perch. I think I was supposed to feel belittled, envious, and inferior. The more genuine communication was in the second half of her narrative. There is a silly cow of a woman who wilfully withholds the food/psychic nourishment provided by her sessions. This seems to be connected to a powerful persecutory anxiety as she anticipates a retaliatory attack from the sister-in-law/therapist. The most enraging and painful part for her is the recognition that she cannot provide the nourishment/therapy for herself. The beginning part of her communication seems to be a red herring—an unconscious attempt to throw us off the scent of her dependence, vulnerability, and, crucially, her envy.

I attempted to offer an interpretation which reflected this.

T: "There has been a break here and . . ."

She cuts me off by putting her hands over her ears and shouting:

P: "I can't stand it when you talk to me like that. I hate it when you insert yourself like that . . . I was talking about K and Easter dinner. K is K, food is food, and my counselling is my counselling. There's no parallel. I wanted to tell you something important, and you distracted me. G and I are going to a gallery this weekend. He is so supportive when I'm struggling to manage K, he always is. . . ."

Characteristically, my attempts to facilitate any thinking are met with unrestrained sabotage. In this example, she becomes concrete: K is K, Easter dinner is Easter dinner, I am reduced to a counsellor, and her psychotherapy to counselling. Her partner is then brought in as a final demonstration that she has no need of me, and she returns to her world of sophistication. I am left behind to do the work alone.

Towards the end of this phase, Ms L brought a dream that provided crucial insight into her internal world. I had needed to cancel three sessions, due to illness. This material came from her first session back:

There was a small aeroplane. A small pink plastic doll, like a baby, was strapped into the seat next to pilot. The doll–baby was completely encased in plastic and was restrained into the seat, so it couldn't move. The pilot seemed to have some bad intent. Although she wasn't sure of the exact location, she felt sure he was flying her to her death. A third person, who sat behind them, was observing and knew what was happening but seemed unable to stop the inevitable catastrophe.

She awoke feeling very distressed.

Ms L thought that she was the plastic doll but wondered why she was not struggling to save herself. I thought this dream was powerfully illustrative. There is a vulnerable/baby part of her that seems to be encapsulated/trapped in plastic and, therefore, cannot breathe. The pilot, with his mischievous qualities, represented the more destructive, murderous part of her. The restraints seemed to represent a slave-like relationship between these two parts of her personality, with the vulnerable part under the domination of the destructive part. The restraints also made it impossible for her to reach out for help/help herself, while the plastic casing also prevented help reaching her. The silent observer is also a part of her: an ego with some capacity for awareness but lacking either the strength or the will to intervene. In my three-day absence I was also not there to intervene. The situation is further complicated by my own illness: I am felt to be far behind her, weak and impotent and unable to do more than observe her plight.

Ms L missed her next session, explaining that that she had stayed up all night drinking vodka. My attempt to talk to her about what seemed to be a negative therapeutic reaction was met with:

P: "I fucking hate when you insert yourself into my mind like that. You're not in my mind at all. . . .

T: "Maybe the three cancelled sessions helped you to recognize the value of your sessions and what I offer. But this disturbs you and so is disguised by cancellations, lateness, hostility, and getting drunk".

P: "Hmm, hmm. Actually, I think that you, and this, are really important to me after all, but I won't allow myself to admit it."

After an unusually long silence she said:

P: "I am not sure why, but suddenly the time when I lost my virginity has just popped into my head. It's the first time I can remember feeling really ugly."

Her first response felt to have been delivered from her perch, aimed at re-asserting her supremacy and supporting her defensive idea that it was she who possessed valuable insights. Her second expression conveyed much more genuine feeling. This was her terror that something ugly happens when something is allowed inside. This seemed to be connected to her use of the word "insert" and her paranoia about what my phallic words were doing to her insides.

Second phase

The next phase of her therapy felt quite different. Ms L gradually began to immerse herself in her therapy in a more serious-minded way. She was able to experience an object capable of surviving. Concretely, her attendance and punctuality improved considerably. I also noticed that her previous habit of removing her glasses had been replaced by wearing them during some sessions, or removing and replacing them interchangeably. Gradually, clarity of sight became possible.

Early on in this phase Ms L presented the following dream:

> *She was in an old house, and she found herself repeating a frustrating cycle of putting a cat outside, which refused to stay outside. Then she found herself with a friend who had a child whom she shot for some reason that she didn't understand. She then found herself in what she described as "two processes". In one she knew she had been responsible for shooting the child. In the other she hid this and involved herself in helping the mother.*

She said:

P: "Being involved in these two simultaneous processes reminds me of when you refer to the healthy and unhealthy parts of me."

T: "Perhaps the cat represents the vulnerable part of you that is desperate to be allowed to stay in this room but keeps being thrown out and is eventually shot as the needy toddler. But we can't attend to this, because a part of you turns a blind eye, and keeps it secret from me by deception."

P: "... Ah, yes, it's a bit like an onion. You know intellectually that it has a very strong smell and the ability to make you cry, but it's not until you start to take the skin off that you actually feel the real texture and realize that it's slippery and you get overwhelmed by the smell and it actually makes you weep."

Again, I was invited to think that the healthy part of her was present and responding thoughtfully. However, I noted the rapidity of her tone, wild gesticulations, and quite frenzied manner. Instead of being concerned by her insight, she actually seemed rather excited.

Ms L began bringing four large, plump cushions, which she would carefully arrange on the couch before lying down, to alleviate her back pain. The arrangement looked very comfortable indeed! A later session enabled me to begin to understand that the cushions seemed to be related to complicated feelings associated with her growing recognition of value and dependence. Having arrived in the building on time, Ms L oddly arrived five minutes late for her session. I spoke to her about her awful dilemma:

T: "On the one hand, there seems desperate need that we should both know that you can provide yourself with your own comfort and have no need of me in managing your pain. However, the fourth cushion maybe represents your wish for a fourth session, and more of the comfort/support that you do feel you get here in managing your pain."

P: "... You're inserting again aren't you? I hate that. I am in constant pain, and this couch seems to make it much worse. It's not so bad when I am lying on it, but the minute I get up to leave, I feel like a cripple".

Ms L had let me know her constant pain was felt more acutely when lying on the couch. However, the really crippling pain is felt when she is required to leave. My attending to this seemed to gradually enable the more crippled and vulnerable parts of her to enter the room and a very different picture to emerge.

Ms L talked about her feeling that her adoptive parents had completely disregarded her emotional state. Unlike the oblivious disregard associated with her birth mother, she felt that they seemed bewildered by the notion that a young child might experience emotional distress. She recalled as a child feeling "inexplicably unhappy" and that her mother's characteristic response to her distress would be to "helplessly" apologize for not being her real mum. I think it very likely that Ms L felt helpless and stuck with an object who was equally helpless in the task of helping her. Possibly, then, her struggle in permitting any dependence on me related to a feeling of being trapped with internal objects who were unwilling or incapable of taking her in and then helping her.

Ms L had been told that she had been a difficult, demanding and wilful baby/child who was difficult to please. I wondered about the mother's own unmetabolized feelings regarding her need/decision to adopt, which might have resulted in a disturbed capacity for reverie and adequate containment. I imagined that my own feelings of disappointment that Ms L wasn't the training patient that I expected or wanted might have corresponded with her mother's conscious or unconscious feeling that Ms L wasn't the baby that she wanted or expected either.

However, despite the progress, there was only so much that Ms L could bear. There continued to be periods when she would return to her perch, and connections with me were severed. Much of the task was making use of my countertransference experience and supervision to track these changes, which could, at times, be so subtle they might very easily be missed.

Over time, a grievance emerged, connected to the idea that it was the lack of a biological link that caused her mother's inability to understand her. This idea was reinforced by her mother's apologies for not being her real mother. I began to understand the pervasive, inauthentic atmosphere in the sessions as a re-creation of an inauthentic world with inauthentic objects. I think I became the adoptive mother who was not the "real deal".

This explained my difficulty keeping myself in mind as a serious and conscientious trainee psychotherapist. Instead, I often felt like a fraud, masquerading as a psychotherapist and "doing" psychotherapy as though I knew how.

The following material illustrates something of the struggle. We had been talking about motherhood.

P: "I thought I didn't have to do anything as a birth mother, that it would all just happen naturally." . . . "I took it for granted. Isn't that sad?" . . . "I thought all those years of warmth and love from my mum was just compensation for something that wasn't naturally there. Isn't that mad? Mad and sad."

This recognition that her mother loved her and probably tried her very best came with a painful sense of wasted opportunities.

Ms L's accounts of her past gradually shifted from depicting idealized or denigrated versions of her childhood and parents. Rather, they conveyed a more ordinary childhood, with ordinary parents who made some mistakes: the recovery of whole objects, whom she was capable of feeling loving and aggressive feelings towards at the same time.

Ending phase

The ending phase of Ms L's therapy was of an entirely different quality. She attended consistently and punctually. Sessions felt slower and quieter, and a sombre atmosphere prevailed.

Some months into this ending phase, she offered the following dream:

> *She had gone to the flat that she and her brother owned to re-negotiate terms with the tenants. Having received no answer, she climbed through a small window. She was horrified to find that the tenants had left and was frantic because they hadn't left a forwarding address. She discovered that they had taken the two beds that were her property and was furious. She rang B and told him that there was no forwarding address. He told her to look by the fruit bowl in the kitchen. She became even more distressed to find out that the fruit bowl, which had been hers and which she had loved, had gone, and the fruit was left lying on the counter. She rang B again and screamed at him that her special fruit bowl was gone. He told her to calm down, and that it was only a bowl. She slammed down the phone after screaming that he didn't understand, it wasn't just any bowl, it was special bowl!*

Ms L could only say that the dream had caused her considerable anxiety. Her account was accompanied by a feeling of utter desolation.

T: "Your therapy will soon end. I will be gone without a forwarding address. The two beds: the couch and my chair will also be gone. There can be no re-negotiation of the terms. The most upsetting thing is that your special bowl is also gone, leaving its contents exposed and uncontained. Maybe you're not sure if I really understand and take seriously the magnitude of this loss for you".

Ms L was silent but cried for some time. She later returned to this dream and my interpretation.

In her external life, much had also changed. There continued to be times when she retreated out of contact and returned to her perch, but somehow her perch didn't feel to be quite as high as it had done previously. Also, the atmosphere that prevailed led me to feel that these retreats now functioned as periods of respite, as opposed to impervious and pervasive defensive retreats.

Towards the end, Ms L was telling me about one of the properties that she and her brother owned, which they rented out:

P: "B raised the question of whether we ought to sell the house. I love that house. I put everything into making it beautiful. It was so much hard work—you remember, don't you? You remember all the heartache and anguish, don't you? B says that it's worth more sold than what we are getting in rent. It could give me the resources I need to manage the rest of my life, a good quality of life. . . ."

I felt extremely moved. I thought she was wondering if I knew just how much hard work she had put into the therapy. As opposed to the contemptuous devaluing of myself and the therapy that had characterized the earlier phases of her treatment, here, there is a recognition and appreciation, not only of the value of her therapy, but that the real value would only be realized if she were able to make use of the valuable resources that she had acquired.

For the next few sessions, she arrived looking haggard and tired, as though she were carrying the weight of the world on her shoulders. She was eventually able to verbalize a feeling of being weighed down by the responsibility and burden of "making this count". Ms L was terrified that, like every other valuable resource that she had possessed in her life, her therapy would be hoarded, wasted, and eventually lost.

Very close to the ending, Ms L's mother died. When she arrived for her next session, the day after the funeral, she went straight to the other chair in the room instead of lying on the couch. Ms L said, very simply:

P: "Perhaps I'll be ready to know what I have lost next time."

In the final weeks, Ms L was talking to me about clearing out a room in her home:

P: "... I was clearing some rubbish, and I came across all these old bowls that I had made, among a load of junk. There was one I had painted, which I thought you might like as a gift when I we end...."

In my countertransference the words old ... junk ... rubbish ... sprang out at me. I recalled just how hard the work had been, how much I felt I had needed to bear and how much I felt she had gained from the therapy, and I thought, "how cheeky". However, in my response, I was able to take up how much she felt she had gained from the therapy. Ms L simply cried in response.

Ms L's final session was very moving. At the end she said she had a gift for me. It was a pretty blue handmade bowl, not the other bowl that she had previously referred to. She said:

P: "It's completely handmade by me for you. I made it in the last few weeks and fired it a few days ago. Now, it's dishwasher- and microwave-safe because it's supposed to be used. I wanted you to be able to make use of it. It's not supposed to be just for decoration or put somewhere and forgotten about. Please make use of it: you will make use of it, won't you? It's not just any old bowl, it's a special bowl!"

Conclusion

The challenges of my training experience often felt painful and insurmountable. I think this was heightened by my sense of the importance of taking on a patient for intensive therapy.

Due to Ms L's initial relentless attacks, her cavalier attitude, and the discourtesy with which I was characteristically treated, I can recognize that, at times, in identification with her own obliviousness, I adopted a similar state of mind. Perhaps this was a way of protecting myself from the ferocity of her denigration and the savagery of her constant, often rather personal attacks. This only served to increase the intensity and violence of her projections. Perhaps at the start we were, for different reasons, trapped in a deadly cycle of clinging on for dear life to our defensive, oblivious states of mind. However, this meant that clarity of sight was often not an option for either of us. I think these times probably correspond to the times when my supervisor observed that I was taking Ms L at face value.

Being my first intensive patient, the type of creative, rich, and developmental experience that I had anticipated and believed to be fundamental to my training experience seemed unachievable. I imagine that my disappointment and discontent would have only served to further galvanize my incapacity for receptivity. The deadly and stagnant environment that often prevailed stimulated a struggle in me to retain any sense of myself as a trainee psychotherapist who possessed valuable capacities.

Through supervision I was gradually able to begin to understand these processes and the position that I was inhabiting. Supervision was crucial to me developing the capacity to receive and bear Ms L's deadly projections and to decipher her confusing and duplicitous communications. As my ability to understand her grew, I found myself experiencing much warmer feelings towards her.

I think that it was only when I could bear to stop taking Ms L at face value, which meant tolerating and understanding disturbing feelings and states of mind, that I could recognize that, in fact, right from the outset I was in immersed in the powerfully rich, creative, and developmental training experience that I had anticipated. As predicted by her assessor, Ms L had turned out to be an "excellent training patient".

CHAPTER THIRTEEN

Should I stay or should I go?

Thomas Hillen

It is generally acknowledged that the patient needs the therapist more than the therapist the patient. I focus, in this chapter, on the peculiar situation that arises in the training context where, in order to qualify, the trainee needs the patient to stay in therapy. This can become a source of intense anxiety for the trainee which colours the transference–countertransference situation.

The title of my chapter encapsulates some of the themes emerging in the analytic work with my patient. There was a constant threat that the patient would drop out. She initially used me like an inanimate automaton into which she could deposit unwanted feelings and orchestrate sympathy for herself. This was a disquieting experience. Reliable and sensitive supervision was crucial, time and again, in helping me recover my analytic stance.

Knowing my patient had to stay for two years so that I could qualify was something that was always in the back of my mind. Many of the discussions among psychotherapy trainees seemed focused on this topic. What kind of patients were we given by our supervisors, will things work out, what are the implications for our training and life if they did not, and how should we manage the situation? My budding identity as therapist seemed to depend on the ups and downs of the work with my training patient. At times this became an obstacle and limited my freedom in the work.

During our preliminary consultation, my patient asked how she should refer to me. She said she called the physician dealing with one of her medical conditions by her first name and called her GP simply "doctor". We were confronted with who I would be to her, right from the start. I was challenged to consider my preconceived ideas about patients coming to me as a psychotherapy expert, and I found myself in a bind sooner than expected. Would we be in a symmetrical relationship, like friends, or would I be the distant professional, both elevated (the Dr) and denigrated (not worth remembering the name) at once? Usually, I would not insist on patients referring to me by my title, but, feeling so alarmed by the invitation to obfuscate the differences between us, I informed my patient I would prefer to be called "Dr Hillen". This seemed to peeve her. Later during the session, she spotted some crumpled-up tissue under the couch and pulled it out with a pen, asking, "Don't you have a bin?" The tables had turned: I no longer felt like the competent professional, and there seemed to be a question about whether I would know how to respond when she became upset and whether her upset would be adequately contained.

The way that I felt about myself had changed: suddenly I was experiencing feelings of shame and inadequacy. I was learning about projective identification from experience, and I was also having to differentiate this from the trainee psychotherapist's very real self-doubt about being up to the job. Later, my supervisor helped me to understand what had been happening in this moment during the preliminary meeting. It began to dawn on me that transference-countertransference feelings can be very colourful and alive and not like faded childhood family pictures.

Should I stay or should I go?

Here I explore how my patient settled into our work and the difficulties that arose in maintaining the analytic frame. Questions like "Do I have a patient?", "How should I hold her?", and "What are we doing here?" featured in our work right from the beginning. Having agreed on a start date and our session times, my patient emailed before her first session, requesting that we should move the session to a later time. She indicated that she could only attend in person three times per week on alternate weeks, because of her work schedule, and she requested that the Friday session should be offered as telephone session fortnightly. She also asked that the clinic should reimburse her travel fares.

We were already wrestling over the analytic frame. Quinodoz (1992) described how the creative maintenance of the frame underpins all psychoanalytic work; it has four facets: spatial, temporal, financial, and "refraining from doing". In other words, from the beginning there were questions whether my patient would come to me/the clinic; whether there was a commitment to regular three-times-weekly work; whether I should reimburse my patient; whether we would refrain from doing things such as moving the session time.

There was an on-going difficulty in establishing a regular rhythm for our sessions. This resembled the lack of a feeding routine that helps the infant to organize her experience and to form a sense of self. There were credible reasons why she missed sessions, such as her sister's death and funeral, and travel for work projects. But there were also missed sessions because she overslept or did not co-ordinate her holidays with mine. The net result was that, except for the first term, we had no uninterrupted run of sessions during the work discussed here. After the first summer break the question of whether my patient would abandon her therapy altogether featured prominently, as she frequently talked about moving to the West Country or abroad. She could not see how much she needed her treatment and, instead, felt she could easily replace me. On reflection, I was drawn into this dynamic and did not fully hold in mind how disastrous this premature termination would have been for her development, and I became worried about the consequences for my own psychotherapy training.

Another question in relation to the frame was how I should manage contact with my patient outside session times. She frequently emailed the clinic, including at weekends. Often, she remained seated on my couch after the end of a session, taking time checking her phone, gathering her belongings, and putting her shoes back on. The administrators in the department forwarded the messages, and they were important partners in helping me to manage the situation.

My supervision helped me to understand that having access to me only during "the hour" brought unbearable feelings of dependency and separateness to the fore—feelings that she could not otherwise allow herself to know about (Bonner, 2006).

Bleger (1967) proposed that the way in which patients respond to the analytic frame is connected to their body schema, their sense of self, and their earliest anxieties. However difficult it proved to preserve the analytic frame, working at it and interpreting it seemed to help my patient towards feeling more at home in her own body and in her therapy.

The concrete physical holding (the clinic, the waiting room, the consulting room, the couch, the regular sessions) had allowed the emergence of a faint idea of continuity of experience (Winnicott, 1953). Becoming more anchored in her therapy, however, also made separations more difficult. By the time my patient had been in therapy for 12 months, she could fathom that our summer break might have an impact on her. One fundamental question occurred, which had previously not featured in her thinking. The question was whether she could feel held in mind and whether she could hold things in mind that might bridge the inevitable external ruptures and facilitate some internal sense of continuity.

A question of power

With this patient, transference and countertransference phenomena included such salient themes as domination/submission, game playing, humiliation, and unpredictability.

I experienced my patient as controlling, touchy, intimidating, and exploitative. I was under pressure to play the narrow role that she had assigned to me, which consisted mainly of validating, reassuring, and appeasing her. She became touchy whenever she felt I did not give her what she wanted.

I still find it hard to acknowledge how much I experienced myself in her presence as weak, appeasing, used, and sullied. It felt precarious having to work with this volatile woman and having to rely on her attendance for my training.

A few weeks into our work, my patient spilled the remains of a cup of coffee as she was leaving. It left a stain on the carpet of the consulting room, which a senior member of staff had allowed me to use for the duration of the therapy. "Oops, I don't know what you do about that", she commented and left. She did not mention the incident in her next session, but I felt it was important to address what had happened. When I brought it up, my patient strongly conveyed that she could not be expected to accept responsibility for what happened. I became so intimidated by the situation that, instead of exploring it, I ended up making practical suggestions about where to place the cup, etc. However, she also picked up how extremely cautious I was when I tried to raise the issue and wondered about how she was coming across. It seemed as if she rejoiced in her intimidating impact on me.

The next day she raged about how I could not be trusted because I was twisting things and manipulating her. At the time I could not fathom what had upset her so much. What sense do I make of it now? I imagine that what provoked my patient was that I had taken the liberty to comment on her behaviour, rather than go along with it. I had my own mind. I had initiative and raised something with her that showed that she did not have total possession of me. She protested that this was not how our relationship should work: I am in control of my objects, and how dare you challenge my omnipotence, you are just an extension of myself (Ruszczynski, 2007).

I began to understand my sense that I had to supply my patient with a perfect—and, therefore, delusional—provision, which was another aspect of the countertransference (Brenman, 1982). For example, I often struggled to end sessions on time or tried to wrap everything up neatly, because I was afraid to leave her with any disquiet and the fury this would cause. It was as if I wanted to eradicate the inevitable impingements that analytic work brings, such as the separations between sessions and the stirring up of conflicts. Without realizing, I felt compelled to provide my patient with an experience free of pain, where I would stay in her good books.

I felt I was in a highly precarious situation. I did not feel that I was there to make interpretations and to help my patient gain deeper insight into her internal world. Instead, I was acting as if my job was to paper over the cracks: her problems had become mine. Any unhappiness arising in her mind became my responsibility and a sign that I was failing her. It felt as if I was being held under water, and my supervision sessions became important moments when I was allowed to surface, breathe, look around, and check in which direction I was heading. I cannot overstate how much it mattered to have a supervisor to whom I could "tell it as it is" during the difficult stretches of the work.

Why was I anxious to avoid painful feelings from emerging? The transference gave repeated glimpses of how she experienced her objects as abandoning and only interested in themselves. For instance, she usually became furious if I remained silent after an unsettling insight had come to her mind and angrily demanded, "I have no data here, why don't you say anything?" She accused me of failing to protect her when she embarked on relationships that seemed to have little hope of going anywhere and would ask, "Why did you not see this coming and warn me?"

My understanding of her history suggested that my patient blamed herself for an imagined inability to evoke awe and love at first sight when she was newborn (Meltzer, 1988). Wanting her mother badly, she could not be sure that her mother wanted her, too, when she descended into postnatal depression. This left my patient feeling ugly and unlovable. Possessing and controlling her objects felt much safer than establishing a psychological link (Bonner, 2006). She felt that she either had to insist on her position without any "give and take" or that she had to blindly comply with others. The possibility of relating to others as whole and separate figures was not possible for her at this point.

This coloured many of our interactions. When my patient experienced me as the junior partner in the work, it could feel as if we were getting on well, and an apparently creative process could unfold, which was quite comfortable for both of us. Whenever she experienced me as a therapist with his own mind, the atmosphere immediately became touchy and volatile. I struggled to think and say anything useful. Interventions acknowledging her fury did not defuse the situation and, instead, seemed to ignite it. Hence, I would slip into the role of a supportive counsellor, mainly validating her experiences. But, with time, I began to become suspicious of my own ease and sense that I was doing good work. I began to realize that I was playing it safe, and that our sessions were failing to have real impact.

I had a dilemma. If we stepped away from the enclave of non-interpretative, supportive therapy and I was no longer just validating my patient's feelings, something much more disturbing might enter the room (O'Shaughnessy, 1992). In other words, if I did not just want to shore up my patient's defences and, instead, undertake a proper piece of analytic work, something had to change. I was in a bind, because I was also aware of the risk that she could drop out if something that was too disquieting was brought to her attention. Again, supervision proved vital here and helped me to realize that I was here to learn about working analytically and that my needing her to stay was a secondary consideration.

The subsequent sessions felt more real and engaged, but also riskier and more unpredictable. Maintaining boundaries seemed vital to keep the work safe. The problem here was that challenging the analytic frame, blurring boundaries, and getting excited about it was part of my patient's defensive system, which seemed to offer protection from psychic pain.

My patient only had very few internal resources for support when her equilibrium became disturbed. As a child, she had tried to control intolerable feelings by restricting her eating, self-harm, using drugs and, later, casual sex. These strategies helped her to reassure herself of the continuity of her physical existence when her psychological survival was under threat (Mitrani, 2007).

As an adult, her most powerful defences against experiencing separation and the catastrophic feelings associated with it were seeking oblivion and excitement (Brenman, 1982). For instance, she reported that she would usually browse dating sites on her mobile in the waiting room. Instead of feeling lonely and excluded, she could feel in charge and decide whether she would give others "likes" or swipe them away.

Any discomfort had to be swiped away too. She informed me in one session that she was thinking of moving with her new boyfriend to New York. She told me that she was worried because she knew the therapy was meant to be for two years. She spoke about continuing with remote therapy and cried, stating that she was anxious that I would kick her out because this might not work. Towards the end of the session, she brought some associations about the beautiful trails that aeroplanes leave in the sky and then left the session feeling calm.

By now I had learned when I could remain silent without her persecutory feelings becoming unmanageable. She wanted to make it my responsibility to protect her therapy and keep it alive by cutting corners with the analytic frame. But I think her association to the white smoke behind aeroplanes illuminates an important aspect of her defensive system, although I did not take this up at the time. The trails were portrayed as beautiful rather than as pollution: the missed sessions could be turned into attended sessions. She could change the meaning of things at will (Bonner, 2006).

The capacity to re-label and blur things gave her a powerful sense of control and, therefore, served a fundamental function in her mental life. Pollution was beautiful. She could tell herself that starving herself was looking after herself. She could tell me that she was desperate to honour her two-year commitment, while organizing her move abroad. She said she had strong feelings (guilt/triumph/sadness?) but showed no inclination to take them seriously and think about them. She could tell herself that nothing mattered, that good and bad were indistinguishable. This was intoxicating, because it made her feel invincible—that nothing would ever hurt her or make her feel anxious. She was looking down on people who anxiously worried about their future and were concerned for their own and other people's welfare. The contempt for people who cared about things included me. I had more "skin in the game" than she; simply walking off because something better had turned up was an option for her but not for me. And she did not owe me anything, because the NHS was taking care of me.

In time, my patient became more open about her sexual life. I felt I could never get it right: I was either misogynistic, intolerant of her sexual preferences, or condoning very risky behaviour. Brenman (1982) explains how the analyst is "blueprinted" to act out sadistic moralizing, masochistic pseudo-tolerance or to supply an ideal, delusional provision. He discusses how the denial of separation and loss leads to the analyst/mother becoming cut off from the knowledge of the valuable aspects of her own baby and from the baby part of herself, which would enable her to empathize with her baby. I think this is why I desperately needed my supervision to bear how I was being used and to maintain something that approximated to an analytic stance. I have mentioned above how my patient looked down at me for trying so hard. But I think it was also crucial that my patient experienced me as a real flesh-and-blood psychotherapist who struggled and doggedly persevered (Feldman, 1997). This gave her a sense that I did care about our work, and this gave her permission to care and, at least temporarily, take off her shield of superior indifference.

Why staying in therapy might feel too dangerous

Meltzer (1992) described how analysis might feel like a "devil of a treatment" to patients. He illustrated how gradually the door opens, and patients must face their history from a different point of view, to look back at their own behaviour and contribution. I feel that my patient reached this difficult stage in the treatment process. She was desperate to be seen, but the seeing eyes of her therapist saw more than she had been bargaining for. And she could see more for herself, which was a similarly mixed blessing. She had begun to think during silences and no longer felt that I was playing games to make her feel small and myself important. She could no longer put her carelessness into others and experience herself as the victim who was overlooked and unfairly criticized by everybody. She realized that she benefitted from our work and that aborting her therapy would bring trouble. However, staying was also problematic, owing to a dawning awareness that she had to ask herself seriously what she was doing to herself and others.

She started to question her belief that she had the perfect right to control her objects. Hitherto, she had related to me and other people in her life with a pervasive "something for nothing" attitude. Other people had been no more than part-objects to be used by her as she saw fit, manipulating them into gratifying her needs. She was acutely aware that she was my training patient, and the idea seemed to be that we both exploited each other's vulnerability.

She continued with her deliberations about going to New York. She commented that she was no longer sure whether she was continuing for her benefit or for mine, and she was unsure whether she should discuss this with me, because I would have a vested interest in her sessions continuing.

What had happened? A negative therapeutic reaction? Our work had seriously started to matter to my patient, and she became aware of her dependency on me. Glasser described how the negative therapeutic reaction can, for some patients, be seen as a self-preservative manoeuvre aimed at fending off the anxiety that the object has entirely colonized the self. My patient became suspicious that I was taking over her mind and subverting the failproof protection against psychic pain that her defensive organization had offered her, and this startled her (Rosenfeld, 1971b).

Furthermore, as we had passed the half-way mark, my patient became more in touch with the reality that it was not only she who would determine the duration of her treatment, and that the two-year end point was approaching.

The situation with New York became more frantic, resulting in her decision that she would be leaving. I would say that intolerable anxieties had come to the fore and resulted in this premature termination. Bleger (1967) helps us to understand that the most primitive and terrifying anxieties tend to get projected into the frame. Because they are buried in the frame, they are exceedingly difficult to get hold of. However, if left unaddressed, they suddenly break into the open and threaten the continuity of the work.

I realized that we had been wrestling over the psychoanalytic frame from very early on in the work, without being able to understand the deeper meaning of it. To see the therapy through to the end, my patient was required to pay an unaffordable psychological price: acknowledgement of dependency and need; conceding that she was not solely a victim and owing up to her own destructiveness; renouncing the right to change all meaning at will and be truthful. It was as if she had entered treatment with the tacit agreement that none of this would be required of her.

I wonder whether, if I had been bolder earlier on in the analytic work, there might have been a different outcome. I had avoided analytic work in favour of supportive therapy, fearing my patient's volatile temper and the risk losing of her as my patient. Brenman Pick (2018) speaks of walking the tightrope between experiencing disturbance and responding with an interpretation that does not convey troubling anxiety. I struggled with this, and I suspect this might be an area where many other candidates might experience difficulties as well.

Conclusion

I discuss in this chapter how the training context and the need to see the patient for a specified duration might impact on intensive psychotherapy. When there are claustro-agoraphobic anxieties, these inevitably become re-enacted during the treatment. For instance, my patient might have looked for a therapist who needed her to stay, and perhaps this was what allowed the work to proceed at all. Both the patient's and my own vulnerability were involved here: perhaps I was too sensitive to being a trainee, and the patient to being a training patient. Not all trainees necessarily inform their patients that they are in training. Still, I do not think this will protect them or their patients from some of the dynamics discussed here.

When the training patient threatens to leave and projects anxieties about catastrophic abandonment into us, it can be very challenging to respond with an interpretation that does not convey troubling anxiety. Supervision and the camaraderie among trainees can be crucial here to manage this difficult task.

CHAPTER FOURTEEN

The shape of things to come

Viv Walkerdine

Ms P, a single woman in her early forties with a history of binge-ing and restricting, was referred to an NHS eating disorders service. The chapter describes her two-year, three-times-weekly psychotherapy, exploring the patient's restricted and limited object relations, where to be known or be dependent were defended against through a form of pseudo-independence. The analytic space was initially experienced, not for containment (Bion, 1962a) or playful experience (Winnicott 1971), but as one where the analyst was drawn into an idealized womb-like experience, with no conflict, hard edges, or difference and where, at first, the patient's words were used not to convey meaning, but to project an empty futility about ever getting through to the analyst. Gradually, the patient develops an internal space or shape that could receive and connect with the mind of another. Symbolic playful images started to appear in the work. These early images were of a small model house, with different keys to the doors, which must be worked out before it can be played with. The house represents the beginnings of the idea of an object that can receive and hold, but with the entrance being fraught with difficulties. Gradually, there is a move towards symbolization and creativity, words start to hold meaning, and emotional expression and dreams finally emerge in the work.

Clinical example: Ms P

Beginnings

The themes of prematurity, of being ready, of being able to take up space, to grow and develop, shaped the early work. Ms P's younger brother had been born prematurely, with significant disabilities. He was a surviving twin, the other brother having died at birth. The patient's early experiences had, therefore, been dominated by her parents' concern for her younger brother and the painful loss of the twin who did not survive. Her earliest memories were filled with her own sense of abandonment as she was left to be cared for by others. She experienced both her parents as unavailable, feeling her mother was blaming and critical and her father fragile. She thought that she should stand back and let someone else take her place at the clinic, as her needs were not serious enough. She was uncertain about having enough "space" in her week, and whether she was quite ready.

My countertransference in these first sessions was of coaxing or trying to feed a baby who turned away at the last moment. I had felt uncertain how much to stay with the process, whether I was in danger of pushing myself at her, that she was not ready, but slowing down the pace and giving more time to thinking about how anxious she felt seemed to help her take a first step.

Ms P seemed "buttoned-up": as if any expression of feelings would leave her overwhelmed or falling apart. Bick (1968) refers to a "second skin", a continuous, containing skin equivalent, a defensive structure that protects the infant from the experiences of psychic disintegration and panic that can arise when the child has had to struggle with the impact of emotional absence. Ms P's buttoned-up manner and her bids for self-sufficiency seemed to be an attempt to hold herself together, creating a pseudo-independence, so that she has no need of others.

What Ms P was also showing me in these early meetings was a first glimpse of her place in the family and the traumatic impact of the birth of the twins.

The brothers arrived at the time when Ms P was still struggling with Oedipal anxieties. She was faced not only with negotiating the loss of an exclusive relationship, for sole possession, but she was then faced not just with a baby, but "special" babies capable of demanding and taking up all the space in her mother's mind. Feelings of loss and deprivation of the maternal object emerge, while hateful and violent phantasies associated with rivalry and envy can seem to come true when a sibling dies or becomes so ill and disabled. This traumatic experience thus conflates internal and external reality, and fears of retaliation from a severe superego can arise (Emanuel 2014).

Crushing self-criticism and persecutory guilt appeared throughout the therapy, where reparation is seen as impossible and with Ms P having little belief that anyone could bear to know or receive any of her "underneath" feelings. Fears of being displaced and excluded by others more needy than herself, or taking what she feels she does not deserve, are managed, as Ms P did in these early meetings, by almost excluding herself from the start and by having a "skin" that was not to be broken through.

Emerging patterns

For about the first nine months of the therapy, Ms P did not use the couch. Although talked about, the couch seemed to represent a more "grown-up" place that she was not quite ready for. The first months of the work were, however, filled with Ms P's self-criticism and what she saw as her stupidity and ineptness, with her belief that I was just seeing her out of charity. In the countertransference, I often felt frustrated and unable to get through, which made me more at risk of pushing forward or being experienced as intrusive. I continued to have the experience of trying to feed a baby, to offer ideas or different ways of thinking, which she repeatedly turned away, telling me that I was just reassuring her and that she would always end up seeing herself as no good. She often told me that she wasn't like a "normal adult"—that it wasn't normal at her age to feel anxious or need reassurance in any way.

A pattern emerged around the three weekly sessions where, by the third session, Ms P would be low, grey, as if a veil had been drawn over any life or steps she may have taken. We would start to get somewhere at the start of the week, but then any steps would disappear. Slowly, I became more focused on her turning away, rather than on my attempts to keep hold of a thread with her: to think about how hard it is to stay connected; to be aware of her fear of being dropped as well as the connection.

There was a sense of Ms P just starting to open out, a coming to life, and then deadening, with any more alive feelings being crushed and closed, with the work being crushed too. In the countertransference I felt sunk. I had an image of a raft, cast adrift, only just keeping afloat. I started to think that her early experience was also of feeling cast adrift, with no way of explaining this other than to blame herself, to feel inadequate and a "failure" in her attempts to reach her mother, whose mind was so occupied elsewhere. The experience in these three weekly sessions, then, was of some ground starting to form but lost as we approached the weekly break. Her early experience was reversed, through the projective identification (Klein 1952b) of the rejected child part of herself, so that I was to be the one who is dropped, and a veil drawn over her feelings of loss and dependency.

What I also found helpful when trying to understand Ms P's image of a "normal adult" was the term "normopath" used by Joyce McDougall (1989) to describe a patient who tries to maintain a presentation of "pseudonormality", to avoid thinking or feeling too deeply about inner pain and conflict that might otherwise be experienced as overwhelming. Ms P could not think or feel too deeply about her internal state but must deaden her inner life to survive, while I, too, was to have little contact with her emotional experience: there was not yet a "fit" between us.

The pink book: the wish for an idealized maternal presence

However, by about seven months, a rhythm gradually started to emerge of Ms P bringing more material, but in a rigid way, as if she was being a good daughter or sister, being responsible and working hard. Within the developing rhythm there was also a pattern that seemed to undermine her therapy, but in a subtle, crafty way. Despite her good attendance and times when I felt she had taken in my interpretations, she started to cancel some sessions, often related to demands at work. She talked of friends questioning the helpfulness of her therapy, that perhaps it was detrimental to her, as she was still struggling with low mood.

A short while later she brought a book to one of her sessions, which she described as "inspirational". The book had a pink cover. I was struck by the pink colour: matte baby pink, and my attention was taken up with this until I realized that it reminded me of calamine lotion: opaque, soothing. There was something in the way Ms P was telling me about her feelings that felt "bookish", that she was giving me an explanation, but with her distress covered over, as if with calamine lotion. In the countertransference, I felt kept out, useless, and drawn away from any disturbance.

Up to this point, I had been struggling with taking things up in a more direct way, her cancellations and her chipping away at the frequency of the sessions, with my going round the houses and pulling back from more definite statements. I had been drawn into creating a soft, "baby pink" place, safely tucked away, free from the intrusion of disturbing emotions: a womb-like place and the longed-for, merged mother-and-baby experience.

I had started to feel "comfortable" in this softer place. Initially, I had failed to notice my role as a comforting maternal presence as, I think, this connected with a version of myself with which I felt at ease.

Feldman (1997) suggests that

> what is projected into an analyst is a phantasy of an object relationship that evokes not only thoughts and feelings, but also propensities to action . . . the projection into the analyst can lead to subtle enactments that do not initially disturb the analyst but constitute a comfortable collusive arrangement. [p. 239]

In a similar way, O'Shaughnessy (1992) refers to the development of an "enclave" where the analyst, under pressure from the patient, can turn the analytic work into a refuge from disturbance.

Ms P did not want to know or want me to know about the more needy and vulnerable aspects of herself, which, she feared, were so disabling and incurable: an understandable fear, given the anxieties and uncertainties surrounding her brothers. She needed to restrict her contact with me, because of her fears of knowing her internal world and of experiencing fuller and freer object relations. She located her dissatisfaction in her friends, and the blame for not feeling better into her "explanations", like in the book. I was only "faced" with her frustrations and fears in a roundabout way. As a transference figure, she did not expect me to withstand her feelings and impulses.

However, as I started to stand back, my association with calamine lotion, with painful skin covered over, helped me to think about what feelings may have lain "underneath". I tried to more firmly take up the negative transference, to address her anger and frustration, to talk about her fear that I could not bear her distress and had to be "soothed". I tried to speak in a clearer, more direct way about her turning away rather than "facing" me when feeling frustrated that she is not progressing. Although at first Ms P denied any angry feelings or turning away, this did seem to "hold her" and help her to stop and think with me about how frantic she had been feeling.

One year on: the model house and the development of the capacity to symbolize

Ms P moved onto the couch. It took some time, however, for her to fully take up this space. Themes around sharing and two people started to come into the work.

There was a move towards using her brother's full name and a developing sense of her brother as separate. I heard more about her family, how no one knew what her brother would be able to do as he grew up, how to "measure" development, which Ms P often connected to herself. She spoke about her concern, too, at having things in her life that her brother could never have and a developing recognition of loss.

At a similar time, Ms P brought an image: a small model house with several keys that open different doors into the house, so that objects can be put inside. She spoke of her frustration when she can't understand or take in what someone is trying to say, as if the keys won't fit the keyholes, and there is no opening to enter the house or take things in.

Ms P had, for a while, referred to a "barrier" to taking in anything good or helpful from me and that, if anything did get through, its "shape" would change to being critical, or she could only have a "taste" and the good shape would fall out and the door close. It often felt that the only "key shape" she could receive was a more concrete, factual form, associated with more structured CBT type of statements, where she could see the actual "evidence" for herself but was stripped of feelings.

Ms P often experienced my words as invasive and "pointed", and so trying to make a link that was thinkable about in words rather than being experienced as an attack was part of the work between us. The emergence of the model house image vividly communicated the difficulties in the first year of therapy, of finding a "fit" between us, with the wrong key meeting the wrong hole. We often ended up in a corner or cul-de-sac, where my words seemed useless. These cul-de-sacs were emptied of feelings but filled with facts and measurements or questions about her progress, like the uncertainty and questions surrounding her brother's development. What I had to learn was to name feelings, to find a language. I started to use her brother's name more and tried to make statements that were less tentative. I became aware of how I would often add a further sentence onto an interpretation, hoping that I could mould it to the right shape to be received.

The emergence of the model house image and the emergence of new words, however, marked a development in her capacity to symbolize and a move towards depressive feelings when separation from the object, ambivalence, guilt, and loss can be experienced and tolerated. The small house represented an object that, however difficult, could take in and receive, as well as the process of opening the door and putting things inside: a representation of the process of introjection and projection. Words could start to represent a separation of the internal from the external world and separation of the object from the self (Segal, 1957).

Bick suggests that the baby has to struggle for the "capacity" to introject and that this capacity is an achievement of both infant and mother. The internal good object described by Klein (1946) as the core of the ego in the paranoid-schizoid and depressive positions, thus has a preceding condition, the capacity to be able to introject at all:

> This internal function of containing the parts of the self is dependent on the introjection of an external object experienced as capable of

fulfilling this function ... until the containing functions have been introjected, a concept of a space within the self cannot arise. [Bick, 1968, p. 484]

The initial achievement of having an "idea of a space" that holds things is shown in Ms P's model house image.

Working through: using words to hold emotional experience

As the work progressed, I often felt drawn to offer a softer-edged place. Although I felt more aware of when Ms P was presenting a picture that covered over (the calamine lotion) her more negative feelings or was trying to be a "good daughter", it continued to be difficult to bring all the picture of her into the room. I often experienced Ms P as younger than her years, trying to be grown up but often preoccupied with measuring her progress, like parents worrying over how a disabled child might develop.

Over the following months, however, the material was richer. At one point Ms P spoke of realizing that she had "boxed" her feelings away, concerned about what she may find inside, but also wished to fling it open and "purge" herself of its contents. I thought she was trying to work out what I would be able to receive so that the sessions were used, at times, to empty herself of all that she felt was unacceptable about herself. She was contemptuous of any feelings she experienced about our breaks, and when I raised this with her, I was the one to be reassured that she was all right. I was to be looked after and protected, to hold all the vulnerability, instead of her.

However, gradually feelings were named, tolerated, and held emotional meaning. She talked about the sad and "horrible place" inside herself where all hope disappeared, and about her fears of unravelling. She was starting to touch on her depressive anxiety about the state of her internal objects, where all goodness is lost and she is left with utter despair.

The naming of feelings, using words to communicate and regulate her internal state, slowly started to develop. About this time, she told her mother about the model house image. She was surprised that her mother received and understood what she said. She started to write notes to herself from the sessions, wanting to keep hold of the words, to keep a thread with the sessions and a thread between us.

Working towards an ending

As we approached the last six months of the work, anger towards her brother's friends and the services that supported him increased. She was furious that they did not help him to have more independence in the future. She was, however, increasingly able to recognize her anger towards the more vulnerable and dependent aspects of herself. She talked about her own fears for the future, her feelings of disappointment and frustration with therapy, and what she felt was now being taken away. Any frustration or anger towards myself was, however, avoided, kept in the box, only appearing in a more roundabout way. In these months leading to the ending, her parents were also going away for several weeks, which provided a place to locate some of her feelings about dependency and loss, as her brother struggled with their absence.

As the weeks progressed, Ms P continued to bring her anger and pain at ending, despite her difficulty in finding words to express this directly. She talked about a work colleague not seeming bothered if all their work wasn't completed, the responsibility she felt for the job even though it was shared, not wanting to leave work unfinished, fearing that she would be seen as lazy or letting people down. I talked about how feelings of loss/let-down are seen in others, away from herself, and I tried to bring it into the transference. She turned this into criticism of herself; her frustration with her own limits rather than mine or the limits of our time together. She moved towards the depressive position but then pulled back to a place where all the badness is hers.

I tried to use more analyst-centred interpretations, to think about what she imagined I might be thinking if she was critical of me, to move away from more patient-centred interpretations, which Ms P experienced as persecutory (Steiner, 1993). She did respond to this approach and started to feel understood. There was a lessening of the harshness of her superego and an emerging ability to recognize the punishing aspects of herself, although at times she slipped back into seeing this as another example of her inadequacy.

The emergence of dreams

Two months from the ending, Ms P had only once before brought a fragment of a dream. I had, however, started to experience some of Ms P's narrative as having a dream-like quality, which enabled me to stand back from the immediate content and think about it more as a dream version about her and me. However, the emergence of some actual dreams showed Ms P's developing capacity to symbolize and the development of her ego, capable of some working through of internal problems through dreamwork.

The dreams were full of "crushing disappointment", of strange worlds where everything had changed, where she felt lost and frightened.

Slowly, over the following sessions, we came back to these dreams. Her crushing disappointment that the ending of her therapy was real, as were her fears and sense of feeling lost in an alien world, with nothing to guide her. We were to be a failed couple: she had not been good enough, and I had not been able to make everything alright.

However, alongside these dreams, Ms P had started to feel more confident at work and felt that her colleagues did offer genuine praise, freely given, with no strings attached. She likened it to finding a key that fits the hole: she could take in and receive their comments but fearful, too, that the hole could close over.

Ms P worried that she would lose her growing openness to the outside world, but there was also a growing idea of an opening that was more personal, located in her body, one that allowed a way through her "skin". This seemed to allow an openness over the remaining weeks, Ms P letting me know her ideas about the ending: that I was disappointed with her; that she was greedy for wanting more and should be satisfied with what she was given. She was able to recognize an aspect of herself that felt that any demand cannot be managed. She told me that it had taken weeks for her to ask whether she could continue to meet with me and then face the knowledge that this was not possible. This had been a painful exchange, and, to some extent, Ms P continued to protect me from the strength of her disappointment and anger. However, it did seem to open up the possibility of a healthy appetite for development rather than greed, and the possibility of her considering further psychotherapy after we ended.

Ms P was anxious about whether the "shape" forming inside her would remain, or whether our separation would leave her falling apart. The limits of our time together painfully echoed her experiences in life, where she was exposed to difficulties she could not make sense of, where she had had to grow up quickly, before she was ready. But the emergence of dreams marked a move from more concrete thinking towards symbolic forms of expression, and the details of the two dreams represented a growing awareness of a mind that has depth, which can be explored.

Discussion

Often, over the two years with Ms P, I found myself thinking about the early handling of a baby, how a mother has to find a way of getting to know and understand her baby, to hear and find a space inside herself to take in the cries, to find a language together that comes before words. I felt that I was like a new mother, having to develop an internal space to receive Ms P, while she, too, was having to find a way to receive me.

Bion's (1962a) model of container-contained shows how "shape" is given to the developing infant's emotions, so that there is an experience of being able to put emotions into something and take them back into the self: a three-dimensional experience of an inside space or shape. Klein (1952b) describes the dependent baby as moving between experiences of integration and disintegration, fearing, at times, for survival. The good experience of being held by the mother's arms and by her mind helps the baby to develop a sense of coherence, a "centre" that can hold, even in temporary absence.

Ms P had been unable to develop this inside space. The "shape" of her experience of being held seemed to be "misshapen", so there had not been established a link or "thoroughfare" (Waddell, 1998) for feelings between mother and child, as was often experienced in the therapy when struggling to find a "fit".

In the absence of a containing presence, Ms P tried to hold herself together in a pseudo-independent, buttoned-up way—a form of primitive omnipotence necessary for survival. The "sticky" quality referred to by Bick in second-skin formation is also shown in Ms P's fitting in with her family culture, to be stoical, like her parents, to put her brother first. She simply stuck to the surface and accommodated her complex family circumstances, without any thoughts about herself. Ms P spoke about having little sense of her internal world, of who she really is.

The arrival of Ms P's "special" brothers had marked a traumatic change in family life. Her anxious parents were overwhelmed, unable to adequately receive and contain Ms P (Williams, 1997). Her own needy feelings were felt to be "ugly" and represented in her body. As a young child, her feelings of rivalry and resentment were thought to only cause damage. Her depressive anxieties were defended against by turning on herself, so that she became full of self-blame, "disabled", and on the edge of depression. In a similar way, she blamed herself for the "restrictions" of therapy. Her own appetite for life had to remain hidden and restricted to avoid feeling greedy. Her own growth and development had to be limited, like her brother's.

What I also came to understand more as the therapy progressed was how much Ms P stepped into the parental shoes, taking on a position where she is the "soother", the grown-up. She did not have an experience of a mother and father together and herself as a third: it doesn't add up in this way. She was always trying to replace her mother, to be the responsible one, to care for her brother, so that a genuine dependency could not be fully experienced. The Oedipus complex and depressive position could not be fully negotiated.

Britton (1998) suggests that when a child perceives the coming-together of his mother and father independently of himself, it unites his psychic world: a third position develops, from which object relationships can be observed. We can see ourselves in interaction with others while being ourselves. Britton referred to the mental freedom provided by this process as "triangular space". Birksted-Breen (1996) also suggests that the development of an "internal space" cannot fully come about until the link between mother and father has been internalized, through the "penis-as-link" function of the father. Unless this link is established, there is a turning towards an omnipotent, no-needs way of being. This was part of the experience with Ms P: her longing to be merged, but a terror of dependence and pulling back, the binge and restriction.

As a "fit" started to develop, she started to experience some "shape" and form being given to her emotions: the unconscious process of symbol formation developed, as did her curiosity about her internal world. There was growing openness and ability to communicate. In a similar way, I started to feel more confident in what I could offer, to start to find my "shape" and come forward in a more definite way. I'd had to find a way to "receive" the teaching, supervision, to take in what, at times, felt painful. Being helped to bear this enabled my own growth and ability to find my voice and "shape" as a psychotherapist.

Ms P started to accept more help from her friends, to be more open with her family. Her eating was more settled and, although she feared at times returning to a more restricting diet, she seemed more able to take in and hold a space inside herself for experiencing and thinking. To some extent, Ms P had come to recognize the responsible and "soothing" position that she took up in her family.

We did talk about the possibility of further psychotherapy in the future. Ms P was both curious to know more about her mind, to look in the "murky water" and see what she could find, but fearful, too. There was, however, a growing sense that she was now "ready" and had, in a way, come to "full term" herself and would be able, in time, to think about starting deeper work.

CHAPTER FIFTEEN

From incorporation to introjection and mourning: parallel processes in both patient and trainee

Diane Turner

The patient, referred for treatment from the pain clinic of a large teaching hospital where she was being treated for chronic pain, was offered intensive psychoanalytic psychotherapy. It was my first case on the M1 training; I saw the patient over three years and was supervised in weekly individual sessions throughout that time.

There was a parallel between the experience of my patient's pain, concretely held in the body, rigid, fixed, and seemingly immutable, which protected her from knowing about the internal psychic pain of facing the death of her mother, and a similar situation I found myself in as a trainee, new to psychoanalytic work, facing my own feelings of inadequacy and loss of my previous professional identity. I argue that, for a successful outcome in the treatment, it was necessary for us both to move from a position of concretization, working through our own internal conflicts and engaging in the process of mourning. I describe how this parallel process was held, contained, and facilitated on the course.

Clinical example

Bion writes:

> In psychoanalysis, when approaching the unconscious—that is, what we do not know—we, patient and analyst alike, are certain to be disturbed. In every consulting room, there ought to be two rather

frightened people: the patient and the psychoanalyst. If they are not both frightened, one wonders why they are bothering to find out what everyone knows. (Bion, 1990, p. 5)

Never is this more relevant than when a trainee begins work with their first training case. The "what we do not know" operates on many different levels. There is the unconscious of the particular patient, and there is the realm of our own unconscious landscape, both relatively unknown at the embarkation on this most intrepid of journeys.

The first phase of treatment

As I reflected on the early phase of treatment, I was reminded of my first training as a general nurse, and the process of moving from beginner to competent practitioner. Benner (1982) describes the stages of clinical competence on the route from novice to expert: a move from rule-governed behaviour to intuitive, contextually determined behaviour. This felt significant in relation to my own reliance on abstract theories and attempts to concretely incorporate my supervisor's thoughts and comments into my clinical work to steady myself in the first disturbing phase of the treatment.

The patient

The patient was 35 years old when she entered treatment; she had been suffering since the death of her mother, 13 years previously, from ovarian cancer. At the time of her mother's death, she had been working, completing a degree, and in a relationship. The following year she was diagnosed with endometriosis, adenomyosis, chronic pain, and, on the first anniversary of her mother's death, she took her first overdose. She experienced a fading-away from life: her relationship ended, she lost her job, her friends drifted away, and, gradually, there was an almost total retreat from life. She had spent the four years prior to coming to therapy mostly in bed, leaving only to attend medical appointments and to do the minimum necessary to maintain life.

She asserted that she had been her mother's "whole world". There was a largely absent father, a merchant seaman away at sea for nine months of the year, leaving her and mother undisturbed, in a perfect union. She was an only child, although she knew that her mother had had a baby boy twelve years prior to her birth, who had been given up for adoption. There were rumours that her father had other children, conceived while on his travels. She described her mother as having been an absolute beauty, with movie-star looks. They had lived in an island community, and she remembered her mother posing on the bow of a yacht in the harbour, adored by everyone, straight out of Hollywood. This Hollywood reference was apt, as the degree of idealization created a two-dimensional figure, with little depth.

During the initial few sessions, a very different picture of her early life emerged. She and mother had lived in poverty on the island. In winter, she remembered mother taking her into her bed in the late afternoons, as they lacked heating and electricity. There, she would tell her daughter stories that distracted them both from the reality of life.

Father was pictured as an alcoholic, a deeply troubled and violent man. She would sleep in mother's bed while he was away at sea, but on his return she was banished to her own room. Her parents eventually divorced when she was 12. Her mother's death when she was 22 years old had been catastrophic, and she had been left alone to manage it, physically, financially, and emotionally.

I was struck by the extreme physical pain that the patient described and the almost complete lack of affect in the room. Her narrative, although dramatic, appeared to arouse very little feeling in her, nor in myself, and I was surprised that she came so compliantly for psychotherapy when she clearly believed opiates to be the answer.

From the beginning, her physical body dominated the space of the consulting room. She readily took up her position on the couch, and the dominant posture was to lie prone, with her knees raised, her hands resting on her abdomen, directing all attention to the internal lesion, which was the site of all her distress. I noticed that her abdomen was slightly protruding, as if in the early months of pregnancy. The death could not be thought about at any level, as if it were too traumatic an event to integrate into her mind, and so it was somehow lodged in the patient's body. All that could be experienced was extreme pain and uncontrollable bleeding, which soaked her bedsheets, which could not be absorbed. The answer was to anaesthetize the pain with stronger and stronger doses of opiates, to retreat to bed, until any capacity to think or feel was annihilated.

In the early sessions the patient gave me a very real experience of having my mind numbed to the pain she was experiencing. By what I now know to be a process of powerful and disabling projective identification, I felt myself anaesthetized by a constant and unremitting attention to the pain of her physical body. There were many different pains, and she had a different idea about each medication and treatment that she received. One medication was for the tension migraines, one for the period pain, one for pain on ovulation, and another for the joint pain in her hips, a side effect of her near total bedrest. There was an analgesic for her "background" pain, and another for her "flare-ups". Her body was hypercathected and split up into "bits", each with a pain and analgesic of its own.

The experience was utterly deadening, and I felt absolutely useless. As the sessions dragged on, I felt pulled down into a state of despair. Perhaps this woman was too concrete for a psychotherapeutic treatment? She almost convinced me that opiates probably were the answer. In tandem with these thoughts was also an anxiety about my own capacity. Was this a projective mechanism that debilitated me, or was it that I was failing in some way? I felt mindless and soporific during the interminable sessions.

Steiner (2011b) describes the way in which the analyst may become preoccupied with the patient's reality, numbed to an awareness of the psychic reality of the transference. I would suggest that in the trainee psychotherapist this is further exacerbated by very limited experience of the vagaries of transference and projective identification. I felt stultified and helpless in the endeavour. It was a painful process, which was significantly at odds with my own narcissistic need to know, to understand, to impress my supervisor, precociously to rescue my patient, not to admit being helpless and hopeless. Looking back, it became clear that the patient's narcissistic withdrawal from life and, in the session, from me was a defensive manoeuvre to protect herself from pain. Her haughty and superior attitude with the pain consultant and myself was an unconscious attempt to protect herself from feelings of dependency, inadequacy, or need. By projecting parts of herself so significantly into me, she was able to deny any dependence, although at the same time she denuded me of any relevance. It was this experience that I found so debilitating at this elementary stage. When I did have something to say, she became irritated, reluctantly acknowledging my existence, before carrying on with her monologue as if I had not spoken. There was a "no entry" roadblock to anything I had to say.

I felt a similar difficulty in relation to my supervisor. I felt the need to take a "good" session to him, as if I didn't need supervision. I struggled to engage with process notes, as the last thing I wanted to do was have to recall these tortuous hours, where I felt I was failing spectacularly.

Over time, I did begin to link the deadening effects in the room with the patient's identification, not with a dead mother, but with a dying mother. In phantasy she incorporated this mother within her own body, causing her extreme physical pain and constant bleeding. An analyst at another institution, whom she had consulted prior to the start of therapy, commented that it seemed as if she were "pregnant with her dead mother". She was unable to lay her to rest, carrying the pain in her body rather than face the psychic pain of mourning. There was a disavowal of reality, which kept her entombed with her mother, in a deadly union.

There was also a particular way in which I was using my supervisor during this period, idealizing him, writing down every word that he said, almost projecting any early capability I had into him, to protect me from the anxiety of not knowing, unaware that that was a necessary state. This reminded me of how some inexperienced practitioners use a manualized form of treatment to simply regurgitate the "correct" interpretation from the pages of a book, rather than risk being alert to what is engendered in the session. On reflection, it mirrored my experience of nurse training, which Menzies Lyth (1960) described, where task orientation rather than patient-centred care was considered to protect trainees from overwhelming anxiety. If the tasks and the patients were broken down into "part objects"—that is, say, the amputation in bed 5—rather than being taken in as whole objects, then anxiety could be spared. Equally, until I was able to build up an internal setting for analytic work, I had my own defences to protect me from experiencing anxiety, my own and the patient's.

An early dream

About six months into treatment the patient brought a dream, which, I felt, shone a light on her internal situation and the nature of her internal objects. It marked a turning point, as there began to be the possibility of a different kind of communication between us. This followed many months of my supervisor reading the internal world of the patient in ways that eluded but fascinated me, and taught me a new language of unconscious phantasy. It enabled me to have a different engagement with the patient and a lessening of anxiety and sterility.

In the dream:

She was in a big, old, frightening house. There was a serial killer on the loose and she had to escape with some children. She wasn't sure who the children were, and they kept changing: one minute a little brother, the next minute it would be her cousin when he was 10 years old. She was so anxious because there was the chance of being caught, and there were dismembered bodies all over the house, stuffed in the cupboards and under the floorboards.

There was an old woman in the house who was seemingly nice, but she was the mother of the serial killer. So, although the woman seemed helpful, she couldn't be trusted.

There was also another person who was helping her, perhaps her best friend. She was trying to get the children out through an open window, but, once outside, she was not sure who was a friend and who was a killer. They made their way to a road and flagged down a car. Just when they thought they were safe, she realized that she was being driven back to the house. At this point, she awoke in a sweat.

I understood the house in this dream to be an unconscious representation of the inside of her body, and the terrible state it is in: bleeding, robbed of its contents. Klein (1946) describes the infant's anxieties around phantasized attacks on mother's body, entering her and robbing her of potential babies, emptying her out. In the case of my patient, primitive paranoid-schizoid anxieties are mirrored in external reality by her mother's premature death from ovarian cancer. In identification with her mother, she also experiences chronic pain, heavy bleeding, and infertility. She defends against these terrifying anxieties by splitting, projection, and clinging to a phantasized ideal object.

In this dream there is distrust in the woman who seems to be helpful but can't be trusted. This seems connected to the transference anxiety about what kind of object I am: ostensibly helpful, but with the potential to turn bad and abandon her in a dangerous place.

The patient responded to my interpretation in a different way. Usually, she would appropriate my interpretations, feeding them back to me as if they had been hers all along. This time she hesitated, seemed thoughtful, and remained quiet. I felt that it was one of the first times that she had been able to consider my thoughts from a place that was not merged with me. She could experience me separately, as someone who had something to offer her.

At the same time, I felt my supervisions change qualitatively, with me feeling less anxious, more able to engage. I was able to take in something from supervision in a new way, moving more to introjection rather than simply incorporating my supervisor's comments. Steiner (2011b) comments that supervision enables the trainee to become aware of their propensity to succumb to projections and, thereby, to be freer and more receptive to underlying unconscious communications.

The middle phase

Although missed sessions were a feature from the start, usually due to the pain or over-sleeping, these increased as we approached the first summer break. As in childhood, she found herself financially and emotionally depleted, without money to top up her electricity.

She attended a July session, having missed two sessions the week before, and not having left messages about her absences. She came into the room clutching her lower right pelvic region, indicating that she was in pain. She said that everything was messed up, that she had no energy and was wiped out. She explained that she managed to get to the dentist, but was so exhausted on her return, she fell into a deep sleep for best part of 24 hours.

P: I've been like this now for about three years, and I am just really worried that my life is passing me by, time is just going and I'm letting it. It's since I gave up work, and the main problem is that I don't have any work to go to, so there doesn't seem to be anything to structure my time. I'm on the bus, and I see people in the street with partners and with children, and I've got no one to go to, I've got nobody, it's just really depressing. *Tears were falling down the sides of her face, and she was wiping her eyes with both hands.*

T: What about the work here? You do have work to do, and you also have somewhere to go. You have here, and you also do have someone: you have me. But it's so easy to wipe out everything that you do have, to feel that you are alone with no one, and retreat to your bed.

P: Yes, I know I do, and I get so angry with myself, because I don't want to do this, but it's just so hard to feel anything since I've been on the higher dose of antidepressants. I don't feel I can access the feelings that I need to. I feel as though I just come here and talk and feel like I'm talking about someone else. If I don't cry, then I feel that I haven't got to anything, and I leave feeling really angry with myself.

T: It isn't my experience that you are unable to access your feelings. You have been feeling very angry in the last few sessions. I wonder whether going to the dentist alerted us to something biting, and maybe your anger with me contributed to not coming to the sessions last week. After all, I recently gave you the dates for my break, which highlights my looking after myself, possibly off with a partner and children, leaving you feeling more alone.

P: I'm not aware of that, only of financial problems, pain, and exhaustion.

T: We have to wonder, because it hasn't been like this until now, with so many missed sessions.

P: No, and it makes me aware of what I'm wasting: wasting my life, wasting this, sometimes I think there just isn't enough time left, that there's no point. *She was crying more as she said this.*

T: It's easier to think that there isn't enough time to do what you need to do than think we do still have time to do something. The emptiness you describe is like the bank being depleted, you can't hold on to the resources that are here for you. The electricity has to be topped up, but there can be a tendency to prefer to remain in the dark, like those times

with your Mum, where you'd be in bed in the dark with no heating, telling each other stories; to not know about reality.
P: Yeah, that's right, we had nothing but we had each other, and that was all we needed.

The patient longed for a state where she would be immune from reality, and she attempted to achieve this by a state of blissful fusion with the object. The sequence above details the consequences when reality shatters the illusion. The presence of breaks was very difficult from the beginning. I think when I introduced a break, I became the mother who welcomes in the father, someone who threatens the perfect fusion of mother and child. In the transference the patient is terrified that she will be annihilated in my mind, where she feels herself to have a tenuous existence at best, and so she protects herself by retreating to her bed, thereby not having to know about the impending separation.

It was clear from the patient's history, and evident in the transference, that something catastrophic occurred in relation to this patient's oedipal situation. The intercourse between her parents, the real and imagined violence, and father's absence and infidelity interfered with her being enabled to give up the mother as her primary love object. Instead, there is a manic omnipotent phantasy where she becomes the desired, potent phallus, mother's defender, and the object of mother's desire. I think the breaks threatened this phantasy, leaving her feeling enraged, desperate, and suicidal. Britton (1989) describes how the hysterical solution entails the use of projective identification to become, in phantasy, one or other member of the primal couple.

She managed to wipe me out, in the missed sessions, pre-empting my wiping her out with my break. By merging with me in phantasy, she denied any dependency on me, as if we were of one mind, or one body. I would experience this in my countertransference: any evidence of me having a separate mind, or a thought different from hers, was not tolerated. Sometimes this would manifest itself in her stripping away the meaning from my words in quite a subtle way. In the session above, when I suggested that she actively prefers to remain in the dark, she responded as though I was concretely confirming that she and mother lived in poverty, rather than symbolically referring to her denial of psychic reality. During this phase of treatment, she oscillated between a position where she could allow me to be separate from her, with the beginnings of feelings of dependency on me, but there would be a sudden retreat back to a merged state.

During the second year, the pain clinic consultant decided to remove all her opiate medication. He had been impressed by the progress that she had made, increasing her activity, running pain management courses, and using her psychotherapy, that he considered opiates were no longer indicated. She was apoplectic.

At the next session, she told me:

> "I found myself getting flooded with more and more of this stuff coming back, and I started crying about it on the bus. I couldn't stop it. And I've had a flare-up of pain, because I've had breakthrough bleeding after the appointment on Thursday that hasn't stopped. I just don't know where it leaves me. I'm just aware that I've lost so much (*crying bitterly*). I'm so old, and fat with wrinkles. I've lost so much time. I realized I've lost myself, I'm not that person anymore, I've lost everything. I've lost so many friends because I never went out. I've lost time. I had still wanted to think about having a child, the chances of me having IVF are so much less now."

There was some evidence of the patient experiencing the beginnings of depressive anxiety. She still projected so much onto the pain consultant who had taken away her one hope of a magical cure, but there was also some evidence of depressive pain (Klein, 1940). This more integrated state represented her capacity to remember and appreciate the whole object, and enabled mourning and pining for the good object. She felt guilt and was exposed to a sense of having squandered the resources that she had. There followed a desire to make reparation and restore the destroyed object back to life.

During this time the patient also reported feeling sad. She described feeling "weird"—a totally different feeling coming over her that had taken her by surprise. Before she knew it, tears were running down her face. This reminded her of when she was 13 years old: she had kept a diary, and, looking back at it now, it was just full of "feeling low", "so depressed".

As the patient developed a capacity to mourn, there was a change in the nature of her internal objects. It was paradoxical that, as she gained the capacity to acknowledge the death of her mother in external reality, her internal mother became more alive and accessible to her. There was a movement from incorporation to introjection (McDougall, 1989). She no longer sounded mechanical or two-dimensional: her reminiscences had depth and moved me; there was an emotional resonance between us.

A dream

In this middle phase, she brought another dream:

> *Her mother and mother's sister were sitting and talking to one another. The patient was standing naked in front of them, but they just carried on talking and ignored the patient. She began screaming at her mother, "WHY WON'T YOU HELP ME?", but they continued to talk as if she wasn't there.*

This dream was pivotal in enabling the patient to get in touch with feelings of anger towards her mother. This was momentous, as she had previously not been able to countenance anything other than idealization. This had protected her from having to acknowledge her aggression, which had been split off and projected, leaving her ego diminished and her internal world impoverished.

Incorporation versus introjection

Failure to introject the object in infancy contributes to the incorporation of the object at the point of death. Introjection enhances the ego: it involves the taking in of the object, appropriating its qualities, desires, and slowly and gradually dispersing it within the ego, enhancing the psychic economy (Torok, 1994). This process was compromised for my patient, perhaps due to difficulties in the early environment. Instead, she relied on the incorporation of the object, which Torok describes as a "fantasmatic mechanism". This process constitutes an insurmountable obstacle to introjection. It is a magical process of appropriating the object and, in my patient's case, protected her from having to acknowledge the loss of the mother.

As she made advances in being able to bear psychic pain and engage with her internal reality, I realized that there was a simultaneous movement in my own development. My personal analysis also enabled me to look at the difficulties in my own internal world that contributed to my difficulties taking this patient in during the early phase. The relationship with my supervisor was significantly different; my process notes improved vastly, as I became keen to explore the week's developments in detail.

I believe that I also had to go through a painful process of mourning my own idealized therapeutic self. Having entered the training from a senior position in the NHS, it was difficult to face my junior status, lack of knowledge, and the vulnerability of learning a new technique. Allowing myself to be dependent on my supervisor, with a shattering of the illusion of precocious competence, I became able to meet my patient where she needed me to be, and we could struggle together with understanding. She felt more contained, just as I allowed myself to be held in supervision.

The ending phase

The ending of the treatment was difficult and painful for us both. It had been successful: the patient had reconnected with her father, who now lived in a different country. She had emerged from her retreat and was reconnected to friends and family alike. She had had an elective surgery to remove the adhesions in her abdominal cavity, which had stopped the bleeding. She had been discharged from the pain clinic on no medication. She told me that the pain consultant had been astounded, and she asserted that she thought she had been misdiagnosed with chronic pain.

She brought a photograph of her mother to the final session, to show me. Previously, she had not been able look at photos of her mother, as it had been too distressing. Recently she got out all her photographs and made a collage to hang on the wall in her flat. In the process she found a picture of herself as a child, in fancy dress as her favourite pop singer, a mixed-race young woman from a popular teen band. She proudly showed me this, saying "Look it's black . . . " (inserting her own name). I found it quite endearing: not an attempt to become me but to introject me, her black therapist—to take me with her internally.

Conclusion

This clinical example demonstrates a parallel process, whereby the movement in the intra-psychic world of the patient occurred simultaneously with my own development, moving from a psychoanalytic beginner to a competent practitioner. Fundamental to this entire process was the "holding" of the trainee by an expert, my supervisor, resulting in a containing environment for the patient, which facilitated her developing capacity to move from a concrete, dissociated state, where her pain and suffering was held directly in her body, through a process of working-through, which enabled her to bear her suffering and to mourn the death of her mother. I argue that I also had to face my own disillusionment, evident at the beginning of the treatment, facing my own inadequacies, acknowledging my limitations, and engaging with the painful reality of my dependence on my supervisor, to mourn the loss of the primitive omnipotence that I came into the training with. I demonstrate this phenomenon using the clinical and supervisory material that I collated throughout the M1 training.

CHAPTER SIXTEEN

On being guided by the countertransference

Carolyn Walker

A careful exploration of the therapist's countertransference serves as a valuable guide to a deeper understanding of her patient, facilitating the development of the therapist's analytic capacity. This fact came to life for me through my work with Ms B, who relied heavily on projective identification to rid herself of unbearable anxieties, as well as to attack and control her object. Tracking my countertransference over the course of her two-year, three-times-weekly psychotherapy, I highlight the significant shifts over three distinct phases of the treatment, to show how my unsettling and sometimes disturbing countertransference enabled me to find my bearings when I became disorientated. It also helped me gain a deeper understanding of the parts of the patient that she herself found unbearable. Ultimately, this approach facilitated Ms B's emerging capacity to face the reality of what belonged to her object and what to herself. Through experiencing separateness and mourning her loss, she could begin the process of taking back her projections and re-acquiring lost parts of herself.

> *Helping an anxious patient regain lost parts of the self through use of the therapist's countertransference: Ms B*

Ms B was referred for help with severe and chronic anxiety, rooted in the trauma of early emotional neglect, which had compromised her ability to work and sustain satisfying relationships. As a child she had experienced harshness and cruelty from her parents. Serious illness within the family had obliged her to take on a carer's role, to the detriment of her own opportunities for development. She recalled bitterly that no one seemed to have noticed or had stepped in to offer help. Despite having benefitted from a good education and being highly qualified in her chosen profession, at the time of referral she was struggling in a job she hated—one that she felt was beneath her capabilities. She craved emotional intimacy, but she was terrified of becoming trapped within a relationship. She was also anxious about the destructive force of her aggressive impulses.

The early months of treatment: the therapist feels useless

From the very first contact with Ms B, I felt a pressure to respond to her demands, rather than have space to think about my new patient. She insisted I should tell her about my qualifications and experience, adding that it was important that her intellectual abilities were appreciated by those seeking to understand her. In early sessions I felt bombarded by detailed accounts of her busy life. She would describe her work to me in a manner that conveyed a sense of her being the expert, with me a student in need of tuition. She complained that she had to do everything herself, let down by slow-witted colleagues, incompetent authority figures, and dysfunctional relatives. I felt required to listen, not to interrupt, nor offer any thoughts of my own. When I did venture an interpretation, I noticed more than once that Ms B would answer "exactly". This did not convey a feeling of being understood, but that she already knew what I was trying to say. I felt put down, the implication being that I was too slow to keep up with her sharp intellect.

What I found particularly disconcerting was that Ms B seemed to know where my own areas of sensitivity lay. She would quote from the classics and ask if I was familiar with the texts, acknowledging that not everyone was as well read as she. Indeed, I was not, and I found myself in the uncomfortable position of being unfamiliar with many of the literary references that peppered her material. I found it difficult to remain engaged, struggling with unsettling feelings of inexperience and incompetence. This was perhaps exacerbated by the fact that, despite being a qualified clinician with many years of experience when I embarked on further psychoanalytic training, my work with Ms B was undertaken in the role of trainee therapist. Ms B was not informed that I was in training, but she nevertheless seemed to sense a valency in me for feelings of inadequacy that she could not tolerate within herself.

During these early months I found it difficult to tolerate the intensity of Ms B's projections, to make sense of my disorienting countertransference, and to distinguish what belonged to me and what to her. Supervision helped me to understand that unconsciously I wanted to evade the disturbing feelings being pushed into me so powerfully by Ms B. She, in turn, needed her grandiosity and intellectualization to prevent me and others from disturbing her psychic equilibrium. Her reliance on projective identification was necessary to defend herself against overwhelming anxieties, and she subtly managed to induce in me those feelings that she was desperate to escape from within herself. I realized that, rather than tackling the here-and-now transference head on, I was tending to keep to safe "textbook" interpretations, in a futile attempt to avoid further derision. Only gradually did I begin to appreciate how this challenging process was allowing me to gain a deeper understanding of the parts of my patient that she could not bear to know about herself.

The middle period of treatment: the therapist feels sceptical

Several months into her treatment, Ms B returned from a break in a less grandiose state of mind. I no longer felt flooded with intellectualized references and lengthy monologues. Often arriving late, her attempts to convince me that she was busy with important work elsewhere lacked conviction. She acknowledged that her habit of turning her back on people left her isolated and alone. She no longer dismissed my transference interpretations about her claustrophobic anxieties, and she seemed more ready to face the reality of her predicament. She began to bring detailed and complex dreams for us to work on together. I felt greatly relieved that she was allowing some genuine contact to take place between us and to let me glimpse, through the dream material, her terror of breaking down irreparably.

This sense of therapeutic progress, although gratifying for both therapist and patient, was relatively short-lived. Tuning back into my countertransference, I became aware of a niggling doubt, which supervision helped me recognize and explore. In Ms B's dreams there began to emerge several figures who were, in some way, manipulative or not to be trusted. A common theme was of something being obscured or hidden below the surface. Things were not what they seemed. Analysis of the dream material provided support for my doubts, and I began to feel sceptical about the apparently rapid improvement in Ms B's personal life. Rather than an indication of genuine psychic development, this could be understood as a flight into health, the offering of false contact as a manifestation of her unconscious resistance to progress. Although Ms B was becoming aware that she had something of value in her relationships, what was emerging was a perverse need to attack and spoil the goodness of these relationships. She would tell me, for example, that she had agreed to help a friend with a difficult task, but then made an excuse to pull out at the last moment. In her sessions she would listen attentively to my interpretations, but would then move away to speak about something else entirely, denying any awareness of the work we had been doing together.

I realized that I felt unable to trust the authenticity of the contact between us. I would occasionally hear of small steps forward in her relationships, but this would trigger claustrophobic anxieties, and she would withdraw to a familiar position of hostility and grievance. Any glimpse of the neglected and vulnerable little girl whose crippling anxiety so disabled her daily functioning was hastily covered over and denied. As she became more aware of me as a separate person, her agoraphobic–claustrophobic dilemma emerged more clearly. She panicked if she allowed herself to venture too far into the therapeutic relationship and to experience genuine emotional contact between us. On the other hand, she was afraid of being isolated and stranded with her anxiety during the gaps between sessions. Terrified of becoming trapped in a claustrophobic relationship with me in her mind, Ms B became increasingly difficult to reach and withdrew into a narcissistic retreat. This served as an idealized safe haven to protect her from intolerable paranoid-schizoid anxieties of fragmentation and persecution. The reality of emotional contact with me and with the outside world had become too much for her to bear.

The final months of treatment: the therapist feels in genuine contact

As the end of the treatment drew near, I began to observe tentative signs of Ms B venturing out of her retreat and risking emotional contact. She described feeling more settled at home and at work. Her emerging curiosity about her objects became evident in the transference as she began to wonder why I did this job and whether I might have children. She admitted to thinking about me between sessions and wondered if I ever thought about her. In a moving session she spoke of her regret that she had behaved in a cruel way to someone she cared about, damaging the trust between them. I felt impressed by Ms B's courage in facing up to this painful realization. She added that she felt ashamed to tell me about this incident and feared I would think less of her, that our relationship would be damaged too. The mood was sad and poignant, and the contact between us felt genuine.

I was becoming aware of a significant shift in my countertransference to a more benign, maternal response. I felt moved by Ms B's preparedness to grapple with painful, frightening feelings that left her exposed and vulnerable. Rushing in very late one day, she was anxious to check that I had received her phone message about being held up at work. Tearfully, she told me how grateful she was that I had waited for her. At such moments Ms B was able to identify with the little girl part of her who could rush towards me as a loving maternal object, appreciating the security and warmth of the relationship developing between us. Inevitably, she was very stirred up by her awareness of this longing within herself; the next session she arrived late, in no apparent hurry. Emotionally unreachable, it was clear that she had let me get too close, then panicked and pulled away again. She continued to struggle with her contempt for the needy and vulnerable part of herself, and there were further attempts to attack the bond between us. However, by this point the quality of the emotional contact between us had deepened, so that it was often possible to reflect on what was happening and re-establish an authentic connection.

During this final phase I felt relieved of the powerful projections that Ms B had previously needed to locate in me. As she began to face the painful reality of the separateness between us, she expressed regret that she had wasted so much time in the earlier months of her therapy. She was angry that I would be leaving her, but alongside an increased capacity to know about her hostility there also came a wish to express her gratitude. We recognized that she was developing her own capacity to look deep inside herself, to recognize her ambivalence, and hold onto her awareness that she could feel both love and hate towards those who mattered most to her. In a moving final session, she told me that she felt something genuine had happened between us, and she hoped I would remember her. I was glad that Ms B had managed to make use of her treatment before it was too late, and I realized that I would genuinely miss my patient. I shared her sadness that the psychotherapy had to end when there was still much work to be done. I also felt gratitude for the rich learning opportunity I had gained through her treatment and the supervision process.

Discussion

Ms B came into psychotherapy seeking a reduction in the severity of her crippling anxiety. Although she did achieve some symptomatic improvement, a more meaningful measure of her progress can be understood in terms of her increased capacity for emotional intimacy. Most significantly, she came to understand the importance of her relationship with her therapist and its development over time as a crucial factor in her progress. When she started treatment, Ms B was heavily reliant on the unconscious defence mechanism of projective identification. This served both as an effective means of disowning unbearable parts of herself and as a powerful way to attack and control her object. It also functioned as a primitive form of communication between us. With the help of my supervisor, I realized that by sensitively tuning in to my countertransference I could use it as a guide to understand and navigate those unbearable states of mind that my patient could not tolerate within herself.

John Steiner describes how developments in analytic understanding following Melanie Klein's discovery of schizoid mechanisms and, particularly, projective identification (Klein, 1946) led to an important extension of the fundamental aim of psychoanalytic treatment:

> We now recognize that projective identification has a powerful effect on the object used to project into, so that it is clearly more than just a phantasy on the part of the patient ... and the patient may make us depressed, angry, excited or sleepy by subtly engaging with those aspects of our personality which are prone to those feelings. [Steiner, 1989, p. 113]

The patient's unwanted parts are split off into the object/analyst, who is affected and altered by the force of the primitive mechanism and experiences the projected affects as his or her own. This leads to a lack of separateness between self and object, and confusion as to what belongs to whom. The classical aim can be understood as helping the patient to find more constructive ways of managing unconscious conflicts between the demands of the id, the superego, and external reality (Freud, 1933a [1932]). According to Steiner, the new aim of psychoanalysis becomes "to help the patient find an integration and re-acquire parts of himself which were previously lost through projective identification" (p. 115). The focus of analytic technique is on the analyst's awareness of what is being projected into him, so that he is "less likely to act out rather than to understand and interpret".

Brenman Pick (1985) emphasizes that at an unconscious level the analyst will not wish to be aware of the powerful feelings pushed into them by patients who use primitive projective mechanisms. Acknowledging Strachey's description of a full transference interpretation as something that the analyst most fears and most wishes to avoid (Strachey, 1934), Brenman Pick highlights the analyst's difficulty in "walking the tightrope" between experiencing such disturbance and needing to respond with a calmly delivered interpretation. She suggests that the analyst must work through the experience of both wanting to know and fearing to know about the "internal buffetings" stirred up by strong countertransference experiences and must avoid the temptation to act out. As a therapist in training, I benefitted from the containment of regular supervision sessions that allowed me to explore the disturbing "internal buffetings" stirred up in me by the impact of my patient's often very forceful projections. While Brenman Pick points to the analyst's need to avoid the temptation to act out, Carpy (1989) argues that some partial acting out is inevitable—for example, in the words used, tone of voice, and so on. He proposes that the patient's observation of this inevitable acting out in the countertransference is valuable, as it allows the patient to see over time how the analyst is affected by his projections and learns to tolerate and deal with his feelings. In this way the patient is helped to gradually re-introject the parts that were projected, along with a capacity to tolerate them. In Carpy's view it is only at this point that interpretation is helpful and links can be made. Interpretations made too soon, before the patient can tolerate any awareness of the projected parts, are "worse than useless" and can leave the patient feeling frightened that projections are being forced back into them.

The understanding of the phenomenon of countertransference has been much developed since Freud's (1910d) original conception as the analyst's unconscious resistance. Heimann (1950) suggested that countertransference was one of the analyst's most important tools, "an instrument of research into the patient's unconscious". She encouraged the analyst to pay close attention to her immediate emotional response to her patient, which was often more accurate than reason in helping select the most significant interpretation from the material. Heimann pointed out that trainee analysts who stifled their feelings, through ignorance or fear, made poor interpretations. My early "textbook" interpretations were safe but ineffective and left me at an emotional distance from my patient. When I did connect to the intensity of my immediate emotional response to my patient, I found it disturbing.

Winnicott (1949) introduced the view that hate in the countertransference is inevitable, as is the mother's hate towards her baby. He suggested that analysis would become impossible unless the analyst was conscious of and understood his hate towards his patients. He wrote: "However much he loves his patients, he cannot avoid hating them, and fearing them, and the better he knows this the less will hate and fear be the motive determining what he does to his patients" (p. 69). For the trainee therapist, feelings of hate and fear towards their patient can be disturbing and difficult to tolerate.

I found it difficult to tolerate periods of not understanding what was going on between myself and my patient. Money-Kyrle (1956) described "periods of non-understanding" as deviations from the normal countertransference experience. He argued that these would inevitably occur when the analyst failed to understand something about the patient, having not yet understood it in himself. In other words, "the patient has come too close", and the therapist "loses the thread". In hindsight, as a trainee I was more susceptible to receiving Ms B's projected feelings of inadequacy and ignorance. This was exacerbated by my lack of knowledge in an area where she had gained expertise. As Carpy (1989) points out, in thinking about projective identification, it would be a mistake to think we are feeling the patient's feelings that they have projected into us. In fact, the patient has been able to induce in the therapist a state of mind very similar to one she is trying to eliminate in herself. When there is a good "fit" between patient and therapist, as there was between Ms B and me, this process can be particularly successful from the patient's point of view. She could then attack me for what was perceived by us both, for a time, as my inadequacy as her therapist.

Pearl King (1978) suggests that the common concern of analytic candidates—that they have made a technical mistake or missed an important clue—may not always be correct. The patient may, in fact, need the analyst to be "a parent who was not able to tune accurately into his feelings, who was continually concerned with his or her sense of failure or inability to cope" (p. 331). King acknowledges that it can feel particularly difficult to be drawn into a role that is not ego-syntonic but suggests that one may be being forced into such roles by the analytic process. She describes how patients like Ms B, who suffered early parental failure, may have been used by their parents unconsciously as an extension of themselves and as a receptacle for unwanted projected parts. In this way, Ms B needed to treat me, unconsciously, as she herself had been treated, identifying with the aggressor–parent and projecting her infantile feelings into me.

The second phase of Ms B's treatment began with a significant shift in my countertransference. I felt less persecuted and more confident in offering meaningful interpretations that she seemed able to take in and make use of. It appeared that the work was progressing well which was gratifying. But my countertransference was guiding me towards less comfortable feelings. Brenman (2006) warns the analyst to be aware of potential narcissistic indulgence, which can lead either to narcissistic fusion or omnipotent detachment. There was an element of narcissistic fusion in the satisfaction I shared with Ms B about her apparently rapid improvement. Brenman suggests that what is most challenging is when the analyst is made to feel meaningless. In retrospect, my eagerness to escape feeling meaningless to Ms B fuelled my readiness to believe that her progress was authentic.

My scepticism and mistrust in the countertransference helped me to recognize that something was not right, that below the surface the apparent progress being made was being subtly attacked and denigrated. Steiner (1989, 1993) describes how the denial of dependency on the object and then of its loss can serve as a protection against envy. Resistance comes into operation, often in the form of a misrepresentation or perversion of reality. He emphasizes the original meaning of perversion as the turning away from what is good and true, and suggests that this twisting of the truth becomes the central obstacle to progress in analysis. I realized that my patient, Ms B, had withdrawn into a psychic retreat. I was subtly invited to join her defensive organization, in a narcissistic object relationship that denied any awareness of me as a separate person who could threaten to disturb her equilibrium. During this phase I provided containment for the projected parts of Ms B's personality that she could not tolerate, particularly her aggression. Careful monitoring of my countertransference and her dream material helped me to gauge her state of mind and keep a watch for any sign that she might be emerging from the retreat. Gradually, through the experience of containment, I think she began to feel understood by her object.

The third treatment phase brought the final shift in my countertransference. I registered a benign maternal concern for Ms B and began to feel that the emotional contact between us could be trusted. I was often moved by the poignancy of our exchanges, in which she grappled with a growing awareness of her vulnerability, fear, and guilt. As she became less reliant on projective identification and on narcissistic or perverse defences, Ms B was able to face the reality of her dependence on me. She became curious about her object and began to tolerate some awareness of the separateness between us. Only through acknowledging the loss of the object and working through the necessary mourning could she start to take back her projections and reintegrate lost parts of herself back into her personality.

Afterthoughts

The process of revisiting this material, many years after it was originally written, has led me to reflect on what it means to develop a secure identify as a psychoanalytic psychotherapist. As Parsons (2006) points out, the analyst has a countertransference not just to the patient, but to the process of psychoanalysis itself. Her work requires her to know about the conflicts and anxieties within her unconscious mind, which consciously she would prefer not to disturb her. Parsons suggests that it is the quality of the analyst's engagement with her countertransference, her "deep inner attitude", that will determine the quality of her engagement with her patient. During my training I found the process of engaging with, and being guided by, my countertransference deeply unsettling at times. However, it was central to the development of the clinical work with Ms B. Beyond this, it has enabled me to develop my identity and capacity to practice as a psychoanalytic psychotherapist.

Note

The original version of this chapter, written many years ago, has been modified for the purposes of contributing to this book at the invitation of the editors.

PART IV

LEARNING THROUGH CLINICAL CHALLENGES

Helen Barker

Part IV brings together six distinct contributions, which we group together under the heading of "Learning through Clinical Challenges." Even under ordinary circumstances, all treatments will bring challenges, dilemmas, and, at times, a sense of painful struggle for patient and therapist alike. It is part of our everyday work to face difficulties. Sometimes these can be worked through and result in a sense of achievement and progress. At other times, there is an impasse or breakdown.

These six chapters, in very different ways, share a common theme of interruption or breakdown and examine what can be learned and understood from the experience. The reader will have gathered by now that learning, and how one learns to become a psychotherapist, is the main theme of this book. The trainees' accounts thus far show that this can be a complicated, disturbing process, even at the best of times. We are now turning our attention to more difficult circumstances, including illness, death, and suicide. In these extreme situations, the trainee will be faced with their own feelings, including grief, shock, guilt, and shame. It is hard to hold onto an analytic attitude in which these feelings can be fully experienced, while also being thought about. It is at these times we need all the help available to us to be open to learning, rather than to foreclose the situation through, for example, denial or the wish to apportion blame. Guilt is a particularly aversive emotion to bear, one that stimulates the strongest defensive responses in us. However, if this can be worked through, there is the opportunity for potent learning to take place.

Louise Barnard (chapter 17) describes working with a patient over a period of ten months, during which time the patient is diagnosed with a recurrence of cancer, becomes ill, and dies. Thanks to the arrangements for remote working during the pandemic, this therapy can continue by phone, whereas, prior to the pandemic, the treatment may have come to an end once the patient could no longer attend in person. This results in some significant challenges to the setting, with sessions taking place in unusual situations: a hospital bed, an ambulance. The task for the therapist is to maintain an internal analytic setting, which she is able to do with the help of her supervisor. In this way the therapist accompanies the patient through the process of dying, which both must learn to face. There is movement from an initial manic denial towards an acceptance of reality—a substantial achievement.

Susan Baldock (chapter 18) also faces the death of her patient, this time through suicide, just at the start of a new therapy. The patient, after a long engagement with the Tavistock, had been offered the chance to have an intensive therapy. The hope of this new treatment was countered by a deadly hopelessness, which rapidly emerged over the first weeks of therapy. As in chapter 17, the therapist here is faced with a shocking and disturbing event, no longer in the realm of intellectual theory but a jolting, alive experience that she, and the wider organization, is required to make sense of. Susan describes the aftermath of her patient's suicide vividly, recognizing the complexities of the psychic task in which guilt, shame, and blame have to be processed at an individual and institutional level. Susan makes some important points about the difficulties she encountered at an organizational level and within the training in supporting her in the aftermath of her patient's suicide. This has shown us how we, as the trainers, must also remain open and receptive to learning.

Every therapist will encounter patients who are ill or suicidal, but most will not experience sudden deaths in the way described here. These statistically rare examples do, however, powerfully illustrate the universal fact that, whatever our level of skill, training, or experience, we have no way of predicting or controlling what will emerge during the course of therapy or during the course of life itself.

Next, Avgoustina Almyroudi (chapter 19) describes the impact of the therapist's pregnancy on the therapy. This is an ordinary event in the life of a woman and yet is quite extraordinary in being one of the few occasions in which the patient is confronted with the bodily reality of the therapist's life and external relationships. Potentially, this will have a disruptive impact and presents the therapy with a crisis. The therapist is faced with both a clinical challenge and a personal one, torn between her wish to look after her patient, her baby, and herself. In this example, the therapy is able to continue, and, moreover, the patient has the capacity to allow herself to be helped with the primitive anxieties provoked by the situation.

We continue this part with a clinical situation that is likely to be much more familiar to all therapists: the patient who ends a treatment prematurely. Devayani Shevade (chapter 20) describes her experience with her patient who drops out halfway through the therapy. Despite a conscious wish to benefit from therapy and a period of progress, the patient becomes increasingly silent and unavailable. The writer links this to an unplanned break in the therapy due to illness and thoughtfully explores the impact of this on her patient. Although the therapist works carefully and sensitively, this rupture cannot be repaired, and the patient ends the treatment. Devayani eloquently conveys the internal difficulties faced by the patient and shows us how his decision to end the therapy reflects habitual defensive structures that protect his mind from a psychotic breakdown.

The Covid-19 pandemic interrupted the world from the years 2020–2022, presenting each one of us with a sudden disruption to our personal and professional lives. For therapist and patient alike, there was an unexpected, abrupt transition from meeting in person to remote working. Almost overnight, we were forced to make adjustments that, days previously, would have seemed impossible. Although this is a book that is focussed on the generalities of psychoanalytic training, it seems important to recognize the specific time during which we started this project. In inviting our contributors to write about their experience of training, naturally enough the impact of the pandemic features as a significant event that has shaped their experience.

Alan Baban (chapter 21) writes a vivid and personal account of working during the pandemic. In particular, he focuses on his relationship with the Tavistock building itself: the Brick Mother which, under usual circumstances, provides the concrete container for the psychic containment of therapeutic work taking place inside. During the pandemic, the Brick Mother turns into the Ghost Ship, allowing the remaining inhabitants to recognize what has been lost: the value of all those informal human interactions in the coffee queue and the corridor. In ordinary times, these are invisible and taken for granted, and it is only when they are absent that their value can be recognized.

Denise Hurst Hastings (chapter 22) also writes about her experience of the pandemic, concentrating on the experience of starting her training and starting work with her first training patient remotely. Although so many treatments have now been carried out online and on the phone,

Denise writes about the particular difficulties faced by her patient, for whom the lack of physical presence promoted a psychotic transference.

These chapters are wide-ranging in their subject matter, but each one show us the value of remaining open and receptive to the unfolding events and, with the help of our supervisors, colleagues, and analysts, the possibilities of expanding our capacities for understanding and bearing what can seem, at times, like unbearable states of mind.

CHAPTER SEVENTEEN

A death during the pandemic

Louise Barnard

I started seeing Ms E, my first intensive patient, in October 2019.

Clinical example: Ms E

Ms E was a mixed-race woman of 45, a single mother to a girl of 11 and a boy of 8. She had divorced the father of her children five years earlier and was, at the time, in a three-year relationship with B. She told me that she had a difficult relationship with her mother, who was a fervent Christian. Ms E described her mother as being on top of everything but who had no space in her mind for Ms E, her needs or her feelings. Ms E felt she could never be angry with her mother, because it could not be tolerated. Ms E's father was from Africa, a charismatic man but also violent and an alcoholic. Her mother fled the family home, while pregnant, when Ms E was 4. Ms E experienced her father as unreliable and abandoning. She recounted childhood memories of being left alone in charge of her brother, not knowing whether her father would return. She was only reconciled with her father about two years earlier, when she helped take care of him as he was dying of cancer.

By the age of 16, Ms E was drinking too much alcohol and taking drugs. To deal with these issues, she joined Alcoholics Anonymous (AA), and she felt very contained, and then constrained, by the Christian ethic of the twelve steps. She stopped taking drugs and, for the most part, drinking.

While at AA, she met her future husband, who later became a substance misuse counsellor. However, he relapsed, and she came to realize that he had serious mental health issues. She described him as being very controlling. There was domestic violence, as well as his own violence towards himself. They divorced, and she described her great anxiety about his access to the children. He wanted to take back care of his children but, in her opinion, he was totally unsuitable as a parent.

On reading the referral, it seems that no one—not the intake meeting, not the assessor, nor I, nor my supervisor—took up the fact that Ms E had completed treatment for bowel cancer just six months earlier. The defence of denial appeared to have worked very powerfully on us all. She had written on her assessment form that she had had part of her bowel removed, had chemo and radiotherapy, but no one then asked about her prognosis. While she was on the waiting list for therapy, she also applied for an NHS psychotherapy training, for which she was accepted. She started the training simultaneously with her therapy. This was a very unusual circumstance, but perhaps speaks to her desperation to get herself into some NHS institutional mental health space.

At the start of therapy, there was a continual movement back and forth: the struggle of Ms E having to know about her want and need of the therapy, followed by her criticism of me, destroying any contact that had been made. While she initially tried to make a good impression on me, it soon came to feel like a battle in the room. She spoke often of her enraged feelings about imperialism and colonialism. It seemed she felt she had to educate me, as a privileged, white, middle-class woman who had no experience of suffering and struggle. At the same time, my sense was of her unconscious wish to defend against me as a white woman who would colonize her mind with my thoughts, as she perhaps felt her mother had done.

Ms E made it clear that she hated my consulting room, the uncomfortable couch/bed she was asked to lie on, the dreadful ceiling and overhead bright lights, which hurt her eyes. She mocked the picture on the wall and then had the thought I might have painted it. Her denigration of me, as the maternal object and what I could provide, was thorough. One session on a Monday at the beginning of February, Ms E started by saying: "I'm fucking angry with you today, I hate this therapy, I hate you. I'm only meant to feel your absence at the weekends and on the break. I hate this place, I hate this room, and I hate you, and I hate the Tavistock." I could understand how painful it was, as she was becoming more aware of her position of need, but I also did feel I had my hands full in trying to contain this mercurial, sometimes hostile, intelligent and talented woman, who was, at the same time, like a lonely child in a great deal of psychic pain.

Although I provided a regular space, and Ms E attended all sessions, I sensed that I was just another untrustworthy, intrusive, controlling object. There were, however, two turning points that somewhat altered our initial relationship. The first was an incident over my failing, in her opinion, to prepare her for a meeting with her ex-husband and a court official. Her fury with me resulted in her getting up from the couch before the end of the session, shouting at me, telling me I was "full of shit", and leaving, slamming the door after herself. The following session she came warily into the room, immediately apologizing for how she had been. She let me know that she felt very angry with herself but was also very worried about how I might react, and that I might hate her. When she felt sufficiently certain that I was not going to retaliate, she was able to continue the session, whereas I felt overwhelmed with distress.

The second incident came a few weeks later. I felt we were being caught up in the politics of difference—the unconscious meanings could not and would not be addressed. It seemed that Ms E felt she needed to educate any white person in her reach about the colonization and enslavement of black populations and the suffering and injustice, which no white person could understand. However, it seemed suddenly to come into her mind that, while she didn't know very much about the Holocaust, she thought that Jews as a group may also have been made to suffer. In that moment, I felt that she was letting me know that, at some level, she recognized that I am Jewish, and that I might be able to join her in knowing what it might be like to be part of a persecuted group.

The early sessions were also filled with her feelings of insecurity with her partner B, her struggles to be a writer, her rage with her mother and her ex-husband. She spoke about her feelings about her children, whom she loved and was proud of and yet, at the same time, experienced as a drain on her resources, a curtailment of her freedom, and a chore to have to think about and with. She was always doubting what kind of a mother she could be to them, comparing herself unfavourably with other mothers at the school gates in terms of what she could provide while, at the same time, disparaging these mothers for their white middle-class attitudes.

At the end of March 2020, as we worked towards the Easter break, we had to stop meeting in person due to the Covid-19 pandemic and the lockdown. The sessions continued by phone. Ms E was very alarmed by a letter from the NHS saying that, as a recent cancer patient, she was at high risk and should shield: she didn't recognize herself as part of that more vulnerable population. On our last session before the break, she mentioned that she was having headaches and finding it increasingly difficult to look at lights. She told me she had spoken to her GP, who was reassuring.

As we returned from the break, she immediately told me that she had had new symptoms. This had led to a full body scan, which had revealed lesions on her brain and further lesions in her lung and spine. She told me she was to have chemotherapy, radiotherapy, and brain surgery very shortly and that she was already on steroids, which, I came to understand, made her sound upbeat to the point of mania. She was researching her prognosis and found that some treatments can hold the illness at bay for years and, in some cases, make the cancer disappear completely. I, on the other hand, felt a sense of shock, deep distress, and fear.

In our own ways we both wanted to run away from this terrible news. She pre-empted my enquiry about her fears by telling me that people were asking her, "Aren't you worried?" She declared she was not frightened and was determined to fight this illness by conventional and non-conventional means.

I enacted my own wish to escape. I arranged a meeting with my tutor, first, to tell him of this sudden development with my intensive patient and, second, to say that since Ms E would no longer be able to be an intensive analytic patient, I would like to be considered for a new patient. My own disappointment and anger ebbed and flowed: this work with a training patient was not what I had anticipated. I discussed these feelings many times with my analyst, again on the phone, due to the lockdown. I railed at my situation and at others, needing comfort and containment for the tsunami of turmoil and distress I was experiencing.

My supervision, also on the phone, remained a solid and containing space for an understanding of the projections that I was being asked to bear. As the work with Ms E continued, I found I was able to put aside my initial reaction to run away and discovered that there was much to be learnt from closely following my patient through the painful struggles of what turned out to be the last months of her life.

Ms E and I continued to meet three times a week. Due to Covid and the fact that we were meeting on the phone, we were able to be in contact with one another in the most extraordinary of spaces and moments in her life. The external frame of the therapy had changed beyond recognition, and I was aware that I had to work hard to maintain my internal setting, to provide a space for her and myself to work.

On one occasion I called her at her appointment time. This was on the day of her brain surgery. I was not expecting her to answer, as she had warned me that the operation and her appointment with me were to coincide. However, I called at her appointment time and was surprised when she answered. She was alone in her isolation room at the hospital, waiting for her pre-meds. It was lunch-time, she had been "nil by mouth" all morning, and, due to Covid restrictions, was completely on her own, with the exception of the occasional interruption from the nurse. Perhaps I could offer her some emotional feeding? She seemed incredibly upbeat, speaking again about being asked by family members if she was afraid and again telling me that she was not. Again, the question of her fear had been in my mind, but, on hearing her view of herself, I was aware I was to be the container for all the anxiety and fear about the coming operation. The following day, I called again at our usual time, again not expecting her to pick up the phone, but, again, she answered and was able to speak for the whole session, to my amazement and humility in the face of her courage and resilience.

The sessions proceeded for some weeks; Ms E still sounded upbeat on the phone, but, in talking about a friend who had "only five weeks to live", I felt that she was beginning to acknowledge what might lie ahead for her. Meanwhile, when I discussed these changes in my supervision, I could acknowledge my anxieties about how I might work with Ms E under these circumstances, and what was expected of me.

I had sent emails to my course lead, my tutor, and the head of my unit, explaining the situation, in the hope of something supportive. My patient was dying, but of cancer, during a Covid pandemic, when death anxieties were all around. It seemed to me that it was difficult to make a space in the minds of others for the idea that my patient's death was a possibility. Ms E was not recuperating well after surgery and the treatments. She did not seem to get much respite, and this was a relentless disease. I felt I could not convey the seriousness of the situation to my team.

I spoke to Ms E at her appointment times, as often as she was able, in various locations, none of which could be described as contained or safe. While at home, there were interruptions from her partner, who had moved in to help look after her and the children. There were phone calls from her mother or nurses, or the children wandered into her bedroom, wanting something from their mother. She spoke from the back of an ambulance on the way to a treatment, from the hospital while waiting for radiotherapy, surrounded by screens and the noises of a busy ward. Several times she picked up my calls from a hospice bed, where she has been sent for respite care. The journeys to and from the hospital and hospice were all taken alone, due to the pandemic, which also meant she could not have visitors while there, another cruel deprivation. I believe that I became a dependable voice that she came to rely on.

On some days it was physically difficult to hear what Ms E was saying, as she was lying in bed, exhausted from her treatments, her voice muffled by pillows. I was witness to the sounds of her retching, coughing, and being sick, the painful struggle to the commode in her room and back to her bed. As time went on, she often did not pick up the phone on a

Monday, which was reminiscent of her feeling that the room at the Tavistock was cold on a Monday. As before, any emotional warmth had dissipated over the weekend. I always left a message and rang back a second time, just in case she couldn't quite get to the phone in time. However, these missed sessions filled me with anxiety and dread, asking myself "What has happened now?" Sometimes she was just too tired to speak, but often there had been a problem requiring urgent medical attention. At times, in the moments when she was too tired to speak, I felt I became an intrusive and demanding object. However, it seemed to me that just the experience of my phone calls and messages, denoting that I was keeping her in mind, seemed to be taken in as evidence of a more concerned and caring object, who could bear what she was going through.

Toward the end of May she told me that she missed the Tavistock, the course, and even the room where we met. As she finished the steroids, she became more depressed and also more tired; she fell asleep in sessions, and there was some sense in me that she felt comforted having me "alongside her" while she rested. However, the fluctuation in her affect returned: the needing and missing her mother and myself was followed by feeling that it was pointless and unbearable to grieve. In that state of mind, the only way forward was to "crack on" and be like her friend, who also had a terminal diagnosis and did not want to know how long she had to live. Immediately, having told me this, she was sobbing: she didn't want to leave her children. Her helplessness was unbearable. In turn, I felt impotent and guilty. I was very aware of the feeling that I was going forward in my life, while she was facing death. She was able to express her envy and hatred of me as someone who is in life, not about to die.

As she started chemotherapy, she became very weak, exhausted; she struggled to accept this more vulnerable side of herself. There was a conflict over the wish to look after her children and the need to be looked after herself.

It became clear that there would be no period of recovery and remission, and in June Ms E was given the news that she had six months to live—maybe more, maybe less. She was moved from the hospital to the hospice, from where she told me she felt well looked after, that they knew about death, and that she needed to mourn. She spoke about not knowing what to do with her anger and asked how she was to deal with the pain of mourning? These questions left me feeling quite helpless myself and filled with a not-knowing how to help her with what was to come. However, in the days after, Ms E described having witnessed the death of someone on her ward: it was peaceful, she heard the machines, she saw the nurse crying. She then took a picture of the sunrise from the ward window, and it gave her comfort: someone dies, people grieve, but the world still turns and doesn't break, "a massive moment", she felt. She later commented that the hospice is near the Tavistock, and I interpreted that perhaps she felt near to me and felt that she had a space in my mind. She told me she had come to feel that she has had a parent, and that she is able to be herself with her children, that it didn't matter if she got it wrong, but that they needed the truth. She spoke of her regret about her lack of capacity to mother her children, but that she had done her best: speaking to me of depressive anxieties at having to face this terrible loss.

These intimate moments of contact slipped away again, and were replaced with frightening thoughts of pain management and palliative care. Since April, I had felt that I had been walking a tightrope of hoping to maintain contact with Ms E's unconscious but, at the same time, being very aware of impinging too much, together with bearing in mind the impact this had on me.

At the beginning of July, Ms E returned home, with a carer. She was depressed, weakened, and often cut short the sessions or struggled to speak. She told me she had spoken to her children about her situation, and their reaction: the 8-year-old had wailed for an hour, but finally could be comforted. Perhaps my capacity to continue to be there gave her a sense that I could survive what she was telling me. In this way she may have felt strengthened and supported in bearing the grief of her children. Her body was colonized by a deadly cancer, but at times her mind could be freer to face the anxieties of her life-and-death struggle.

Towards the end of July, she discovered that her ex-husband was applying for full custody of the children—the very thing she wanted to avoid. She talked about how painful and tiring it was to speak to me at this time, how there was an unseemly rush to complete a process of custody, how difficult it was to keep her medications down, and my growing sense that she was removing herself from therapy and there was nothing to be done about that. This observation brought more feelings of guilt and a further sense of her envy of my health as the number of lumps and bumps in her body increased.

My sense of anxiety grew every time she didn't pick up the phone. I struggled with feeling that I might be left not knowing what had happened to her, and that I might not ever be able to find out.

In the last week of July Ms E missed the first two sessions of the week, and we had our final conversation on the last Thursday in July, for about 15 minutes. She told me she had been hospitalized with septicaemia and that, if stable, she would be moved to a hospice over the weekend. She was struggling to breathe and to speak, and I could hardly hear her. She told me that the kids were in good shape. We agreed to speak again on Monday, and she said "Yes, I'd like that."

When I rang Ms E at her appointment time the following Monday, my call went to answerphone. As usual, I left a message, saying that I had rung and that I would call again. When I called and she still did not pick up, I said, as usual, that I would call again the following day, at her appointment time. When she did not pick up again on the Tuesday, a sense of foreboding overtook me, and I rang the hospital ward, and then the hospice. Finally, I received a phone call from a doctor who told me that she had died that morning.

I was overwhelmed with feelings.

I had already arranged an appointment with my supervisor, and we spoke about my sense of shock and grief. We spoke about Ms E's life and my experience of working with her. However, there is an inescapable void in such circumstances: there is no one else who knew the patient, with whom her life could be celebrated and her death mourned. I was helped with some of the paperwork by the head of unit. By fulfilling the bureaucratic requirements, I felt I was involved in something more ordinary that happens after the death of an individual.

Since Ms E's diagnosis, I had experienced many complex feelings about the loss of my chance to have an ordinary experience with a training patient. However, at her death I was overwhelmed with feelings of grief at the loss of Ms E, the loss of this brave woman with whom I had shared the last ten months of her life in an intimate and emotional way. I hope this chapter in some way pays tribute to her in her courage and struggle to the end of her life.

CHAPTER EIGHTEEN

When the worst thing happened

Susan Baldock

My patient, whom I will call Ms M, committed suicide not long after therapy began. In writing about this shocking event, the impact on me is explored. I describe the aftermath: of navigating and participating in the enquiries that took place—both within the Institution (Serious Incident Review) and externally (the inquest into her death). As a trainee whose former career had been in law, as a barrister, this experience brought to life unexpected connections between my current training and my earlier professional life. The chapter tries to convey how the processing of this very painful experience and what followed was, while very challenging, ultimately enriching of my learning and was a valuable part of my training experience on the M1 training.

It was an ordinary Tuesday morning when I came into the Tavistock building and into the fourth floor Common Room, to check my emails. Nothing much was on my mind, and I had time before a scheduled meeting to undertake some routine tasks on my mental to do list. In my inbox was an email forwarded by one of the admin staff a few hours before, subject line "Your Patient". When I read it—or, more importantly, when I read it properly—I learnt of something shocking: something that changed everything, in a moment, inside and out.

I was a fourth-year M1 trainee. I felt very engaged with and immersed in my learning and in the work of the department. In short, if asked, I think I would have said that morning that all was going well, that I had the beginnings of a sense of the end of my training somewhere on the horizon and of what might come after.

Clinical example: Ms M

I had recently begun to work with my second intensive training patient, a woman I shall call Ms M. We had met for the first time a couple of months before, but she had been in my thoughts for some months before that, since I was first asked to see her. She had been waiting a long time, for various reasons. I had read the extensive records on the Carenotes system and discussed her with the therapists previously involved in her care. Her history as a patient with the Tavistock was a long and complicated one. Looking back now, I can see that, while I felt aware that Ms M would be an interesting but complex patient, I was gratified by being viewed as someone who was capable of being her therapist, feeling that this was evidence of being well thought of as a trainee. I think this blinded me to the magnitude of the risks I was assuming, including the risks for myself.

Ms M was a woman in early middle age, from a Southern European country, but who had lived in the United Kingdom most of her adult life. Her childhood as she described it was emotionally abusive, seriously neglectful, and Ms M had suffered many traumatic experiences, separations, and losses. Her relationships were often problematic and distressing to her, particularly those with close family members whom she experienced as uncaring and unavailable. She had struggled with her mental health throughout her life, since her teenage years, especially with bouts of severe depression. She had made several suicide attempts in the past, and had once been sectioned under the Mental Health Act, because of the serious and imminent risk she presented to herself. This was another very traumatizing experience for her, and she was terrified of this ever happening again. It was after this detention and in this context that Ms M had made a solemn vow to her partner that she would make no further attempts on her life, and this had remained true for over 15 years. There were many positives and strengths in Ms M's history, not least her long and committed relationship with her partner, her determination to overcome her emotional difficulties, and her wish to live a full and creative life. She had made good use of her previous therapy.

By the time I had a vacancy to offer Ms M, her situation had deteriorated considerably. She was very depressed, unable to work, increasingly isolated, agoraphobic, and in poor physical health. Her reviewer—who knew her very well—was concerned, but it was agreed that it was still appropriate to go ahead as planned. The reviewing therapist was to remain involved in the capacity of care co-ordinator. It was agreed, too, that the therapy would begin once weekly, to see how Ms M responded, with a plan to increase to three sessions a week. In fact, I only saw her for six sessions in total over a two-month period, due to her extreme difficulty in attending.

Ms M and I did not have the chance to get to know each other very well, but the contact between us was immediate and close in the sessions she was able to come to. In the moment of our very first meeting at the fourth-floor lifts, she "claimed" me with an intense and hungry gaze. At the end of our second meeting, she told me there was no need to remind her of her next session, as she knew deep inside her already that I was her person, and this was her place, and this was her time. I was very moved by her plight, impressed by her poetic and lyrical use of (her second) language, alarmed by the severity of her depression, and very affected by her profoundly bleak and hopeless feelings, which pervaded the atmosphere of the consulting room during each session and stayed inside me and with me for some time after. To be with Ms M was to really feel the force of her projected deathly feelings. After most of our meetings I had a severe and debilitating headache, and sometimes also felt very sick indeed for a few hours. In our fourth meeting, Ms M cried in a bleak and affectless way for most of the session. She only broke off to say, repeatedly and in slightly different ways, that the terrible state she was in now had gone on for too long, that she was "a long, long way down a deep, deep hole. Maybe a well. But I'm not well. I know and feel you want to help me, but no one can rescue me from such a distance, you don't have arms long enough. No one does." She said that she was full of despair and beyond repair.

From the outset it was clear that Ms M was often plagued with suicidal thoughts and at times by a fixed certainty that there was nothing that could be done to alleviate her deep depression, that it was too late for her. On the other hand, there were glimmers of curiosity, of a wish for something more on the side of life, and her conscious wish was to take up the offer of intensive therapy in the hope—however slight—of this being helpful to her. It was possible to begin to explore the mixed message of her resolutely bleak feelings of hopelessness that she so impressed on me and the fact that she was nevertheless coming to her sessions with me, despite it being extremely difficult for her to leave her house. More than once she was hungry for more, wanting to move quickly to more sessions each week.

Ms M remained very aware of the vow she had made not to act on her suicidal feelings, and she felt still bound by this solemn promise. She did tell me that she was in the process of putting her affairs in order administratively, but this was something that had been going on for over a year and did not feel acutely alarming in itself at the time. There was an explicit fear and threat that if attempts were made to detain her again as an inpatient, she would feel compelled to take her own life.

What I learnt first that Tuesday morning from the forwarded email was that Ms M was missing. This was in the aftermath of emergency services attending her home to carry out a mental health assessment. Her partner had written to tell me this and to ask me whether she had been in contact with me. Above this email in my inbox was what looked, at first glance, when I opened it in a state of shock, like a duplicate email. It was this second email that I quickly printed off. My instinct (with no or very little thinking involved) was to see if my supervisor was available to share this news with and so I went to his room and was relieved to find that he was free. I told him what I knew and referred to the exact wording of the printed copy. It was in doing this that I realized that what I had in my hand wasn't a duplicate message but contained a second email as well as the first. This further email, written in the early hours of the morning, conveyed the news that Ms M had been found by the police, that she was dead, believed to have taken her own life.

It was by chance, not design, happenstance rather than forethought, that I learnt this awful news in the presence of another rather than alone, and that this other was someone who knew both my patient and me well. And yet . . . not complete chance? What felt instinctual perhaps included something of a premonition of where this news would end and a self-protective reflex of not bearing the shock of it alone. It was such a relief in retrospect that this moment of learning that the worst thing had happened was a shared moment.

As part of my M1 training and previous study, I had learnt about suicide and risk in a theoretical way, and through my involvement in the clinical work of the Adult Complex Needs Service these were topics that came up in some form or other in almost every supervision and clinical discussion I took part in. Assessing, noting, and recording risk was a routine element, too, of the case record for every patient I worked with. I don't think it was that I had become in the least blasé or inured to these issues, but I do think that there was an element, perhaps, of my losing sight of the real horror and enormity of what was involved, that something very frightening was made abstract and conceptual by its everyday repetition and normalization and became something that might be "managed". I had had much more personal experience of acts of suicide in my extended family, too, albeit many years previously. These events were something that felt far away, something that belonged mostly in the past, even if they were often felt reverberating in the present, brought alive again in unexpected ways and at unforeseen moments. The shock and horror surrounding those very personal experiences was all too easy to recall, yet, when I reflect on these things now, had been split off from, were mostly disconnected from these experiences as a training clinician.

In the moment of learning of Ms M's death and likely suicide, they were revived with sudden and real force. The disbelief, the numbness, the distress was about Ms M but had in it, too, feelings that belonged to these previous traumatic losses. It was a repetition of something that I thought I had over time been able to make sense of, to assimilate, but which was powerfully shown to be far less processed and digested than I had let myself believe.

My initial shock was swiftly followed by disbelief and then anxious feelings of shame, guilt, and responsibility: shame, I think, for being so closely involved in a suicide—something that remains so taboo and imbued with shame; guilt, I think, for the fantasy of being accused and blamed for this awful event; responsibility, I think, from feelings that I could have or should have both predicted and prevented this death, of someone I was indeed responsible for as my patient and with whom I was in close emotional contact, however briefly. With the benefit of hindsight, with the ability to look back over the period leading up to Ms M's death only afforded by the completed act, her suicide remained completely shocking but also, simultaneously, no shock at all, given the depth of her despair and the whole of her troubled history. Both existed, and both were true.

What helped me immeasurably to bear these raw feelings in the days, weeks, and months that followed was the help, kindness, and containment offered by many individuals in the department: my supervisor, the senior management in the service, the other therapist still involved as care coordinator, as well as that of those fellow trainees and friends I chose to share this with. My own analysis, too, was invaluable in offering a space where my thoughts and feelings could be aired and shared outside my role as trainee, with my analyst, who knew me and my own history so well. I was grateful for all this support and felt protected, both as a trainee clinician and as a person.

Over the time that elapsed between the immediate aftermath of the news and its accompanying flurry of activity, I became slowly aware of a very different parallel process at play, best described perhaps as taking place at an organizational level, and which felt in direct conflict with the thoughtful individual responses. This might be conceptualized as a stark splitting in the face of life and death anxieties. Examples of what I am describing involved what I would characterize as a focus on (faceless, impersonal) bureaucracy. For instance, the way in which the original emails were simply forwarded to my inbox for me to discover as I did; a senior administrator whose only response to the news was to tell me that I would need to complete a number of lengthy forms "immediately" and must record the fact of my patient's death on Carenotes "straight away", another senior manager who, days before the inquest, became involved in a heated discussion with me (in fact more a heated argument!) over the question of whether my anonymized process notes for supervision legally belonged to me or to the Trust and therefore whether I was able to take them from Trust premises.

I think what was at play in what felt at times like dizzying and confusing treatment was the effect of the very disturbing event on all those who encountered it in their different roles. There was also, I think, an unconscious ambivalence and conflict about whether I was to be treated as "just" a trainee, or as the clinician carrying clinical responsibility for a patient who had taken their own life. The difficult reality was that I occupied both positions. So, I believe, there was at times a wish to protect me from further anxiety and at other times a wish to locate responsibility in me.

These difficult experiences were not limited to or solely located in admin staff but were, I realized, more systemic, within and throughout the organization. Examples included, but were not limited to, my having to insist repeatedly that I be included in relevant email correspondence about the legal process around Ms M's death. I found again and again that while I might be included originally in discussion about some topic, I would subsequently be "dropped" from the conversation, or, conversely, would only be included in the last stages of some conversational thread that directly involved me and had been going on without me. Each time this became apparent, I would be offered a sincere apology and a reassurance that this was a complete oversight. It was hard not to feel excluded and left out and did nothing to allay my more persecutory anxieties. I felt simultaneously powerless and responsible.

The most glaring example of this more unthinking, unfeeling organizational response (or so it felt to me) was finding out that a service-wide event had been planned to discuss risk and risk management, one that would use two recent examples of patient deaths by way of illustration. One of the examples to be used was Ms M's treatment and death (anonymized, of course). I found out about this from a chance remark a week beforehand. No one involved in the planning had thought I might need to be made aware of this before finding myself in a large meeting discussing these things that so concerned me. Again, once raised, I received an apologetic response, but one that carried within it a slight but palpable puzzlement: one that conveyed the idea that after a year or so I should perhaps be less "sensitive". I did at this point feel once again very upset, angry, and disturbed and that my professional integrity as a clinician and the appropriateness of my response as a trainee were both in question.

This event, when it did take place, was interesting. The meeting focused so much on the other clinical example, of a death that was, in fact, determined to be from natural causes, that there was almost no time at all to discuss this death by suicide. It received a brief mention (the facts) at the very end of the meeting, with no time at all available for any thinking, any feelings. From feeling cross beforehand, then anxious, I was left feeling both relieved and frustrated afterwards.

I do think that what I encountered in this organizational response speaks to the horror of a completed suicide and the powerful unconscious defensive manoeuvres employed to avoid the awful anxieties stirred up by it: by turning away from the human tragedy to something impersonal and by turning to action in concentrating on a form, a legal issue, a learning event. The paradox of this taking place in and playing out in an NHS institution whose primary task is to provide thoughtful and safe care to those with mental health problems is that the heightened sense of failure prevents or works against a consistently thoughtful response. The examples I have given were all, I think, attempts to achieve some distance from the messy, frightening feelings suicide evokes and to "manage" them in a particular way.

Ms M's death as a patient in the care of the Tavistock required a prescribed formal response in the form of an internally conducted Serious Incident Review (SIR), and I was interviewed for this part of the process quite soon afterwards. This was helpful in requiring me to gather my thoughts in order to give an account.

The ensuing external inquiry was protracted. Waiting for the inquest to begin was painful. Originally scheduled to take place just over a year after Ms M's death, the hearing was postponed indefinitely soon after the Covid-19 pandemic began. In the early confused and confusing weeks of the first lockdown I didn't give this much notice, but when I did find space to think about it, I realized that this was not a welcome reprieve from an unwelcome commitment but, rather, that I had in fact been holding on to the idea that this formal inquiry would mark an ending of sorts to what had happened and to my continuing involvement in the events surrounding Ms M's suicide. Now there was, abruptly, no imagined endpoint to have in mind. By the time word came that the postponed hearing would now take place, another six months had passed, and I was very aware of the details of events being less clear and less in focus, the more time elapsed.

I think, too, that the effects of the pandemic played a part in this: my work with Ms M and the fact of her death belonged to the "time before", to a way of working and a way of life that I now felt disconnected from and abruptly separated from in an infinite number of ways. Like so much else in this new world, it was remote from me and to me. The inquest eventually took place 18 months after Ms M's death, nearly a year after I had completed my statement for the legal proceedings.

Attending the inquest was a strange experience. I was glad I made the decision to attend in person rather than participate by video link, which was an option. I was worried that, without actual participation, the proceedings would seem more virtual than real, and I needed them to feel real. I was certain, too, that I didn't want to be speaking about the details of Ms M's death from my own living room or to have my private space left full of these distressing and highly emotive details when I turned my laptop off. I was glad, too, that the other colleagues involved in giving evidence made the same decision, and this meant that we were together in facing this, physically close with our shared anxieties and nervousness.

Before beginning to train as a psychotherapist, I had worked for some 20 years in a previous career as a barrister and part-time judge, specializing in family law. The reasons behind my desire to retrain were many and complicated but included an increasing dissatisfaction with the structures and strictures of a legal system in which there was little room for uncertainty, for not knowing, and often a very binary, black-and-white approach that the system relied on and imposed. A contested court hearing must reach a conclusion, a judgment, with an apparent clarity and certainty, which, in many circumstances, did not seem either possible or comfortable. There were many things I missed about this former working life and felt the loss of, but, in this respect, it was a welcome change to have room for doubt and uncertainty, curiosity and exploration.

During my (re)training to be a psychotherapist, I had to do a lot of learning and a lot of unlearning too. There were deeply ingrained skills and ways of doing things appropriate to my professional life as a lawyer that had to be relinquished or adapted, a new culture to find my place in. These things were more challenging to me than assimilating theoretical knowledge. An important moment came when I was presenting in a Unit Meeting. Talking to a large group of my peers and senior staff in this way came quite easily to me, being so used to appearing in Court and "presenting" there. I also responded to anxiety-provoking situations with a protective show of confidence as second nature. When I finished describing my assessment, the patient's history, and the material from a consultation meeting, others offered their thoughts and associations. I continued (as I would in answer to questions from judges in a courtroom setting) to engage and answer, taking up much of the time and space available. My Unit Head was sitting next to me. He touched me on the arm and told me, quietly and kindly but firmly, that I needed to be quiet now and to listen. He was absolutely right, and the moment stayed with me.

What I was unprepared for and taken by surprise by at the inquest was how much my familiarity with the Court system and my legal training would come to my aid in this awful situation. My practice as a barrister had never directly included taking part in an inquest, and the details of the legislative framework for such proceedings were unfamiliar. Likewise, I had never given evidence as a witness in any proceedings. Yet, a bit like discovering a physical action is facilitated by a muscle memory that you are consciously quite unaware of, I instantly felt "at home", albeit in an "uncanny" way, in this courtroom, surrounded by lawyers, presided over by the Coroner. Speaking in this formal and perhaps potentially intimidating setting was not difficult for me, even if I was now standing in an unfamiliar place, having switched places from being one of the lawyers in the courtroom to standing in the witness box. The atmosphere was one in which I had spent so much time that it didn't just alleviate my nerves, it shifted me into another state of mind in which I felt part of a process with a role to play, one that I understood and felt capable of. It suddenly felt more possible to feel like and be a witness, to give my account of what had happened.

I was able to defend against anxiety by arming myself with my legal knowledge and professional experience from my former career, still there for me to draw upon when needed, not erased but overlaid by my new professional identity. In addition, the reality of finally being at the inquest mitigated against the powerful fantasies that had grown up in the space between Ms M's suicide and this date. These included not being up to the task, of "performing badly" in front of my senior colleagues, and of being blamed and criticized for my actions and/or inactions. I knew I wasn't on trial, wasn't the accused, but it felt as if I was or might be, until the reality of the experience interrupted and replaced these fears. Beforehand, the reality of the inquest was twisted and distorted by the projections from my own internal psychic courtroom.

I was fortunate, I think, in being the first witness at the hearing, and once I had repeated the well-worn words of solemnly and sincerely declaring and affirming that I would tell the truth, the whole truth, and nothing but the truth and had begun to answer the questions posed to me by the coroner and the legal representatives, I felt focused and calm. There was a satisfaction in being able to give a full and, I hope, thoughtful account of my involvement with and thoughts about Ms M, her treatment, and her death. Again, my old skills kicked in and enabled me to recall dates and chronology and to remember details with surprising exactitude and to convey these as well as more abstract ideas and thoughts about the events in question. The Coroner was a measured man with a warm manner towards all involved, and this facilitated feeling able to give a full account. Although I knew intellectually that this was an enquiry into the events surrounding a death, not a contested hearing between combative parties with competing interests, I hadn't been able to believe this at an emotional level. My expectation at some level was of a criminal court, of prosecutor and defendant, of being "on trial". I think a big part of my anxieties in this respect involved the sense of being also on trial before my Tavistock colleagues—as an unqualified trainee—whose approval and good opinion I wanted and needed. The actual experience largely displaced those more primitive expectations.

I was left afterwards feeling drained but relieved, aware of a feeling almost of an anticlimax that was proportionate to the enormity that giving evidence had grown to assume in my mind. The findings of the inquest included a formal recording of suicide. The Tavistock was not considered to have fallen short in Ms M's care and was commended for aspects of that care. The relief of this was immense too.

I am writing these words a year after the inquest. It remains the case that while much of my distress and anxiety about what happened has receded and while the verdict of the Coroner's Court was significant in facilitating this, the experience, of course, very much remains with me. At a professional level it affected me in various ways. Most obviously, I became much more frightened of any of my patients' suicidal thoughts and feelings, often too quick to step out of my role into active "risk management": any waiting and thinking with and about my patient felt too little, too dangerous. At an unconscious level the reassurances of the verdict cannot allay the feelings of shame and guilt that persist. Over time, I have allowed myself to grieve, too, for the loss of the more ordinary, less shocking training experience that I didn't have in working with Ms M.

I desperately wish Ms M had not acted as she did. For her own sake, of course, but also because of the effect of her suicide on so many people, me included. None of the self-reflection and undoubted growth and learning that has come from these events could possibly make me wish other than that they had never happened. When I think of Ms M now, though, it is not only this last violent act that fills my mind. I can also vividly recall more of her: her warmth and humour can be included in the picture. I will always remember her, but not only her fate.

CHAPTER NINETEEN

The impact of the therapist's pregnancy in a training case

Avgoustina Almyroudi

Clinical example: Ms K

"I am swimming in a small and tranquil lake, surrounded by green hills. I put my head underwater. I think: this is where I want to be!" Ms K moved her arms gracefully, as if she were swimming on the couch. She was telling me about a dream she had the previous night. "But then", she continued, with a sudden rush of anxiety, "I feel an intense need to pee. I don't want to do it. I fear I am going to spoil the water but, if I keep it inside, it will leak inside my body and poison it. I have no choice. Suddenly the walls of the lake turn rocky, the trees lose their leaves. The landscape around me becomes arid. Now I feel trapped...."

Ms K was my first training patient: I describe my experience of the challenges my pregnancy posed on the therapeutic relationship with her. I explore how negotiating a therapist's pregnancy can facilitate emotional growth and development in patients and provide the student with a rich experience of managing a challenging clinical situation.

Background

When I met Ms K, she was in her late fifties. She had been referred to our service for chronic depression. She lived with her partner of five years. There was a lot of conflict in their relationship. Ms K did not have any children, but her partner had a daughter from a previous marriage. Ms K felt close to her mother, who lived nearby; she was elderly but in good health and quite independent. Ms K worked in a highly responsible admin position and was competent in her job. Apart from this, she was quite socially isolated.

In our sessions, Ms K often found being listened to containing. Yet, as soon as there was any indication of my separateness, she would dismiss me. She left little room for me to get a word in, interrupted me, ignored or corrected my interpretations. She would, occasionally, forget the dates of my breaks, turn up in the clinic, and then would feel angry with me not being there. I often felt heavily controlled and scrutinized. In the months preceding my pregnancy, I was gradually able to talk with her about that way of interacting with me. We explored how it served to fulfil a wish of merging with me, of feeling harmoniously fused with me. This phantasized union protected her from awareness of our separateness, giving her relief from her profound loneliness without the need to acknowledge her dependence or envy. The prospect of relating to a real, separate other made her feel confused and terrified of being abandoned.

Pregnancy

I became pregnant when Ms K had been in intensive psychotherapy for a year and a half. It was a difficult pregnancy, with uncertainty about the wellbeing of the embryo, requiring frequent check-ups, particularly in the first and second trimesters. As expected, this challenging situation left me feeling vulnerable and anxious. My supervisor's support was crucial in helping me to mitigate the potentially disturbing effects on the transference.

Prior to becoming consciously aware of my pregnancy, Ms K began expressing phantasies about a frail figure who could not hold her. "My manager looked exhausted today, like a ghost", she said, sounding apprehensive. I noticed she had crossed her arms around her chest, as if she were hugging herself. "On my way here today, I felt certain that the receptionist would tell me my sessions for this week had been cancelled; that you could not see me", she added. As Ms K talked, I felt pervaded by anxiety. In hindsight, it was anxiety about my own vulnerability at that moment, given the complications in my pregnancy and a worry that Ms K had grasped something about it. Driven by a desire to alleviate anxiety for both of us, I quickly commented that her sessions that week were on as usual. The session moved on, but I was left feeling unease; on reflection,

I realized that rather than containing Ms K's anxiety by interpreting her phantasy about a frail therapist who might abandon her, I had provided reassurance to her.

Later that week, I explored with my supervisor what had led me to do this. Ms K's phantasies at that moment resonated deeply with my own. I was feeling less robust than usual. I was fearful of the effect this could have on my holding capacity towards my patients. Would I be able to hold onto Ms K and contain her, should she break down? I realized that I had concerns that my pregnancy would inflict a kind of trauma on her. Not only would it mean that she would not be offered an extension in her treatment, which she had requested and needed, but it would face her with her "infertile" way of being with others, something that she was doing that had deprived her of having creative relationships. Perhaps an unconscious wish to avoid the painful reflection on all these issues had influenced the way I had responded to her.

The following week she talked about her worry that her mother, who was undergoing some medical investigations, would eventually become older, frail, and die. She added, in passing, that I looked tired too. I commented that she was worried *I* was frail and might be unable to hold her. She said, "I have felt close to you recently, but I find it difficult to rely on you, to trust you. I wish I could make you safe and always available. I wish there was no ending." I commented that the solution she had found in her mind to the problem of whether the other, including her mother and myself, was trustworthy was a wish for an unchangeable, never-ending closeness, which she knew was not possible. I thought of how a pregnant body always changes, evolves. Our setting would become inevitably less stable and less containing for Ms K in the coming months. I felt a wish to hide my pregnancy for a little longer from her.

In fact, the question of when I was going to tell her came up soon. I had now entered the second trimester. I had the dilemma that the pregnancy was starting to show, yet there was still uncertainty about its outcome. In discussion with my supervisor, we decided not to discuss it yet openly with Ms K. However, in the material, there were indications of unconscious awareness of it: "I was invited to a colleague's birthday party on Saturday. She has young children. Another colleague had brought her children too. For a while I enjoyed watching them playing and moving around the living room, but then I started thinking that they were filling up all the space around me and I felt anxious and dizzy!" I commented that she was anxious that all the space in my mind was taken by others, leaving little space for her when she needed it so much. And indeed, I thought about how there had been a third person in our room, a little baby, for some time now. I had recently started feeling a quickening inside me, her presence becoming livelier. Ms K's wish for exclusive, almost merged relationships came to my mind. Would she feel able to trust that we could still have a relationship when she found out there was third in our space?

A few weeks later I was finally reassured by the medical team that my pregnancy was progressing satisfactorily. In the meantime, Ms K had had an argument with her partner, leaving her furious. He had insisted that he and Ms K spend Christmas with his daughter and her family, ignoring Ms K's wish to book a holiday, in an effort to revive their relationship. She became very preoccupied with this argument. She complained that her partner was prioritizing his needs over hers. This argument seemed to me, at least partly, to be an enactment of feelings triggered by the unconscious awareness of my pregnancy: fury at the inability to control the other, to have them all on her own. However, when I tried to focus on our relationship, she kept ignoring me. I commented that perhaps she wished to block out a change in me, confronting her with the prospect that I had prioritized my needs over hers. After a long pause she muttered, "Are you expecting a baby?" On my confirming this, Ms K covered her face with her hands, as if wishing not to see me but also preventing me from seeing her. She remained silent for a long time. There was an atmosphere of deep sadness in the room. My mind drifted to a picture that I had seen earlier that week as I was walking through the park. A mother was breastfeeding her baby on a bench, while her older child, a toddler, was pulling her clothes, trying to prompt her to play with him. She asked him to wait; she could not attend to him. The toddler, though, could not wait. He became increasingly frustrated, tears pouring down his face, now walking away from her, looking lost and angry.

In the following sessions, Ms K told me she felt envious that I was moving forward when she felt stuck in depression, with no children and little hope for the future of her relationship. Seeing me with my bump, she continued, made her feel miserable and disposable. I commented that she felt angry with me for what felt like my rubbing her nose in it. "What troubles me most", she replied, "is that I am not only angry with you. I caught myself having angry thoughts about the baby, envying your involvement with him, even wishing bad on him. These thoughts are torturing me." I found myself feeling intensely uncomfortable and conflicted. On the one hand I was relieved by Ms K's courage to talk openly about this and felt empathetic of her predicament. I remembered how disturbing it was when I had experienced negative feelings about my pregnancy, particularly during the first trimester, when there had been a lot of uncertainty surrounding it. At the same time, I felt an irrational worry about the effects of her envy and anger on my pregnancy and felt protective of my baby. "I feel that I have no other option but to leave you", she continued. "However, if I were to leave, I would have no one to talk to . . . My problem . . . is that you are not mean." I commented that if she perceived me as mean, she could just feel resentful at me, rather than being troubled by her hateful feelings, her ambivalence, or even feel any gratitude. I thought of how mixed what I had offered Ms K was. I had worked hard for her, and we were both aware of this, but she also felt that I had provoked her, "displaced" her, stirred up her envy, and would now unavoidably desert her.

Staying in contact with such painful emotions proved to be unbearable. The following week, she drifted into a confused state: "I am worried I will end up in a care home, mindless and deserted by others." She sounded fragmented to the point where I found it difficult to make sense of what she was saying, thus sharing her confusion. I commented that she had found my pregnancy so disturbing that she felt she was losing her mind. The atmosphere in the room was painful for both of us. I could only be there with her, knowing that my pregnant figure was hugely provocative, yet being fully aware of my strong desire to protect her. This situation, which continued for a week, evoked deep sadness and guilt in me. I became concerned that she would have a breakdown. My concern increased further the following week, when she missed all her sessions without leaving any messages. I was left feeling acutely concerned about her.

She came back the following week, having recovered from her confusion through an enactment. She had a brief sexual encounter with a colleague with whom she had gone for drinks after work. She decided to leave her partner and went to stay temporarily with her mother. In our sessions, she was completely preoccupied with phantasies about a future with her colleague, alternating with angry monologues about her partner. When I tried to make links with her hope that *we* would stay together and her anger and disappointment that this could not materialize, she invariably rejected what I had said. "I can't see why you keep coming back to this, I don't think it is significant. Therapy is the last thing on my mind at the moment!" I realized that she had found relief from the painful mental state of the previous weeks by projecting the disturbing feelings of exclusion and abandonment on to me. I was made to feel insignificant. Trying to talk to her about this proved difficult. I started feeling that we had reached an impasse. I felt doubtful of what could be achieved, disappointed, and lacking a sense of hope: feelings that were shared by her.

Things became even more complicated when we entered the Covid lockdown, four weeks before the date set for the end of therapy. We switched to telephone sessions. She adapted quickly, and, to my surprise, they felt indistinguishable from our face-to-face ones. I noticed that the awareness of loss and the wish for less distance between us was held by me: she would rather continue with phone sessions. I thought that she was perhaps feeling relieved by not having to see any longer my, by now close to full-term, pregnant body.

Soon I realized that, in her mind, the lockdown had come to rescue her from the ending of therapy. External circumstances had brought a situation where the wish she had always harboured was fulfilled: she was now in a fused state with her mother, staying at home with her, perfectly sealed off from external world.

I thought that she had fled symbolically into the womb, perhaps identifying with my baby. She was inside her object, avoiding awareness of our forthcoming separation. My calls were unwelcome—an intrusion that reminded her that the fused state she was in, rather than being idyllic, lacked creativity or development. She kept saying that her therapy had been meaningless and futile. This situation left me feeling despondent. I started imagining the possibility that we would reach the end of therapy with such hostility. I commented that she was attacking our work, perhaps to protect herself from pain triggered by the ending. She told herself she had nothing to lose. However, by doing so, she deprived herself of the care I could provide and prevented us from thinking together about the ending.

As we moved towards the final weeks of her therapy, this defensive structure gradually lessened. Ms K became more aware of the good things that the therapy had given her, her sadness at ending, and her need for more support. She resumed contact with her partner, and they started having honest discussions about their feelings and the future of their relationship. In our last sessions she reflected on what a challenge it had been for her to allow herself to feel close to me and to continue the therapy, despite my pregnancy and knowing that our relationship was bound to end. We acknowledged that this was, perhaps, evidence of her progress: managing to stay with me despite feeling hugely provoked, reminded regularly of our differences and the ordinary nature—rather than ideal—of our relationship. I was left feeling that, despite the challenges, emotional growth had been achieved for Ms K and learning and development for me as a therapist. However, I was also very aware of what had been left incomplete and of my leaving my patient with it, at a time she really needed me.

Discussion

Female psychotherapy trainees and their patients often face the challenges a therapist's pregnancy imposes on the psychotherapeutic process, including the disruption of the psychotherapy setting and changes in the dynamics of the patient–therapist relationship. Personal information about the pregnant therapist is inevitably exposed, interfering with the anonymity and neutrality of the psychoanalytic frame. Often, especially in the public sector, there is a premature ending of treatment, or transition to another therapist. Patients must cope with tempestuous infantile feelings aroused by the universal phantasies of exclusion and displacement (Gibb, 2004). They respond differently according to their patterns of object relationships and past histories (Etchegoyen, 1993). The therapist must contain her patients' feelings, managing, concomitantly, her anxiety about her baby's safety. Thus, it is little surprise that in the literature it is generally argued that a therapist's pregnancy intensifies the transference and countertransference (Fenster, 1986). For the trainee at the beginning of her career, with relatively little experience, this is a daunting time. The role of supervision in supporting her to manage complex dynamics and gain a clear understanding of the unconscious conflicts is crucial.

For Ms K, my pregnancy constituted a crisis that acted as a catalyst, elucidating themes that we had been exploring for months, giving us another angle from which to examine them. In this way, I feel, it facilitated a deeper understanding.

Ms K had brought, at the outset of her therapy, a powerful phantasy of a symbiotic fusion with an omnipotent, idealized mother. This fused state, in her mind, protected her from the dread of collapsing into a state of fragmentation and profound confusion about her object. It was her solution to the problem of feeling a lack of "structure in herself"; without it, she felt fragmented, impoverished, and lost (Riesenberg-Malcolm, 1999). This phantasy also served as a defence, protecting her from feelings of dependence, loneliness, and envy, which emerged when she was more consciously aware of separateness from her object (Rosenfeld, 2002).

There was a strong pressure to enact this fused state in the transference, through a controlling part of her ego, which scrutinized me and observed our relationship almost incessantly (Joseph, 1989). I was warned, implicitly and explicitly, that if I failed to conform to her expectations, she would cast me off. Controlling me through projective identification protected her from an awareness of my differences, my relationships with others, or my breaks. Indications of my separateness, including evidence of my relationships with a third object, were difficult to bear. This included my efforts to consult with my analytic self and my supervisor to produce objective interpretations (Britton, 2000). Ms K would usually ignore them, interrupt me, or tell me she knew in advance what I was going to say. If she heard them, her initial momentary relief from feeling understood would usually be quickly replaced by feeling humiliated and frustrated that I knew something about her that she had not thought of. Awareness of my difference would frequently lead to my devaluation and an attack on our relationship. She then felt that I was not good enough for her and that she could not trust me. Therefore, Ms K alternated between seeking in the transference an idealized object, which could make her feel understood and contained and with which she could merge, and a devaluation of her object, creating a denigrated object, which she could not trust to bring the parts of herself that needed help (Brenman Pick, 2018).

Progress in working through this material was slow. The recognition of her attempts to control the object made her feel persecuted by guilt. Furthermore, this narcissistic retreat precluded creativity, which requires a recognition of difference. The creative process, the result of the joining of different elements to form a new conclusion (Chasseguet-Smirgel, 1985), was replaced by a joining with no freedom, which allowed her to be inside the object. The picture that would come into my mind was of a desire to be interminably inside a wooden womb, whose containment was the stability of its frame. But the potential of growing had been halted. The parental couple's intercourse, the joining of two different objects in their separateness, and its result, the new baby, was detested. I wondered whether this was because exclusion by the parental couple felt so painful and gave rise to unbearable feelings of dependence, jealousy, envy, aggression, and fear of badness of the self.

My pregnancy made her aware, violently and rather concretely, that I was not under her control. She saw that I had relationships with others (third objects) and that I was able to have a procreative relationship, different from her idealized fusion of mother and child. She was forced into the third position, where she could only be a witness, rather than a participant (Britton, 2000). This was a blow to the narcissistic organization I have described, with high risks. As an initial reaction to my pregnancy, Ms K experienced a collapse into a fragmented state of mind, a sense of disintegrating that was terrifying for her.

For my part, the dynamics created by my pregnancy were difficult to contain, particularly as I was feeling vulnerable, anxious, and less clear-headed than usual. I found that highly charged feelings in the transference, such as envy, anger, and hatred, were more disturbing than usual. They aroused irrational fears in me that they could potentially affect my baby, a need to protect it, and negative feelings towards Ms K. It was tempting to turn a blind eye to them, to avoid the difficult situation, both internally and in the room. However, this would have had a detrimental effect on Ms K's need to be understood and accepted. I also noticed that it was more difficult than usual to keep an open mind about how I was being perceived in the transference (Etchegoyen, 1993). It was easier sometimes to jump to conclusions driven by my own feelings rather than doing the detailed and, at times, painful work of disentangling my own state of mind from what was really playing out in the transference. An example of this was when I thought that Ms K had perceived me as a cruel mother abandoning her child (perhaps due to my own guilt for leaving her in a state of need). I interpreted along these lines.

Later, in supervision, we realized that Ms K had identified herself with the abandoning mother, projecting her feelings of exclusion and displacement onto me. The help of my supervisor was invaluable in helping me to gain a clearer understanding of the unconscious processes and conflicts. My analyst's help was also crucial in helping me to work through the primitive anxieties activated by the pregnancy, such as anxieties about the inside of the body, fears of loss of identity, fears of damaging or being damaged by the foetus, or of the effects of the envious attacks of others on the pregnancy.

However, despite these difficulties, I also found the pregnancy to have a positive effect. It intensified the psychotherapeutic process, and it gave us a paradigm, through which we could examine and symbolize some of the themes that we had been exploring slowly for many months. Grievance about the inability to control her object, pain at the loss of the illusion of unity, the realization that the ideal is immaterial and thus of no real value, painful feelings of exclusion, the hatred of couples for their creativity: all these were felt intensely by Ms K and could be looked at through the angle of my pregnancy. For me, bearing the guilt of leaving my patient when she needed me to care for my baby, exploring the position of a maternal object who must manage sibling rivalry, and learning to manage crises in a psychotherapeutic environment were significant positive learning experiences.

Overall, I think that, with the help of robust supervision, which helped me to manage the disturbance of the setting and to retain psychoanalytic thinking in the face of difficult dynamics, my pregnancy enriched my experience as a trainee psychotherapist. Most importantly, it formed a substantial part of Ms K's therapy, with a facilitating effect on her development. Hopefully, it will be the fertile grain that can enhance further growth through a new psychotherapeutic process or psychoanalysis in the future.

CHAPTER TWENTY

"I would prefer not to": a man in terror of his own mind

Devayani Shevade

I saw my patient, Mr D, for a period of 18 months in three-times-weekly psychoanalytic psychotherapy. Although I had offered to see him for three years, he decided to terminate his treatment after 18 months. The chapter is, therefore, an endeavour to understand what the difficulty was in making and keeping contact with Mr D. I describe my realization that he was terrified of having thoughts and feelings—in fact, of having a mind of his own. Through the work with him I realized not just the meaning and importance of projective identification and countertransference, but also the way in which I could use it to understand his states of mind.

Clinical example: Mr D

Mr D reminded me of the character Bartleby in the short story by Herman Melville (1924). The story is narrated by a lawyer who employs Bartleby, a scrivener in his office. Bartleby lives in a screened-off area in his employer's office and, over the course of the story, disintegrates into deathly stillness. There is an insistent turning away from anything lively, and he responds to requests to work with "I would prefer not to". His passivity arouses curiosity, a wish to help, pity, impotency, and anger in his employer. However, Bartleby remains impassive, mechanical, and withdrawn, as though locked into something deadly inside. He stands motionless in the corner of the office staring at a blank wall, not eating, not relating, refusing any help, not saying anything apart from "I would prefer not to".

Background and preliminary meeting

Mr D, a 50-year-old man from Asia, was referred by the local NHS talking therapies service due to longstanding depression, OCD, and anxiety. He had tried, both in his home country and here, various therapies and anti-depressants, none of which were helpful. He lived with his wife and his daughter.

Mr D felt that he had been depressed and anxious from an early age. In his early life there was a rather bleak picture of a little boy feeling frightened and anxious, with no one to help him. He was the only child of his parents, who were described as having a violent relationship. He would often get in between to keep the peace, at the cost of being cruelly beaten. He described his father as an alcoholic and unpredictably violent. His mother was described as aggressive, tyrannical, often contemptuous, hitting him, wanting perfection.

He was shy and lonely as a child, struggling to make friends. At school he was average. He thought himself intelligent but lacked confidence and left with poor marks. He started a degree but gave up, despite studying for several years.

Mr D had not worked for a long time. He took up a traditionally feminine role at home while his wife worked. He had belonged to a religious sect since the age of 16. What appeared to comfort him about being a part of this community was that he was told how to live, whom to meet, what to do, whom to choose as his partner. No questions or doubts were allowed. In time I realized that coming to see me felt dangerous—as though he had done something forbidden.

Brain fog

For the first five months of treatment, Mr D attended most of his sessions. There was a ritualistic quality to his sessions. He would always arrive half an hour early and would always come in wearing huge headphones that covered not only his ears, but half of his head too. It looked like a bizarre protective helmet (I was reminded of the aliens in Star Wars).

Mr D always dressed in black. He had a peculiar way of getting on and off the couch, removing his shoes at the far end and sliding in reverse up the couch. At the end of the session, he would slide down on his palms to the bottom. I came to feel that this behaviour was a way of avoiding my gaze. For him, the act of looking and being looked at felt fundamentally dangerous, as though something violent and invasive was being done to him or me.

The striking thing in this phase of treatment was that, although these behaviours felt bizarre and suggestive of a more primitive or even psychotic aspect to his personality, I responded to him as though he was an ordinarily neurotic patient. This may have had to do with my wish to have a "good" training patient, but I came to feel that it was my identification with an internal object who was impervious to him.

Mr D would fill in the space with concrete details of his life or talk about theories about the mind. I felt that I was either listening to a timetable of his day or a textbook explanation. Imaginative and spontaneous thinking was absent. Most sessions would end in me feeling that he hadn't told me much, and there was very little affect in the room. His speech induced what I can best describe as "brain fog". At such times I would give him inadequate interpretations, responding in an intellectually cutoff way, missing obvious cues about the state of his mind.

I felt that he was dominated by a cruel, tyrannical object who demanded that he tell me all the facts. He spent many sessions masochistically berating himself for not being able to "free associate" (his term), and nothing I would say could mitigate that. It was painful to watch him do this. I came to understand the brain fog as a countertransference response: an identification with the part of Mr D that was unable to think. He found this part of himself intolerable, filling him with shame and guilt.

In the fifth month of the treatment, Mr D brought a memory of his mother asking him to clean the kitchen when he was nine. He had put in a lot of effort, but his mother had looked around contemptuously, pointing out the things he had left out. He had begun crying, feeling that he had failed her, while she remained watching him in a way that left him feeling that she was "impenetrable". Mr D narrated this in a matter-of-fact way, not giving any associations. Having spoken, he simply waited, as if watching me. I said to him that I thought that he was like his mother, watching as I, like he at nine years old, made various efforts to help him. He was briefly silent after this interpretation and went on to say that he did not know how to feel. He said that his basic position was one of feeling fearful. He appeared sad when he said that, and I found myself very moved. This was followed by a long silence, and, when I asked him what he was thinking, he said that he was blank. He had no recollection, either of the interpretation I had just given or of his associations which followed.

I felt that my interpretation had resonated with him because he was able to tell me something about his terror. This admission was then attacked by a tyrannical part of him that could not allow for any vulnerability. I found the concept of the "internal mafia" (Rosenfeld, 1971a) helpful in understanding this aspect of Mr D. The tyrannical part of him seemed to offer protection from psychic pain to his more needy, vulnerable self.

Whose mind is it anyway?

The session above brought changes. I felt more able to understand and recognize his terror and the different ways in which he would make himself impenetrable in the session. Simultaneously, he seemed to have erected stronger defences against my attempts to reach him.

Mr D no longer filled the sessions with concrete facts. Instead, he remained silent. He—or, rather, his wife—also started cancelling sessions. When I tried to speak about both the meaning and the manner of the cancellations, Mr D would insist that I was reading too much into this. He also responded to planned breaks as though they hadn't taken place and was rather dismissive of my attempts to link this to his anxieties.

There were long silences in the sessions: 20 minutes to half an hour. Eventually, he told me that his mind was "filtering". The need to say the perfect sentence was so overwhelming that in the end he wouldn't say anything. When he did talk, he would tell me about his frustration that I wasn't telling him what to do and wasn't helping him. At other times, he told me that the problem was with the model, that it would be the same whoever the therapist was. He was scathing when I pointed out that he lived in a world where people got replaced very quickly. In yet another session, he told me that his mind was a computer, and perhaps the way to feel better would be to just replace one damaged part with something else. I began to feel frustrated and useless at what I saw as my failure to make contact with him. Sometimes I would feel dread when waiting for him and, at other times, angered by his constant blocking of my attempts.

In her thought-provoking paper on projective identification, Roth (2005) suggests that, when patients use projective identification, it is because it is "lifesaving" and "the best possible solution for what are experienced as uncontainable psychological pressures" (p. 206). Mr D's excessive use of projective identification seemed to be his way of communicating his experience of being a child, trying desperately to connect with a parent who either doesn't respond or responds violently.

I found that, in these silences, I began to have personal associations in the form of memories. Almost all of these associations centred on violence and trauma. For example, in one session, I remembered being eight years old, sitting in my classroom with my friends, chatting and laughing, when suddenly a pigeon flew through the window, right into the ceiling fan. The pigeon was cut to fragments, the benign classroom transformed into a scene of blood and gore, all of us transfixed with horror. In another session, a memory surfaced of being in an earthquake with people being buried alive and others watching with helpless horror, but also a perverse curiosity. Such memories not only felt disturbing, but I also felt intruded upon, as if the memories were not actually mine.

Brenman Pick (1985) describes how the analyst can defend against the patient's communications when this touches on the analyst's own primitive anxieties. She stresses the importance of the analyst's capacity to remain open to the countertransference responses. I found this paper helpful in thinking about my powerful countertransference responses, which reflected the state of Mr D's mind and its violent fragmentation. I also realized how massively he had projected not just his early experiences into me, but also the functions of his mind: his curiosity, the ability to associate freely and observe. He was functioning in the treatment primarily by living inside me and through me. It was as if he had abandoned his own mind. In time and with the help of supervision, I found a way of talking to him about these countertransference responses, as shown by this session on a Thursday, the last session of the week. We were now in the 14th month of the treatment.

> Mr D remained silent for a long time at the beginning of the session. He lay very still, as though frozen. I began to drift in my thoughts, and a memory came to my mind, from a day out with my family to see an old fortress when I was 6 years old. I had run off to play in the ruins with the other children, but being curious, I had drifted away and had got lost in the labyrinth inside the fortress. No one had noticed my absence initially, and I had felt cold, lonely, and extremely frightened as I waited for someone to come and find me in the dark and confusing labyrinth.
>
> I said to Mr D that, in the silence, he seemed to feel stuck, on his own, as if I was not present. He agreed, appearing surprised that I had understood something about his state. I thought he sounded sad, but this quickly changed to his usual intellectualizing. I wondered if he felt curious about his stuckness, and he was able to tell me that he did not. He talked about his lack of curiosity as a fact, rather than being puzzled by this lack. I commented that he seemed to find curiosity to be something dangerous: he was terrified that it would lead him to frightening places, and that he might get lost there. He told me that he was feeling very tired and that talking was an effort. When he was silent, he did not have any thoughts. Then I would say something, and then he could have a thought and respond. He went on to say that he was doing something called "mirroring" in the session. When I said something, he said something. He felt that mirroring was being like the other and that

he used it to empathize with others, for a sense of better connection. It felt clear to me that this was no ordinary empathic mirroring. I said to him that I thought what he was calling empathy actually masked his feeling that the other would not be able to bear it if he was not the mirror image, and vice versa. Mr D responded by describing how he would consciously change his feelings to fit the feelings of the other person, believing that this led to a "deeper connection". He had learned this in childhood. Later, he could tell me that if he was not exactly like the other, then the mirror would reflect nothing, and there would be no image. He sounded very sad when he said this, and I felt a sense of his profound emptiness. I thought that, in this emptiness, he was left with just silence and absence. This made sense of his silence in the sessions and also his response to the breaks and his cancellations.

My countertransference association/memory seemed to be a link to Mr D's state of mind. He wasn't having the associations, I was! The old, ruined fortress was an image of his mind, where both he and I felt stuck, cold, and frightened. The labyrinth stood for the "internal mafia" (Rosenfeld, 1971), cruelly blocking freedom from that dark, cold place. There was a sense that playing and curiosity were dangerous. However, my interpretation seemed to free something, and he was able describe his belief that the only way he could exist was in a complete fusion with his object. His stillness at the beginning of the session made sense in this context. Any thought or feeling of his own (even a breath of his own) that indicated that he had a separate mind left him feeling terrified and anxious.

The dream and the rupture

In the following session, a Monday, Mr D brought his first and only dream. In the dream,

he had entered a room to see his daughter, Jane, lying dead. He was horrified and tried everything he could to revive her, but then he found that he was actually stabbing her with a knife. There were other people in the room too, but no one noticed what he was doing, and that was horrible.

Mr D woke up crying.

When I asked for his associations to the dream, he gave me a textbook explanation of how dreams represent the unconscious. I asked him what he thought the dream said about *his* unconscious? Mr D was silent, then said, sounding sad, that he didn't have any thoughts about the dream. He told me that, in the silence, he had been wondering about what thoughts he might have, but all he kept thinking of were textbook explanations.

I said that I thought the dream was about the death of the part of him that could spontaneously and imaginatively play. He desperately wanted to revive this dead part and yet found himself repetitively killing it off. He was terribly worried that I had not noticed, either his wish to revive it but also the killing off.

There was another long silence, but it felt to me that Mr D was thinking about what I said. He then told me that what had come to his mind was how accident-prone Jane was. Once she had fallen outside her school, banging her head, and there had been a lot of blood. He didn't have a tissue or anything to staunch the flow. There had been a woman nearby who had given Mr D a tissue and explained to him that he needed to hold it tight to stop the bleeding. That had helped, and she had also called an ambulance. He had felt grateful to her, but in the chaos had forgotten to thank her. She had stayed in his mind. I said that he was very frightened that if he allowed himself to play, then something violent would happen, but that he also felt that I had been able to understand that. He had felt that my interpretation had helped him, for which he felt grateful, but also worried that he couldn't find a way to show me.

I felt that this had been a profoundly moving session in many ways. He had been able to bring a dream that was linked to the session before, in which something was freed up in him. He was able to retain this link. His dream represented his fundamental psychic struggle: the violence that killed off any sense of life in him. I felt that in the session we were able to make real emotional contact.

At the same time, I remained unsure whether there would be a negative therapeutic reaction. Initially, it felt as if Mr D had retreated into his defensive place, and yet I noticed small but significant changes. Although Mr D still got on the couch in his usual fashion, there would be a moment when he would make eye contact. Sometimes he would give a slight smile. At times, when leaving the room, his eyes would pass onto the bookcase near the door. Not only had he begun noticing me and the room, curiosity was also present. There were fewer cancellations, and he would call to cancel rather than asking his wife to do so. He would leave an apology and a reason for cancelling, letting me know that he would be back for the next one. These changes felt like small green shoots of life.

It was extremely unfortunate that, a month following the session above, I had to take three weeks off due to ill health. The week I came back, Mr D's wife called and left a message, cancelling all his sessions for the week. So, by the time he came back, we had not seen each other for four weeks. As Mr D came into the room, I noticed that he had lost weight. He came in as usual, lying still and being silent for about ten minutes or so. I broke the silence by acknowledging that we hadn't met each other for a long time. He said that he wasn't sure that I would be there today. His wife had called the Tavistock but hadn't got an answer, and there were some missed calls from withheld numbers, but no messages. After a brief silence I said that I had withheld my presence by not being here when he expected me, and, perhaps, he was left with a massive sense of confusion about what was going on. I then said that I thought he was very worried about what had happened to me, and this worry made it difficult for him to come back last week. He was silent for a while, and then, in a rather contemptuously amused tone of voice, said that, as usual, I was making too much of everything. He had, of course, wondered if I was ok, as he had been told that I was ill. That was that. He had then gone on with his tasks: cleaning, cooking, looking after the house. He didn't think much beyond that. There was a long silence, during which I felt quite drowsy and had to fight to stay awake. Mr D then told me that, since I was not going to tell him about my illness, he wanted to tell me a few things that happened in the last month. The first thing was that his cat had had kittens, six of them. They were shut up in a room, and his wife was dealing with what they should do with them, as he didn't want to have any part in it. The second thing was that he had started a new diet in the last month. It was a raw vegetarian diet, and he had already lost weight and felt quite good about that. He, again, fell silent, and I said that there were many things in what he had said. I thought that a part of him really wanted to know what was going on with me, but, if he allowed himself to be aware of this, he ended up feeling needy and dependent, like the kittens who could be dispensed with, and he hated feeling this way. Therefore, the needy part of him was kept out. At some point in the session Mr D said that he blocked all the private numbers from his phone, because they are generally about useless things. He then went on to say, angrily, that he didn't understand why the Tavistock number was private, and that he had reason to be suspicious, as his wife's identity had been stolen some years back. I said to him that he was suspicious and hurt and rightly so, because I disappeared for three weeks. He then remained silent until the end of the session.

I felt that my sudden absence left Mr D with intolerable feelings of rage, longing, and curiosity, which he had to shut away, like the kittens. He was also frightened of having done something dangerous and violent to me. I was in a fragile state of mind in the session and managing a loss of my own. I also felt guilty and worried about what I had done to him. All this created a certain dissonance in the session. I felt that we were touching on relevant things, and yet I was not fully in touch with how awful it had been for him. I think it felt too unbearable, hence my drowsiness.

Through the new diet, he was also letting me know that he was treating himself and didn't need the food/treatment I was giving him.

The unplanned break had ruptured something that couldn't be recovered. Over the following sessions, Mr D retreated into a narcissistic state: impenetrable and contemptuous. He remained silent, but my mind remained empty of any associations. Instead, I would find myself unable to think, frozen or drowsy. He also started cancelling sessions regularly, so that we would end up having two or sometimes one session a week. When I tried to talk to him about the meaning of these cancellations, I was either met with an impenetrable silence or a batting-away of my inquiry. Not only did Mr D fear that he had done something dangerous to me, but he also felt that I had done something deadly to him—perhaps tricked him or manipulated him, as he felt his mother had often done. He gave me the experience of what it is like when one's mind is taken over: in this period I had no associations or thoughts in the silence. Instead, there was just drowsiness and, after most sessions, a sense of having failed him. It was unnerving, even frightening at times. Supervision was a strong anchor, which helped me to navigate this and to continue to think about him.

Three months later, Mr D terminated his treatment. He did come to see me for a final time, remaining standing by the door for almost half the session, repeating that treatment did not help him and he was wasting his time. I linked his wish to leave with my sudden break three months previously, when he felt that I had left him in a broken-down state. He dismissed this and remained this way for most of the session, where I felt it was impossible to make contact with him.

This was a very painful session. I felt that Mr D had come to the session feeling frightened and paranoid. He seemed terrified that I would somehow trap or trick him, but he was also frightened by what he was about to do to himself. A more accurate way to take this up might have been to suggest that he now doubted whether I had actually returned and recovered, but perhaps I found this too painful because of my own state of mind. Perhaps there was a part of him that was aware that he might be cutting himself off from the lifeline I tried to offer him. But a larger, more dominant part was determined to kill off this lifeline. He veered between feeling that I was not giving him the right sustenance and feeling that he was not the right type of patient. Either way, we were not the mirror image of each other. I felt that my unplanned break had left him with a wish to return to a painless state. Following this session, Mr D did not return, despite my making efforts to contact him. Finally, I wrote to his GP, informing him of the premature termination of the treatment.

Conclusion

My sense of Mr D was that he had profoundly lacked a mother who was able to think about him—that is, an adequate maternal container. This left him with unbearable primitive anxieties: a fear of falling apart, perhaps, and breaking down. In response, his mind seemed to have become populated with violent objects, ones that destructively attacked not just his desires, but also his curiosity and his capacity to make emotional links. I felt that Bion's (1959) notion of an ego-destructive superego was helpful in understanding the relentless attacks I observed. Mr D was caught between a cruel, violent internal parental couple, resulting in a belief that intercourse was dangerous, even murderous. This led to a profound restriction in "triangular space" (Britton, 1989), the consequences of which were a profound impairment in his capacity for reflection and reciprocity. Organizing his experience through splitting and projecting seemed to be a necessary survival strategy but also reduced his capacity to function in his relationships and get on in life.

The mirroring that Mr D idealized was not the ordinary kind of empathic mirroring leading to a deepening of emotional contact. The mirroring he sought was one where he could only mechanically and concretely reflect the other, while believing that he was being an authentic friend, husband, father, and patient. In fact, having feelings, thoughts, and sensations of his own terrified him, and he dealt with his terror by resorting to this type of mirroring, which, while rigid and unchangeable, also helped maintain some contact in his relationships.

In the treatment, Mr D displayed a disdain for my curiosity, while he held himself aloof. His memory of his mother jeering at him for offering her a gift was profoundly sad. Yet, in different ways, this was replayed in the sessions, with him being attacking and contemptuous of my efforts. Through my countertransference, I was able to know something about his violent fragmentation and anxiety.

When I was able to interpret the meaning of this mirroring, I felt that I had made emotional contact with him. This was further evidenced by his bringing to the session a dream that showed his core pain. This was then followed by my unexpected break, which put him in a state of deep terror. He felt that he was in bits, like the six kittens, and this felt intolerable.

I think he really did feel as though he was not able to get in touch with the good object/therapist, and this exposed him to fears of a psychotic breakdown. This seemed to be the reason he was unable to stay in treatment.

In conclusion, Mr D used powerful defences as a way of managing his deep terror of fragmentation and disintegration. The dominant part of his mind was like Bartleby, who, throughout the novel, keeps saying "I would prefer not to". Mr D preferred *"not to"* because he was terrified of knowing something fundamental about his mind: the violent manner in which he attacked himself, his objects, and life itself.

CHAPTER TWENTY-ONE

The Ghost Ship: a reflection on working in the Tavistock during the Covid-19 pandemic

Alan Baban

Every Thursday during lunch the members of our clinical unit used to meet in a medium-sized room on the fourth floor of the Tavistock. I remember the first time I sat in that room—the sun that filtered through the windows and touched the heads of the senior staff, lending them a faint but unmistakable glow in my mind. Someone said something about the good breast. In response, someone else said something back about the bad breast, because the good had to be counterpoised by the bad. It was inevitable, like clockwork. We could not escape the inevitability of a mild depressive state or a state of fragmentary confusion, whichever would come for us first. Many of us in that room were very hungry. A trainee with a haggard and hypoglycaemic look muttered something about "container-contained" as he slowly patted Doritos chips from his belly.

Ah, I thought to myself, *the home of psychoanalytic psychotherapy. I have finally arrived.*

Quite strange now to look back at those times and remember, not so much what we said, but how we said things, what we embodied with our speech. In other words: *how our speech came out of us.* What echoes it made. The little homes it found in faraway corners of the building that are now empty. The footsteps and faint breaths and familiar lift-pinging sounds that signalled someone was either coming or going. Now we (or a microphone-muffled version of us) existed in that vague apparatus we call The Cloud. I didn't really know what The Cloud was, but I wanted to avoid it.

Like many, I imagine, I started a psychotherapy training in order *not* to be swallowed up by The Cloud. In my mind, Clouds both belonged to and facilitated the world of e-mails and Outlooks and hastily forwarded "cute sloth" memes. They did not belong in the room with the patient. Unless they were psychic clouds, or mere cloudings of consciousness—those were OK.

Of course, all of this—the humour, the ribald commentary, and constant kvetching about Zoom—was our way to *not* think about things. And by things, I mean the real things, the things that matter, which in 2021, as I write this chapter, still feel difficult to articulate and make sense of without a sense of anger or resentment sewering up. Thinking about the first year of Covid conjures up a sort of mental sludge of press conferences, images of hospital staff working in spacesuits, and a public-at-large recast as bands of masked wanderers heaving bags of toilet paper and precious detergent.

And yet, if you asked me now "what happened", I can't say I'm sure. Even a year later, I still do not think I can see clearly what has happened to my life, let alone your life, or anyone else's life amidst this global crisis. The dust has not yet settled on our mass confusion.

What I do know, though, is that there was a brief period of time in the Tavistock during 2020 when I was at war with a Starbucks machine.

The Starbucks machine, No.1

I met a systemic therapy trainee as she waited for a hot chocolate. We spoke about the different coffee machines we'd encountered in NHS care settings: the St Charles Centre for Health and Wellbeing in Notting Hill had a Douwe Egberts, while those in St. Pancras had to make do with Costa.

The Starbucks machine was something new for both of us. We had never seen a Starbucks machine in an NHS setting before. It was a gleaming, industrial-grade nightmare whose nozzle spewed milky steam into corporately labelled paper cups. This became our conversation piece, a bulwark against our own fears about the virus.

Over the next few weeks, as the world outside reconfigured itself around the threat of an "invisible enemy" (the virus particle made to look sinister and spiky on TV, with red tips, like a gnarled medieval torture device), we always had our coffee conversation. The queues began to dwindle, as fewer people came into the building.

The systemic trainee pointed out that we no longer saw the woman with the Birkin bag any more. For me, that was a good thing, as she always held up the queue. Only later did I realize that she might have been seriously unwell; that the absence of people in the building carried this new, awful weight. We were working in a hospital where there were no patients and, increasingly, no staff, and it felt *haunted*.

One day, as we waited, the systemic trainee commented that the space between us was becoming less and less peopled. I struggled internally between my concern for others and my secret urge to have the Starbucks coffee machine all to myself.

Pretty soon I got my wish.

And then, just like that, it was over. One day I came into the building, and the Starbucks machine was nailed shut. Where coffee once was, there would now be . . . nothing.

Ghost Ship, No. 1

The French psychoanalyst and psychiatrist Henri Rey famously called the Maudsley Hospital the "Brick Mother", and the term has since represented ideas of safety, continuity, stability, and institutional forbearance—the safe structure that quite literally houses patients' minds, allowing them, within its walls, to fall apart and re-form anew.

Of course, hospitals and clinics can have the same containing function for the staff that work there, allowing staff to securely occupy and explore internal states of confusion that are important parts of the work at hand. This is provided, in the symbolic sense, by supervisions, team meetings, and other avenues where we can learn to be curious about our own sense of "not knowing", so that it might develop into something creative. In a more concrete way, there is something very centring about the presence of other people, thinking, working, biting on the same sandwiches, beset by the same IT-related conundrums. It is a tangible thing that is psychically felt: and I don't think I truly understood how important this all was until it wasn't there anymore.

There was a period at the start of the pandemic when no one really knew what was going on. The Tavistock Centre still stood in all its architectural heft, but things inside were crumbling, any ideas about "containment" bleeding into our new language of "isolation" and "self-isolation". Those of us remaining in the building kept two metres apart and looked at each other rabbit-eyed under masks. Needless to say, it was a profoundly disturbing time, but also, after a while, one we could begin to be curious about.

In the opening chapter of his 2019 book, *Psychoanalysis and Anxiety*, the Kleinian analyst Chris Mawson draws on the work of the Roman philosopher Lucretius, who suggested that the mind is analogous to a vessel "polluted with foul taste/Whate'er it got within itself". The sense is that it is not only the nature of the vessel itself that acts on and modifies its contents, but it is also the contents therein that can, in turn, alter the structure of the vessel itself.

As with the mind and the continual process of projection and introjection we undergo with our own internal objects, we can also have an effect—and be affected in turn—by our relationship with the objects in the outside world, and whatever they mean to us.

I want to suggest in this chapter that, during the pandemic, interesting changes occurred in how the Tavistock Centre, as an object and sturdy repository of safe meaning, was experienced by the staff inside it and how those staff, as harbourers of the multifarious feeling states we experienced in relation to the loss of Covid-19, re-experienced and re-fashioned the building anew.

Because, in my estimation, what was once the "Brick Mother" became, for a brief period of time, the "Ghost Ship."

To elucidate this further, I must return to the Starbucks machine.

The Starbucks machine, No. 2

I was furious. I couldn't believe the machine had been shuttered. It didn't make sense to me that during a time of lurching and sudden change, and change happening in a centenary year, when things were already roiling, the Institution would take this step. For me, it was a big issue, one whose wider, symbolic import I had no access to at the time. I simply wanted to have my automatically engineered Cappuccino. I wanted my coffee.

I brought my issue to the unit meeting, which was, by that point, on Zoom. The early days of Zoom unit meetings were exercises in mass bewilderment. We are all on these large Zoom meetings both about to say something and scared of interrupting one another, as if doing so would break an awful spell. That day, someone may have said something about the good breast. Perhaps the bad breast came up. Feeling brave, I sallied forth, and formulated my thinking about the lost Starbucks machine.

Did anyone hear me? Could we hear each other?

Communication in large groups is challenging at the best of times. But it all gets weirdly modulated in the floating, flat-screen tundra-verse of Zoom. Our communications there enter a new, distorting dimension— one that, unlike our own unconscious predilections, is all too manifest to see. Words get mangled, broken up, frozen, then stretched like taffy in various states of mid-buffer.

It may be that, during my contribution to that unit meeting, as I said "Starbucks", some people only heard the "Star", while others, with different connectivity issues, heard me for some strange reason repeatedly say the word "bucks", like I was asking for more money.

In any case, the response came. The Toza Cafe was still open, and the staff there were doing heroic work. Was this actually an important issue? As one of the younger members on the team, could I not walk the 300 metres to the real Starbucks on Finchley Road, where I might also have some in-person contact: a rare commodity in those days? I didn't know what to say. We quickly returned to speaking about symbolic breasts.

But I couldn't quite get the Starbucks machine off my mind. Like the sea captain Ahab in Herman Melville's *Moby-Dick*, who is psychically assailed by the eponymous whale and pursues it relentlessly, in the face of all good reason and logic, I, too, could see that this wasn't really about some elusive and absent beans, at least not concretely. As Melville puts it in his famously convulsive prose:

> . . . all evil, to crazy Ahab, were visibly personified, and made practically assailable in Moby Dick. He piled upon the whale's white hump the sum of all the general rage and hate felt by his whole race from Adam down; and then, as if his chest had been a mortar, he burst his hot heart's shell upon it. [Melville, 1851, p. 262]

Is Melville not speaking here of an absent object massively projected into, until, suffused with a new and terrible light, it hangs in and imbues the psyche with its own persecuting presence?

After a brief moment where I did try, with some conviction, to wrench the plastic barrier that covered the machine, I paused to reflect. It wasn't just me. In those early days, people were furious. It might have been at an awkwardly designed laminated poster or at an inexplicable neon-lit sign welcoming people to the library when no one could enter the actual library: these objects were little synecdoches for something wider that was going on in the building at large, and in the mind it housed a split, where everything good was projected into the vaunted ideal of what the Tavistock Clinic *had once been* (that we might go back to, sometime, somewhere), whereas we were left with something unfamiliar and bad.

The Brick Mother had become the Ghost Ship, and it was haunted by strange new objects that teased us with their light and warmth.

Somehow the work continued.

There was something surreal about sitting in the same offices we had previously been in: occupying those same analytic chairs, but staring over now at empty cushions; phoning our patients, whom we could hear but not see and who were, in their own way, navigating the same issues: who? what? where? How to get through?

Clinical example

> A 41-year-old woman, who was then in a once-weekly psychotherapy that had recently been moved onto the phone, contacted the Adult Department's duty service in a state of terror and confusion. She wanted to speak to the duty clinician, reporting suicidal thoughts that were intensifying at work. When I called her, all I could hear were squawks and shrieks. The noise completely overwhelmed my headphones, pressing in on my ears to the point where I could feel nothing but building pressure. I said "Hello" over the din but was unsure if anyone could hear me. Was there anyone there? Eventually, through the animal noises, I could hear a small voice speaking faintly. The patient said she worked in an animal enclosure; she was cleaning out the bird cage. She was sorry. Could I call back later? When I did, I could hear animal grunting; she was cleaning out the foxes' dens. Later I heard the pigs. In this way my patient led me around the zoo. At some point, in some quieter place, and after I had sat (in the figurative sense) with her for a period of time, she felt she could speak to me in words about her suicidal thoughts.

In this example, the patient used her immediate environment—and its deafening, cacophonous qualities—to communicate something about her own primitive state of mind. If she were in the room, and in a more coherent place internally, she might have spoken to me about the zoo and described the aggrieved and instinctive, penned-in creatures with which she identified and into which she projected parts of herself; but, of course, she wasn't *in* the room with me. She was quite literally in the zoo. For the first few minutes of our contact, words became beside the point. All I had to hear, and understand, was threatening noise, and, in this way, to experience what the patient experienced herself—as became clearer later on during the phone call, when she alluded to a series of tyrannical and primal internal figures that persecuted her. I do not believe we would have been able to have this quality of interaction in the room, where the centring presence of bodies may have prevented something so disturbing from erupting.

It could also be said, and I believe this has been true for many patients, that having sessions or therapeutic contact on the phone has meant a reckoning with and compensatory response to what is lost: down four of our senses, we are only left with speech. The bandwidth is severely limited, and patients who might otherwise communicate through their physical presence, or smell, a quick flash of their eyes, are now left with having to communicate, and compress, all of that data, somehow, through sound only. That results, as in this interesting example, in the patient literally co-opting piercingly loud environments to put forward in noise what cannot yet be put into words.

When one doesn't have a sense of where, who, or what the object is, one might attempt to reach it *more* aggressively.

It was so important, then, dealing with this level of demanding clinical work that we, as clinicians, knew where we were.

Ghost Ship, No. 2

It is very strange working in and moving around a mostly empty building. Even as I knew, on a rational level, why there were no people in the building, another part of my mind still expected people and presence—and searched for it. Much like the opening scene of Cameron Crowe's *Vanilla Sky*, where a helmet-haired Tom Cruise wakes up to find Times Square deserted, his initial sense of freedom and elation (blasting his Porsche through what were once busy thoroughfares) transforming over time into anxiety and then blind panic. Where is everyone?

In those early days, one could walk long stretches of the building without coming across another person. The thin, dimly lit corridors of the Adult Department, with their blind turns that led into more empty spaces, put one in mind of the uninhabited Overlook Hotel in *The Shining*—a film where, infamously, the protagonist has a psychotic breakdown. To add to the surreal sense of existing in a "Ghost Ship", when one exited the building, the world outside was in the same arid and evacuated state—with some exceptions. The Tavistock's car park became, for a few months, North London's coolest "skate park", as teenagers performed whirlies and drifts on the tarmac. I also noticed a few times that there were little pockets, usually outside the library, where local kids congregated to smoke weed. There was actually something centring about this: the world stops, but adolescent boundary-pushing continues unfazed.

More worrying were the reports of random people walking into the building and stealing alcohol gel and toilet roll, which led, after a while, to reception being reconfigured as a security station where one had to sign in and show ID on entry. Security guards patrolled the corridors, which, obviously, became one-way. Discomfiting as it was—and it was discomfiting—the new systems provided a much-needed sense of structure that, I think, made it easier for people to come together and speak to each other. The staff I spent time with seemed to share the same strange thoughts I had. If no patients were coming in, why were we there?

Was it that we were, from an administrative standpoint, keeping the building alive by demonstrating that there continued to be "bodies on the ground", that work at the Tavistock persisted, it did not fold in on itself, as many other psychotherapy services did at the time? Or was the building, as a place to be, actually the thing that kept us going as staff? I don't think it's an either/or.

In an article for the *International Journal of Psychoanalysis*, Michael Parsons unpicks and elucidates some of the late ideas of the French psychoanalyst André Green, whose work is bound by ideas of absence and negation. Most useful is his explanation of Green's term "the negative hallucination":

> The hallucination is to compensate for the absence of the wished-for object. If we can give up the hallucination and bear the object's absence, that is, if we can accept the negative, we can then find other, constructive, ways of dealing with our sense of lack, including the growth of new object-relationships. [Parsons, 1996, p. 405]

In other words, it is not only that we come to know heretofore unknown facets of the object only in the object's absence, but that, if we can truly accept and bear this absence, we might open ourselves up to knowing the object (and other objects) in a new way. As Parsons neatly puts it: "We become who we are by how we deal with the fact that we cannot have what we want nor be who we wish to be" (p. 404).

It has become clear through this period that there are aspects of the work and the training whose importance we are only now coming to understand. Staff speak about the loss of so-called "corridor conversations", and all the interstitial happenings around and in between patient contact and supervisions, which enrich those processes because they enrich *us*.

Equally, and movingly, the slow shift back to working in person with patients has led to important developments in the work around loss and absence, and if these matters can be adequately worked through, as I show in the example below, both patient and therapist can understand each other in new ways.

Clinical example: Mr R

> I had been seeing Mr R once a week for five months before the pandemic struck. Fey and unassuming, he had been referred by a psychiatric team who had struggled to alleviate his depression, which, he said, was crippling: it was so crippling that he made it clear, in various ways, that if it did not lift, he would kill himself on a specified date. The clock was ticking. At the start of our treatment, Mr R would not say very much, and his speech was deadened and washed of colour and tone. Nothing of worth happened in his life. No one existed. His friends had long abandoned him. I was his only human contact, and

then, of course, he stopped seeing me. Five or six sessions would go by with no contact whatsoever, and then, like that, he would re-appear, as if nothing had happened. There was a real sense of hopelessness, and despite my efforts, I did not feel Mr R was in a position, at that point, to understand his sado-masochistic way of relating to the object, the fear and terror he instilled in me (was he dead?), and his need to set up a system of control where I would be very much under his thumb—he the one leaving me, and not the other way around.

When we moved to remote work, I noticed a shift. Mr R began to sound frightened and scared. Of course, on one level this was to do with the pandemic; but on another level, I believe he was terrified of what he might have done to me, that I would now no longer see him in person. When I put this to him, he seemed to come in touch with reality and understand the damage he had been doing, through his many missed sessions, to his opportunity at an NHS-funded psychotherapy. He began to turn up and to speak to me in a deeper way about his experience and to let me into his phantasy world. What I did not realize at the time was that there was a "me in his head" that was being built up, and fortified, during this time of remote work—an idealized voice in his ear, which he continued communicating with between sessions—but which, of course, had its differences from the "me in the room".

It was only when we returned to the room after many months that these divergences and disjuncts could be explored. Mr R was chastened—my hair was different, I was slimmer, he did not remember me wearing contact lenses. Equally, I found myself re-orientating myself to him, forgetting how tall he was, or the ungainly way he ducked and shouldered himself into the room. My absence (in one sense) had allowed him to make contact with me (or some sense of me) in a new way. Coming back meant having to face up to more of a reality of who I was, which he seemed now able to do (as opposed to at the start of our treatment, when I believe I was experienced by him as a bundle of projections). In short, he could realize that we had a real therapeutic relationship.

In our last session, in the very last minutes, Mr R gave me a gift that was clearly very important to him. It was an outline of a person made out of wire—two arms, two legs, a body, and a head. He did not tell me who this person was, but that he wanted to say thank you to me and for me to keep this as a memento of the work we had done. It was a terribly moving moment for us both.

In hindsight, I feel this gift encapsulates something very important, both about Mr R's treatment (where a real object, even in outline, could start to be apprehended), but that it says something useful about both his and everyone else's experience of the pandemic, where we were, whether we liked it or not, driven very deep into our own heads—speaking to people on phones, watching heads shudder and freeze on Zoom, but missing and having to make up for so much. In the same way as our patients could not be with us in the same way, we would not be with our patients (and other people) as we used to be, but in a modified, sketched-out, "outline" form, where things like consistency, stability, forbearance were very hard to achieve and maintain (especially in a pandemic, where the lay of the land shifted every few weeks). It is only now, as we come back in, that we are starting to fill things out again, and re-draw some of the contours of these strange shapes we made. The "Ghost Ship", as a concept, invites a bit of colouring in.

Conclusion

The original brief of this chapter was to give an account of what it was like to be working in the Tavistock during the Covid-19 pandemic. I hope that, by using the concept of the "Ghost Ship", I have been able to give some idea of some of the thoughts stimulated by that experience: that, in the end, a reckoning with the absences allowed for something new to emerge, but that he emptiness and the void had to be contended with first. It is maybe strange, but true, that my thinking around all this seemed to centre on a Starbucks machine (which, as it happens, is still not available for staff use). I can say now, though, that it was never really about the coffee. I realize that I never really wanted the coffee from the Starbucks machine. What I actually wanted and missed was the queue.

CHAPTER TWENTY-TWO

Lost in the dark: my first training patient and working on the telephone

Denise Hurst Hastings

At age 60, I came to the M1 training late in life. Already a psychodynamic psychotherapist, the training appealed to me for its psychoanalytic rigour, coupled with its application to public sector working. I was very much looking forward to my first training case and prepared for the challenges I expected to experience. What I could not have anticipated were the radically altered working conditions I would encounter: the lockdown conditions resulting from the Covid-19 pandemic.

Clinical example: Mrs D

Mrs D, my first once-weekly case for the M1 training, had a complex early history of emotional deprivation and sexual abuse. She was referred to our service by her GP, as she had been suffering from anxiety, low mood, and deep frustration. She told her assessor that previous counselling had been helpful and that she wanted to work on her struggle with intimate relationships, but had recently abruptly terminated treatment with a colleague.

The therapy started in November 2020, early in the Covid-19 pandemic, and it was understood that we would work remotely until we could meet in person. My supervisor told me that it was Trust policy to offer the patient a choice of the telephone or Zoom. Mrs D was adamant that she couldn't work on Zoom, so we agreed to work on the telephone.

Initially, I wasn't unduly concerned by working on the telephone. My own analysis had moved to being on the phone, and this had been a good experience. Similarly, I had been working with private patients on the telephone, and we had been able to do some very helpful work. I also had considerable experience of many NHS patients in very disturbed and disturbing states, so I felt reasonably well equipped to start. The difference, however, was that I had never met or seen Mrs D.

I realize now that I had no idea at the start how different, new, and, at times, alarming this experience with Mrs D would be: how she would take me into uncharted territory; how her way of making use of the remote setting of the telephone would leave me feeling completely blind, wandering about feeling de-skilled and, literally, lost in the dark.

Mrs D had a strong regional accent and at times spoke quite softly, which made it hard to hear her. Not being able to hear her without any visual cues to help left me at times feeling quite handicapped and frustrated that she wouldn't allow us to see each other.

Furthermore, from the start Mrs D used this situation in a very particular way, telling me that she needed to "get into her feelings" and proceeding to do so, with character voices, strange sounds, and unexpected silences. If I spoke, she would become furious, and, without any visual cues to help, I felt shut out, silenced, and given the role of only being allowed to witness.

Some background

Mrs D is middle-aged and single. She grew up in a small town in the countryside, the middle child in a large family, where the parents struggled to make ends meet. Her mother had suffered a great trauma herself in childhood, and Mrs D told me that she was often unavailable, sad, and withdrawn. Father was the dominant parent at home and was regularly brutal with his children, shouting at them and lashing out physically.

As a teenager, Mrs D was sexually abused by an older cousin over an extended period of time, and this experience, combined with the difficult relationship with her father, was something that Mrs D loosely seemed to understand had impacted on her own intimate relationships.

Straight in

Mrs D told me straight away that she had "googled" me and was satisfied that I was qualified and experienced. I noted that she would have then also seen a photograph of me, whereas I had not seen her. She acknowledged this and seemed to be quite pleased about it.

In our first telephone call, she introduced me to her "child" self, as a different persona that takes over: "The adult is there and she's really good and people like her, and all-of-a-sudden she's gone, and the child is there waving her arms around and doesn't know what to do . . . where does the adult go to? Where the hell has she gone to when I need her?"

From the start, there were two versions of Mrs D in our sessions: the "adult" her, who seemed to want to work with me and speak about the important events and relationships in her childhood, and the "child" her, whom she personified with a different voice and an excited manner, full of expletives.

Mrs D's "adult" communication was intelligent, open, and engaged, and I felt warm and empathetic towards her, but when her "child self" took over, I had no idea what was going on. In an early session, Mrs D told me that she had a sore throat and needed to "breathe into it to see what it says . . . my child wants to speak out", and this was followed by panting, tapping, and sounds such as "Oooo, oooo."

After only four sessions, Mrs D expressed very strong feelings about me, and her experience of the first break surprised me: "This bit of me wants to say, into a cushion, you're a fucking bitch . . . it's not fair to go off and leave me all alone."

I started to feel anxious, fearful, and confused. I had enough experience to recognize my feelings as powerful projections of her own feelings, but this didn't help me in the heat of the session: if I tried to speak about what she might be feeling, she became enraged and tried to silence me.

The value of supervision

Starting with Mrs D, I was also starting work with my new supervisor.

Both from my own Kleinian analysis and from my two past Kleinian supervisors, I started this work knowing something of the importance of addressing what was going on in the transference and finding ways to speak and interpret this to the patient.

With the same aims, my new supervisor introduced me to a different way of working. She introduced me to the ideas of Patrick Casement and Winnicott. She felt that in this case it was important to "learn from Mrs D: hold back, say less, don't interpret".

But neither approach seemed straightforward with Mrs D. I found this work very difficult, and, under fire, I would say more. Mrs D herself constantly complained about my interventions, saying "You talk too much" and "I'm going to have to teach you how to be a therapist!" While she laughed and there was even a feeling of warmth between us, there was hostility in this communication too, and I also felt fearful that she might be right.

My supervisor encouraged me to "stay with the affect" but the affect in the sessions with Mrs D was wild and overwhelming and very hard to understand. Very, very slowly, with the support of supervision, I started to hold back a bit more in an attempt to understand her—when I could.

Working with Mrs D

Mrs D told me about a dream in which *I* (her therapist) *was in a big hole, and she was standing back at a safe distance.* When I asked for her thoughts about this, she told me that the hole was her darkness, and she didn't want to get in. When I tried to think about this a bit more with her, she complained that I talk too much, that I am too dominant, and that I have a strong voice, like her father: "I don't need those explanations . . . I need more space."

I spoke to Mrs D about how a part of her felt that she could work with me and wanted to try, but how another part felt that this is impossible and that I wouldn't be able to understand her. Mrs D acknowledged this, but told me that, although she liked me, she didn't like my way of working, because it left no space for her feelings.

Her idea that she does "feelings" and I do "thinking", and that these are incompatible, became a recurrent theme, a special logic that felt powerful and left me de-skilled and unable to think.

I found the sessions really difficult and especially confusing when I was being cast as not *like* her father, but *as* her controlling, dominant father. I was struggling with being the bad object. When Mrs D attacked me, for example, as too "posh" or having "had a good life", I imagined that if she could see my face in the room or on Zoom, she would see my empathy and would not feel these things.

Supervision helped me to untangle these thoughts and feelings, to understand my defences against being the bad object, and, patiently, my supervisor continued to encourage me to hold back, give her space, and gently explore the feelings in the session.

We also discussed the reality of the telephone setting and how Mrs D was using it. Would her transference to me, which was so concrete, have been the same if we had been meeting as two physical bodies in the same room? Would Mrs D's phantasies have been impacted by the reality of an actual therapist in the same room together?

Brief link between us

I managed to speak to Mrs D about how frightening it was to connect with me and how much she would have liked to push me away, and for a while there was a shift that allowed a bit more contact, warmth, and humour between us.

For a while, Mrs D used the sessions in a more ordinary way, talking about difficulties in her past and her current life situation. She told me that she felt safe with me and opened-up about her intimate relationships, where she had been hurt emotionally and sexually abused. She was thoughtful, and I was deeply moved when she told me that her experience of sexual abuse, from which she had never been protected by her mother, was something that she felt had pervaded all her subsequent relationships. When it felt as if we were working collaboratively, I became more able to stay quiet and just listen.

Mrs D told me about a close male friend whose company she enjoyed and with whom there had always been a possibility of becoming more intimate. I noticed that I was holding a wish for her to have a relationship with this man, and that the more I felt this, the more she spoke about different reasons why this could never happen.

Mrs D acknowledged that she couldn't allow people to get too close to her, and that then she ends up a loner. I tried to talk to her about how getting close to others stirs up huge anxiety, how she then finds reasons to shut things down, and how this was what she does with her friend, as well as with me. Proving my point, Mrs D became angry as I "got closer" to the problem and told me that this therapy wasn't working for her.

Beginning of the end

In the last few months of treatment, Mrs D used the sessions to "get into her feelings", often without words, using sounds, and whenever I tried to follow her, comment on the feelings, or try to make sense of things, she would become increasingly furious.

Whenever I spoke or even took a breath, she would angrily tell me that I was interfering with her process, because my thinking "gets her away from feelings". In one session, Mrs D entered into a noisy, visceral, wordless description of her "blackness", which left me feeling lost, as usual, but also quite alarmed for her state of mind.

The Tavistock Unit meeting is a weekly clinical meeting for trainees and senior staff, and each week someone will present a case for the group to think about. These meetings, like the supervision sessions, were all on Zoom, and, while I missed the corridors of the Tavistock, the befores and afters of supervisions, the coffees and teas with colleagues, I nevertheless felt supported in my work with Mrs D.

My colleagues expressed their empathy with the struggle of working in this way; someone spoke about Mrs D being more appropriate for the Trauma Unit, and one of the senior staff cautioned me not to interpret or go in too deep. The other senior supervisor encouraged me to stay with my countertransference feelings and to work with these.

For Mrs D "getting into feelings" meant experiencing those feelings viscerally and uninterrupted in the session, through tears, movements, and sounds, which would then lead to "releasing" those feelings. My trying to name these feelings or talk about what was happening only infuriated her more, because it disturbed her process. What she seemed to mean was that I was interfering with her unconscious wish to have an impact on me, one in which she could project something of her disturbance and have me know about it, viscerally rather than cognitively. She told me that "psychodynamic" was not helping her and she wanted to stop.

In person?

In September 2021, 11 months into the treatment, I returned to face-to-face work in the clinic. Mrs D made it clear that she did not want to meet me, adamant that there was no point "starting something new". She continued to express her wish to end treatment and continued to attend the sessions on the telephone. Meanwhile, I was back working "in person" at the Tavistock Centre.

During one of our last sessions, there was a very loud car honk outside my window, and Mrs D asked me where I was and was then very surprised to hear that I was at the Tavistock. She then briefly wondered with me whether she could come in to meet me in person, and then gave several definitive reasons why this wouldn't work.

Finally, following a serious health scare, Mrs D ended the treatment prematurely in October 2021. In the last session Mrs D expressed warmer and more ambivalent feelings towards me.

Mrs D, M1, and me

In supervision, we discussed the episode of the loud car honk and my momentary excitement that Mrs D and I could meet and work together. We understood that in that moment reality was introduced: I was a real therapist in a real clinic, and she briefly entertained the idea of meeting and working together. I had a moment of hope that seeing me and being in the same room might be containing enough to mobilize a more neurotic part of her, so that we might begin to do some work together.

My supervision helped me to understand that Mrs D unconsciously needed me to be a bad object, whom she could then continually destroy in fantasy and, therefore, not have to engage with the reality of me or our task. With working on the telephone, it was often as though I had literally become a voice in her head. In her experience, this was not me being *like* her father in the transference, but of *being* her father.

Working on the telephone, as two disembodied voices, we lost the reality of knowing each other as two people in a room. Not having to see me or be with me in person enabled Mrs D to avoid real contact with me. In this way, the telephone setting itself was unconsciously used by Mrs D as a kind of psychic retreat so that her illusory, omnipotent world might be maintained. John Steiner speaks about how, in cases of extreme external trauma, patients struggle to face reality and firmly hold on to the structure of an illusory world. In not allowing us to see each other on Zoom and then not allowing us to be in the same room together, Mrs D could control how much reality she allowed in, so that she could maintain her status quo and avoid feelings associated with both depressive and persecutory anxiety.

With the help of my M1 supervisors and colleagues, I have tried to make sense of an experience that I wasn't expecting and couldn't make sense of at the time. The outcome was, in many ways, a painful failure for us both, with the remote nature of the treatment proving to be an insurmountable obstacle to the unfolding of an analytic process. My experience was one of being denied access to a full view of the patient, which might then have enabled better understanding. Although experience has shown that many treatments have been successfully conducted remotely during the pandemic, it seems to me that the fact that Mrs D and I had never met in person resulted in my remaining a frighteningly ambiguous figure: one who might be abusive but who also might stir up longings and feelings of dependence that needed to be kept at a safe distance.

PART V

DIVERSITY

Francesca Hume

In Part V, we turn to the subject of diversity in clinical training. In these chapters, there is something of a shift of focus. Whilst they continue to highlight the experience for the trainee for whom this topic has particular personal importance, these chapters address the culture of the institutions themselves and their capacity and willingness to embrace issues of diversity. In some cases, these issues could be addressed helpfully but in most, there were significant struggles arising from factors that lay within the institution itself and an unwillingness to take stock of the trainee's experience. All these chapters offer sobering reflections on what it is to feel that an aspect of one's identity is not accepted or even rejected and the pressure on the trainee to "blend in" with whatever is felt to be normative for the institution.

In chapter 22, Poul Rohleder provides an excellent overview and an introduction to the subjects of inequality, diversity and inclusion in psychoanalytic training.

In chapter 23, Poul Rohleder focuses on sexual diversity. He outlines some points for consideration about teaching on sexual diversity in psychoanalytic training, as well as considering the trainee experience. There is a brief overview of the anti-homosexuality and heteronormative bias in psychoanalytic theory, and the use of this theory and texts in psychoanalytic training. There is an exploration of how difficult it may be for LGB trainees to "come out", to be able to engage with discussions on theory and in supervision, and to be able to freely and safely voice their perspectives.

In chapter 24, Diane Turner explores her personal experiences of undertaking psychoanalytic training as a black trainee and the "blending in" that was required of her.

In chapter 25 Reziya Harrison explores her personal experiences of undertaking psychoanalytic training as an elderly female trainee as well as her earlier experience of being female in a different profession where women were very much in the minority.

CHAPTER TWENTY-THREE

Insiders and outsiders: some thoughts on diversity and psychoanalysis

Poul Rohleder

There is an increased focus in society and institutions on matters of inequality, diversity, and inclusion, spurred on by events and socio-political movements such as Black Lives Matter. In psychoanalysis, too, there is an increased focus. In the United States, the American Psychoanalytic Association initiated the Holmes Commission on Racial Equality. In the United Kingdom, the British Psychoanalytic Council (BPC) have established an Ethnicity, Culture and Racism Task Group and a Sexual and Gender Diversity Task Group. The theme of the BPC's 2022 annual "Psychoanalytic Psychotherapy Now" conference was *"Insiders and Outsiders: Navigating Identities and Divisions Inside and Outside the Consulting Room"*. There was a day and an evening of excellent papers and discussion, stirring up much thought about what is "inside" and "outside" what we do as psychoanalytic practitioners, and who is "inside" and "outside" the profession. The following chapters in Part V, on diversity in psychoanalytic training and reflecting experiences of ethnicity, age, gender, and sexuality, touch on matters of insiders and outsiders in psychoanalysis. In this short comment, I provide some thoughts on diversity and psychoanalysis by way of introduction to the next chapters.

As Lisa Baraitser (one of the speakers of the PPNow 2022 conference) points out, Freud advocated psychoanalysis not only as a mental health treatment, but also as a project of emancipation and social and political change: a "psychoanalysis for the people" (Baraitser, 2022). But, as Baraitser so powerfully asks, what constitutes "the people"? How is it decided who benefits or needs psychoanalysis? Who is psychoanalysis for? She argues how psychoanalysis, as an institution and part of the structures of society, is unavoidably implicated in deciding who is included and excluded from activities: decisions that are shaped by normative "patriarchal, colonial, ableist, and hetero- and cis-normative" regimes. Some reference is made to this in this section of the book, as some of the authors comment on what has been written about or what has been verbally uttered in relation to psychoanalytic patients and who is treatable or not. The chapters also note how issues of prejudice and discrimination might be considered by some psychoanalytic practitioners and institutions as "outside" (sociopolitical) matters, secondary to the consulting room's primary focus of the internal world.

Baraitser (2022), in writing about the history of "social clinics" in psychoanalysis, considers what constitutes "the people" primarily in considerations of access to psychoanalytic treatment—how it is decided who would benefit and be helped by psychoanalytic treatment and who not. But the same can be asked of who are "the people" *inside* the profession? And what happens when those that are "outside" the norm, come in?

Through my involvement in various professional and institutional committees, I am aware that most psychoanalytic institutions in the United Kingdom are actively thinking about and concerned with addressing issues of diversity and inclusion in their trainings. I have seen several training institutes having public "diversity and equality statements" and committing themselves to addressing inequality. When the topic of diversity and psychoanalytic training is discussed, attention can rapidly be given to matters of accessibility—for example, bursaries for people who could not otherwise afford it. Such people are often constituted as ethnic minorities—and statistically this is not wrong: ethnic minorities, by reason of their minoritized status, are more likely to live in conditions of social and economic disadvantage. Suggestions are also made about the need to review the curriculum and include more papers about diversity. These are important considerations for trying to address diversity and inclusion and inviting in people on the outside. However, sometimes there is a risk that this becomes little more than window-dressing, and more fundamental issues may not be addressed.

When it comes to accessibility considerations, *who* are those people outside that the profession wants to invite in and whom do they not? In past years, when it came to homosexuality, for example, training institutions *might* have considered allowing a "good gay" to train—a "good gay" who would be discreet and who may have had some homosexual experiences in the past, but was not actively so (as suggested in the research by Ellis, 1994). Some applicants might have been considered "too old" to train, others perhaps too culturally different, or too disabled. Of course, not everyone will have the required qualities and competencies to train as and be a psychoanalytic practitioner, just as not everyone could be a pilot, an architect, or a neurosurgeon. However, one should not confuse required and necessary qualities, skills, and competencies with value judgements about the "right kind of people". There may be primitive anxieties at the entry gates, with "insiders" fearing being colonized by outsiders and their thoughts and practices destroyed. We see this fear in social prejudices on a frequent basis.

Furthermore, thought is needed about the institutional environments applicants are being invited into. The "political" issues of racism and other forms of prejudice do not just happen "outside"; they are very much "inside" too. By focusing only on matters such as accessibility and curriculum, the hope may often be that change will come for the next professional generation. But what about now? What about existing problematic dynamics, relationships, and structures within the profession and individual institutions? Will the person outside even *want* to come in? How white, straight, and middle-class is the senior management and training committee? What positions do ethnic minority members hold within an institution? Most importantly, how are differences handled and responded to? The chapters in this part offer various recollections of moments where differences could not be tolerated, where people were left silenced, and topics could not be openly discussed. There is little point having a "welcome" mat at the front door but for there to be little sense of welcome once inside. The chapters also offer some reflection of more welcoming, more open, and more constructive experiences.

If we want to be an open, contemporary profession for "the people", then we need to take a good look inside our profession and trainings and make changes from within, and not just look outside for good people of diversity who can be persuaded to come in, and for change to eventually come one day. The chapters in this part, reflecting on issues of ethnicity, age, gender, and sexuality, and psychoanalytic training, partly invite you, the reader, into the personal space of the author. For some readers, what is written in these pages may be all too familiar. For others, it will be unfamiliar. After reading these chapters, what thoughts do you have? What feelings are you left with? Why do you think you might be feeling that? What does it make you want to do next?

CHAPTER TWENTY-FOUR

Thinking about sexual diversity in psychoanalytic training

Poul Rohleder

In my experience as a clinical psychologist and psychoanalytic psychotherapist, involved in the education of psychologists and psychodynamic counsellors and psychotherapists, it has felt easier and more straightforward to be out as a gay man to colleagues and students/trainees in the world of psychology than it has been in the world of psychoanalysis. I don't think I am alone in experiencing this.

When I was invited to write this chapter, I observed the ambivalent feelings it stirred in me. I was honoured to be asked; I felt keen to write about a topic I consider important, but anxious and reluctant to write from a personal perspective. Initially, I thought I would write from a theoretical perspective and my observations as a lecturer on matters of sexual diversity. But that is not good enough. We need to think about the actual experience of lesbian, gay, and bisexual (LGB) individuals in training. However, I was sitting with the anxiety of writing about this topic as a gay man and thus "coming out" in doing so. I grappled with dilemmas and consulted with a colleague and friend to help me think this through.

This is the first time I have described myself as a gay man, in writing, in a psychoanalytic text. I may have not felt it necessary to explicitly state it before, but more importantly, I had always thought I *should* keep this private: private from other psychoanalytic colleagues I did not know well, and in case a current or potential future patient might read it. After a lot of thought and reflection, I have taken comfort in the realization that my identity as a gay man is really no secret and that I have the respect of those colleagues who know me as such. If a reader or patient did a simple Google search and came across my academic and professional profile, published work and stated interests, they would be able to make a well-informed guess. Nevertheless, I suspect some more conservative psychoanalytic colleagues may bristle at my openness.

So why have I decided to open the chapter this way? For the simple but important reason that I can make this choice to "come out" a bit more comfortably and with less sense of risk than a trainee can. The editors of this book informed me that they were not able to find trainees who might identify as LGB willing to write about their experiences of training. I was not surprised at all. I know of LGB individuals in psychoanalytic training who have not felt comfortable speaking openly about their identity. I find it is not the same for psychology students and trainees who, by comparison, seem able to be more open. We really need to think about why the psychoanalytic profession can seem an uncomfortable and unwelcoming place for LGB people to enter, and the dilemma LGB trainees sit with about being able to talk openly about sexuality in psychoanalysis.

In this chapter I outline some points for consideration about teaching on sexual diversity in psychoanalytic training, as well as considering the trainee experience. First, I provide a brief overview of the anti-homosexuality and hetero-normative bias in psychoanalytic theory, and the use of this theory and texts in psychoanalytic training. Second, I explore how difficult it may be for LGB trainees to "come out" and be able to engage with discussions on theory, and in supervision, and be able to freely and safely voice their perspectives.

When considering sexual diversity, we are used to referring to the LGBT (lesbian, gay, bisexual, and trans) community. In this chapter I am focusing specifically on sexual diversity, referring to the experiences of LGB trainees (which may include individuals who identify as queer). I do not wish to exclude consideration of transgender individuals, but I cannot talk about trans experience from a personal perspective, and I cannot draw on having learnt from colleagues or trainees who identify as trans. I could also find no published literature on the experience of transgender trainees in psychoanalytic training. So, while I focus on sexual diversity, it is important to bear in mind how much more difficult the experience of transgender individuals considering psychoanalytic training may be. I use the terms "psychoanalysis" and "psychoanalytic" training to refer not just to trainings in four- or five-times-weekly intensive treatment, but to all trainings grounded in psychoanalytic thinking.

Psychoanalytic theory on homosexuality: from perversity to diversity

There is a history of pathologizing homosexuality in the various mental health professions—psychiatry, psychology, and psychoanalysis—viewing homosexuality as a disorder of the mind requiring psychiatric or psychotherapeutic treatment. In the United States psychoanalysis was inextricably linked to psychiatry, as only doctors could train as psychoanalysts in the last century. In the United Kingdom there was a tradition of admitting "lay" candidates into psychoanalytic training—that is, individuals without a medical training. Thus, the psychoanalytic pathologizing in the United States is more clearly documented, in its relation to psychiatry, whereas in UK psychoanalysis it is a bit murkier. While in the United Kingdom some sympathetic views were held in the past (e.g., some psychoanalysts were involved in advocating for the decriminalization of homosexuality in the Wolfensen report: Newbigin, 2013), others were vocal in their views that policies should reflect the pathology of homosexuality (e.g., some UK psychoanalysts spoke in support of Section 28, a series of laws effective from 1988 to 2000, prohibiting the "promotion" of homosexuality in schools, and thus any teaching on same-sex sexuality: Ellis, 2021).

In the United States homosexuality was included as a personality disorder in the first edition of the American Psychiatric Association's *Diagnostic and Statistical Manual of Mental Disorders* (DSM; APA, 1952). This was around the time that the Kinsey research reports on human sexuality (Kinsey, Pomeroy, & Martin 1948; Kinsey, Pomeroy, Martin, & Gabhard, 1953) were published, beginning a move to consider homosexuality and bisexuality as a normal variant of human sexuality. This inspired renewed thinking about the conceptualization of homosexuality as a mental disorder within US psychiatry. However, the reports were largely ignored within psychoanalysis, being viewed as "outside" what is relevant for psychoanalytic thinking (Lewes, 1995). Homosexuality as a mental disorder was eventually removed from the *DSM* in 1973 (APA, 1968). However, groups of psychiatrists, many of them psychoanalysts, continued to advocate for the possibility of providing "treatment" for homosexuality for LGB patients who sought a cure (Bayer, 1987). Thus, the diagnosis of "ego-dystonic homosexuality" was proposed and included in the *DSM* until its eventual removal in 1987 (APA, 1987). The World Health Organization followed similar lines in their revisions of the *International Classification of Diseases* (ICD), removing homosexuality in the 10th edition of the ICD in 1992 (WHO, 1992), but replacing it with the diagnosis of "ego-dystonic sexual orientation". The conceptualization of the diagnosis of "ego-dystonic homosexuality" rested on the consideration that heterosexuality, in contrast, is not something that could, or indeed should, be changed. While the DSM is published by the American Association of Psychiatry, it nevertheless has considerable influence in the United Kingdom.

Psychoanalysis has been much slower in changing its views on homosexuality. Lewes (1995) outlines different phases in the psychoanalytic theorizing of homosexuality, from Freud's humane and liberal, albeit tentative and ambivalent theorizing on homosexuality, through a long period of more pejorative theorizing (notably on the part of American psychoanalysts such as Edmund Bergler, Irving Bieber, and Charles Socarides), to emerging counterarguments against the pathologizing of homosexuality and eventual curiosity and openness. Lewes reviews how, before the 1980s, psychoanalytic theorizing formulated homosexuality as psychopathology and perversion. More has been written in relation to male homosexuality. In the United Kingdom, O'Connor and Ryan (1993) review psychoanalytic theorizing about lesbian women.

Lewes (1995) observes how the most vociferous authors reflect an unexamined and unchecked hatred in the countertransference in their writing. Take, for example, this passage by American psychoanalyst, Bergler (1956), written in a book about homosexuality:

> I have no bias against homosexuals; for me they are sick people requiring medical help. . . . Still, though I have no bias, I would say: Homosexuals are essentially disagreeable people, regardless of their pleasant or unpleasant outward manner . . . [their] shell is a mixture of superciliousness, fake aggression, and whimpering. Like all psychic masochists, they are subservient when confronted with a stronger person, merciless when in power, unscrupulous about trampling on a weaker person. [p. 29]

Some British psychoanalysts seemed sympathetic to such views, reflected in the invitation to Socarides (a strong advocate for conversion therapies to treat homosexuality) to give the annual lecture of the Association for Psychoanalytic Psychotherapy in the NHS in 1995 (Ellis, 2021).

Various British authors have outlined how British psychoanalysis has historically tended to formulate homosexuality as pathology and observe a heteronormative narrative against which homosexuality is regularly problematized (e.g., Barden, 2011; Fonagy & Allison, 2015; Lemma & Lynch, 2015; Newbigin, 2013; Twomey, 2003; Hertzmann & Newbigin, 2023).

Psychoanalytic theories that pathologize homosexuality tend to conceptualize it as an abnormality and deviation from "normal" heterosexual development, reflecting an underlying disease, or as immaturity, reflecting a developmental fixation or arrest at a pre-Oedipal stage of development (as reviewed by Drescher, 2008; Lewes, 1995; Twomey, 2003). Melanie Klein (1932) and Gillespie (1946), for example, regarded male and female homosexuality as an oral defence against heterosexuality. Fairbairn (1952) and Limentani (1979) regarded homosexuality as perversion, and as a symptom of borderline or narcissistic characters. It is important to note that psychoanalysts may have been writing case studies of homosexual patients, who, in terms of their individual psychology, may have had interpersonal and intimacy difficulties. However, the formulation about "the homosexual" patient became a formulation about all homosexuals, and homosexuality itself.

Contemporary psychoanalysis no longer regards homosexuality as pathology and perversity, understanding homosexuality, rather, in terms of diversity of sexuality. There are many new publications that observe the problematic past and offer new approaches (Giffney & Watson, 2017; Hertzmann & Newbigin, 2020; Lemma & Lynch, 2015; O'Connor & Ryan, 1993). The British Psychoanalytic Council has also produced a helpful bibliography of relevant books and papers for thinking about sexual and gender diversity (Full, 2021).

In my experience of teaching trainees, many are unaware of this history of pathologizing homosexuality. There have been more discussions about the pathologizing of homosexuality in psychoanalysis in the United States. In the United Kingdom, by comparison, there has been a notable silence and stubborn resistance. Mary Lynne Ellis's recent publication (2021) gives an important historical account of the actions taken to de-pathologize homosexuality in UK psychoanalytic professions. She rightly points out that there is still some way to go.

In addition to this historical pathologizing, there is also a heteronormative bias embedded in psychoanalytic theory. Our theories are saturated with heteronormative assumptions, with frequently used binaried organizing concepts such as male vs female, masculine vs feminine, active vs passive, heterosexual vs homosexual, and so on. The Oedipus complex, which remains a cornerstone of psychoanalytic theory, is formulated along heteronormative lines, with identification with the same-sex parent and desire for an opposite-sex object being regarded as the "healthy" resolution of the Oedipus complex. Although Freud made some attempt at formulating the homosexual Oedipus complex, it was conceptualized as a solution to castration anxiety and thus interpreted as a heterosexuality that was not achieved. Gay psychoanalysts like Richard Isay (1986, 2009) have offered alternative revisions of the Oedipus complex for understanding the sexuality of gay men, with formulations of the father as the primary object of desire.

There is renewed interest in Freud's theory of psychic bisexuality (e.g., Perelberg, 2018), which might open the possibility of thinking about sexual and gender fluidity. However, some of the writing on psychic bisexuality retains a heteronormative focus, missing an opportunity for thinking more creatively about sexual diversity and, indeed, bisexuality itself (Gulati & Pauley, 2019).

Such theoretical biases are hard to shift, and any challenge to our core theories may be met with anxiety about "being told how to think". Clarke and Lemma (2011) comment on this stubborn resistance to change anti-homosexuality and heteronormative biases:

> The obstacle of institutionalized homophobia for psychoanalysis is different from other causes of a long-term retreat from the public sector. Not only does it have deep roots in our trainings, and is ingrained at the most senior levels, it is also inextricably embedded for many as a cornerstone of theory via the centrality of the Oedipus complex [. . .] British psychoanalysis has been turning a deaf ear to the changing socio-political and mental health landscape of sexuality [. . .] over the past 25 years, the UK object relations tradition has struggled to make sense of contemporary concepts of gender and sexual identity. [p. 304]

So, what does this mean for teaching on sexual diversity and psychoanalysis?

Teaching sexual diversity

Too often, psychoanalytic trainings teach sexual diversity by including a short series of seminars. The same can be said for teaching on race, culture, and ethnicity. These "diversity" seminars are treated as additional topics, conveying a message that diversity is something extra, existing in work with "other" patients. Making it a separate topic continues to render it to the margins, rather than at the centre, in all aspects of our teaching and the theories we draw on.

When it comes to sexual diversity, some psychoanalytic practitioners and trainers feel anxious that we must "throw away" past papers and theories. In the era of "cancel culture", they envisage an Orwellian nightmare of rewriting history. Some trainees, on the other hand, have questioned why some papers are even taught at all. I would not necessarily advocate cancelling "old" papers and theory, although thought should be given to why we would want to teach about homosexuality using classic papers without any consideration to contemporary understandings of homosexuality. Psychoanalysis, like any profession, involves the continual revising and expanding of theory through research and practice. Our contemporary theories make sense by understanding what it has developed from. Furthermore, some papers may be "old" but contain theoretical cornerstones of our profession.

It is not what is taught and what is not taught, but *how* it is taught that matters. Psychoanalysis invites us to meander and explore with a sense of curiosity and openness. Yet, so often we find psychoanalytic theories being dogmatically followed as gospel truths. There are enriching opportunities for learning in engaging with texts with a critical lens. We might engage with a text while pointing out any heteronormative and other (e.g., sexist) biases embedded in it. Social constructionists observe that these texts are written within a particular social, historical, and political context. Freud's writing, for example, is partly a product of his time. He was revolutionary, regarded by many as subversive. Freud was, indeed, open and curious, not shy about commenting on what he didn't know or was unsure of. We run into trouble when theories become used in dogmatic ways and contribute to a closed, conservative mode of thinking.

Rather than "throwing away" such papers, they can be useful for thinking about how assumptions and prejudice interfere with working in an ethical way. We learn how to do things better by learning how *not* to do things. But this requires creating a space safe enough for a critique to be made. Classical texts may be open to refreshed readings and interpretations. For example, new readings of early versions of Freud's *Three Essays on the Theory of Sexuality* (1905d) show that he seemed to place greater emphasis on sexual drives and pleasure-seeking and psychic bisexuality than on the Oedipus complex, offering a potential for thinking about sexuality in non-heteronormative ways that is, thus, of great relevance for contemporary psychoanalytic understanding (Van Haute & Westerink, 2020).

Psychoanalytic teaching emphasizes understanding the internal world, sometimes with the exclusion of the external world and its impact. Too often a false distinction is made between that which exists "inside" the consulting room (phantasy, transference, intrapsychic conflict) and that which exists "outside" it, with a sense that, psychically, we all have the same internal structures. As with race and racism (Morgan, 2021), homophobia and anti-homosexual prejudice are seen to exist "outside" psychoanalysis, in the realm of the social and political, whereas psychoanalysis is focused on the internal. We fail to understand our patients if we ignore their external realities. For example, past psychoanalytic case studies about "the homosexual" emphasized their mental disturbance as signs of their character pathology, with little, if any, consideration of the impact of homophobia, oppression, and discrimination (Lewes, 1995).

Training experiences

In 2015, a gay man wrote anonymously about his experience of training for *New Associations*—an article entitled "a gay trainee". He said he could not identify himself out of a sense of fear for his career. At that time, I was entering my final year of intensive training. I remember reading that article and feeling angry and sad: why did he write it anonymously? To understand this, we need to bear in mind the historical theorizing of homosexuality, and we also need to understand the institutional experience for the LGB trainee.

A history of exclusion from training

For many years, openly LGB individuals were excluded from psychoanalytic training. Freud himself did not believe that homosexual individuals should be excluded, disagreeing with Ernest Jones, who wrote to him in 1921 that he was rejecting an applicant to training on the grounds of his manifest homosexuality. Jones regarded it as an intractable condition that could not be analysed, and thus the applicant could not be entrusted with the analysis of others (quoted in Lewes, 1995).

In the United States, the exclusion of LGB individuals from psychoanalytic training was quite explicitly known (Drescher, 1995). In the United Kingdom, while not explicitly stated as a policy, many LGB individuals were excluded, based on the understanding of homosexuality as pathology and perversion. In 1991, Rachel Cunningham published a paper exploring the exclusion of homosexual individuals from psychoanalytic training, where she stated that UK training institutions have an unwritten policy of exclusion or are "affected by prejudice, making it difficult for a homosexual to brave the choppy waters of training without compromise and discomfort" (Cunningham, 1991, p. 48). It is interesting to note that Rachel Cunningham was a pseudonym, suggesting that the author wrote under a culture of fear for speaking out.

In 1994 Mary Lynne Ellis, an openly lesbian psychotherapist, published a report on her research into homophobic attitudes in selection and training in three intensive UK training institutions. She found no explicit policy on exclusion but, nevertheless, found prejudiced attitudes expressed by the interviewees: members of the three institutions involved in selection of trainees. For example, she reported that the Chair of Admissions at the Institute of Psychoanalysis stated that they "wondered about a homosexual's ability to work intensively with a lot of issues of a heterosexual nature such as relationships with children" (Ellis, 1994, p. 511). The chair stated that they "would worry if someone had made a firm choice of homosexuality as their sexual orientation and didn't feel that was something that needed to be considered in their lives" (p. 512). Ellis also interviewed applicants who reported experiences of being judged and felt that their exclusion was based on their sexuality. For example, one gay applicant was reportedly told by a training institution that "homosexuals can't be psychotherapists". Another lesbian woman was told that "we don't train homosexuals . . . well certainly not male homosexuals. We might take a woman if she were very discreet" (p. 513).

More recently, Wayne Full (2020), investigating attitudes on homosexuality and psychoanalytic practice among BPC registrants, details psychoanalysts' and psychotherapists' awareness of LGB individuals being excluded from training in the past. This is not the case today, with the BPC and its member institutions having published official position statements condemning any form of discrimination, including on the basis of sexual orientation. However, this past (recent) history is important to note' because it is often known to LGB individuals who may be considering training but feel potentially unwelcome.

The dilemma for LGB trainees

Returning to "a gay trainee" (Anonymous, 2015), the author observed his discomfort and fear of speaking up about how homosexuality was taught and thought about in training, and his encounters with the texts that referred to homosexuality as perversion. I could relate to what he was talking about. The author wrote an invitation to the reader:

> "I wonder what you think of my experience and my relating of it. I'd like to know—really I would. I'd also like to hear your story and to use that to inform me better about mine." [Anonymous, 2015, p. 9]

I so wanted to write a letter in response because I sensed a loneliness in this invitation. If I could join him, then maybe it would be OK. But I could not. I was in the final stages of training myself, and I understood why he had to be anonymous. I thought about that article when sitting with my dilemma about writing this chapter. Seven years later, I feel I can afford to not be anonymous, but for some LGB trainees not a lot has changed. There are some openly LGB psychoanalytic practitioners in the United Kingdom, but not many. This article remains the only one from a gay man writing about his UK psychoanalytic training experience that I could find.

A dilemma for LGB trainees is that, to be able to talk authentically about their responses to texts that pathologize homosexuality, it may require being open about their sexuality, and their minoritized experience. Unlike many other characteristics, being LGB requires disclosure: "coming out". Other characteristics are observable and do not require such personal disclosure: having a visible disability; the colour of one's skin and one's racialized identity; accent and language denoting one's nationality;

title such as "Mrs" or wedding band denoting marriage; accent and terminology that may denote class.

I am not talking about disclosing to one's patient. I agree with the analytic stance of neutrality, abstinence, and anonymity, although this is not entirely possible because, as just mentioned, some characteristics are immediately visible and, thus, known to the patient. The question of therapist's self-disclosure of sexual orientation is debated, however, with more relational approaches recognizing therapeutic merits in self-disclosure (Drescher, 1998). Nevertheless, there is often a sense (whether actual or perceived) that this extends to training, too. We are taught that one should strive to be as much a "blank slate" as possible, and there is a "don't ask, don't tell" culture around homosexuality (Drescher, 1995; Ellis, 2021). This risks keeping LGB trainees and professionals "in the closet"—a historically lonely and painful experience for many. When it comes to clinical work, how can one reflect on one's countertransference if an aspect of one's personhood must be kept silent?

Part of the difficulty for LGB trainees is a fear of negative repercussions. As with race, it is often those who are themselves oppressed and marginalized who must do the work of anti-oppression and anti-marginalization. Too often they are met with resistance or defensiveness when speaking from honest experience. As Davids (2011) and Morgan (2021) state in relation to anti-racism work, the one doing the diversity work then becomes the troublemaker, or the one with "the problem". It can be similar when it comes to sexual diversity. Attempts to discuss the validity or relevance of theory becomes perceived as a personal grievance (Drescher, 1995). I have been in meetings talking about past anti-homosexuality attitudes in psychoanalysis, only to be angrily told that it is not like that at all. So, for trainees, it can feel difficult, if not impossible, to speak, as they risk alienating their peers and being labelled as troublesome or "woke". At best, there may be a sense of anxiety and fear from others that a wrong thing has been said. I recall in my training making comments about my response to reading a text where homosexuality was written about as perversion. I once tried to put into words my discomfort, my anger, at the homophobia I was reading. Although I knew I had sympathetic peers, I felt a sense of panic in the tutor, who seemed unsure of what to say or what to do. And so no further discussion took place.

As Dalal (1998) states, in writing about race and racism and the marginalization of black people:

> The point about being at the margins is that the centre finds it hard to hear, partly because of the psychological distance, and partly because what is

being said is inconvenient. And so the marginalized are forced to shout until hoarse, and can end up sounding shrill [. . .] those at the centre feel themselves to be innocent, unfairly assaulted from without. [p. 207]

Talking about homophobia (as with racism) can often turn into being perceived—and experienced—as being one's "personal issue" and grievance, rather than being responded to in any helpful, open way.

Another dynamic is, where there is an interest in speaking about diversity, trainees (and teachers) may be keen to hear from the minoritized members of the class. For example, when talking about racism, I have observed how white trainees (and teachers) look to their black peers to speak. This is done with good intention and with a sense of wanting to be inclusive. Yet, it puts the black trainee on the spot and places pressure on them to become the spokesperson for "the black experience", to carry the burden for talking about diversity issues, and to "teach" their white peers. This has been written about by black and Asian minority trainees in clinical psychology (Shah, Wood, Nolte, & Goodbody, 2012). The same can be said for sexual diversity, when the LGB member of the cohort carries the voice for an entire population group. I make the parallels with race, because it is how "difference" is perceived. Those identities located in the centre do not experience their identity as different, and so the difference is located in the other, in the margins. Racism is often perceived as being about blackness, and whiteness does not get considered (Morgan, 2021). Similarly, sexual diversity is about "the homosexual", and heteronormativity does not get considered.

The dilemmas for a trainee about being open about their sexual orientation may be particularly difficult in supervision. Drescher (1995) reports how some trainees find themselves working with supervisors who formulate homosexuality as pathology. Out of anxiety about advancing in their training, some felt unable to challenge their supervisors' views.

Richards (2020) observes that

the psychoanalytic supervisory tradition has not tended to allow for, let alone encourage, the active use of the supervisee's sexual identity within discussion of clinical work; even less encouraged is any acknowledgement that the supervisor has a sexual identity. [p. 57]

Richards reflects on what gets enlivened in the work if the sexual identity of the supervisee and/or supervisor becomes available for discussion.

Concluding thoughts

As mentioned at the start, I sat with a dilemma about how to write this chapter and how open to be. I wondered whether I should include some discussion about my sexual orientation and experience and thus risk "making an issue" of it. I wondered whether readers would think that I was voicing a personal grievance about psychoanalysis and psychoanalytic institutions, or whether I was making some valid observations. There was a lot that I could have written, and I found myself writing sections over and over again.

Too often diversity is addressed institutionally in a "tick-box" fashion, adding a series of seminars and making position statements (such as the flurry of statements that were brought out during Black Lives Matter). These are not unimportant, but if we are to be serious about diversity and inclusion, it must be central to everything we do. When it comes to sexual diversity, as "a gay trainee" (Anonymous, 2015) states, sexuality and homosexuality is for everyone. And as Donald Moss (2002) states, homophobia is of relevance not only for gay men, but for straight men, too, who restrain what would be labelled as their "feminine" aspects. Issues of diversity are difficult, because they challenge the norm. As the saying goes, "Diversity is a reality, inclusion is a choice."

CHAPTER TWENTY-FIVE

Hiding in plain sight: a personal experience of being black on the M1 course

Diane Turner

Being a black trainee on the M1 training was, at times, a disorientating and disturbing experience. There was an immersion into a world where the human condition was examined in the most fascinating and considered of ways, by sensitive and insightful practitioners who imparted understanding that I had not previously known possible. This created a heady mix of excitement and idealization of these purveyors of truth, who were prepared to pass on the skills of their trade to me. And I wanted to learn.

It was clear that a scrutiny of myself was going to be a necessary part of this journey. I realized this from the beginning, when I emerged from one of the two personal interviews, astounded that I had been reduced to tears, having disclosed deeply personal information. However, I accepted that this was part of the process of being "known" on this most exceptional of journeys and I was in.

I then found it disturbing to be sitting in a clinical meeting chaired by respected senior staff who were considering a black British female patient, someone not unlike myself. Their comments struck to the core: "Well, of course, these women do not make good analytic patients"; "*They* are unreliable, *they* won't turn up, it's all too much, *they* need something different"; "Well, I'm just an old softy, I tend to see *them* forever . . . but just once a month!" This was my first experience of something utterly discombobulating. How did this one "unreliable" patient come to suddenly represent "these patients" reminiscent of the "those people" of old? How was I seen? Did anyone realize that I was in the room? I found myself wanting to disappear. Although new to psychoanalytic training, I was an experienced clinician, with 20 years' experience of working in the multicultural central London NHS. I was no shrinking violet and didn't struggle to find my voice on the training, but in this situation I was rendered mute. The overwhelming feeling was one of shame, which was familiar and reflected certain experiences deeply held within me, which I had never expected to be reawakened on the fourth floor of the Tavistock Centre.

In the early days, I thought the only way to psychically survive the training as a black trainee was to split off my racial self, to shed my black skin, leave it at the door, and put it back on, along with my coat, at the end of the day. There was no place for it. It was only going to be a problem. Or, worse, it would be totally unacknowledged, an embarrassment: best not to draw attention to it. It did not seem to make any sense to me, on a training where we were challenged at every level, where everything was there to be interrogated and thought about, where the deepest recesses of the mind were explored—how could something so obvious be so off limits? I lost count of the times that our attention was drawn to the fact that Freud stated that the first ego was the body ego, and yet here was an aspect of my body that could not be more present, and it didn't exist. It was, at best, meaningless, ignored, irrelevant, at worst a problem and had to be hidden in plain sight, as it might just exclude me from analytic relevance.

This experience wasn't new to me, but one that I had buried deep in my psyche. It was a remnant from my personal history that I thought had been banished, along with the Robinson's golliwogs and the black-and-white minstrels of childhood. Adopted at three months, a mixed-race baby, into a white family, in a white street, in a white town up North, it was a familiar experience to be perceived as *other*, with all that that entailed. Racism, exclusion, black shame, guilt, and difference making me so visible, alongside an ancient desire to disappear, were inscribed on my being. But times had changed: a life in a major cosmopolitan town, multiculturalism, many years in analysis, a solid career, and family had changed everything—or so I thought. Here I was, in my late forties, at what should have been the pinnacle of my development, confronted with an unacceptable part of myself again split off, reminiscent of that abandoned baby, unwanted and unacknowledged.

I was familiar, from theoretical work on the Tavistock's D59 (Race, Culture, and Psychoanalysis) course, with the hatred of difference, the infant having to navigate its growing awareness of separation from the object and the privations that entailed. In my view, the adult department, and M1 specifically, were not interested in the growing analytic literature on race and racism—having to experience the separateness of the object as the basis of the hated other and the implications for the genesis of othering, more generally, and racism, in particular.

White (2002) described three ways of thinking about hate as it derived from racism. First, being hated, being the object of pernicious, destructive attributions and projections. As black trainees, these came directly and indirectly. There were ways in which the absence of thinking about the dynamics of race wiped us out. We were subjected to the presence of absence: our skin colour did not exist within the discourse of psychoanalysis. There was no "race" in the unconscious, therefore no structure for thinking. This left a hole, a void, an absence that was deeply troubling for those of us who felt that absence acutely. On my previous course, I looked forward to a lecture on race and psychoanalysis, but I was left dumbfounded when the lecturer did not, at any point, refer to skin colour as a relevant phenomenon in a discourse on race. I felt utterly wiped out when the entire lecture referenced only anti-Semitism as relevant, incapable of knowing how to even begin to open a dialogue as the only black face in the room and totally in collusion with the whitewash.

In those early days on the course, I used a familiar strategy of "integration": keeping my head down, blending in. Being mixed race and raised "white", it was possible for me to engage in a disavowal of my difference. It was obvious that I had a different-coloured skin, but the least said about it, the better, and this strategy was working well. I felt respected, my experience was valued. I was certainly not about to rock that boat!

The one situation where this strategy was of no use was with patients. Undertaking one of my first consultations, I met a new patient at the lifts. She was a black, West Indian woman, the same age as me, and on realizing that I was the therapist there to greet her, she immediately screwed up her face, sucked on her teeth, rolled her eyes to the ceiling, and barked "REALLY!" Fortunately, in my supervision it was possible to address issues of race in a serious-minded way when these situations arose. In contrast to the situations when I felt invisible and wiped out, when it mattered most, I was able to ask for help and receive careful, considered attention. Whether that was blatant racism from the patient or, equally, the patient who expected me to be "at one" with them due to our shared skin tone, I felt that this was the beginning of my being able to think about and engage with my racial self in a new way.

White's second way of thinking about hate in relation to race is "hating the self": the internalizing of pernicious, destructive attributions and projections that result in self-hating. It is with shame that I remember arguing for the right of patients to refuse to be seen by a black therapist.

It sounds ridiculous to me now, and I will never forget the look of despair on the face of a racially aware, fellow black trainee on the course.

On another occasion, I remember being in a "race" training event where we broke into small groups to discuss the issues of racial discrimination in employment at the Tavistock. Again, I remember my rather "manic" self, extolling the virtues of the clinic, and my denial of any form of discrimination in my time there, overshadowing the quiet voice of dissent coming from a black administrator, who was calling out the racism she had experienced. I am reminded of the character played by Samuel L. Jackson in Quentin Tarantino's *Django Unchained*: the appalling manipulative head house slave, who turns on his fellow slaves to preserve his status in the household. I abhor this position but also think about the acting-out necessary to survive in such an unenlightened situation. It was perhaps an attempt to integrate (ingratiate), as the small group included two senior members of the department, neither of whom had anything to say about the unfolding dynamics. I think now that this is an example of the difficulty of thinking under fire, with racial politics being the battle that raged.

The third way of thinking about race, according to White, is the re-externalizing of the malignant projections and regarding the projective source with extreme hostility. This speaks to the enactments that were a result of the projections we were subjected to.

When discussing this chapter with two black colleagues, we were struck that this was the first time that any of us had come together to have a frank discussion about the nature of being different on the training. It was a taboo that we each seemed to accept in our own way. Rather than supporting each other, we seemed to further project into each other in a damaging way, at times idealizing, but more often denigrating. We each did what we needed to survive. One of us had been described in a report as "mindless" but we, each in our own way, needed to split our minds, as well as our objects, to maintain our progress on the course. We employed different strategies. I heard repeatedly that the nurses on the multi-disciplinary training were "workhorses", and this presented itself to me as a good strategy to survive, to become indispensable. I took on all work presented to me, often far more than was healthy, mindlessly, and I was often out of my depth. It was detrimental to my training, and I was hurt by remarks on reports saying that I took on too much. One senior member of staff commented that "the nurses" were asked to do much more and that the other professional groups were much more able to protect their time. It was important to hear it acknowledged, but I didn't feel that I had a choice. I certainly didn't feel able to say no. The only other black British trainee and I both came from a nursing background, and it was significant, in terms of intersectionality, that our invisibility was related not only to race, but also to sex, class, and core profession.

Melaku (2020) references the "invisible labour clause". This is the added "invisible labour" that marginalized groups are required to perform to navigate their daily existence within social and professional spaces. She also introduces the "inclusion tax"—a concept to describe the additional resources "spent", such as time, money, emotional and cognitive energy, just to adhere to the norms in these white spaces. All these contribute to the silencing and whitewashing of the experience of the black trainee, but, more significant in an analytic setting, this also produces an inauthentic and fragmented state.

Towards the end of my time in the Trust, a new race strategy was launched. I had never involved myself with the actual work of race strategies, as every organization I had ever worked in only seemed to pay lip-service to meaningful change in relation to race, so I didn't waste my energy. This time, following much work on the couch, something seemed different. The strategy was launched with quite a fanfare: a packed conference room seemed to signal a new energy and I, uncharacteristically, decided to join the BAME (an acronym I despise!) working group. The new strategy required each department to have a volunteer "race champion" to think about how race was addressed in clinical meetings, to have someone to disseminate new policies and procedures, to provide a listening ear for staff with issues related to race. I decided to put my head above the parapet and volunteered for the role in the adult department. We had a new progressive head of department, who seemed committed to diversity and who seemed keen to see change. He would get back to me. He worried how the new policies would be received by the senior staff. After several months of waiting, he finally let me know that his own line manager had told him that the role should be dropped.

However, this time did mark a turning point for me personally. Something was beginning to change: the institutional race strategy corresponded to a more personal engagement with an internal race strategy that was no longer fit for purpose. I was emerging from the shadows, engaging with my racial self, not prepared to split my mind and body in quite the same way. It was a gradual development, but I felt emboldened to inhabit my racial self in a more authentic way. I don't want to idealize this process, but I think it was part of a more general developmental process that was underway.

It is important to outline moments during the training when race was addressed in a thoughtful, analytic way, commensurate with the spirit of enquiry that we were immersed in. A senior analyst who had left the department returned to head a scientific meeting in which he presented one of his patients. In the clinical material he presented a patient's dream. In the detailed dream, the patient recalled getting on to a bus and seeing a black woman sitting on the bus. I became anxious: how would this dream be interpreted? I braced myself for the usual conceptualization. Instead, he simply said that he didn't know why the woman on the bus was black. I was shocked and deeply moved. I think it was the fact that he allowed himself to simply not know. He did not launch into the familiar and derogatory list of attributes so easily projected into black skin. I will never forget that moment, made so significant by its rarity: a true analytic moment of thinking about race. He allowed himself to not know what was represented, while remaining curious. He did not project the contents of his own mind. I did not need to disappear. I felt validated. I may be accused of over-egging this moment, but this illustrates how rare these moments were.

Again, in a Fitzjohn's Unit group supervision led by a very senior, distinguished psychoanalyst, I had detailed a very negative countertransference towards a patient whom I had been seeing. A member of the group explored this difficult and disturbing feeling, asking me what it was that had happened at the beginning of the treatment that had left me feeling so negative towards her. In that moment, my mind went blank—I simply could not remember what had happened. There was an awkward silence. Then the supervisor said "Well, I remember what happened: she was racist." She said it directly, in a way that I had not experienced any senior staff acknowledge previously. It was a fact, and it was important that it be acknowledged in a meaningful way. It had a significant effect on me that needed to be thought about seriously. This was another moment when race and racism could be thought about and contained, when I also felt able to be myself, not having to hide or deny a part of my existence. It also had the effect of enabling me to reclaim what was split off and to go back to the patient, feeling supported, to continue what was ultimately a meaningful piece of work.

The M1 training espouses a tripartite structure, where the clinical work with the patient and supervision of that work is built around a solid theoretical structure, with the entire enterprise underpinned by a training analysis.

The theoretical component demanded a close reading of Freud's original writings. I had had a taster of these while undertaking less intensive trainings, and I was keen to be fully immersed and guided through the canonical texts. What I had not anticipated was the emotional impact of the conceptualization of the "dark" continent and the repeated references to the "primitive", which was synonymous with black skin. There were the more aware teachers, who would occasionally make a remark about

Freud being a man of his time when the casual racism or sexism arose, but there was little acknowledgement or understanding of the impact.

Again, I feel shame when I think of my own behaviour when these situations arose. I sat silently, feeling sure it would be addressed but then, realizing that it would not be, just allowed things to move on. I now feel that this was much more damaging. When I think of my black peer's clinical report stating that she did not have a mind, how easily this becomes reality when our teachings repeatedly refer to the primitivity of the black mind. Also, structurally within the organization, individual attitudes among our policy makers, our service leads, our supervisors are shored up by the theoretical underpinnings of psychoanalysis. Brickman (2018) eloquently deconstructs colonial anthropological attitudes that Freud drew on in the development of his theory of mind. I agree with her that the baby should not be thrown out with the bath water, that the theory and practice of psychoanalysis is rich with the potentiality of fundamental emancipation, but that does not mean that ideas and language that reinforce structures of racialized object relations should not be challenged.

In a particularly challenging small group supervision, the discussion touched on the importance of the use of language in relation to race. The supervisor spoke of "the black . . ." and went on to make a generalized point about black people. By this time, I felt emboldened by the developmental work I had undertaken, and it suddenly struck me as important to challenge this objectification and generalization. With some trepidation, not wanting it to be "interpreted", nor argued away, I challenged its use. I spoke respectfully but earnestly about this. He responded in a thoughtful way, thought that maybe something had been lost in translation, his having English as a second language, how it had landed with me was not what had been intended. I surprised myself at feeling able to take this up. I was engaging with this part of myself in an unapologetic way, communicating directly. He received it well. We spoke further, and he apologized. This moved me and deepened something in our relationship. Despite the criticisms I had of the training and the department, I don't think that I would have been able to have a conversation like this without the internalization of a good receptive object, reflecting many experiences of this kind during my time on the course.

Having completed the M1 training and having secured a teaching post on the D59, a qualifying course built around race and culture, I was impressed by a group action brought by a younger generation of students, who refused to remain silent about the casual racism, sexism, and homophobia in their theoretical texts. There seemed to be a courage and confidence in them that I did not possess at their stage of development, possibly not until now! It was part of an international movement in academia that seriously challenged the status quo in universities. It seemed to be overshadowed in our own institution by the explosion of transgender issues, but it marked an important time, together with the Black Lives Matter movement, in challenging institutional racism. Academic and political institutions were being held to account, and psychoanalysis was to be no exception.

During the collating of these personal experiences, the question was asked: how have we not only survived, but thrived, developed, moved on to successful careers? One of us has set up a training institution in her home country, others have secured solid posts in the NHS, and I have a thriving private practice, alongside an NHS post in psychosomatic medicine.

I would say that having my personal training analysis was fundamental. I was given excellent advice at the beginning of the training that the most important part of the training was the analysis. I was a black trainee in analysis with a white analyst, but the most important thing was that this was a space where I could be seen. Of course, I needed to rant and rave, to disavow, defend, delude, and deny until I was able to find myself in relation to another who could bear my rage, challenge the more ridiculous aspects of myself, withstand the storms and standoffs and ultimately survive, and still be there. It remains a work in progress.

When White (2002) writes about the process of surviving hating and being hated, she talks about having a home for her rage. But this was a place where she was told not to come back crying to, but to stand up for herself out there. The analysis has absolutely been a place where I could run home crying, where so much could be poured out in relation to racism, but also, where the important working-through could begin.

The M1 course and Adult Department was another home where it was possible for me to emerge from the shadows as a competent practitioner and a more authentic version of myself.

In the final session of a three-year psychoanalytic therapy, my patient, a young white woman who had bravely faced the task of mourning for the first time, brought two photographs: one of her mother and another of herself, in fancy dress as a 12-year-old. She had loved a pop group that featured a young mixed-race singer, and her mother had turned my patient into her young mixed-race idol for the party. The transformation was incredible, as she herself was pale-skinned with blonde hair. She looked stunning and beamed as she showed me the picture, announcing, "Look, I'm black!" I'm sure much could be made of this. However, I simply smiled at her parting gift to me and her desire for a closeness and identification with me at the point of separation.

CHAPTER TWENTY-SIX

On my diversity and the M1 training

Reziya Harrison

If there are diversity wars, I have been a foot-soldier in them most of my life. I am ethnically mixed, a woman, and now also old. All these are perfectly all right things to be. But the context is all. Those characteristics can be quite out of the question if you are in a group that is predominately white/male/younger, as the case may be. One defence against prejudice is to try to blend in. I have employed this defence with my ethnicity. I do not hide it: I tick the box "White and Asian", and I announce it if not to do so would be misleading. But I do not advert to it much. Does it work? I do not really know—perhaps I am being like a child who covers his face and believes no one can see him. And, of course, the Jews in Germany in the 1930s blended in. But ethnic characteristics are not a complete definition, and if there are enough concordant characteristics between me and the group, I believe it works, to an extent. The characteristics you can't fudge seem to me harder.

My experience of sexism

I encountered sexism in my last job, as a Chancery barrister; but gender is only part of what defines me, and prejudice did not prevent me doing the job, enjoying it, having good relations with colleagues, and learning a great deal. Nonetheless, as a young woman I became used to evoking responses from some colleagues I found puzzling and infuriating. There was an assumption

I must *know* it was impossible for me to be there, that no real explanation was needed for that view, it was too obvious. "Of course, women's brains are unsuited to Chancery work", was said to other women as well as me. There was an idea that, if we were in court, we couldn't be relied on not to burst into tears and run home to our children. There was displacement onto others: "The solicitors wouldn't cope with a woman in chambers." And we did seem to be regarded as dangerous, despite our efforts to fit in: "Why are you trying to take the bread out of men's mouths? Surely your husband can support you?" Not everyone said that sort of thing; and for everyone like that, there were others who actively encouraged me. I gained a lot from the group, as I said.

Much later, and a relatively old woman, I left the Bar after the death of my husband and two siblings in quick succession. I felt I needed a break. I had become interested in understanding unhappiness. After a while, I thought of psychoanalysis, but first I did a psychology degree. I had the notion that psychoanalysis might be a matter of belief and not necessarily consistent with what was known about the brain. I found, happily, that that was wrong: psychology mainly works with group averages that tell us useful things but may not be true of any one individual in the group; while psychoanalysis focuses on individual (and sometimes group) behaviour as it manifests in the encounter with the analyst/therapist. So, I started a training to enable me to see patients once a week. The atmosphere was not one of prejudice, but it was an avowedly eclectic course, and after a while I felt that I needed more in-depth psychoanalytic teaching.

My experience of ageism

I applied to an organization which I believed to offer a really good training, but which I feared was rather ageist. (I am not giving its name, because I should like to think that, like the Chancery Bar, it has moved with the times and would be different now.) I applied first to do a weekly introductory course, to see what it was really like. I was warned off applying to train but accepted onto the course. I liked it, admired the people who taught it, felt perfectly comfortable in the group, and could not see why I should not train there—particularly so in that age discrimination was by then against the law. So, I applied. It was a mistake. It did not end happily. I was told that I was too old and was rejected at an initial stage. I tried reasoning: I looked out average mortality statistics, the purpose of the ageism directive, and so on, and I wrote a polite letter, asking if their initial decision to exclude me could be revisited. It *was* revisited, but,

I think, with ambivalence. I was allowed to apply, but I think the letter only increased my dangerousness in their eyes. I was rejected as being "not ready" but encouraged to try a second time. I did and was rejected again, this time on purely age grounds.

The strange thing about these applications was that the prejudice I encountered felt strangely familiar. There was the same idea that I must *know* it was impossible; there had to be something terribly wrong with me, some omnipotence or worse, that I contemplated applying at all. There was the same displacement onto others: "What would happen to the patients if you *died*" (I was given to understand my death was imminent). There was also some magnification of my dangerousness. I had a quandary. Barristers have a duty to uphold the law, just as doctors have a duty to do no harm. This doesn't really stop when you are no longer practising. So, when I was faced with ageist reasons for my rejection, I couldn't very well say, "Oh. All right." I attempted to reason, to ask for a meeting, assuming some compromise would be arrived at. All to no avail. There is a strict deadline for discrimination claims, so I had to take it to a tribunal before long. Of course, this *is* potentially dangerous, and usually people try at this stage to see if the case can be prevented—they seek to talk, to negotiate. It is highly unusual to refuse to talk, as happened. It is hard to know why this course was chosen, but my guess is that the unconscious was at work: I had become so dangerous that rational discussion did not seem possible. Like pitch, I could not be touched.

So, to my surprise and horror, the case went to a hearing. I have a family, and I didn't think I could justify the considerable expense of legal representation, so I represented myself. It is lonely and burdensome, acting for oneself without a solicitor or a clerk, in an area of law I was unfamiliar with. And there is something disagreeable about being the subject matter. But I won, was awarded some damages, and the organization issued an apology and agreed to various measures, including equality training of those who dealt with potential applicants. While I had found it upsetting and could hardly see it as a triumph, as some did, it was a duty done: I hoped I could put the whole business behind me. I had fortunately been accepted on to the Tavistock M1 course by then and thought to get on with it.

The Tavistock M1 course

This kind of course is emotionally taxing, I think for everyone. And I probably underestimated how annihilating it feels to be rejected by a group I had wanted to be accepted by, for something I could do nothing about: my age. Perhaps it is some ancient fear of rejection by a group, like our instinctive fear of spiders and snakes, or perhaps it just does feel annihilating to one's identity. But that was not really what damaged me, I think.

There had been one difference between the Chancery Bar and the first training organization I applied to, other than the fact that one accepted me and one rejected me. At the Chancery Bar there were individuals who maintained their distaste for women colleagues, and there were also those who helped me; but I do not think anyone tried to do both at once. This, however, is I think what happened with the first training organization. I encountered a strange mixture of what seemed, and I think was, a genuine wish to help me, but more or less *fused* with adherence to what appeared to be a strong group culture of ageism. This unconscious fusion of inconsistent approaches inside the same people made for extremely confusing interviews: you could, as I can see now, pick up strands of these entirely opposite feelings at different times in the same interview.

I think it was the strands of real kindness I had encountered, followed by the increasingly implacable rejection, that keyed into a latent emotional fault-line from the very beginning of my life. (I wonder, too, if it had been partly why I had decided to try a second time—some instinct to try to repair or repeat or just flush out the unthinkable). Aged 3, I had been rejected by my depressed mother after a miscarriage that was one too many for her. Suddenly, she could no longer bear the sight of me. It had been unbearable to me at the time, despite a loving father; but, after a year or so, my mother became pregnant again, we were reconciled, and she taught me how to read. I thought no more of it. Now, in old age, I experienced the exploding of a latent pocket of terror and helplessness in me I had not known was there.

I must have tested my M1 supervisors' patience and empathy for at least a year or two, and I am sure I survived on the course narrowly. I lost what metaphorical ability I had had and really struggled to feel in the role of a therapist at all. It was, for a period, as if some inner censor had banned the exercise of what skills I had, leaving me with nothing much but observation and a sort of background kindliness. Worse still, part of it was that I could not properly face what was happening to me and unconsciously behaved as if I was unaware of anything untoward. I think this infuriated at least two of my supervisors, who thought I was not making an effort. But their reaction wasn't "It's your age, better give up", but more like "For goodness sake, make an effort to put this right." I am grateful for that.

I did not know for sure if the problem afflicting me could be got over—probably nobody knew. But my analyst remained professional, skilled, and undaunted. I owe her a great deal. Gradually, I improved. It took time, and there were obstacles along the way. When two of my supervisors of once-a-week patients retired from supervision, I felt it unconsciously as another betrayal, and I was set back. It helped when I began to realize in analysis that my 3-year-old self had believed the abandonment was all her own fault. This made clearer the way I had been affected by a kind of imposed inability while trying to acquire new therapeutic skills. Finally, I started with an intensive (three times a week) patient, and then another. Gradually, I began to get better, more able to take in what my supervisors had to offer. I began to get the hang of the complex, pleasurable skill that is psychoanalytic therapy. It is amazing. It draws on both main systems of our brain—the intuitive, bodily "default mode" system and the rational system—at the same time. There can be a remarkable crossover moment, when you have noticed something with your body, and it meets your rational mind. I used to get something like it in my old job when cross-examining a witness, or when suddenly realizing how a complex argument might be built up; but it is more ubiquitous in therapy. One of my grandsons passionately wants to be a footballer; I suspect something similar happens in that.

So, I completed the training and qualified, and here I am—an old woman—though still fortunately what actuaries call "young–old"—who has been enabled to practise a second profession and given a training I can build on to do it as well as I can and for as long as I can. It feels like a huge achievement.

Towards a peaceful solution

Most people who have been discriminated against want to prevent it happening to anyone else. So, I am going to set out some thoughts derived from my experiences that may possibly be helpful.

First, I think it is a powerfully unconscious thing, and, perhaps because we all need to distinguish basic difference in everyday life, any of us can do it. There were exceptions, but I generally liked and admired the professional skill of the people who went on to discriminate against me on grounds of my sex or age. They were mostly clever, distinguished people, far from crazed lunatics. Yet the lack of joined-up thinking characteristic of what the psychologist Daniel Kahneman (2011) calls "System One" and psychoanalytic psychotherapists, following Freud (1915e), call "the Unconscious" seems to emerge in both my discrimination experiences. A hallmark of the Unconscious is managing to believe two inconsistent things at once—so that, for example, on the one hand, almost total valuelessness was attributed to me; on the other, I was felt to be powerfully dangerous. System Two, or our rational, fact-checking brain function, didn't get much of a look-in.

Second, it seems to me to be most powerful as a group thing. I do notice that there is much talk generally of "rooting out" discrimination. It makes me think of patients who, at first, want to "chop off" parts of their psyche. I don't think it can be rooted out. We know from psychology how powerful the group can be over the individual members, enough for them to agree that the opposite of what they perceive is true. There was an extraordinary similarity of the responses I met with in these two highly respected and respectable groups. So, I would be inclined to treat it like rage or lust or fear—part of being human but needing to be guarded against. And one hopeful thing I have found is that discrimination largely melts away when there is genuine contact between individuals. That helped me at the Bar: the chambers where I was a pupil had a year to get to know me as a person. All my Tavistock supervisors, too, had a job—to teach *me*, not some abstraction—and they got on with it. If they were tempted to fit me to some stereotype, I certainly wasn't aware of it. I think group responsibility should be abolished in favour of individual responsibility of group members. Each one should sign their names to group decisions. (Preferably they should also print their names in capital letters. At the Bar it was customary for us to sign certain court documents called "pleadings" with our names in capital letters. It made you think twice about what you were putting out into the world over your name.)

Third, I wonder if discrimination by groups may not be linked to underlying anxiety about change. I think now that it contributed to the sex discrimination at the Bar when I was young. Barristers are self-employed on a kind of piece-work basis, and there is a feeling of financial precariousness at every level. And, at that time, the comfortable unbuttoned masculine world of dusty rooms and posters of Page Three girls on the walls of the clerks' room, and lunches of meat and two veg and spotted dick in Hall, was changing, if very slowly. So, perhaps, a few females felt like harbingers of ruin in some instinctive unconscious way. Certainly not in any other way; we tried hard to fit in. Perhaps there was some similar unconscious feeling of threat in the air felt by the group at the training organization I applied to? Yet clearly discrimination *can* be avoided, even where the group is threatened. I did not experience any at the Tavistock, yet it became apparent later that those who taught us had been under huge pressure following misguided management decisions. It is a puzzle. Perhaps we can only say that, in times of transition, institutions may need to be especially aware of the potential for discrimination.

Fourth, I do think the law has a useful place in any civilized solution. I don't mean going to court, which is very much a last resort, though a necessary one when all else fails. I mean making ordinary rules that become routine, part of the culture, and keeping some ordinary records to check adherence. I use the word "ordinary" to mean that such rules need not be long or arduous, they just need to bear in mind the organization's usual practices, to see where the risk lies. (The training organization I had trouble with not only insisted on whole-group decisions but seemed to lack any rules calculated to avoid discrimination and kept terrible records.) If discrimination is merely condemned or disavowed, excesses can grow in the dark, unnoticed.

What now?

I have found the M1 course to be an amazing training. Like others, I want to pay tribute to the skill of our supervisors and tutors. I also pay tribute to their patience, in my case. And equally or more important has been the skill, professionalism, and devoted care of my analyst. I felt a brimming-over sense of gratitude on qualifying. Then came mourning, as the reality of the cuts to the department in which the M1 is embedded began to take effect: as if it had swallowed a kind of Alice in Wonderland Shrink-me potion, winding up smaller, also beleaguered, and apparently starved of resources. Now, two years on, I still feel grief and resentment about that shrinking. But for myself, the old bruises seem to have healed, and I feel a quiet, enduring pleasure in being able to exercise—and build on—the skills I have learned. It feels like a precious possession, allowing me in old age to hold up my head and make a small contribution to society.

I do not normally talk much about having been discriminated against. However, I have felt moved to give this candid account, partly as a thank you to the Tavistock M1, but also in the hope that it may help other older people who may want to train for something new. Perhaps, also, I may hope that it may give potential discriminators some slight idea what it feels like, how much it can affect our lives.

And my hopes for the future of psychoanalysis? That discrimination will utterly cease to stain the lustre of any psychoanalytic institutions, that psychoanalysis will be recognized as the superlative method of achieving mental health and wellbeing that it is, and that our M1 training will somehow, like a Phoenix, grow back to its former health and strength.

PART VI

SOME FINAL REFLECTIONS

CHAPTER TWENTY-SEVEN

A changing NHS and threats to the integrity of the M1 training: can we keep a culture of enquiry?

Francesca Hume

So far, the focus of this book has been on the psychoanalytic learning that can evolve through an immersion in the clinical work and its challenges, provided that the trainee is open to this. With the exception of the section on Diversity where we wanted to highlight shortcomings in our institutions, the book has been written from the perspective of the individual and assumes that the institutional environment will be reasonably conducive to this experience.

The focus has been on the personal attitudes and suitability of the trainee and how these interact with what is provided in supervision, and elsewhere. But in this chapter, I change focus. I address the state of the Institution itself and its essential role in either fostering or impeding such learning. I refer to Tom Main's concept of a "culture of enquiry" (1967) to look at how a culture characterized by thoughtfulness and creativity can become corroded and degraded or even disappear altogether.

I suggest that psychoanalytic psychotherapy trainings that are rooted in the particular context of Britain's National Health Service now face significant threats, both to their future existence and, more immediately, to the survival of a culture of enquiry. While I am focusing here on the M1 training at the Tavistock and the impact of recent economic and political vicissitudes, I understand that there are similar struggles going on elsewhere in the NHS, with similar outcomes.

The NHS is an institution in peril. At a wider ideological level, successive governments have reshaped it, and this has taken place alongside relentless underfunding and cuts. While the New Labour government in the 1990s were bounty years for the NHS, the same government also ushered in a managerialized approach to an institution that was originally founded on socialist principles. A more benignly paternalistic culture in the NHS, in which students and patients were looked after by senior staff, who were themselves looked after by the containing structure of the NHS, has largely been replaced by a culture dominated by market forces, with NHS trusts effectively being told to regard themselves as akin to corporations in the private sector. Under the years of Conservative government, the NHS has faced increasingly lean times, with loss of funding deleteriously damaging both clinical services and the training provision accompanying them. The NHS is arguably one of the most successful ever socialist enterprises, and therefore the idea of an internal market is inimical to it and cannot but change the nature of the whole beast.

Add to this a pandemic that has hugely impacted overstretched public services, and it is no surprise that the NHS finds itself in difficulty.

All this has been true at the Tavistock, as elsewhere. Austerity measures have meant that our budgets have been cut by 5% each year, unless the Trust could find ways of growing new business. The reality, of course, is that there is little money to be made, either from NHS clinical work or from clinical training. Some years ago, in the hope that, instead of cuts, the Trust might make more business from its activities, it was argued that training activities might fare better at this than clinical ones, but only if they were free of their ties to the clinical services—so, two activities that had been inextricably tied to each other and could not survive without the other were separated, and a Department of Education and Training was established to manage all training activities. Each had its own management structure and budget, immediately creating internal competition for resources between the two service lines. This corporatization of our management set up internal contradictions that meant that the existing model of training could not continue. The hope was that we would have a more efficient and money-generating structure. But there were now two competing services, each with their own priorities, income concerns, and, to some extent, different aims, and the impact of this on clinical staff in the Adult Department was keenly felt. Senior staff who, until now, were also de facto trainers and had used their time flexibly across both clinical and training activities, prioritizing whatever was more urgent at any given time, were suddenly servants to two masters, each wanting different things from their staff. In an NHS service that, like so many, depended upon the goodwill of its workers delivering over and above their hours, a new culture of tighter management seriously impacted staff morale, with the unforeseen consequence that many of the senior consultants chose to relinquish their training obligations and stop being involved in training activities at all. Further strain came later, with the reduction and eventual loss of the National Training Contract. (This contract was the mechanism by which Health Education England entrusted health providers to undertake healthcare education and training activities.) The National Training Contract financed many of our courses, and its loss has meant a significant reduction in the number of salaried training posts. While medical posts were better protected (paid for externally at a national level), the other disciplines have suffered. There are no longer any nurses or social workers in M1 posts, and the remaining psychology posts will be lost, as the present incumbents leave. The pressure to deal with immediate economic and clinical considerations has also led to massive cuts to senior staff posts, making succession planning almost impossible. This has damaged the prestige of an institution whose national and international reputation as a centre of excellence for training and clinical work has largely depended upon its notable and plentiful consultant figures. Anxiety among students about who remains of the senior staff, as they witness the gradual but steady exodus, is not only because they are attached to us and benefit from our teaching and supervision, but because they correctly sense that, with the loss of experienced analytic figures, the cultural knowledge around the training and its ethos disappears as the critical mass of senior leaders who understand the importance of an immersive type of learning is depleted.

On M1, we responded to the imperative to create a new income stream by opening up the training to fee-paying trainees. We had always had a trickle of foreign fee-payers (mostly doctors from Japan, who had for a long time been interested in psychoanalysis and the work of the Tavistock), but we were able to increase our numbers significantly from the 2000s by accepting fee-paying students from across the United Kingdom and elsewhere in the world. We were glad to be able to open up the training more broadly, and, over time, we expanded our remit, offering the training to mental health professionals from outside the four core disciplines. A more diverse group of students brought new talents and ideas enriched from previous careers in other fields (law, academia, the arts, etc.) as well as from other countries. The training became available to a larger number of people, and these students often hoped that on qualification they would make a career for themselves in the NHS. But there have been problems, too. Cuts to NHS clinical services have also meant that formal posts for qualified adult psychotherapists have been increasingly hard to come by, especially for those without a mental health background, and, while many who have qualified have been industrious in achieving positions for themselves in the NHS, many have not done so and have been lost to the private sector.

Another consequence of opening up the M1 training to fee-paying students was that we now needed to make M1 competitive with other fee-paying analytic trainings. While the rich breadth of a training experience based in the NHS was—and still is—precisely what attracted many fee-paying students, the M1 clinical "requirements" for qualification were well over those required for professional membership of the British Psychoanalytic Council (BPC). We therefore decided to make the additional requirements optional rather than mandatory, while stressing the value of engaging in as many clinical roles as possible. Under my course leadership, we developed a "core training" to stand alongside the "broader public sector training" to encourage students to train with us, when they might otherwise be drawn to less demanding training schemes elsewhere. The core training consisted of the same academic teaching, clinical seminars, and intensive cases as the broader training, but students were now strictly required to work with only two non-intensive patients before starting with intensive training cases, with the express purpose of gauging their readiness for the more intensive work. As is true of other psychoanalytic trainings, core training students were no longer required to learn the skills involved in undertaking assessments or to work with a large number of once-weekly patients or to run a psychotherapy group. We were pleased to find that the appeal of M1 remained in its having breadth of clinical (NHS) exposure as well as its analytic depth, and, for a while, the fee-payers took part in as many clinical activities as they could manage. But this has changed, and we have found an increasing number of fee-paying trainees opting to take on the minimal core requirements needed for BPC registration. Today, it is mostly the very few remaining salaried post-holders who still undertake the full public sector.

With hindsight, I have had to reflect upon how these and other changes aimed at protecting the future of M1 have placed it at risk. The move away from the broader training has weakened its standing as a full apprenticeship education along the lines described in chapter 1. There is a danger now that the broader training is regarded more as a "luxury" afforded only to those in salaried posts and not important for all. Ironically, fee payers are often less clinically experienced when they start training with us and, therefore, have a greater need of a broad clinical education. There is a risk that we will have a future workforce who are less clinically educated and experienced and less able to attend to the complex clinical situations encountered in the public sector.

A culture of enquiry

In his paper, "Knowledge, Learning and Freedom from Thought" (1967), Tom Main stresses the importance within institutions of maintaining a "culture of enquiry", so that ideas that start out as thought-provoking or as creative attempts to improve a clinical situation don't become degraded into meaningless rituals or even dogmas to be worshipped. Organizations are particularly vulnerable to this happening at times of anxiety and uncertainty about the future. A thoughtful, enquiring culture becomes replaced by ritualized practices as a defence against the primitive dread of "not-knowing" (what will happen next). Omnipotent solutions to manage doubt and uncertainty replace the pursuit of knowledge, and a tyrannical atmosphere can develop in which persecutory anxieties and a fear of being blamed dominate. I would add that what purport to be creative solutions are often panic-laden, desperate measures in which attempts at repair are characterized by destructively manic thinking and actions.

Main describes how handing on information (e.g., the rationale for an idea or new way of working) gets replaced by a superego function: "You *will* do this or that . . .", etc. David Bell, in his discussion of Tom Main's paper, gives an example of this sort of transformation in the common hospital procedure of "feeding back". He says:

> An understandable wish to encourage the free flow of information concerning patients . . . turns into a demand for endless meetings where information is fed back from other meetings. The feedback process swells up until there is no room for discussion or thought. [Bell, 1990, p. 76]

Bell suggests that while anxieties about "not-knowing" may initiate this sort of process, it is the dread of being blamed for something going wrong (e.g., a suicide) that comes to drive the process. He agrees with Main that an "ego-function" gets replaced by a "superego" function and suggests that the character of this superego has much in common with the superego found in the psychotic patients described by Rosenfeld: a superego that may purport to protect, but is actually inimical to life and creativity.

Returning to M1, I think we see a stark example of a degradation of thinking and creativity into thoughtless dogma and ritualized practices: our very attempt to protect the M1 training by introducing a more flexible approach to meeting the clinical requirements (the two routes to qualification described above) has become the vehicle by which the training is undermined. The less demanding "core" training, which, at first, simply meant that if a trainee was unable to fulfil all the broader requirements, they might still qualify, provided they had comfortably met the BPC requirements, has become "the thing that fee-payers do". In this way, this group of trainees are seen as no longer needing to attend clinical unit meetings—after all, "other BPC trainings don't require that". M1's unique selling point (to use uncomfortable corporate language) is that it offers a broad exposure to all the applications of analytic work to NHS patients as well as the opportunity to work intensively, three times per week. Other trainings do one or the other, but not both. But now, for the vast majority of M1 trainees, this has become degraded. The "restructuring" that now means that fee-payers no longer attend the clinical units is, I believe, deeply antithetical to learning and hard to justify on financial grounds, but, at some level, an attempt to fix a problem that feels too broken to be mended properly. Those M1 trainees who no longer attend a clinical unit feel displaced, without a home at the centre of their training. To quote Main (1967): "What had originally been a useful idea and a break from thoughtless discipline was itself becoming a new kind of thoughtless discipline. . . . A fixed procedure had developed out of a flexible technique" (p. 66). The persecutory anxiety being managed is that the training will not survive unless we can continue to recruit fee-payers. An ego-function (creative thinking) has been replaced by a superego function (a non-negotiable fixed procedure), and this process is driven by a fear of being blamed when things fail.

In *Nostromo*, Joseph Conrad says, "Something inherent in the necessities of successful action carry with it the moral degradation of the idea" (p. 433). I believe that this is what we are suffering from at the Tavistock, both in relation to the M1 training but also at the level of the institution as a whole. It is, of course, an affliction that has permeated the whole of the NHS and, some would argue, beyond that too: we have all been subject to a neo-liberal economic philosophy and have been damaged by that. The Tavistock had to become financially viable: a "Foundation Trust Hospital", secure in that position, comfortably in the black and not the red. So, we did what successive governments told us to do. We corporatized. In the end, I don't believe we had a choice in this. But in the process of what was deemed to be "successful action" (restructuring, corporatizing, cutting,) supposedly to maximize the bankable impact of what the Tavistock stood for, the essence of what the Tavistock has *actually* been about (its original stated and unstated aims and objectives) has been drained away. The very thing we had been seeking to maximize the profit upon has been degraded.

When our NHS managers are under great pressure, thinking in terms of profits, costs, and austerity measures, they cannot think primarily from the perspective of this or that clinical service (including the service "users" and the staff who are training and treating them). Strenuous attempts are made to do so sometimes, but it is very difficult. In this way, the central point of reference, the in-depth understanding of what is essential in running psychoanalytic clinical and training services—the beating heart of the Tavistock upon which its reputation depends—is kept out or, at best, marginalized from management discourse and decision making, and those making financial decisions become alienated from the idea that the centre is decided by the clinical work. Sometimes, there is covert animosity between the hard-pressed managers and the clinicians who feel their authority to be undermined and who feel they are trying to defend the existing clinical culture. Moreover, as Main describes, members of one group are apt to present degraded caricatures of the ideas of another group: "Groups generate disciples . . . and it is not easy to suspect ardent followers of one's own ideas as having little capacity for thought or understanding" (in Bell, 1990, p. 78). The pressures on all the individuals involved is significant, and what it adds up to is deeply regrettable at the level of the Institution.

Somehow our predecessors avoided this fate. Perhaps their bureaucratic battles were less intense and were conducted in a less hostile environment, and they were looking ahead towards better post-war times. The NHS, at that time, was the precious new post-war baby, and from its inception by Nye Bevan in 1948, and for several decades thereafter, the likes of Jock Sutherland and John Bowlby (both psychoanalysts) recognized that management battles would deplete their energy from what they regarded as "higher" things (clinical activities and training). They were in the more fortunate position to keep that focus firmly in mind.

So, we have to conclude that the M1 training, with the exceptional breadth and depth it offers, is steadily becoming eviscerated and hollowed out. This hasn't yet happened completely, but, unless all concerned can come together to face this possibility, it is likely that this will be the outcome. The students feel the loss of a solid centre around which they can learn. The feel it, and they protest about it.

Some positive strategies have been found on the M1 training. Over several decades we have been able to recruit senior external psychoanalysts to teach theory and supervise, and this has been of great help and support. And, of course, trainees are all in their own psychoanalysis. So, what is lacking at the core, is somewhat ameliorated by this external scaffolding. There has recently also been a change of leadership at the

Tavistock helm, with experienced clinicians in key roles: on the board and as governors. There seems to be some energy and goodwill to get through the current crisis, but it will need colleagues to come together thoughtfully in a spirit of proper collaboration.

Finally, I am forever impressed by the trainees themselves: their passion for the work, their determination to train under difficult circumstances and when they face an uncertain professional future. Much of this book is concerned not just with the students' learning, but with a willingness to put aside (unlearn) what was there before, when it is interfering with approaching a new problem in a new way. And here, I think the "parents" might learn the same lesson from the "children". We seniors also need to learn from our mistakes, to recognize when our thinking has gone awry and become defensive and to recover our culture of enquiry.

CHAPTER TWENTY-EIGHT

Final reflections

Francesca Hume

Learning through experience

When Einstein wrote "Imagination is more important than knowledge ... imagination encircles the world" (1929), I think he was inviting us to hold our knowledge more loosely: to search beyond important facts and be alive to our imaginative associations as these come up. This strikes me as close to Freud, who didn't talk of imagination as such, but emphasized curiosity and initiative: the experiential learning that involves facing difficulties as they emerge and working them through. And this is what our book has tried to illustrate. Bion's interest in thinking as a human link (as described earlier) sees this as, first and foremost, an emotional experience: one that involves trying to know oneself or someone else, so as to comprehend the reality of both (Bion, 1962b). His, by now, familiar idea that we can distinguish coming to know oneself through such experience (or *getting to know*) from the more static position of being *in possession* of knowledge has inspired others to richly elaborate upon this theme, and it is what we try to describe here. Along with other aspects of the setting and the analyst's stance, it is what we think of as a *psychoanalytic attitude*.

Many of the contributions of our trainees vividly describe their experience of feeling lost at the start of their training and recognizing that their existing knowledge (of psychoanalysis) was bookish and formulaic and didn't help them in its static state. In her chapter 7, Malika Verma writes:

"At this early stage of my training, I had thought that patients were supposed to talk about their life and that I was supposed to bring in the transference. She, however, could only ever talk about me, and I would find myself paralysed by her. It took time for me to understand that this *was* the transference, being lived out between us rather than talked about."

I describe how to some trainees the disruptive impact of new learning could feel overwhelming, leading to the experience of anxiety, doubt, and even fragmentation (Ms A in my chapter 10, on supervision, provides an example of this). Most, however, convey how, in the end, they understood the opportunity that this state contains.

Era Trieman (chapter 4) writes: "Once things began to unravel, flooded by anxieties, feeling lost at sea, I, too, felt the turmoil and despair of uncertainty. Yet it is only by negotiating that journey that we can (eventually) emerge from it."

At various points in the book, I take up Tom Main's notion of a "culture of enquiry". He stresses the tension that exists within institutions to remain alive and creative in the thinking that goes on, so that ideas that start out as thought-provoking can continue to be developed imaginatively, rather than degrading into stagnant or ritualized knowledge. In this regard, I describe something of the history of the M1 training: from its hesitant beginnings, to how it became an exemplary clinical training, enabling its graduates to think flexibly about the application of psychoanalytic principles across wide-ranging clinical situations. I hope that the reader will have gained a sense of a training at its very best—the learning that is possible in these circumstances. Regrettably, however, I also felt it was important to describe how the training has been undermined in recent times by political and managerial decisions—the erosion of a culture of enquiry.

Institutional learning and embracing diversity

My chapter on a changing NHS and threats to the integrity of the M1 training (chapter 27), as well as the chapters in Part V, on diversity, address the culture of the institution itself and how this determines the learning that it can provide. As described, the knowledge held by an institution is always in a state of flux. When thinking and reflection are protected, it can evolve flexibly. At other times, especially when threats to the survival of the institution dominate, knowledge and learning are at risk of becoming degraded. Holding tight to a particular intellectual position is one response to facing external change, and the result is often an intellectual stagnation or rigidity—one that is inimical to the self-scrutiny needed to recognize a prejudicial attitude to minority groups. A trainee's freedom to evolve and learn in the way this book describes depends upon the culture of the institution and its capacity to demonstrate a comparable willingness and openness to learning.

All three of the contributors to Part V allude to the prejudice they had experienced and the "blending in" that was required of them or others like them at different points in their careers (though not always on the M1 training). Poul Rohleder talks of the acceptable "good gay" who might, these days, be allowed to train. And both Diane Turner and Reziya Harrison use the same expression—"blending in"—to describe the way in which core aspects of their identity had to be made to disappear or become invisible.

Diane Turner's chapter 25, on race, vividly describes the actions she felt obliged to take in order to fit in when she was training some years ago: "In the early days, I thought the only way to psychically survive the training as a black trainee was to split off my racial self, to shed my black skin, leave it at the door, and put it back on, along with my coat, at the end of the day. There was no place for it."

This *blending in* can at times feel like a betrayal to an essential part of one's identity—"*the only black face in the room and totally in collusion with the whitewash*" (to quote Diane Turner again). We don't image that the drastic action she felt obliged to take will have been conducive to her being able to assimilate a new analytic identity when such a core aspect of her own identity felt shunned or repudiated. It is to her credit that, despite this, she evolved into a gifted analyst.

Later she asks: "on a training where we were challenged at every level, where everything was there to be interrogated and thought about, where the deepest recesses of the mind were explored—how could something so obvious be so off limits?"

How, indeed?

The Tavistock has done a lot in recent years to embrace some fundamentally important areas—especially issues of racism and exclusion. This has been true of the M1 training too, with important developments taking place on the structure of the training and teaching and also the active inclusion of black and non-heteronormative trainees. But this kind of knowledge and insight is particularly vulnerable to degradation. Poul Rohleder describes the agonizing involved in "writing sections [of his chapter 24] over and over again", always fearing that he would be seen simply as voicing a personal grievance rather than hoping for more thoughtfulness within the psychoanalytic profession.

As he quotes: "Diversity is a reality, inclusion is a choice."

Clinical challenges and guilt

In Part IV, on clinical challenges, we look at what learning is possible in more difficult circumstances. As Helen Barker says, while the subject matter in these chapters is wide-ranging, they demonstrate the value of remaining open and receptive to the unfolding events when the temptation is to foreclose things. Mostly, the accounts we received demonstrated learning that was possible through adversity. But not all. For some, the challenges proved too much.

Denise Hurst Hastings (chapter 23) says this of her experience: "The outcome was, in many ways, a painful failure for us both, with the remote nature of the treatment proving to be an insurmountable obstacle to the unfolding of an analytic process."

For other trainees, and, indeed, for the patients too, the experience of being able to get on with the work through lockdown was very important. For some it worked better. But for all, there was great relief in returning to the consulting room, and an acknowledgement of the added struggle in understanding the patient, especially at such an early stage in their own development. In the words of one trainee, Holly Hassell: "I felt an immediate relief in having access to his full range of embodied non-verbal communication. I realized that, in the absence of this to triangulate with his verbal material, I had felt overly dependent on his verbal communication and had lost my sense of authority and objectivity while working exclusively online. Once this was exposed, I felt more confident in identifying and processing Mr M's projective identification, and less afraid of his hostility and contempt."

Jane Milton, who read and commented on the whole book in draft form, observed that in Part IV, on clinical challenges, we had not addressed the issue of guilt. Helen Barker subsequently added a note, and I was also prompted to think about it further. But the oversight interested me. When I looked again at Part IV, the issue of the trainee's guilt was very apparent, but mostly not explicitly acknowledged. The guilt of feeling luckier than the patient; of being a pregnant therapist treating a childless older woman; or of being alive and healthy, when a patient is dying; or simply having had a better start in life, are all examples. And, most obviously, the guilt involved when faced with a patient's completed suicide. But another aspect struck me too. Many trainees referred to feeling guilty at their failures in understanding their patients without their familiar recourse to offering relief and reassurance. They found themselves having to tolerate pain and sorrow while they struggled with their own development and understanding. I wondered again what, as editors, our own omission had been about. I believe that, for myself, it had to do with leaving my role as Course Lead at a time when the Institution was facing unprecedented challenges. Over many years, and often at considerable personal cost, I had done what I could to look after the trainees and safeguard the quality of the M1 training. Mostly, I felt that, along with a close team of colleagues, we managed to keep things afloat, sometimes against the odds. Increasingly, however, I realized that the forces we were up against were too big. So, leaving the Tavistock after many years was an action to protect my own interests; at times, it felt like abandoning a sinking ship—leaving it now for others to try to rescue and take care of. The struggle to remain thoughtful and reflective when managing the frustration of being unable to rescue and repair one's damaged objects is always hard to bear. Most mental health practitioners have chosen such a profession precisely because we want to mend things—the patients around us reflecting a deep need in us to repair our own internal damaged objects. When we cannot, we feel guilty and despairing and, sometimes, persecuted. Many of the clinical challenges described here were felt to be so precisely because they frustrated that deep-seated desire for reparation that the trainees hoped a training of this kind would offer them.

Finally, while this book has been about the learning involved in becoming psychoanalytically educated, there are some sceptics who question whether psychoanalysis can be taught at all. Reik, for example, suggested that a psychoanalyst is born, not made: "I would say that a therapist has to be born with a certain disposition" (Reik, 1968, p. 17). Against this, I would cite one of Britain's most brilliant psychoanalysts, Betty Joseph, who might have been thinking about Reik's comment when she insisted that she was an analyst made not born, having struggled in her training, nearly giving up three times: "So if people think one has to have a calling to do psychoanalysis, it is not quite true" (Joseph, 2006, p. 5). For most of us, we hope that this more optimistic view—that learning of the right kind may foster talent—holds true. And whatever an individual's analytic endowments, there is always a journey of development, and, as teachers within institutions, we hope to do what we can to encourage that.

REFERENCES

Anonymous (2015). A Gay trainee. *New Associations*, 17: 9.

APA (1952). *Diagnostic and Statistical Manual of Mental Disorders (1st Edition)*. Washington, DC: American Psychiatric Association.

APA (1968). *Diagnostic and Statistical Manual of Mental Disorders (2nd Edition) (DSM–II)*. Washington, DC: American Psychiatric Association.

APA (1987). *Diagnostic and Statistical Manual of Mental Disorders (3rd Edition, Revised) (DSM–IIIR)*. Washington, DC: American Psychiatric Association.

Armstrong, D., & Rustin, M. (2020). Psychoanalysis, social science and the Tavistock tradition. In: S. Kraemer & M. Waddell (Eds.), *The Tavistock Century: 2020 Vision*. Bicester: Phoenix.

Baraitser, L. (2022). "Time" for "the people": Reflections on "Psychoanalysis for the People: Free Clinics and the Social Mission of Psychoanalysis". *Psychoanalysis and History*, 24(3): 375–392.

Barden, N. (2011). Disrupting Oedipus: The legacy of the Sphinx. *Psychoanalytic Psychotherapy*, 25 (4): 324–345.

Bayer, R. (1987). *Homosexuality and American psychiatry: The Politics of Diagnosis*. Princeton, NJ: Princeton University Press.

Bell, D. (1990). Comment by David Bell on Tom Main's paper. *Psychoanalytic Psychotherapy*, 5: 74–78.

Bell, D. (2010). Psychiatry and psychoanalysis: A conceptual mapping. In: A. Lemma & M. Patrick (Eds.), *Off the Couch: Contemporary Psychoanalytic Applications*. London: Routledge.

Benner, P. (1982). From novice to expert. *American Journal of Nursing, 82* (30): 402–407.
Bergler, E. (1956). *Homosexuality: Disease or Way of Life*. New York: Hill & Wang.
Bernfeld, S. (1952). On psychoanalytic training. *Psychoanalytic Quarterly, 31*: 453–482.
Bick, E. (1968). The experience of the skin in early object-relations. *International Journal of Psychoanalysis, 49*: 484–486.
Bion, W. R. (1959). Attacks on linking. *International Journal of Psychoanalysis, 40*: 308–315.
Bion, W. R. (1962a). *Learning from Experience*. London: Karnac.
Bion, W. R. (1962b). A theory of thinking. *International Journal of Psychoanalysis, 43*: 306–310.
Bion, W. R. (1967). Notes on memory and desire. *Psychoanalytic Forum, 2*: 272–273, 279–290.
Bion, W. R. (1979). Making the best of a bad job. In: *Clinical Seminars and Four Papers*, ed. F. Bion. Abingdon: Fleetwood Press.
Bion, W. R. (1990). *Brazilian Lectures: 1973, Sao Paulo; 1974, Rio de Janeiro/Sao Paulo*. London: Routledge.
Birksted-Breen, D. (1996). Phallus, penis and mental space. *International Journal of Psychoanalysis, 77*: 649–657.
Bleger, J. (1967). Psychoanalysis of the psychoanalytic frame. *International Journal of Psychoanalysis, 48* (4): 511–519.
Bonner, S. (2006). A servant's bargain: Perversion as survival. *International Journal of Psychoanalysis, 87*: 1549–1567.
Brenman, E. (1982). Separation: A clinical problem. *International Journal of Psychoanalysis, 63*: 303–311.
Brenman, E. (2006). The narcissism of the analyst: Its effect in clinical practice. In: *Recovery of the Lost Object*. London: Routledge.
Brenman Pick, I. (1985). Working through in the counter-transference. *International Journal of Psychoanalysis, 66*: 157–166.
Brenman Pick, I. (2012). Working through in the countertransference revisited: Experiences of supervision. In: *Authenticity in the Psychoanalytic Encounter: The Work of Irma Brenman Pick*, ed. I. Brenman Pick, M. Fakhry Davids, & N. Shavit. London: Routledge, 2018.
Brenman Pick, I. (2018). *Authenticity in the Psychoanalytic Encounter: The Work of Irma Brenman Pick*, ed. I. Brenman Pick, M. Fakhry Davids, & N. Shavit. London: Routledge.
Brickman, C. (2018). *Race in Psychoanalysis: Aboriginal Populations in the Mind*. London: Routledge.
Britton, R. (1989). The missing link: In R. Britton, M. Feldman, & E. O'Shaughnessy (Eds.), *The Oedipus Complex Today*. London: Karnac.

Britton, R. (1998). *Belief and Imagination*. London: Routledge.
Britton, R. (2000). Subjectivity, objectivity and triangular space. In: *Belief and Imagination*. London: Routledge.
Carpy, D. V. (1989). Tolerating the countertransference: A mutative process. *International Journal of Psychoanalysis, 70*: 287–294.
Centre for Economic Performance's Mental Health Policy Group. (2006). *The Depression Report: A New Deal for Depression and Anxiety Disorders*. London: London School of Economics.
Chasseguet-Smirgel, J. (1985). *Creativity and Perversion*. London: Free Association Books.
Clarke, J., & Lemma, A. (2011). Editorial. *Psychoanalytic Psychotherapy, 25* (4), 303–307.
Conrad, J. (1904). *Nostromo: A Tale of the Seaboard*. New York: Harper & Brothers.
Crick, P. (1991). Good supervision: On the experience of being supervised. *Psychoanalytic Psychotherapy, 5* (3): 235–245.
Cunningham, R. (1991), When is a pervert not a pervert? *British Journal of Psychotherapy, 8* (1): 48–70.
Dalal, F. (1998). *Taking the Group Seriously: Towards a Post-Foulkesian Group Analytic Theory*. London: Jessica Kingsley.
Davids, M. F. (2011). *Internal Racism: A Psychoanalytic Approach to Race and Difference*. Basingstoke: Palgrave Macmillan.
de Maat, S., de Jonghe, F., Schoevers, R., & Dekker, J. (2009). The effectiveness of long-term psychoanalytic therapy: A systematic review of empirical studies. *Harvard Review of Psychiatry, 17*: 1–23.
Dicks, H. V. (1970). *Fifty Years of the Tavistock Clinic*. London: Routledge & Kegan Paul.
Drescher, J. (1995). Anti-homosexual bias in training. In: T. Domenici & R. C. Lesser (Eds.), *Disorienting Sexuality: Psychoanalytic Reappraisals of Sexual Identities*. New York: Routledge.
Drescher, J. (1998). *Psychoanalytic Therapy and the Gay Man*. Hillsdale, NJ: Analytic Press.
Drescher, J. (2008). A history of homosexuality and organized psychoanalysis. *Journal of the American Academy of Psychoanalysis and Dynamic Psychiatry, 36*(3): 443–460.
Einstein, A. (1929). What life means to Einstein. Interview by George Sylvester Viereck. *The Saturday Evening Post*, 26 October.
Ekstein, R. (1969). Concerning the teaching and learning of psychoanalysis. *Journal of the American Psychoanalytic Association, 17*: 312–332.
Ellis, M. L. (1994). Lesbians, gay men and psychoanalytic training. *Free Associations, 4* (32): 501–517.
Ellis, M. L. (2021). Challenging identities: Lesbians, gay men, and psychoanalysis. *Psychodynamic Practice, 27* (3): 241–258.

Emanuel, R. (2014). The impact of sibling loss and illness. In: D. Handle & S. Sherwin-White (Eds.), *Sibling Matters*. London: Karnac.

Etchegoyen, A. (1993). The analyst´s pregnancy and its consequences on her work. *International Journal of Psychoanalysis, 74*: 141–149.

Fairbairn, W. D. (1952). *Psychoanalytic Studies of the Personality*. London: Tavistock Publications.

Feldman, M. (1997). Projective identification: The analyst's involvement. *International Journal of Psychoanalysis, 78*: 227–241.

Feldman, M. (2007). The illumination of history. *International Journal of Psycho-Analysis, 88* (3): 609–625.

Feldman, M. (2009). *Doubt, Conviction and the Analytic process: Selected Papers of Michael Feldman*. London: Routledge.

Fenster S. (1986). *The Therapist's Pregnancy: Intrusion in the Analytic Space*. Hillsdale, NJ: Analytic Press.

Fonagy, P. (2010). The changing shape of clinical practice: Driven by science or by pragmatics? *Psychoanalytic Psychotherapy, 24:* 22–43.

Fonagy, P., & Allison, E. (2015). A scientific theory of homosexuality for psychoanalysis 1. In: A. Lemma & P. E. Lynch (Eds.), *Sexualities*. London: Routledge.

Fonagy, P., Rost, F., Carlyle, J., McPherson, S., Thomas, R., Fearon, P., et al. (2015). Pragmatic randomized controlled trial of long-term psychoanalytic psychotherapy for treatment-resistant depression: The Tavistock Adult Depression Study (TADS). *World Psychiatry, 14*: 312–321.

Freud, E. L. (1960). *Letters of Sigmund Freud*. New York: Basic Books.

Freud, S. (1905d). *Three Essays on the Theory of Sexuality. Standard Edition, 7*: 123–245.

Freud, S. (1909b). Analysis of a phobia in a five-year-old boy. *Standard Edition, 11*: 139–152.

Freud, S. (1910d). The future prospects of psycho-analytic therapy. *Standard Edition, 11*: 139–152.

Freud, S. (1913c). On beginning the treatment. *Standard Edition,12*: 121–144.

Freud, S. (1914d). On the history of the psycho-analytic movement. *Standard Edition, 14*: 1–66.

Freud, S. (1915e). The unconscious. *Standard Edition, 14*: 159–215.

Freud, S. (1925f). Preface to Aichhorn's *Wayward Youth. Standard Edition,19*: 273–275.

Freud, S. (1926e). The question of lay analysis. *Standard Edition,20*: 179–258.

Freud, S. (1933a [1922]). The dissection of the psychical personality. In: *New Introductory Lectures on Psychoanalysis. Standard Edition, 22*: 57–80.

Full, W. (2020). *Psychodynamic Psychotherapy and Same-Sex Sexual Orientation: An Empirical Investigation*. Unpublished Doctoral dissertation, University College London.

Full, W. (2021). *BPC Bibliography on Gender, Sexuality and Relationship Diversity.* London: British Psychoanalytic Council. Available at https://www.bpc.org.uk/professionals/diversity

Garland, C. (2002). *Understanding Trauma: A Psychoanalytical Approach.* London: Routledge.

Garland, C. (2010). *The Groups Book. Psychoanalytic Group Therapy: Principles and Practice.* London: Routledge.

Gibb, E. (2004). Reliving abandonment in the face of the therapist's pregnancy. *Psychoanalytic Psychotherapy, 18* (1): 67–84.

Giffney, N., & Watson, E. (Eds.) (2017). *Clinical Encounters in Sexuality: Psychoanalytic Practice and Queer Theory.* Galeta, CA: Punctum.

Gillespie, W. (1964). Symposium on homosexuality (I). *International Journal of Psychoanalysis, 37*: 396–403.

Goethe, J. W. (1808). *Faust.* New York: Verlags-handlung, 471 Pearl St, 1837.

Gulati, R., & Pauley, D. (2019). The half embrace of psychic bisexuality. *Journal of the American Psychoanalytic Association, 67* (1): 97–121.

Heimann, P. (1950). On counter-transference. *International Journal of Psychoanalysis, 31*: 81–84.

Hertzmann L., & Newbigin, J. (Eds.) (2020). *Sexuality and Gender Now: Moving beyond Heteronormativity.* London: Routledge.

Hertzmann, L., & Newbigin, J. (2023). *Psychoanalysis and Homosexuality: A Contemporary introduction.* London: Routledge.

Isay, R. A. (1986). The development of sexual identity in homosexual men. *Psychoanalytic Study of the Child, 41*: 467–489.

Isay, R. A. (2009). *Being Homosexual: Gay Men and Their Development.* London: Vintage.

Joseph, B. (1982). Addiction to near-death. *International Journal of Psychoanalysis, 63*: 449–456.

Joseph, B. (1985). Transference: The total situation. *International Journal of Psychoanalysis, 66*: 447–454.

Joseph, B. (1989). The patient who is difficult to reach. In: *Psychic Equilibrium and Psychic Change.* London: Routledge.

Joseph, B. (2006). *Interview with Betty Joseph.* London: Melanie Klein Trust. Available at: https://melanie-klein-trust.org.uk/wp-content/uploads/2019/07/Interview_with_Betty_Joseph.pdf

Kahneman, D. (2011). *Thinking, Fast and Slow.* New York: Farrar, Straus and Giroux.

Keats, John (1899). *The Complete Poetical Works and Letters of John Keats,* Cambridge Edition. Houghton, Mifflin and Company. p. 277.

Keiser, S. (1969). Psychoanalysis—taught, learned, and experienced. *Journal of the American Psychoanalytic Association, 17*: 238–267.

Kernberg, O. F. (1996). Thirty methods to destroy the creativity of psychoanalytic candidates. *International Journal of Psychoanalysis, 77*: 1031–1040.

Kernberg, O. F. (2010). Psychoanalytic supervision: The supervisor's tasks. *Psychoanalytic Quarterly, 79 (3)*: 603–627.

King, P. (1978). Affective response of the analyst to the patient's communications. *International Journal of Psychoanalysis, 59*: 329–334.

Kinsey, A., Pomeroy, W., & Martin, C. (1948). *Sexual Behavior in the Human Male*. Philadelphia, PA: Saunders.

Kinsey, A., Pomeroy, W., Martin, C., & Gabhard, P. (1953). *Sexual Behavior in the Human Female*. Philadelphia, PA: Saunders.

Klein, M. (1921). The development of a child. In: *Love, Guilt and Reparation and Other Works, 1921–1945*. London: Hogarth Press, 1975.

Klein, M. (1928). Early stages of the Oedipus conflict. In: *Love, Guilt and Reparation and Other Works, 1921–1945*. London: Hogarth Press, 1975.

Klein, M. (1932). *The Psycho-Analysis of Children*. New York: Delacorte.

Klein, M. (1940). Mourning and its relation to manic-depressive states. In: *Love, Guilt and Reparation and Other Works, 1921–1945*. London: Hogarth Press, 1975.

Klein, M. (1946). Notes on some schizoid mechanisms. *International Journal of Psychoanalysis, 27*: 99–110.

Klein, M. (1952a). The origins of transference. *International Journal of Psycho-Analysis, 33*: 433–438.

Klein, M. (1952b). Some theoretical conclusions regarding the emotional life of the infant. In: *Envy, Gratitude and Other Works, 1946–1963*. London: Hogarth Press, 1975.

Klein, M. (1957). *Envy and Gratitude: A Study of Unconscious Sources*. London: Tavistock Publications.

Layard, R., Clark, D., Knapp, M., & Mayraz, G. (2007). Cost-benefit analysis of psychological therapy. *National Institute Economic Review, 202*: 90.

Lawrence, M. (2008). *The Anorexic Mind*. London: Routledge.

Leichsenring, F., & Rabung, S. (2008). Effectiveness of long-term psychodynamic psychotherapy. A meta-analysis. *Journal of the American Medical Association, 300*: 1551–1565.

Leichsenring, F., & Rabung, S. (2011). Long-term psychodynamic psychotherapy in complex mental disorders: Update of a meta-analysis. *British Journal of Psychiatry, 199:* 15–22.

Lemma, A., & Lynch, P. E. (Eds.) (2015). *Sexualities: Contemporary Psychoanalytic Perspectives*. London: Routledge.

Lewes, K. (1995). *Psychoanalysis and Male Homosexuality*. Hillsdale, NJ: Jason Aronson.

Limentani, A. (1979). Clinical types of homosexuality. In: I. Rosen (Ed.), *Sexual Deviation*. Oxford: Oxford University Press.
Lowe, F. (2013). *Thinking Space: Promoting Thinking About Race, Culture and Diversity in Psychotherapy and Beyond*. London: Routledge.
Main, T. (1967). Knowledge, learning and freedom from thought. *Australian and New Zealand Journal of Psychiatry, 1*: 64–71.
Marzillier, J., & Hall, J. (2009). The challenge of the Layard initiative. *The Psychologist, 22* (5): 396–399.
Mawson, C. (2019). *Psychoanalysis and Anxiety: From Knowing to Being*. London: Routledge.
McDougall, J. (1989). *Theatres of the Body: A Psychoanalytical Approach to Psychosomatic Illness*. London: Free Association Books.
Melaku, T. (2020). You don't look like a lawyer: Black women and systemic gendered racism. *Sociological Inquiry, 9* (4): 993–995.
Meltzer, D. (1988). The apprehension of beauty. The role of aesthetic conflict. In: *Development, Art and Violence*. Strath Tay: Clunie Press.
Meltzer, D. (1992). *The Claustrum: An Investigation of Claustrophobic Phenomena*. Strath Tay: Clunie Press.
Melville, H. (1851). *Moby-Dick*. London: Vintage Classics, 2007.
Melville, H. (1924). *Billy Bud, Bartleby and Other Stories*. London: Collector's Library, 2016.
Menzies Lyth, I. (1960). A case-study in the functioning of social systems as a defence against anxiety. *Human Relations, 13*: 95–121.
Meyerowitz, R., & Bell, D. (2018). *Turning the Tide: The Psychoanalytic Approach of the Fitzjohn's Unit to Patients with Complex Needs*. London: Routledge.
Milton, J. (1997). Why assess? Psychoanalytical assessment in the NHS. *Psychoanalytic Psychotherapy, 11* (1): 47–58.
Milton, J. (2001). Psychoanalysis and cognitive behaviour therapy—rival paradigms or common ground? *International Journal of Psychoanalysis, 82* (3): 431–447.
Mitrani, J. (2007). Bodily centred protections in adolescence. *International Journal of Psychoanalysis, 88*: 1153–1169.
Money-Kyrle, R. E. (1956). Normal counter-transference and some of its deviations. *International Journal of Psychoanalysis, 37*: 360–366.
Money-Kyrle, R. E. (1968). Cognitive development. *International Journal of Psychoanalysis, 49*: 691–698.
Morgan, H. (2021). *The Work of Whiteness: A Psychoanalytic Perspective*. London: Routledge.
Moss, D. (2002). Internalized homophobia in men: Wanting in the first person singular, hating in the first person plural. *Psychoanalytic Quarterly, 71* (1): 21–50.

Newbigin, J. (2013). Psychoanalysis and homosexuality: Keeping the discussion moving. *British Journal of Psychotherapy*, 29 (3): 276–291.

NICE (2004). *Depression: Management of Depression in Primary and Secondary Care.* Clinical Guideline 23. London: National Institute for Health and Clinical Excellence.

NICE (2009). *Depression: The Treatment and Management of Depression in Adults (Update).* Clinical Guideline 90. London: National Institute for Health and Clinical Excellence.

Obholzer, A. (1994). *The Unconscious at Work: Individual and Organizational Stress in the Human Services.* London: Routledge.

Obholzer, A. (2021). *Workplace Intelligence: Unconscious Forces and How to Manage Them.* London: Routledge.

O'Connor, N., & Ryan, J. (1993). *Wild Desires and Mistaken Identities: Lesbianism and Psychoanalysis.* London: Virago.

Ogden, T. H. (1992). Comments on transference and countertransference in the initial analytic meeting. *Psychoanalytic Inquiry*, 12 (2): 225–247.

O'Shaughnessy, E. (1983). Words and working through. *International Journal of Psychoanalysis*, 64: 289–290.

O'Shaughnessy, E. (1992). Enclaves and excursions. *International Journal of Psychoanalysis*, 73 (4): 603–614.

Parsons, M. (1996). Recent work by André Green. *International Journal of Psychoanalysis*, 77: 399–407.

Parsons, M. (2006). The analyst's countertransference to the psychoanalytic process. *International Journal of Psychoanalysis*, 87: 1183.

Perelberg, R. J. (Ed.) (2018). *Psychic Bisexuality: A British-French Dialogue.* London: Routledge.

Pitt Aikens, T., & Ellis, A. T. (1989). *Loss of the Good Authority: The Cause of Delinquency.* London: Penguin.

Poincaré, H. (1914). *Science and Method.* London: Thomas Nelson and Sons.

Pynchon, T. (2009). *Inherent Vice.* New York: Vintage.

Quinodoz, D. (1992). The psychoanalytic setting as the instrument of the container function. *International Journal of Psychoanalysis*, 73: 627–635.

Racker, H. (1953). A contribution to the problem of counter-transference. *International Journal of Psychoanalysis*, 34: 313–324.

Racker, H. (1968). Psycho-analytic technique. In: *Transference and Countertransference, Vol. 73* (pp. 6–22). London: Hogarth Press.

Reik, T. (1968). Theodor Reik speaks of his psychoanalytic technique. *American Imago*, 25: 16–20.

Rey, H. (1994). *Universals of Psychoanalysis in the Treatment of Psychotic and Borderline States.* London: Free Association Books.

Richards, D. (2020). Working with sameness and difference: Reflections on supervision with diverse sexualities. In: L, Hertzmann & J. Newbigin (Eds.), *Sexuality and Gender Now: Moving Beyond Heteronormativity*. London: Routledge.

Riesenberg-Malcolm, R. (1999). The mirror: A perverse sexual phantasy in a woman seen as a defence against psychotic breakdown. In: *On Bearing Unbearable States of Mind*. London: Routledge.

Rizq, R. (2014). Perverting the course of therapy: The fetishisation of governance in public sector mental health services. *Psychoanalytic Psychotherapy, 28* (3): 249–266.

Rosenfeld, H. (1971a). A clinical approach to the psychoanalytic theory of the life and death instincts: An investigation into the aggressive aspects of narcissism. In E. Bott Spillius (Ed.), *Melanie Klein Today. Developments in Theory and Practice, Volume 1: Mainly Theory*. London: Routledge.

Rosenfeld, H. (1971b). Contribution to the psychopathology of psychotic states: The importance of projective identification in the ego structure and the object relations of the patient. In: P. Doucet & C. Lauri (Eds.), *Problems of Psychosis*. Amsterdam: Excerpta Medica.

Rosenfeld, H. (2002). Narcissistic patients with negative therapeutic reactions. In: *Impasse and Interpretation*. London: Routledge.

Roth, P. (2005). Projective identification. In: S. Budd & R. Rusbridger (Eds.), *Introducing Psychoanalysis: Essential Themes and Topics*. London: Routledge.

Roth, P. (2009). Where else? Considering the here and now. *Bulletin of the British Psychoanalytical Society, 45*: 13–22.

Ruszczynski, S. (2007). The problem of certain psychic realities: Aggression and violence as perverse solutions. In: D. Morgan & S. Ruszczynski (Eds.), *Lectures on Violence, Perversion and Delinquency*. London: Karnac.

Sandler, J. (1976). Countertransference and role responsiveness. *International Review of Psycho-Analysis, 3*: 43–47.

Segal, H. (1957). Notes on symbol formation. *International Journal of Psychoanalysis, 38*: 391–397.

Shah, S., Wood, N., Nolte, L., & Goodbody, L. (2012). The experience of being a trainee clinical psychologist from a black and minority ethnic group: A qualitative study. *Clinical Psychology Forum, 232:* 32–35.

Spillius, E. (2007). Developments in Kleinian technique. *Encounters with Melanie Klein*. London: Routledge.

Steinberg, B. S. (1993). The need to know and the inability to tolerate not knowing. *Canadian Journal of Psychoanalysis, 1*: 85–103.

Steiner, J. (1989). The aim of psychoanalysis. *Psychoanalytic Psychotherapy, 4*: 109–120.

Steiner, J. (1993). *Psychic Retreats: Pathological Organisations in Psychotic, Neurotic and Borderline Patients*. London: Routledge.

Steiner, J. (2011a). Embarrassment, shame and humiliation. In: *Seeing and Being Seen: Emerging from a PSYCHIC retreat*. London: Routledge.

Steiner, J. (2011b). The numbing feeling of reality. *Psychoanalytic Quarterly, 80*: 173–189.

Steiner, J. (2011c). *Seeing and Being Seen: Emerging from a Psychic Retreat*. London: Routledge.

Steiner, J. (2012). *Henri Ray*. London: Melanie Klein Trust. Available at: www.melanie-klein-trust.org.uk/rey

Stokoe, P. (2010). The theory and practice of the Group Relations Conference. In: C. Garland (Ed.), *The Groups Book. Psychoanalytic Group Therapy: Principles and Practice*. London: Karnac.

Stokoe, P. (2019). Where have all the adults gone? In: D. Morgan (Ed.), *The Unconscious in Social and Political Life*. Bicester: Phoenix.

Strachey, J. (1934). The nature of the therapeutic action of psychoanalysis. *International Journal of Psychoanalysis, 50*: 275–292.

Stubley, J., & Young, L. (2021). *Complex Trauma: The Tavistock Model*. London: Routledge.

Tarrant, R. J. (Ed.) (2004). *P. Ovidi Nasonis Metamorphoses*. London: Oxford University Press.

Taylor, D. (2017). *Talking Cure: Mind and Method of the Tavistock Clinic*. London: Routledge.

Temperley, J. (1984). Settings for psychotherapy. *British Journal of Psychotherapy, 1* (2): 101–111.

Torok, M. (1994). The illness of mourning and the fantasy of the exquisite corpse. In: N. Abraham & M. Torok, *The Shell and the Kernel*. Chicago, IL: University of Chicago Press.

Twomey, D. (2003). British psychoanalytic attitudes towards homosexuality. *Journal of Gay & Lesbian Psychotherapy, 7* 1–2): 7–22.

Van Haute, P., & Westerink, H. (2020). *Reading Freud's Three Essays on the Theory of Sexuality: From Pleasure to the Object*. London: Routledge.

Waddell, M. (1998). *Inside Lives: Psychoanalysis and the Growth of the Personality*. London: Duckworth.

White, K. P. (2002). Surviving hating and being hated: Some personal thoughts about racism from a psychoanalytic perspective. *Contemporary Psychoanalysis, 38*: 401–422.

WHO (1992). *The ICD-10 Classification of Mental and Behavioural Disorders: Clinical Descriptions and Diagnostic Guidelines*. Geneva: World Health Organization.

Williams, G. (1997). *Internal Landscapes and Foreign Bodies: Eating Disorders and Other Pathologies*. London: Duckworth.

Winnicott, D. W. (1949). Hate in the countertransference. *International Journal of Psychoanalysis, 30*: 69–74.
Winnicott, D. W. (1953). Transitional objects and transitional phenomena: A study of the first not-me possession. *International Journal of Psychoanalysis, 34*: 89–97.
Winnicott, D. W. (1963). The development of the capacity for concern. *Bulletin of the Menninger Clinic, 27* (4): 167–176.
Winnicott, D. W. (1969). The use of an object. *International Journal of Psychoanalysis, 50:* 711–716.
Winnicott, D. W. (1971). *Playing and Reality*. London: Tavistock.

INDEX

abandonment
  catastrophic, 134
  childhood fear of, 256
  exclusion and, 193
  sense of, 136
acting out, 58–59, 60, 107, 163
adoption and adoptee, 113
  case of Ms L, 113–124
ageism, 253–254, 255
alcohol abuse and alcoholism 64, 80, 148
  case of Mr D, 199
  case of Ms E, 171
Alcoholics Anonymous (AA), 171
Alcohol Services, 81
Almyroudi, A., 168
  See also, pregnancy
American Psychiatric Association (APA), 234
  See also, Diagnostic and Statistical Manual of Mental Disorders (DSM)
analytic
  apprentice, 11
  apprenticeship, 91
  attitude, 88, 167
  candidates, 164
  capacity, 157

chairs, 213
change, 106
consultation, 110
couple, 41
culture, at Tavistock 8
figures, 263
frame, 126–127, 130–131
functioning, 112
group psychotherapy, 9
ideas, 92
identity, 90, 99–100, 102, 271
learning, 14, 17
literature, 246
patient, 174, 244
persona, 99
position, 41
principles, 270
process, 42–43, 164, 225
relationship, 37, 109
self, 195
session, 105
setting, 168, 248
space, 135
stance, 84, 125, 131, 241
teachers, 91
technique, 91, 162
theory, 62, 90

traditions, 90
treatment, 104, 107
understanding, 90
work, 89, 96, 109, 125, 129–130, 133, 139, 150, 266
analytic knowledge and expertise, 13
passing on of, 21
analytic perspective
on challenge of learning, 28–31
analytic training and trainees, 12, 14, 30
fee-paying, 264
selection of, 27
animals, 37, 214
antidepressants, 56, 152, 199
anti-homosexuality, 227, 233, 237–238, 241
anti-oppression, 241
anti-racism work, 241
anti-Semitism, 247
anxiety(ies)
avoiding, 114, 185
Bion on, 32, 101
castration, 236
chronic, 157
claustrophobic, 150
crippling, 161
defending against, 187
depressive, 141, 144, 154, 177, 225
earliest, 18, 127
experience of, 29
fending off, 132
infant, 18–19, 151
intolerable, 133
life and death, 183
managing of, 11–12, 48–49
Mawson on, 211
Mr D, 199, 201, 202, 207
Mr E, 64, 65
Mrs D, 219, 223
Ms A, 93, 95, 101
Ms B, 157, 159–161
Ms D, 70
Ms E, 172, 175, 177
Ms K, 191, 195
Ms L, 114, 117, 121
Ms O, 33–34, 36–42
Ms P, 139
Oedipal, 136
persecutory, 117, 184, 225
of pregnant therapist, 190–191

primitive, 42, 169, 197, 202, 207, 231
projection of, 59
psychological therapy for, 63
shared, 186
status, 47
superego, 89
survival, 86
trainee, 2, 20, 91, 96, 98, 125, 134, 150
troubling, 133
unbearable, 70, 157, 207
unconscious, 166
APA, *see* American Psychiatric Association
apprenticeship, 9–11, 264
analytic, 11, 91
salaried, 10
aqueduct, the (Makin's painting), 45
Brick Mother and, 53–54
automaton, 125

Baban, A., 12, 24, 169
See also, "Ghost Ship"; psychiatry, unlearning
baby(ies)
Bion on, 144
breastfeeding of, 97
development of sense of coherence by, 144
doll-baby, 117
mixed-race, 245
mother's hate toward, 163
Ms P and, 136, 137, 143
struggle to introject by, 140
See also, infant
baby-part of patient (Ms L), 114, 118, 120, 131
baby pink, 138
Baldock, S., 168
See also, suicide and suicidality
Baraitser, L., 229–230
Barker, H., 4, 272
See also, clinical challenges
Barnard, L., 168
See also, cancer, death of patient by
barriers, 140, 213
Bartleby the Scrivener, 198, 208
beggar-queen, 53
Bell, D., 10, 64, 265
Benner, P., 147
Bergler, E., 235

Bernfeld, S., 16
betrayal, feelings of, 256, 271
Bevan, N., 267
Bick, E., 8, 136, 140–141, 144
Bieber, I., 235
binge eating, *see* eating disorders
Bion, W.
  on container-contained, 144
  on creativity and "catastrophic change," 101
  on ego-destructive superego, 207
  on the "emotional storm," 32, 105
  emphasis on learning from experience, 3, 8–9, 22
  on "negative capability," 30
  "Notes on Memory and Desire," 29
  on projective identification, 69
  at Tavistock, 9
  theory of thinking of, 19–20, 269
  on the unconscious, 146–147
  on unprocessed interpretation, 68
Birkin bag, 210
Birksted-Breen, D., 145
bisexuality, 234
  psychic, 237–238
  See also, LGB
"black experience, the," 242
Black Lives Matter, 229, 243, 251
blackness, of mood, 223
black racial identity and black people
  on being a black trainee on the M1 course, 228, 244–251, 271
  identifying with, 156
  marginalization of, 241
  racism and, 242
blame, 73, 129, 137, 139
  analyst's processing of, 168
  dread of, 265
  fear of, 266
  self-blame, 144
  wish to apportion, 167
Bleger, J., 127, 133
"blending in," by Black trainees, 228, 246, 271
body schema, 127
borderline personality disorder, 65, 236
Borderline Workshop, 10
Bowlby, J., 8, 267
BPC, *see* British Psychoanalytic Council
BPS, *see* British Psychological Society

Brenman, E., 131, 164–165
Brenman Pick, I., 36, 51, 92, 96, 104, 109, 133, 162–163, 202
Brexit, 51
Brickman, C., 250
"Brick Mother," 12, 211–213
  the aqueduct and, 53–54
  as the Ghost Ship, 169, 213
British Confederation of Psychotherapists, 10
British psychoanalysis, 235, 237
British Psychoanalytic Council (BPC), 9, 10, 229, 236, 264
British Psychological Society (BPS), 9
Britton, R., 52, 145, 153

cancel culture, 237
cancer
  death of patient by, 168, 173, 174, 175, 177
  death of patient's father by, 171, 172
  death of patient's mother by, 147, 151
Carpy, D., 163–164
castration anxiety, 236
CBT, *see* cognitive behavioural therapy
centre
  holding of, 144
  margins as opposed to, 237, 241, 267
Child Psychotherapy training, 8
Clarke, J., 237
clinical challenges
  guilt and, 272–273
  learning though, 167–170
clinical competence, stages of, 147
clinical examples of patients
  Mr D, 198–208
  Mr E, 55–66
  Mr M, 272
  Mr R, 216–218
  Mrs D, 219–225
  Ms B, 157–166
  Ms D, 67–74
  Ms E, 171–178
  Ms K, 189–197
  Ms L, 113–123, 124
  Ms M, 179–188
  Ms O, 32–43
  Ms P, 135–156
  Ms Z, 48–53
clinical vignettes of trainees

Mr B, 92, 96–99
Mr C, 99–100
Ms A, 92–96, 270
cognitive behavioural therapy (CBT), 56, 63, 84
   "bootcamp," 85
   structured, 140
condescension
   defensive, 114–115
Conrad, J.
   Nostromo, 266
container (psychological), 19, 41, 53, 175
   emotional, 94
   maternal, 207
   psychic, 169
container-contained, 76, 144
contempt
   of mother towards her children, 199, 200
   of oneself, 161
   of patient for therapist, 49, 55–56, 103, 205–207
corpse
   toxic internal, 104
"corridor conversations," 216
countertransference
   analysts' own, 92
   association/memory, 203
   being guided by, 157–166
   being open to, 202
   brain fog as response to, 200
   homophobia as form of, 235
   learning about transference and, 103–104
   projective identification and, 198
   therapists' (Ms B), 157–158
   therapist's pregnancy and, 195
   therapist's, towards patient, 249
   transference and, 4, 32, 35, 36, 41, 96, 105–112
COVID-19 and COVID-19 pandemic
   "brain fog" from, 94
   death from cancer during (case of Ms E), 171–178
   death from suicide right before lockdowns due to (case of Ms M), 186
   impact on and aftermath at NHS of, 12, 82
   impact on therapists and patients of, 169, 193
   impact on trainees of, 4
   lockdown conditions (case of Mrs D), 219–225
   remote working and remote therapy during, 12, 87, 168–169, 217, 219–220, 225
   trainee Ms A's developing of "long Covid," 93–95
   working at the Tavistock during, 12, 169, 209–218
Crichton Miller, H., 7
Crick, P., 86
Crowe, C., 215
Cruise, T., 215
"culture of enquiry," 4, 22, 261, 270
   M1 at NHS and, 265–268
Cunningham, R., 239

Dalal, F., 241
Davids, M. F., 241
death
   COVID-19 pandemic and (case of Ms E), 171–178
   of mother, 104, 146–148, 151, 154, 156
   Ms Z's experience of death of friend, 48
   of newborn, 80
   of patient (case of Ms M), 4, 168, 179–188
   of sister, 127
   up or down and life and, 44–54
   See also, suicide and suicidality
De Jongh, F., 64
Dekker, J., 64
De Maat, S., 64
denial, 78, 167, 168
   defence of, 172
   of dependency on the object, 165
   of need, 115
   of psychic reality, 153
   of separation, 131
Dennis, M., 10
dependency 17, 39, 103, 127, 132–133, 138, 142, 144, 149, 153
depression, 64–65
   case of Mr D, 199
   case of Mr R, 216
   case of Ms K, 189, 192
   case of Ms L, 113
   case of Ms M, 180–181

case of Ms P, 144
chronic, 189
postnatal, 129
severe, 113, 180
Tavistock Adult Depression Study (TADs), 64
Depression Report (Layard), 63
depressive
anxiety, 141, 144, 154, 177, 225
breakdown, 33
experience, 44
feeling, 140
functioning, 114
illness, 10
pain, 42, 154
position, 29, 39, 44, 70, 110, 140, 142
state, 209, 280
symptoms, 65
Dicks, H., 7–8
Diagnostic and Statistical Manual of Mental Disorders (DSM), 234–235
disease, 175, 235
See also, *International Classification of Diseases* (ICD)
disembodiment, 94, 225
disillusionment, 38, 70, 156
disordered eating, *see* eating disorders
disruptive events impacting therapy, 168
disruptive patient, 15, 103, 115
dissatisfaction, 139, 186
diversity, 227–228
gender, 236
institutional learning and, 270–271
M1 training and, 252–258
See also, race and racism; sexism; sexual diversity
Django Unchained (dir. Tarantino), 247
dread, 22, 53, 176, 195, 201, 265
Drescher, J., 242
DSM, *see* Diagnostic and Statistical Manual of Mental Disorders

eating disorders, 10, 104, 135
education, 21, 87
clinical, 88, 264
healthcare, 263
of psychologists, 232
psychoanalytic, 14
at the Tavistock, 7–13
See also, M1 training

ego, 94, 108, 114, 118, 140, 142, 155
body, 245
See also, superego
ego-dystonic homosexuality, *see* homosexuality
ego-function, 265, 266
Einstein, A., 27, 269
Ekstein, R., 14, 16, 21
"elephant and string"
case of Mr E, 55–66
Ellis, M. L., 231, 236, 239
"emotional coalface," 84
enquiry, *see* "culture of enquiry"; "spirit of enquiry"
envy, 52, 73, 117, 136, 165, 176–177, 190
baby envy 192–193, 195–196
exclusion
abandonment and, 193
displacement and, 195, 197
parental, 196
phantasies of, 195
racism and, 271
exclusion from training, of LGB and minoritized individuals, 239–240, 245
external and internal pressure, 79, 86
external reality, 72, 151
death of mother as, 154
demands of id and superego and, 162
internal and, 137
of patients, 238
external world, 19, 115
being sealed off from, 194
bridging internal and, 45–46
extra-transference interpretations, 106

fantasmatic mechanism, 155
fantasizing, 62
fantasy(ies), 46, 183, 187, 224
anxious, 58
faun, 95
Feldman, M., 30, 139
"Illumination of History," 108
feminine vs. masculine, 236, 243
Flaying of Marsyas (Titian), 95
fluidity, sexual and gender 237
Fonagy, P., 64
Freudian analytic tradition, 90
Freud, Sigmund
advocation of psychoanalysis, 229

casual racism and sexism of, 250
classical approach of, 107
on countertransference, 163
on curiosity, 269
on ego as body ego, 245
Goethe's influence on, 22
   on historical reconstruction and transference, 106
homosexuality theorized by, 235–236
on infantile sexuality and curiosity, 18–19
on inherited unconscious guilt, 22
on the response to novelty, 18
on teaching psychoanalysis, 14–16, 21
theory of mind of, 250
theory of psychic bisexuality of, 237
Three Essays on the Theory of Sexuality, 238
on transference, 108–109
on the Unconscious, 256
views regarding homosexuals, 239
Full, W., 240

Garland, C., 10
gay man as psychoanalyst, 232–233, 236, 238–240, 243
   as a "good gay," 230, 271
gender 46, 229, 231
   identity and, 237, 252
   transgender, 233
gender diversity, 236
gender fluidity, 237
"ghost ship" (Tavistock) 12, 209–218
   the Brick Mother turning into 169
   Starbucks machine at, 210–213, 218
Gibb, E., 10
Gillespie, W., 236
Goethe, J. W., 22
good breast, 212
"good child," 33
"good daughter," 141
"good object," 37, 41
   internal, 140
   pining for 154
"good gay," 230, 271
"good object/therapist," 207
"good patient," 200
grandiosity, 12, 72, 115, 159
Green, A., 216

guilt 13, 17
   aversive emotion of, 167
   awareness of, 165
   clinical challenges and, 272–273
   experience of, 140
   feelings of, 38, 60, 68, 80, 131, 154, 167, 176–177, 183, 200, 205
   inherited unconscious, 22
   maternal, 71
   persecutory, 114, 137, 196
   processing of, 168
   suicide and, 183, 188, 272
   therapist's or analyst's feelings of, 183, 188, 193, 197, 205, 272–273
   unresolved, 80

hallucinations, 64, 216
Harrison, R., 228, 271
   See also, "blending in"; diversity and M1 training
Hastings, D. H., 169, 272
   See also, COVID-19: lockdown conditions (case of Mrs D)
hate, hatred, hatefulness, 40, 136
   analyst's hate of own patient, 163, 173
   envy and, 176, 196
   expressed by Ms E, 172, 176
   expressed by Ms K, 193, 196
   love and hate, 161
   Klein's views on, 73
   mother's hatred of baby, 163
   Ms D's feelings of, 72
   White's views on racism and, 246
   Winnicott's views on, 163
Health Education England, 263
Heimann, P., 73, 109, 163
heteronormative bias, in psychoanalytic theory, 227, 223, 236–238
heteronormative narratives, 235
heteronormativity, 242
heterosexuality, 235–236
Hillen, T., 103, 126
   See also, premature ending of therapy by patient
historical reconstruction, 106
hoarding, 113
Hobson, P., 10
Hodgins, R., 12, 24, 25, 49
homophobia, 237–239, 241–242, 250
homosexuality, 230

ego-dystonic, 234, 235
   pathologizing of, 234, 236, 242
   as perversion, 236
   psychoanalysis and psychoanalytic theory of, 234–237, 239–241
   See also, anti-homosexuality; homophobia
homosexual, the, 236, 238, 242
Hume, F., 10

ICD, *see International Classification of Diseases* (WHO)
id, 162
illusion, 70, 153
   shattering of, 155
illusory world, 225
imagination
   as more important than knowledge, 269
   Ms A's, 95–96
   patient's, 50
   Segal's, 91
immaturity, 235
incorporation and introjection, 146–156
   introjection versus, 155
infantile
   defences, 33
   experiences, 100
   feelings, 164, 195
   needs, 98
   sexuality, 18
infant observation, 8
infants, 19
   cognitive development of, 20
   mother experiences of, 106
   object experiences of, 104, 107
   self-formation of, 127
information
   as distinct from knowledge, 27
insiders and outsiders, 229–231
instinct, 182
   epistemophilic, 18–22
   sexual, 18
instinctive fears, 255, 257
institutional learning
   embracing diversity and, 270–271
International Classification of Diseases (ICD) (WHO), 75, 234
International Journal of Psychoanalysis 216
introjection, 19, 104, 105, 140, 141
   from incorporation to, 146–156
   incorporation versus, 155
introjective identification, 76
intuition and the intuitive response, 16, 83–84, 91, 102, 147, 256
"invisible enemy," threat of, 210
"invisible labour" clause, 248
invisibility
   feelings of, 246, 271
   irrational fears and worries, 192, 196
Isay, R., 236

Jackson, S. L., 247
Johannesburg 45–46
Jones, E., 239
Joseph, B., 44, 51, 91, 105, 110–111, 273

Kahneman, D., 256
Keats, J. 30, 101
Keiser, S., 21
Kernberg, O. F., 47, 86, 89
King, P., 164
Kinsey research reports on human sexuality, 234
Kleinian analysts, 211, 221
Kleinian analytic tradition, 90
Klein, M., 17–19
   on analysts' getting caught up with patient's love, 73
   Bion's use of concepts borrowed from, 29
   on countertransference, 109
   on the dependent baby, 144
   on depressive pain, 154
   depressive position as understood by, 29, 70
   on infant anxiety, 151
   on the internal good object, 140
   on male and female homosexuality, 236
   "Origins of Transference," 106–107
   on projective identification, 162
   on the rejected child, 138
   schizoid mechanisms discovered by, 162

Layard, R., 63–64
Lawrence, M., 10
learning
   didactic, 16

experiential, 16
See also, institutional learning
learning and unlearning
    identity and citizenship and, 82–87
    not-knowing and, 23–25
Leicester Conferences, 8
Leichsenring, F., 64–65
Lemma, A., 237
lesbian, gay, bisexual (LGB), 227, 232–234, 239–242
lesbian women, 240
    psychoanalytic theorizing about, 235
    See also, Ellis, M. L.; LGB
Lewes, K., 235
LGB, *see* lesbian, gay, bisexual
libidinal drive, 19
libido, 18
Limentani, A., 236
longer-term psycho-dynamic psychotherapy (LTPP), 64–65
Lowe, F., 10
LTPP, *see* longer-term psycho-dynamic psychotherapy
Lucretius, 211

M1 training 2, 271
    1970s establishment of, 5
    Baban's experiences with, 77, 79
    Baldock's experiences with, 179, 182
    as broad education for a career in the public sector, 9–11
    changing NHS and, 261–268
    current context of psychoanalytic training at NHS and, 11–13
    current form of, 8
    diversity and, 252–258
    fee-paying students, 263, 264
    future of, 13
    Harrison's experiences with, 252–258
    Hastings' experiences with, 219, 224–225
    history of, 3–4, 270
    Hodgin's experiences with, 82–87
    McKay's experiences with 46, 48, 53
    personal experience of being black on, 244–251
    threats to the integrity of, 261–268
    Tavistock M1 Course, 254–256
    trainees, 27

Turner's experiences as black trainee, 244–251
Turner's first case on, 146, 156
Main, T., 12, 16–17, 265–267
    "culture of enquiry" of, 4, 22, 261, 265, 270
Makin, J., 45
mania, 174
manic
    approach to patients, 24, 78
    defences, 114
    denial, 168
    excitement, 73
    omnipotent phantasy, 153
    optimism, 72
    self, 247
    thinking, 265
marriage
    analysands who have been previously married, 48, 113, 190
    LGB trainees and markers of, 241
    Tavistock training with groups and, 8
masochism, 51, 131, 200
Maudsley Hospital, 211
Mawson, C., 211
McDougall, J., 138
McKay, A., 15, 24
    See also, "one-up" or "one-down" position; up or down and life and death
medical doctors, 9, 78
"medical model," 63
medical training, 81, 234
medicine
    profession of, 10
    psychosomatic, 251
Melaku, T., 248
Meltzer, D., 132
Melville, H., 198, 213
    Moby-Dick, 213
Mental Health Act, 180
    assessment of patient, 77–78
Menzies Lyth, I., 150
Milton, J., 84–85, 272
money, 7, 117, 151, 213, 248, 262
Money-Kyrle, R., 104, 164
Morgan, H., 241
Moss, D., 243
mourning, 39, 147, 154, 157, 258
    necessary, 165

pain of, 150, 155
process of, 146
real, of loss, 52
loss of mother (Turner's anonymous
    case), 146–156
task of, 251

narcissism, 28
    unchallenged, 70
narcissistic
    characters, 236
    defences, 24
    fusion, 164
    indulgence, 164
    object, 165
    retreat, 160, 196
    states, 56, 206
    withdrawal, 149
National Health Service (NHS), 1, 8
    aftermath of COVID-19, 82
    annual lecture of the Association for
        Psychoanalytic Psychotherapy
        1995 at, 235
    application of psychoanalysis at, 9
    battles over money at, 7
    career (potential) at, 10
    clinicians at, 83, 85, 86
    coffee machines at, 210
    counsellors, 56
    current context of M1 psychoanalytic
        training at, 11–13
    eating disorders service at, 135
    finances of, 66
    institutional mental health services
        at, 172
    long-term analytic treatment at, 24
    M1 system and, 261–268
    McKay's experience at, 46
    psychoanalysis clinic at, 53
    psychological therapies at, 49, 52, 63
    psychotherapy training, 172
    resource provision, 65
    talking therapies service, 199
National Institute for Health and Clinical
    Excellence (NICE), 63–65
negative capability, 30, 101
neuroses, 7
    analyst's own, 109
neurologist, 94
neurosurgeon, 231

neurotic
    defences, 110
    patient, 200, 224
newborn, 129
NHS, *see* National Health Service
NICE, *see* National Institute for Health
    and Clinical Excellence
non-heteronormativity, 238, 271
non-receptive mother-therapist, 95
non-understanding
    periods of, 104, 164
non-verbal communication, 110–111, 272
"normal adult," 137, 138
"normal" heterosexuality, 235
normopath, 138
not-knowing, 3, 20, 22
    anxiety of or about, 150, 265
    being open to, 86
    inability to tolerate a state of, 102
    on learning and unlearning and, 23–25
    legal system's lack of space for, 186
    Ms E as case of, 176–177
    pressure between "knowing" and, 78
    remaining in an anxious state of, 96
    sense of, 211
    sitting with, 53
    Trieman on (case of Ms O), 23, 32–43

Obholzer, A., 45
object
    absent, 213
    bad, 37, 38, 91, 222
    denigrated, 196
    fragile or frail, 33, 41
    indifference, 85
    internal, 84, 212
    transference, 89
    See also, "good object"
object/therapist. 69
O'Connor, N., 235
Oedipus complex, 136, 144, 236–238
Ogden, T., 42
omnipotence, 24, 56, 70, 78, 129, 144–145,
    225, 254
    magical, 104
    manic, 153
    mother's, 195
    primitive, 156
"one-up" or "one-down" position, 24, 44
O'Shaughnessy, E., 111, 139

overdose, 79, 147
　See also, suicide
Ovid
　Metamorphoses, 95

pandemic, *see* COVID-19 pandemic
paranoia, 118
paranoid-schizoid
　anxieties, 151, 160
　position, 29, 42, 110, 114, 140
Parsons, M., 165–166, 216
penis-as-link function of the
　　father, 145
personal analysis, 16, 100, 111, 155
personal experiences of being black,
　　244–251
personal grievance, 241, 242, 243
personality disorder, 234
personality(ies), 28, 111, 162
　meeting of two, 32, 105
　Mr D's, 200
　Ms B's, 165
　patient's, 109, 115
personality disorder, 10
"personal relationship" of therapy, 52
persona, 221
　analytic, 99
perverse
　defences, 165
　curiosity, 202
　excitement, 44
　need to attack, 160
　organizational solutions, 86
　psychoanalytic theory of
　　homosexuality, 234–237
perversion, 165
perversity, 64
phallic words, 118
phallus 153
phantasy, 3, 18, 32, 38, 107, 108, 149–151,
　　190–191, 193, 238
　manic, 153
　unconscious, 91, 105, 112
　universal, 195
　violent, 136
phantasy life, 114
Pitt Aikens, T., 45
Poincaré, H., 29
pregnancy
　appearance of, 148

of therapist, impact on patient of, 168,
　　189–197
premature ending of therapy by patient
　Hillen's anonymous patient, 103–104,
　　125–134
　Shevade's case of Mr D, 198–208
premature knowledge, 41
primal
　couple, 153
　internal figures, 214
primitive
　anxieties, 34, 42, 133, 169, 197, 202, 207,
　　231
　dread, 22, 265
　expectations, 188
　experience, 95
　idealization, 115
　modes of functioning, 114
　object relations, 41
　omnipotence, 156
　projective mechanisms, 162
　self, 111
　state of mind, 214
　thoughts, 19
primitive, the, 249
projective identification, 36, 76, 104–105,
　　111, 126, 148–149, 153, 157
　Carpy on, 164
　Klein on, 162
　Mr D, 198
　Mr M, 272
　Ms B, 165
　Ms K, 195
　Ms P, 138
　Roth on, 201
pseudo-independence, 135, 136, 144
pseudonormality, 138
pseudo-understanding, 34
psychiatry
　unlearning, 75–81
psychoanalytic attitude, 269
psychoanalysis, 18
　insiders and outsiders in, 229–231
psychoanalytic knowledge and attitude,
　　14–22
"Psycho-Analytic Technique" (Racker),
　　109
psychoanalytic psychotherapy training
　adult, 1, 5, 7–13
psychoanalytic training, 20, 21

NHS, 11–13
  education rather than, 14
  process of, 3
  sexual diversity in, 232–243
  uncertain rewards of, 44
psychotic
  breakdown, 64, 169, 215
  crisis, 78
  patients, 10, 265
  processes, 24, 77, 78
  projections, 78
  states, 78
  transference, 170
  transient psychotic symptoms, 56
psychopathology(ies), 20, 28, 93, 99, 104, 109–110
  homosexuality as, 235
  somatic pain as, 104
psychoses, psychosis, 46
psychosomatic disorders, 46, 93, 104
psychosomatic medicine, 251
psychotherapist, *see* psychoanalytic psychotherapist
psychotherapy 12
  D59 Psychodynamic Psychotherapy training, 83
  Heimann on, 73
  individual, 56
  intensive, 57, 62
  psychoanalytic, 47, 65
  as relationship between two people, 73
  trainee, 63
  training, 77
  treatment, 80
  See also, LTPP
Pynchon, T.
  Inherent Vice, 77

Quinodoz, D., 126

Racker, H., 109
race and racism, 238, 241, 246, 271
  calling out, 247
  casual, 250
  challenging, 251
  containing, 249
  exclusion and, 271
  hate and, 246
  homophobia and, 242
  language and, 250

mixed-race, 156, 171, 245, 251
  otherness and, 245
  perception of "difference" and, 242
  "political" issue of, 231
  prejudice and, 231
  psychoanalysis and, 246
  sexuality and aging and, 4
  strategies on, 248
  teaching on, 237
  thinking about, 249
  Task Group on, 229
  training event on, 247
  trauma of, 26
Rees, J. R., 7
regression, 89, 96
Reik, T., 273
repressed memories, 106
repression, 20, 101, 110
Rey, H., 211
Richards, D., 242
Rizq, R., 86
Rohleder, P., 4, 271, 231
  See also, diversity; "good gay"; sexual diversity
Rosenfeld, H., 56, 71, 265
Rosenthal, J., 10
Roth, P., 32, 201
Ryan, J., 235

sado-masochism, 24, 56, 60, 217
schizoid mechanisms, 162
second skin, 136, 144
Section 28 (on homosexuality), 234
Section 136 (on mental health), 79, 180
Segal, H., 91
self-harm, 12, 64, 65, 130
self-hatred, 146
sex, *see* sado-masochism
sexism, 46, 250, 252
sexist bias, 238
sexual
  abuse, 219, 220, 223
  curiosity, 18, 19
  encounter, 193
  instinct, 18
  orientation, 55, 241, 243
  preferences, 131
  problems, 18
  thoughts, 71
sexual diversity, 227

in psychoanalytic training, 232–243
  teaching, 237–238
sexuality
  ageing and race and, 4
  bisexuality, 234, 237, 238
  infantile, 18
  Freud on, 238
  gender and, 46, 229, 231
  human, 234
  Mr E, 56
  in psychoanalysis, 233
  same-sex, 234
  See also, homosexuality
sexually explicit material
  Mr E and, 59–60, 62
shame, feelings of, 15, 49, 70, 71, 72, 126, 167–168, 183, 188, 200
  black, 245
  racism and, 246, 250
  Steiner on, 70
sharing space with a patient
  Verma's work with Ms D, 67–74
Shaw, S., 12, 15, 24, 66
  See also, "elephant and string"; sadomasochism
shell
  around the heart, 213
  emotional, 235
shell-shock, 7
Shevade, D., 169
  See also, premature ending of therapy by patient
Shining, The (King), 215
Socarides, C., 235
social constructionism, 238
Spillius, E., 33
"spirit of enquiry," 21
St Charles Centre for Health and Wellbeing, 210
Steinberg, B., 20
Steiner, J., 10, 50, 70, 149, 151, 162, 165, 225
Stokoe, P., 87
Strachey, J., 104, 106, 162
Stubley, J., 10
suicide or suicidality in patients, 4, 12, 64–65, 167–168
  attempted, 80, 180
  case of Ms M, 179–188
  therapists' dread of being blamed for, 265
superego, 37–38, 90, 96

ego-destructive, 207
friendly, 104
overly critical, 28
superego function, 265, 266
Sutherland, J., 7–8, 13, 267
symbiotic relationships, 9, 195
symbolization, 104, 135

TADS, *see* Tavistock Adult Depression Study (TADS)
Tarantino, Q., 247
Tavistock
  Bion at, 9
  brief history of education at, 7–9
  COVID-19 pandemic at, 209–218
  D59 Psychodynamic Psychotherapy training at, 83
  education at, 7–13
  inception of, 5
  Institute of Psychoanalysis and, 1
  psychoanalytic training at, 5
Tavistock Adult Depression Study (TADS), 64
Tavistock M1 Course, 254–256, 261
Tavistock qualification in adult psychotherapy (TQAP), 9
Taylor, D., 10
Temperley, J., 84
terror of one's own mind
  case of Mr D, 198–208
Titian, 95
Torok, M., 155
TQAP, *see* Tavistock qualification in adult psychotherapy
transference
  countertransference and, 4, 32, 35, 36, 41, 96, 102, 105–112
  elephant and string scenario of, 60
  positive, 37
  scenario, 42
  shifts in, 38, 39
Transference Workshop, 10
transgender, 233
Trieman, E., 23, 31, 270
  See also, not-knowing: (case of Ms O)
Turner, D., 104, 228, 271
  See also, blending in; mourning

unconscious
  actions, 96
  communication, 32, 38, 114

conflict, 162, 195, 197
drives, 19
fusion, 255
guilt, 22
meaning, 173
mind, 166
phantasy, 91, 105, 112
processes, 3, 89
process of symbol formation, 145
resistance, 163
responses, 20
stress, 45
struggles, 100
terror, 114
thought, 107
wish, 172, 191, 224
Unconscious, the, 42 109, 111, 146, 147, 254
    dreams and, 203
    Freud and, 256
    new language of, 150
    "race" and, 246
United Kingdom, 1, 46, 180, 239, 263
    Brexit and, 51
    views on homosexuality in, 234–236, 239–240
    See also, British Psychoanalytic Council; National Health Service
United States
    views on homosexuality in, 234–236, 239
    See also, APA
up or down and life and death, 44–54

Verma, M., 24, 269
    See also, sharing space with a patient

Walker, C., 103
    See also, countertransference
Walkerdine, V., 10
    See also, eating disorders
Wallace, D. F., 32
Washington, M., 15, 103
White, K., 246–247, 251
White Rabbit (Alice in Wonderland), 24
whitewashing (racial), 246, 248, 271
WHO, *see* World Health Organization
Winnicott, D., 53, 70, 163, 221
Wittels, F., 14
Wolfenson report, 234
World Health Organization (WHO), 234

For Product Safety Concerns and Information please contact our
EU representative GPSR@taylorandfrancis.com Taylor & Francis
Verlag GmbH, Kaufingerstraße 24, 80331 München, Germany